CLERICAL
CELIBACY

CLERICAL CELIBACY

THE HERITAGE

WILLIAM E. PHIPPS

continuum
NEW YORK • LONDON

The Continuum International Publishing Group
Madison Square Park, 15 East 26th Street, New York, NY 10010

The Continuum International Publishing Group Ltd.
The Tower Building, 11 York Road, London SE1 7NX

Cover art: Priest Praying/Corbis

Cover design: Lee Singer

Quotations from the Bible are often the author's own translation, but indebtedness to a variety of versions can be found.

Library of Congress Cataloging-in-Publication Data

Phipps, William E., 1930-
  Clerical celibacy : the heritage / William E. Phipps.
    p. cm.
  Includes bibliographical references and indexes.
  ISBN 0-8264-1617-9 (pbk.)
  1. Celibacy—Catholic Church. 2. Catholic Church—Clergy. I. Title.
  BX1912.85P48 2004
  253'.252—dc22
                                    2004003704

Printed in the United States of America

04 05 06 07 08 09   10 9 8 7 6 5 4 3 2 1

To Teresa Reddington, a Catholic sister from Ireland,
who expresses the gospel with lilting voice and gracious deeds.
She has helped me realize that women ministers are indispensable.

CONTENTS

TIMELINE FOR TRACING
CELIBACY IN CHRISTIANITY

(most dates approximate)

Before Christian Era (BCE)

400 Hebrew Scriptures affirm sanctity of marriage
300 Vestal virgin cult becomes prominent in Rome
200 Buddhist monasticism begins to affect Mediterranean cultures
100 Greco-Roman sexual asceticism influential for centuries to come

Christian Era (CE)

30 Jesus teaches about sexual desire, marriage, and eunuchs
55 Paul acknowledges being an exception to the married apostles; assuming the nearness of the world's end, he recommends celibacy for Christians like himself whose sexual drive is not strong
70 Jerusalem razed; the church's center moves toward Rome and is less influenced by the Semitic rejection of celibacy
70–90 Stories recorded in four Gospels; two refer to Jesus' "virgin" mother and one refers to his disciples renouncing wives
80 Pastoral Letters stipulate marriage for church leaders
140 Heretic Marcion requires celibacy of Christians
150 Apologist Justin Martyr endorses Hellenistic sexual asceticism
160 Heretic Tatian first to view Jesus as celibacy paradigm
190 Clement of Alexandria advocates marriage for all Christians
200 Tertullian, Latin patristic and misogynist, berates marriage
220 Eunuch Origen associates sacredness with sexlessness
250 Persian prophet Mani establishes a syncretism of Christian ideas and Buddhist monasticism that affects Western celibacy
300 Egyptian hermit Anthony attracts followers who mortify the flesh

310 Elvira Council imposes sexual abstinence on Spanish priests
312 Emperor Constantine converts to Christianity, removing the primacy of pagan priests in Roman Empire
330 Pachomius develops rules for separate male and female monasteries in Egypt
380 Bishop Ambrose preaches that purity requires coitus abstention
385 Pope Siricius declares clerical intercourse defiling
390 Monk Jovinian defends moral equality of celibacy and marriage
400 Monk Jerome champions celibacy's superiority to marriage
410 Bishop Augustine argues all sex sinful due to Adam's fall
530 Benedict establishes renunciation rules for Western monks
540 Emperor Justinian institutes laws regulating sexual practices
590 Pope Gregory replaces virginity for martyrdom as ultimate witness
692 Eastern church's Trullo Council accepts the married for ordination
1050 Cardinal Peter Damian denounces "sodomy" among clergy
1054 Schism between Roman Catholicism and Eastern Orthodoxy, due in part to disagreement over celibacy of priests
1080 Pope Gregory VII demands that clergy abandon sexual companions
1110 Peter Abelard's tragic romance due to celibacy requirements
1130 Lateran Councils declare clerical marriage invalid
1250 Monk Thomas Aquinas views passionate love of women as wicked
1484 Pope Innocent VIII approves persecution of alleged witches
1500 Renaissance scholar Erasmus extols the purity of marriage
1525 Martin Luther and Protestants repudiate failed clerical celibacy
1550 Reformer John Calvin shows Bible sanctions marriage for all
1563 Council of Trent rules marriage is inferior to celibacy
1954 Pope Pius XII's Holy Virginity encyclical lauds Trent ruling
1964 Vatican II Council acknowledges that celibacy is not essential to priesthood and accepts married deacons
1965 Beginning of precipitous decline in priests worldwide
1967 Pope Paul VI reaffirms obligatory celibacy for priests
1969 Paul VI begins accepting priests who are converted Protestant clergy
1980 Proportion of homosexual priests begins to rise rapidly
1990 Most Catholics think celibacy should be optional for priests
1995 Clerical pedophilia scandal becomes prominent
1998 Resignations of bishops who protect abusive priests rather than their victims begin
2000 Catholic catechism continues to treat homosexuality and masturbation as perversions
2002 Priestly predators provoke large lawsuits from victims
2003 Pope John Paul II declares celibacy rule nonnegotiable

Chapter 1
INTRODUCTION

☙❧

My Approach

Two things motivated me to write this book: a current awareness and a historical understanding. Like all who follow news of religious organizations, I have been reading the almost daily disclosures of sexual abuses by professed celibates. Headlines call our attention to tawdry deeds of clerical predators and prelate cover-ups. The scandal is tarnishing all religious organizations. My wife, knowing that my research focus for several decades has been celibacy issues over the two millennia of the church, encouraged me to relate my data to the appalling misconduct that is at last becoming public.

Defenders of celibacy anchor their doctrine in what they allege to be "the word of God." Since my academic specialization is biblical interpretation, considerable attention will be given here to analyzing scriptural passages that celibacy advocates claim to be relevant to their cause. As Richard McBrien acknowledges in his magisterial book entitled *Catholicism*, my understanding of the subject results from my probing of ancient religious texts. My investigation of the alleged biblical authority for celibacy gives distinctiveness to this study. No other treatments scrutinize relevant biblical texts with the methodology of modern literary-historical criticism.

My curiosity over celibacy in Christianity began in 1967 while I was studying at the Hebrew Union University in Jerusalem. Only after discussions

1

with Semitic scholars did I come to realize how offensive Roman Catholic insistence on priestly celibacy has been to Jewish and Muslim traditions. Recognizing that Jesus was a Jewish rabbi somewhat like his immediate predecessor Rabbi Hillel, I began to examine church history to understand why celibacy has been attributed to him and to many prominent church leaders who have worshiped him.

I appreciate the scholarly outlook of the Apostle Paul, on whom I wrote my doctoral dissertation.[1] He acted on his own advice by testing those who claimed to be religious spokesmen (1 Thess 5:20–21). Even though Peter was, as Paul describes him, an "acknowledged pillar" of the church, Paul boldly denounced him as a hypocrite. While Paul was aware that everyone, including himself, had faults, he did not let that keep him from criticizing a particular social practice of Jesus' most prominent disciple that was contrary to the gospel (Gal 2:7–14). Paul was inspired by Jesus, who used the proverb, "Practice what you preach" (Matt 23:3). In a similar spirit, I find it necessary to confront candidly many who claim to be Peter's successors and the bishops they have appointed.

As a Protestant minister, I share the view of reformers Martin Luther and John Calvin—that compulsory celibacy should no longer be tolerated because it has corrupted Christian theology and practice. I sympathize with the many active and inactive priests who are alienated by the Vatican's anachronistic sexual code for ordained Catholics. We agree that the inhumane papal law of celibacy falsifies Christian core values and is Catholicism's own worst enemy. Even when bishops speak out against priestly misconduct, most of them refuse to recognize that it is in part caused by the celibacy requirement. This indicates a need for someone outside the Roman Church to examine and reveal what the magisterium refuses to debate.

Since I belong to a non-celibate branch of Christianity, in this book I frequently quote Catholic spokespersons in church history to represent their positions accurately. Letting both celibacy advocates and critics state their positions in their own words should provide readers with a balanced approach to the subject. As much as possible I have exercised caution in using journalistic anecdotal material, which is often gut wrenching but may not be representative. Not having engaged in sociological or psychological investigations myself, I have ferreted out studies that provide factual assessments of the general individual and cultural consequences of celibacy.

Celibacy has not been mandated for Catholic leaders for most of the church's history and has been a failure from its beginning until now. During the past millennium, there has often been a wide gap between pledge and practice. In the United States, hundreds of Catholic priests have been removed from office in recent years and some have been imprisoned because of what is mildly labeled child sexual abuse. Required celibacy has resulted in immorality, criminality, female subjection, hypocrisy—thus, a basic misunderstanding of the gospel.

In previous generations, awareness of cancer was usually not perceived until a tumor appeared on the surface of the body. Now, tests have been devised to detect malignancy when it first develops internally. This study will demonstrate that various clerical sexual abuses are the surface symptoms but that celibacy is the systemic disease. The media has described the ugly eruptions but has given little attention to the disquieting underlying historical causes. This dysfunctional crisis cannot be alleviated without surgical treatment. In an institution as historically oriented as Catholicism, a new path for the future cannot be laid out until the church comes to terms with past failings. After the current superannuated pope is replaced, much attention will no doubt be given to the modification—if not to the discarding—of the celibacy law in the largest Christian church. Recognizing this, I have given much attention to understanding and evaluating how celibacy began and developed. Much of this material has never been widely known.

My position is conservative, not radical. Mandatory celibacy is relatively newfangled, having been made Vatican policy in spite of much opposition by traditionalists, not only in Eastern Orthodoxy but also among the lower echelons of Roman Catholicism. The innovation was imposed in the feudal and crusading era, which was a dark period for the church.

Defining Terms

"Celibacy" comes from the Latin word *caelebs,* meaning "alone." It is an inexact term for this study because it pertains simply to singleness, not necessarily to sexual abstinence. Nor does it suggest any motivation for singleness, religious or otherwise. *Caelebs* does not correspond closely to any biblical term. The ancient Hebrew language had no word for bachelor, and the single state was not treated as a lofty goal for dedicated individuals. Also, the Greek term *monos,* meaning "alone," from which "monk" and "monastic" were derived, is not associated in the New Testament with monks or hermits.

In this investigation, "celibacy" will be used as defined by Catholic officialdom to refer to the commitment priests must make to renounce all sexual intercourse for life. Catholic canon law states that a candidate cannot be admitted to the priesthood "unless in a prescribed rite he has assumed publicly before God and the Church the obligation of celibacy."[2] The purpose of celibacy is described in another law: "Clerics are obliged to observe perfect and perpetual continence for the sake of the kingdom of heaven and therefore are bound to celibacy which is a special gift of God, by which sacred ministers can adhere more easily to Christ with an undivided heart and are able to dedicate themselves more freely to the service of God and humanity."[3] Accordingly, a bishop asks the ordinand, "Are you resolved to remain celibate for the sake of the kingdom and in lifelong service to God and mankind?" Mandatory celibacy is a redundancy because the word celibacy itself, as used by Catholics, pertains to a required sexual abstinence. The seriousness of the solemn promise is reinforced by the sacrament of Holy Orders, placing it on a par with the sacrament of Holy Matrimony. Priests, like witnesses in a courtroom who have publicly sworn to tell the whole truth, are obligated to be faithful to their religious oath or be subject to divine and ecclesiastical penalties. Motivation and commitment are necessary components in the concept of celibacy, the practice of living without sexual relations as a means of devoting one's life to God's service. Sexual abstinence is a consequence of the pursuit of this lifelong ideal. In Catholicism, it involves a religious vow to give one's body exclusively to Christ.

Celibacy is not defined in this study as the mere avoidance of marriage, for many people who avoid marriage are sexually active. To be a confirmed bachelor, who may or may not be involved in sexual activity, is distinct from being a celibate. Approximately 10 percent of American male adults have never married or fathered children, but few in that population segment are Catholic celibates. For centuries, the Vatican decreed that married priests be celibate, meaning that they were expected to be sexually continent while living with wives. But sexual abstinence is not the equivalent of what Catholicism defines as celibacy. A person may be abstinent because of erectile dysfunction, preoccupation with other matters, disgust with sex, or the absence of opportunity.

Sexual fasting for a limited period by the married or the unmarried should also be distinguished from the perpetual discipline of celibacy. Youth frequently abstain from genital intercourse before marriage, but they should not be called celibates. Temporary personal commitment to sexual abstinence by single people is usually commendable, enabling an individual to find a partner interested in more than immediate gratification. Abstinence may also result from recognizing the danger of promiscuous behavior, especially because of sexually transmitted diseases that range from mild to deadly. Popular magazines often carry stories such as these: a woman writes that being "celibate" for weeks at a time has taught her how to relax without having sex; or a couple acknowledge that after a month of "celibacy," they have learned that abstinence makes the heart grow fonder and intercourse more ecstatic.

This book is also not about those who choose not to marry, temporarily or permanently, for nonreligious reasons. Some with ecological concerns do not wish to engage in reproductive partnership. Others have remained single for professional reasons, or because they not been able to find suitable mates. Still others may not marry because they are suffering from psychological, behavioral, or genetic problems. Celibacy is not a synonym for virginity, because Catholic celibates often have had prior sexual experience. Nor should celibacy be confused with chastity, a word that comes from the Latin *castus,* meaning pure. Chastity refers to living with sexual faithfulness that is morally appropriate for one's situation, whether with or without a partner. Marital chastity, which does not mean sexual abstinence but commitment to an exclusive relationship, is expected of all believers in most religions.

The term "Catholic" will be used as a shorthand way of referring to Roman Catholics, and usually to those of the Latin Rite who make up the vast majority of all Christians in the world. In the lower case, "catholic" means "universal" and encompasses Christians of the Roman Catholic, Eastern Orthodox, and Protestant churches, who all confess: "I believe in the one, holy, catholic and apostolic church." Also, although "priest" is a vocational designation used in a variety of Christian denominations as well as in some other religions, here it will refer to those whom the Catholic hierarchy ordains as priests and bishops, even if they resign from their diocesan assignments and marry. The saying "Once a priest, always a priest" expresses Catholic doctrine,[4] so "ex-priest" is an improper designation. "Clergy" includes deacons and subdeacons as well as priests, but the latter are distinguished by having the right to say Mass.

"Pagan" is another word with varied meanings. The term was first applied to those who clung to Greek and Roman religions after the advent of Christianity. Though often used pejoratively to refer to an irreligious or hedonistic person, in this study the word will be used in accord with its primary dictionary definition to refer to someone who does not belong to the monotheistic religions of Christianity, Judaism, or Islam. Therefore, classifying Buddhism as a pagan religion is not intended to convey a negative judgment, as the word "heathen" might do.

Sex and religion are two areas of human life that tend to be highly disturbing emotionally. They can be as destructive as dynamite when used foolishly. Both are overlaid with taboos, making it difficult to make rational judgments about either one, and even more difficult to relate one to the other. Even so, it is imperative to try to overcome the neurotic reaction that many have when attempts are made to relate these hot-button issues. In what follows, attention has been given to clarity of terminology and to accuracy of information sources. I have provided voluminous notes so that scholars and the public can judge for themselves the truth of what is presented. Hopefully this approach will defuse misunderstandings.

Notes

1. William Phipps, "The Attitude of the Apostle Paul toward Scripture," (PhD diss., St. Andrews, Scotland, 1956).

2. *Code of Canon Law,* 1037.

3. Ibid., 277.

4. Ibid., 290.

Chapter 2

THE PRE-CHRISTIAN ERA

❧

Jewish Culture

Knowledge of the anthropology contained in the Genesis creation stories is basic for understanding the place of sex in the Jewish tradition. In both the separable Genesis 1 and the Genesis 2 accounts, God's creative acts climax when man and woman unite. This high place in the order of creation shows that human sexuality is "very good"—as is stated—and is endowed with more grandeur than other aspects of the natural world. By contrast, the single state is the first thing to be pronounced "not good." The Lord said, "It is not good for the man to be alone" and a fit partner is created to fill that need. When man's solitariness is cured, he bursts into song, "This at last is bone of my bone and flesh of my flesh!" The composer of the garden of Eden myth believed that the delight of such companionship explains why a man leaves his parental home in order to cling to the nude completion of himself. The unmarried state is viewed as deficient and sex is seen as a means of mutual fulfillment. Masculine and feminine interdependence is exquisitely recognized in that best-known story of world literature.

Celibate Ruud Bunnik finds confirmation in this creation mythology of the scientific judgment "that an unmarried person is in some way unfinished, and truncated; both his biological and psychological structure ask for a complementary partner."[1] Based on his psychiatric research, Sigmund Freud writes, "A man shall leave father and mother—according to the biblical precept—and cleave to his wife, then are tenderness and sensuality united."[2] Concerning the relationship between Freud's judgment and the Jewish outlook of his ancestors, David Bakan states: "Freud had as a norm the so-called 'genital' form of sexuality, most adequately realized in marriage. The Talmud and the whole orthodox tradition had pressed the marital form of sexuality into normative position."[3]

Hebrew religion did not attempt to affirm the supremacy of the spiritual by depreciating the physical. Biblical men and women were represented as having spirited bodies. The stuff of their humanity is essentially neither spirit nor flesh. The Latin term *spiritus* means "breath" and is associated with liveliness and energy. The spirit in bodies was not thought of as a separate substance grafted on to life, but rather as the divine percolating through matter, making the Israelites enthusiastic participants in the sensuous as well as in the spiritual aspects of life.[4] Sex was not idolized as something ultimate—as in the fertility cults of Canaan—nor was it debased as something devilish—as in some other pagan cults.

Sociological practice with respect to marriage was in accord with the creation story in the biblical culture. The burning love between a couple was admired by the poets of ancient Israel. Their loveliest song was entitled the "Song of Songs," using the Hebrew idiom for expressing superlative degree. It can be viewed as an expansion of the concluding portion of the second chapter of Genesis, for both tell of naked wedded partners clinging together without shame.[5] The ardent lovers savor every part of one another's bodies. The lyrics affirm that humans are created for the close companionship that can be found through intimate male and female relationships. The two become one flesh not primarily to reproduce, but to express their mutual love. The fact that procreation is not mentioned in the Song indicates that the tie between the lovers has an intrinsic value apart from breeding capabilities.

This monogamous bonding is "till death do us part." Near the end of the Song of Songs, the theme of steadfast love leaps to a blaze. The couple exchange these vows:

> Stamp me as a seal upon your heart,
> For love is as strong as death,
> And passion is as unyielding as the grave.
> Its flashes are bolts of lightning,
> A holy flame.

Raging rivers cannot quench love,
Nor can floods drown it.

The Song of Songs expresses love sentiments similar to those found in other books that the Jews included in their canon of holy books. For example, the Song is echoed in this poem:

Have pleasure with the wife of your youth!
A lovely deer! A graceful doe!
May her breasts always intoxicate you!
May you ever find rapture in loving her! (Prov 5:18–19)

Although the paradise of Eden and the renewed paradise of the Song of Songs do not allude to procreation as one purpose of marriage, that has been the prime concern for cultures on the margin of survival. Through much of the century when Judaism and Christianity separated, 60 percent of people who were born alive in the Mediterranean area would have died by their mid-teens, 75 percent by their mid-twenties, and 90 percent by their mid-forties.[6] Bleak longevity awareness underscores why the Israelites continually recalled the divine mandate to "be fruitful and multiply" (Gen 1:28; 9:1; 35:11).

The Israelites regarded a life sans marriage and parenting as a disgrace, so virginity was associated more with lack of fulfillment than with purity. According to a Genesis story, a craving to have children caused Lot's daughters to trick their father into impregnating them (19:30–38). The tale of an Israelite judge illustrates that being killed was not a girl's greatest angst. Jephthah's daughter, on learning that she would be sacrificed because of her father's rash vow, lamented that she would die before marrying and starting a family. She requested time to bewail her virginity with her companions (Judg 11:37–38). Virginity in girls was as lovely to the Hebrews as the virgin earth, which was more valued after it was tilled to grow plants that provided sustenance for survival and delight to the senses. Since virginity was only a temporary stage that culminated in childbearing, the Hebrews had no word to denote a permanent virgin. Underpopulation was an acute problem because of the high mortality rate from disease, harsh environment, and war. In such a situation, it was irresponsible for someone to avoid marriage; sexual relations were viewed as a necessary good, not as a necessary evil.

On some occasions, ancient Israel practiced temporary sexual abstinence. Moses asked all his people to refrain from sexual intercourse during the days that God's revelation was being given on Mount Sinai (Exod 19:15). Semen discharge and menstrual flow were believed to cause ritual pollution (Lev 15:16–19). Priests were ceremonially unclean on days of ejaculation and did not handle cultic items at the tabernacle altar until after they bathed in the evening (Lev 22:4–6). The priests in Israel shared with some neighboring pagan cultures the notion that sacrifices in worship might not be acceptable to God if those administering them had engaged in sex on the day prior to the ritual. When priests were initiated into office, they stayed in the sacred place of worship for seven days and were separated from their families (Lev 8:33). Also, on the Day of Atonement, sexual abstinence may have been one of the ways of practicing self-denial (Lev 23:29). According to the Mishnah, eating, bathing, and sexual relations were forbidden on that annual day for all Jews; in addition, conjugal abstinence was required of the high priest while he lived in a chamber at the temple during the week before the Day of Atonement.[7]

In the biblical culture, marriage was expected of all, including priests. They procreated sons to inherit their office, so abstention from sex for ceremonial purposes was temporary. A priest was required to marry a virgin of his own people rather than a foreigner, widow, divorcee, or prostitute (Lev 21:13–14). Regarding that Levitical requirement, Judith Wegner comments: "Unlike religions that elevate celibacy above marriage, Israelite religion insisted that even its highest religious functionary take a wife and beget children. Sexuality was an integral part of human life, and marriage and paternity were indispensable aspects of 'complete' manhood."[8]

Sacred and sexual activities were regarded as mutually exclusive in tabernacle worship and in holy war. This rule is stated in the Torah:

> When you are encamped against your enemies you shall avoid any foulness. If one of you becomes unclean because of a nocturnal emission, he shall go outside the camp. . . . He shall wash himself with water, and at sunset he may come back into the camp. . . . Because the LORD your God travels with your camp, to keep you safe and to hand over your enemies to you, therefore your camp must be kept holy, so that he may not see anything indecent among you and turn away from you. (Deut 23:9–11, 14)

When David was leading his troops against the Philistines (or "Palestinians" as later written), he attested that his hungry men were worthy to eat the tabooed consecrated bread of the holy place because they had abstained from sex (1 Sam 21:4–5). Similarly, after David became king, his commander Uriah refused to have sex with his beautiful wife Bathsheba while his unit was on a military expedition. That integrity blew

David's scheme for having the public presume that Uriah, not David, had impregnated Bathsheba (2 Sam 11:2–11). It appears that Israelite army officers, like some current athletic coaches, thought sexual indulgence before a contest weakened their men's ability to triumph over adversaries.

A verse in one of the Hebrew psalms seems to Westerners to suggest that coitus pollutes holiness. A penitent confesses, "I was brought forth in iniquity, / and in sin did my mother conceive me. . . . Create in me a clean heart, O God" (Ps 51:5, 10). But psalmists had a hyperbolic way of expressing their moral deficiencies. When the psalmists speak of sinfulness from conception onward, or of lying at birth (Ps 58:3), their poetry should not be taken literally. They were not referring to congenital evil transmitted by sexual generation. Rather, they were reflecting on the way humans start making wrong choices early in life.

The cultic impurity concern that occasionally resulted in abstinences for some Israelites was unrelated to a belief that marriage is morally contaminating. In the entire Hebrew biblical history, there are no instances of lifelong voluntary celibacy. But one case of alleged celibacy needs to be examined to defend that categorical assertion. Lucien Legrand's review of virginity in the biblical era begins with Jeremiah, whom he believes to have been the first Jew to renounce marriage.[9] John Meier also contends that Jeremiah shows "the Old Testament was not lacking in at least one celibate."[10] Contained in his prophecy is this testimony: "The word of the LORD came to me: 'Do not marry or have children in this place. I will tell you what is going to happen to the children born in this place and their parents: . . . They will perish by sword or famine'" (Jer 16:1–4). That prophet was confronted with a Jerusalem citizenry who stubbornly believed that God would not allow their city to be destroyed. They would not listen to him when he urged his people to surrender to the invading Babylonians and thereby avert death by disease and by swords.

In a desperate attempt to get the Jerusalemites to change their military policy, Jeremiah dramatized their impending plight in nonverbal ways. For a time he walked about wearing an oxen yoke to portray the bondage that would come if they continued to resist the enemy. During the traumatic period when Judah was on the verge of being wiped out, he also remained unmarried in an effort to shout forth from his personal situation that ordinary life as Jews knew it was ending. He knew that marriage was universally associated by his people with the fulfilled life, so his abstaining from marrying or from remarrying was calculated to have a shock effect. Jeremiah thought that the symbolic action might make the lethargic public take the grim future more seriously, since to be without wife and children was a terrible disgrace. Such deprivation could obviously result in the extinction of one's family. Jeremiah's actions at the time of the siege of Jerusalem and the emphasis on not marrying "in this place" show the temporary nature of his sexual abstinence.[11] Far from conveying that the single life was a good life-long option, he was attempting to communicate that tragedy was ahead but it would not necessarily be a permanent disaster to Judaism.

Hebraist M. D. Goldman plausibly interprets several passages in Jeremiah's prophecy as alluding to his marriage.[12] He purchased a plot of land, indicating that he planned to settle down to normal life if he survived the destruction of Jerusalem (Jer 32:6–15). He probably intended to act on the advice that he gave to the exiles to build homes, take wives, and bear children (Jer 29:5–6). The city was destroyed and the Babylonian conflict ended not long after Jeremiah's peace demonstrations. When that tragedy had passed, there would have been no point in his continuing his protest, either by wearing the undesirable oxen yoke or by refraining from the desirable connubial yoke. There is no indication in ancient Jewish literature that Jeremiah never married.

Hirschel Revel is not indulging in overstatement when he asserts, "The voluntary renunciation of marriage is a conception utterly foreign to Judaism."[13] The attitudes of the ancient Jews toward sexuality were positive and meant much more than the mere avoidance of celibacy. The many-splendored purposes of connubial love were extolled, but the extremes of undisciplined license and sexual deprivation were abhorred. With the support of biblical quotes, a Talmudic scholar sums up Judaism's position on marriage: "Any man who has no wife lives without joy, without blessing, and without goodness."[14] A Jewish sage, living in the second century BCE, expresses suspicion of unattached men who travel about:

> He who acquires a wife gets his best possession, a helper fit for him and a pillar of support. Where there is no fence, the property will be plundered; and where there is no wife, a man will become a fugitive and a wanderer. For who will trust a nimble robber that skips from city to city? So who will trust a man that has no nest, but lodges wherever night overtakes him? (Sir 36:29–31, NRSV)

Marriage was considered a sacred obligation in Judaism, to be fulfilled at an early age. Marcus Cohn stresses, "The most important common obligation of the married couple is the performance of the marital act."[15] The Mishnah elaborates on the Torah's injunction on spousal duty by specifying the frequency of sexual intercourse: every day for the unemployed, twice a week for laborers, once a week for ass drivers, and once a month for camel drivers.[16] Since the sacred is associated with the sexual, the Talmud recommends conjugal intercourse as a good way to begin the holy Sabbath.[17] In his sociological study of Hebrew sexuality, David Mace comments: "The Hebrews so ordered their community life that no one was likely to be left in the condition of prolonged sexual frustration. Sex was a gift of God, and it was given to be used."[18]

Pagan Cultures

Much of the sexual outlook in Western civilization has been filtered through ancient European philosophers who championed moral dualism and its concomitant asceticism. That theory and associated practice is a legacy received mainly from the Greek culture. Moral dualism can be traced to the Orphic cult, and Greeks used a pun for one of the metaphors to describe it, "The body [*soma*] is the tomb [*sema*] of the soul . . . and the body is a prison in which the soul is undergoing punishment for sin."[19] *Psyche,* the Greek term traditionally translated as "soul," might better be rendered "mind." Pythagoras, the first Greek to call himself a philosopher, adopted this mind-flesh dichotomy in the sixth century BCE, and the fraternity he founded lived by his principles. He was reported to have said, "Keep to the winter for sexual pleasures, in summer abstain; they are less harmful in autumn and spring, but they are always harmful and not conducive to health." Asked when a man should consort with a woman, Pythagoras replied, "When you want to lose what strength you have."[20] Females were associated with qualities such as dark, evil, odd, and crooked.[21]

Democritus and Plato, Athenian admirers of Pythagoras, denounced sexual activity.[22] Plato referred to sexual desire as a diseased part of the personality. In contrast to the appetite for food, which cannot be completely rejected if a person desires to survive, he thought genital gratification expendable. Plato pictured the well-balanced person as one who sublimates all his amorous energies to intellectual pursuits.[23] In his *Symposium,* two kinds of love are separated as far as possible: noble, heavenly eros is perfected to the extent that it is removed from vulgar, earthly eros. The former seeks after clear knowledge; the latter is "of the body rather than of the mind" and is experienced in heterosexual relations. According to Plato, woman has no part in the creation of heavenly love.[24] Greek philosophy specialist Benjamin Fuller states that for bachelor Plato, sex was "the archenemy of the life of the spirit."[25]

Asceticism, the by-product of the Greek mind-body dualistic philosophy, maintains that bodily appetites should be severely repressed for the health of the soul/mind. *Askēsēs,* the Greek root of "ascetic," first meant the training an athlete receives. Later it came to connote a life of abstaining from the natural enjoyments of life as much as survival permitted. Sensual pleasures, especially those experienced in sexual relations and from some foods, were denied. They were deemed inherently evil because they are stimulated by the flesh-craving part of the psyche. Athletes with moral convictions consciously tried to rid their minds of the contamination incurred by contact with physical substances. Hellenistic expert Eric Dodds observes that sexual asceticism not only originated in Greece, but also "was carried by a Greek mind to its extreme theoretical limit."[26] Only after the pervasive impact of pagan asceticism is recognized can we distinguish and appreciate the distinctively different sexual viewpoints that prevailed among participants in the biblical milieu.

Some religions in the Mediterranean area extolled virginity as the superlative virtue. Ephesus featured the well-organized cult of Artemis, who was called "the virgin goddess and the immaculate one." The Athenians crowned their city with the Parthenon (virgin-temple), and the center of adoration within was the gold and ivory statue of Athena. In the Greek culture, sexual fasting before approaching a temple area was expected. At Pergamum, Athena devotees had to abide by this purity rule: "Whoever wishes to visit the temple of the goddess . . . must refrain from intercourse with one's spouse that day and from intercourse with another than one's spouse for the two preceding days."[27] "The Greeks were particularly insistent on the sexual purity of priests and innumerable cults demanded the absolute chastity of the priest or priestess."[28] Edward Schillebeeckx writes:

> In areas round the Mediterranean . . . laws of purity for pagan priests were very prominent: "Anyone who approaches the altar must not have enjoyed the pleasures of Venus the night before." . . . The Stoic ideal . . . was widespread at that time (in antiquity sexual intercourse was called a "little epilepsy": . . . it robs people of their senses and therefore is not "in accord with reason"). Neo-Pythagoreanism and later, above all, Neo-Platonic dualism also played a part: the Neo-Platonist pagan Porphyry wrote a book entitled *On Abstinence,* which enjoyed great popularity.[29]

The veneration of virginity was as prominent in Roman as in Greek civilization. For centuries of Roman history, the "most sacred of priestly offices," according to Cicero, was that of the vestal virgins.[30] The virgins selected for the office were regarded for virtually all of their lives as personifications of the virgin goddess Vesta. Virtuous vestals had great influence, but the unfaithful ones were buried alive.[31] So in Rome, ideal purity was inseparable from sexual continence. Celibates were also associated with Mithraism the popular mystery religion of the Roman Empire and the chief rival of early Christianity.[32]

"Beginning in the first century B.C., a wave of asceticism swept over the whole Greek world, which became more and more powerful as time went on. World-flight and other-worldliness were the characteristic features of the thought of decaying Greece."[33] The Epicurean and Stoic schools were the most popular philosophic schools during the long Greco-Roman era. "Sexual intercourse has never done a man good," Epicurus said, "and he is lucky if it has not harmed him."[34] Lucretius, who championed Epicurus's philosophy in the Latin culture, asserted that sexual craving cannot be cured by intercourse: "At length when the pent-up desire has gone forth, there ensues a short pause in the burning passion; and then returns the same frenzy, then comes back the old madness."[35] A wise man should avoid sex altogether, for it does not contribute to the ideal, unruffled life.

"Endure and abstain" was the motto of Epictetus, the famous Stoic of the first century CE.[36] He taught that the impulse to indulge in sensual love should be counteracted by an opposing discipline of renunciation.[37] The Stoics believed "the wise man is passionless [*apatheia*]" and classified love, along with hate, as irrational conditions to shun.[38] Seneca, a Roman Stoic, said: "A wise man ought to love his wife with judgment, not affection. Let him control his impulses and not be borne headlong into copulation. Nothing is fouler than to love a wife like an adulteress."[39]

Indian culture had begun to influence the Greco-Roman civilization before the beginning of the Christian era. From the time of the Persian empire onward, historical records show significant cross-cultural contacts between India and the Mediterranean areas.[40] In the third century BCE, Emperor Asoka of India sent Buddhist missionaries as far abroad as Macedonia and Egypt, transforming an Indian sect into an international religion.[41] In the first century BCE, Alexander Polyhistor described for the Greeks the celibate practices of Hindus, Buddhists, and Jains who "think sexual relations are unnatural and unlawful."[42] Egyptologist Flinders Petrie, who finds no encouragement of celibacy in Egypt prior to the period of Indian influence, asserts, "There is no difficulty in regarding India as the source of the entirely new ideal of asceticism in the West."[43] The heat and dry climate of Egypt attracted hermits and monks of different religions. At the beginning of the Hellenistic era, Ptolemy I established the cult of Serapis to unify his empire. Its cloistered priests at the Egyptian temples devoted themselves to sexual and dietary austerities.[44] Chaeremon, the librarian at Alexandria, wrote a treatise on Egyptian priests who abstained from wine, meat, and intercourse with women.[45]

The ancient religions of India sanctioned family life for the many but encouraged the single life for those in pursuit of a nobler and more arduous path. The Hindu god Krishna advised, "Firm in the vow of celibacy, subdued in mind, let him sit, harmonized, his mind turned to me and intent on me alone."[46] Patanjali, who gave yoga its classic formulation in the second century BCE, asserted, "Vital force is established through sexual abstinence; purity involves a disdain for one's physical body and a cessation of contact with others."[47] The retention of semen is thought to increase a man's spiritual energies. But celibacy is not required for Hindu priests, and marriage is a requirement for those conducting certain ceremonies.

The most ascetic of all Indian religions is Jainism. Mahavira, its celibate founder, lived some six centuries before the Christian era. Making sexual abstinence a cardinal obligation, he admonished: "The greatest temptation in the world are women. . . . Men should not speak to women, nor look at them, nor converse with them, nor claim them as their own." One of the basic vows of the Jainist ascetic is, "I renounce all sexual pleasure."[48]

Siddhartha the Buddha, whom Queen Maya is alleged to have miraculously conceived without having sex with her husband, was a contemporary of Mahavira in the Indian culture. After coming to think of marriage as an entrapment, Siddhartha permanently abandoned his wife and baby. One of the more reliable historical sources states, "The monk Guatama [Siddhartha] . . . is celibate and aloof, and has lost all desire for sexual intercourse, which is vulgar."[49] In the hermitage to which he had withdrawn, he endured years of austerity and temptation before he managed to extinguish all sensual passion and become "enlightened." The Buddha then left the forest to instruct Hindu ascetics how they, too, could reach the state of nirvana. He persuaded them that freedom could be found by breaking loose from family entanglements and by establishing permanent residence in a monastery. Late in his life, a monk asked him for advice on the proper conduct toward the opposite sex. This exchange ensued: "What should be our attitude toward women?" "Avoid the sight of them." "But if we should see them, Lord, what must we do?" "Do not speak to them."[50]

In Buddhist monasteries, the first commandment is continual coital abstinence.[51] Buddhism's regulation of sexual activities has remained constant, as a contemporary monk explains:

Celibacy is an important element in Tibetan Buddhist monasticism. It is taught as a value from the earliest years and is one of the four musts in terms of monastic vows. The four initial vows are not to steal, not to kill, not to have sexual relations, not to lie. The breaking of any one of these four is cause for immediate expulsion. . . . If any incident between males did happen, it would mean the end of one's monastic life.[52]

Since humans of every culture share the same strong sex drive, there is a yawning gap between what is professed and what is practiced. The editor of the *Bangkok Post* finds it scandalous that many Buddhist monks today are not adhering to their celibate vows.[53] Reports that some of them are infected with AIDS attest to this. While recognizing the lapse in carrying out their theory, devotees of the dominant Indian religions believe that withdrawal from sensuous experiences tends to charge one's inner sanctum with psychic and cosmic energy. Disengagement from all enticements of sex pervades the concept of spirituality in these religions.

Zoroastrianism is the pagan religion bearing the closest resemblance to the Jewish outlook on sexuality. The Persian religion had considerable influence on the ancient Jews after their liberation from exile by Persian King Cyrus. Although Zoroastrianism is based on avoiding defilement, conjugal sexuality was not considered contaminating. Prophet Zoroaster was married to a woman named Hvovi and had children. John Hinnells comments on Zoroastrian ethics: "People have a religious duty to expand God's material creation as well as to support his spiritual creation. A man should get married and have children. . . . In Zoroastrian belief a monk is as great a sinner as a lecher—both deny what God wills."[54] Miles Dawson adds, "Zoroaster and his followers condemn celibacy utterly and find no warrant for it in nature; the unmarried of both sexes are looked on with disfavor and there is no celebration of continence as purity."[55] Zoroastrians believed that the pleasures of the world should be enjoyed in moderation.

Notes

1. *Cross Currents* (Winter 1966): 91.
2. Sigmund Freud, *Collected Papers* (New York: Basic Books, 1959), 4:206.
3. David Bakan, *Sigmund Freud and the Jewish Mystical Tradition* (Princeton: Princeton University Press, 1958), 272.
4. William Phipps, *Recovering Biblical Sensuousness* (Philadelphia: Westminster, 1975).

5. William Phipps, *Assertive Biblical Women* (New York: Greenwood, 1992), 139–44.

6. Bruce Malina and Richard Rohrbaugh, *Social-Science Commentary on the Synoptic Gospels* (Minneapolis: Fortress, 1992), 305, 338.

7. *Yoma* 1:1; 8:1.

8. Carol Newsom and Sharon Ringe, eds., *The Women's Bible Commentary* (Louisville: Westminster/John Knox, 1992), 43.

9. Lucien Legrand, *The Biblical Doctrine of Virginity* (New York: Sheed & Ward, 1963), 23–26.

10. John Meier, *The Marginal Jew* (New York: Doubleday, 1991), 1:339.

11. Josephine Ford, *A Trilogy on Wisdom and Celibacy* (Notre Dame: University Press, 1967), 24–25.

12. M. D. Goldman, "Was Jeremiah Married?," *Australian Biblical Review* (1952): 43–47.

13. "Celibacy," *The Universal Jewish Encyclopedia* (New York: Ktav, 1948).

14. *Yebamot* 62b.

15. "Marriage," *The Universal Jewish Encyclopedia.*

16. *Ketubot* 5:6; Exod 21:10.

17. *Ketubot* 62b.

18. David Mace, *Hebrew Marriage* (London: Epworth, 1953), 144.

19. Plato, *Cratylus* 399–400.

20. Diogenes Laertius, *Lives of Eminent Philosophers* 8:9.

21. Aristotle, *Metaphysics* 986a.

22. Stobaeus, *Anthology* 3:18, 4:24.

23. Plato, *Republic* 402–5, 485, 559; *Phaedo* 66–67.

24. Plato, *Symposium* 180–81.

25. Benjamin Fuller, *History of Greek Philosophy* (New York: Holt, 1931), 446.

26. Eric Dodds, *The Greeks and the Irrational* (Berkeley: University of California Press, 1951), 155.

27. Frederick Grant, *Hellenistic Religions* (New York: Liberal Arts, 1953), 6.

28. Joseph Swain, *The Hellenic Origins of Christian Asceticism* (New York: Columbia University Press, 1916), 9.

29. Edward Schillebeeckx, *The Church with a Human Face* (New York: Crossroad, 1985), 242.

30. Cicero, *De domo suo* 53, 136.

31. Elizabeth Abbott, *A History of Celibacy* (Cambridge: Da Capo, 2001), 39–42.

32. Tertullian, *Prescription against Heretics* 40.

33. Swain, *Hellenic Origins,* 143.

34. Epicurus, *Symposium* 8.

35. Lucretius, *The Nature of the Universe* 4:1115–18.

36. H. W. Smyth, ed., *Harvard Essays on Classical Subjects* (Cambridge: Harvard University Press, 1912), 120.

37. Epictetus, *Discourses* 3:12, 24.

38. Diogenes Laertius, *Lives* 7:117.

39. Vern Bullough, *Sexual Variance in History* (New York: Wiley, 1976), 166.

40. William Phipps, "Did Ancient Indian Celibacy Influence Christianity?" *Studies in Religion* (January 1974): 46–47.

41. *Rock Edicts of Asoka* 13.

42. Clement of Alexandria, *Miscellanies* 3:60.

43. Flinders Petrie, *Egypt and Israel* (London: SPCK, 1923), 134.

44. Porphyry, *On Abstinence* 4:6–9.

45. Jerome, *Against Jovinian* 2:13.

46. *Bhagavad Gita* 6:14.

47. *Yoga Sutra* 2:38, 40.

48. *Gaina Sutras* and *Akaranga Sutra,* in *Sacred Books of the East* (ed. Max Muller; Oxford: Clarendon, 1884), 22:21, 48, 207.

49. *Digha Nikaya* 1:4.

50. *Maha-parinibbana Sutta* 5:23.

51. *Pratimoksha Sutra* 1.

52. Richard Sipe, *Sex, Priests, and Power* (New York: Brunner, 1995), 134–35.

53. *National Catholic Reporter,* May 26, 1995, 13.

54. *Eerdmans' Handbook to the World's Religions* (Grand Rapids: Eerdmans, 1994), 87.

55. Miles Dawson, *The Ethical Religion of Zoroaster* (New York: Macmillan, 1931), 147.

Chapter 3

A CELIBATE JESUS?

❧

The lifestyle of leaders in all religions is greatly affected by the presumed marital status of their founders. Jews and Muslims have expected marriage of their rabbis and imams, in large part because of the hallowed stories pertaining to Abraham, Moses, and Muhammad. Likewise, the traditional view in Judaism and Islam that confirmed bachelors lack completion has been influenced by an awareness that those originating leaders were espoused. Correspondingly, monastic life has been elevated in Buddhism as the holy ideal because the Buddha was celibate. Was Jesus more like Siddhartha or more like Abraham?

Church celibacy is like baptism in that neither was sanctioned by practices described in the Hebrew Bible. Virtually all Christians presume that they were begun and continued by the church mainly because Jesus himself was baptized and celibate. Vatican II followed centuries of tradition in commending priests who "have freely undertaken sacred celibacy in imitation of Christ."[1] John Paul II has cited the example of Christ as the primary reason why Latin Catholics should preserve obligatory celibacy for priests.[2] This recent Vicar of Christ, like his predecessors, believes without a doubt that Christ was celibate, and thus most Catholics have long been convinced that the more spiritual persons are celibate.

In his essay on the roots of celibacy in the church, Benedictine monk Ignatius Hunt observes, "The life of Jesus has been one of the great factors in presenting to Christians, and especially to priests, the ideal of celibacy."[3] The appeal to Jesus' lack of a spouse as a model for priests continues to resound in books recently written by Catholics to defend priestly celibacy. Cardinal Alfons Stickler, a participant in Vatican II, regards celibacy as "indispensable to the priesthood" and, in dealing with its "theologian foundation," appeals to the example of Jesus as its inspiration.[4] Theologian Stanley Jaki writes, "It cannot be emphasized enough that Jesus was a celibate and that this was part and parcel of the superhuman fullness of his character."[5] James Martin, an editor of the national Jesuit magazine, concludes his defense of sexual abstinence for priests by pointing to Jesus and some of his apostles as models.[6] Catholic journalist David Gibson, even though he does not approve of mandatory celibacy, acknowledges, "The most powerful argument for celibacy, of course, is that Jesus, the model for the perfect Christian life and for priests in particular, was himself unmarried and chaste."[7]

Protestant as well as Catholic clergy usually affirm that Jesus was a celibate and seem to accept that axiom as self-evident, as needing no proof. German Lutheran theologian Helmut Thielicke asserts: "Jesus himself was unmarried. He also demanded of his disciples the renunciation of family ties."[8] Protestant monk Max Thurian writes: "Christ did not experience marriage, physical love and sexual union. His life is therefore the valid foundation of the vocation of celibacy in the new era."[9]

On the other hand, consider several Catholics and Protestants who think that Jesus was probably not celibate. Charles Davis, a leading Catholic theologian in Britain during the Vatican II era, acknowledged that the "historical probabilities favor marriage rather than celibacy" for Jesus.[10] German Catholic theologian Uta Ranke-Heinemann states: "Today we take it for granted that Jesus never married, whereas there is not the slightest hint about this in the New Testament."[11] American Catholic theologian Anthony Padovano likewise argues "the evidence for the lifelong celibacy of Jesus is nonexistent" and that a married Jesus is "a high probability."[12] Also, Protestant Stephen Twycross provides arguments "establishing the probability that Jesus, like most Palestinian Jewish males of his time was, in fact, a married man."[13]

According to the "table-talk" recorded by one of his disciples, Martin Luther assumed that Jesus fully expressed his sexual impulses with some women companions.[14] Few Lutheran spokespersons have been as brash as Luther on this matter, but Elisabeth Moltmann-Wendel wonders if his judgment about Jesus might not have been right.[15] Lutheran clergyman Richard Langsdale has written a historical novel in an attempt to illustrate Jesus' continual awareness of both his "God-nature" and his full humanity. In Langsdale's story, a young woman from Magdala with psychological difficulties is healed by "Yisu." He subsequently strolls with Mary Magdalene along the Sea of Galilee, and his "Yahweh Spirit" sanctions falling in love with her. "With Mary I saw a whole new dimension of compassion, understanding, patience and forgiveness," acknowledges Langsdale's Jesus. Having been encouraged by his fellow Galileans to take Mary as his wife, he experiences in marital intercourse the full-orbed "breadth and length and height and depth" of love that the New Testament emphasizes (Eph 3:18–19). Jesus reflected during the honeymoon:

> Long ago and in another place I had watched my father Joseph hone and plane and mold the jointure of two olive boards until, with nod of perfection gained and satisfied, he closed the jointure and bound the olive wood from two parts into one. So here in this night I drew this Mary, this handicraft of God, into human jointure with myself, and through the night we honed the union to its height and depth and breadth of intended perfection. We two became one.[16]

Arguments Pro and Con

In spite of a few notable disagreements, Christians are generally agreed that Jesus was celibate, but there is no consensus as to why. Unlike dogmas regarding Mary of Nazareth's virginity, church bodies have never established definitive doctrines pertaining to Jesus' sexual or nonsexual life. What follows is my collection of the main reasons for and against a celibate Jesus.[17] As a method for examining this issue critically, I will use an informal version of what is found in Thomas Aquinas's *Summa Theologica*. In that intellectually stimulating and highly influential compendium of Catholic thought, Aquinas first states a proposition contrary to his own and lucidly summarizes all the arguments he can find in its favor. Then he gives counterarguments against the proposition. The form of Aquinas's reasoning will be borrowed, but no use will be made of any ideas he might have had on the topic at hand. For Aquinas and his medieval era, the celibacy of Jesus was unquestioned, so he does not debate the subject.

1. The New Testament states that Jesus encouraged eunuchry.

Pro

According to Matt 19:12, Jesus taught: "There are eunuchs who have been so from birth, and there are eunuchs who have been castrated by others, and there are eunuchs who have castrated themselves for the sake of the kingdom of heaven. Let anyone accept this teaching who can." A thorough examination of this bizarre and enigmatic saying follows.

In the nineteenth century a Russian sect called *Skoptsys,* meaning "emasculated ones," appealed to that eunuch verse as one of the two giving them authority to castrate male converts with a red-hot iron. The other gospel verse was, "If your hand causes you to stumble, cut it off!" (Mark 9:43). In Hebrew Scripture, "hand" could be a euphemism for male genitals (Isa 57:8). Skoptsy's founder Szelivanov interpreted the sayings attributed to Jesus to mean that amputating the sin-stimulating genitals was necessary for salvation. Also, the prediction that Jesus would baptize with fire in Matt 3:11 was interpreted to mean that he would cauterize the apostles' castration surgery. Thousands of Skoptsys thought they were imitating Jesus, whom they believed actually made himself a sexual cripple.[18]

Nearly all other Christians have interpreted the eunuch saying differently from the Skoptsys. It would be antithetical to the compassionate spirit of Jesus to think that he encouraged his followers to maim their bodies to overcome temptation. Even literalistic fundamentalists avoid viewing Jesus as a self-amputated gelding. Surgery on diseased limbs can save lives, but Jesus did not intend his words about cutting off a hand or foot or tearing out an eye to be taken literally. Jesus often indulged in absurd exaggerations to make a point,[19] and the eunuch text illustrates this. After the hyperbole is removed, the residual meaning is that the rule of God entails stringent sexual self-discipline.

In the third century, Tertullian was among the first to assume that Jesus was speaking figuratively when he commended those who have made themselves eunuchs. He asserted, "The Lord himself opened the kingdom of heaven to eunuchs and he himself lived as a virgin."[20] For the Latin church leader, "eunuchs" designated not only virgins but spouses who became sexually abstinent after converting to Christianity. He stated, "How many there are who, by mutual consent, cancel the debt of their marriage; eunuchs of their own accord through the desire of the kingdom of heaven."[21]

Pope John Paul II has declared that this gospel reference to eunuchs provides the ultimate ground for designating as "apostolic teaching" Catholic pronouncements on celibacy.[22] The Pope makes these comments on the eunuch text: "That preference given to celibacy and virginity 'for the kingdom' was an absolute novelty in comparison with the Old Covenant tradition. . . . Does Christ perhaps suggest the superiority of continence for the kingdom of heaven to matrimony? Certainly."[23]

Presbyterian exegete Floyd Filson presumes that Jesus, in his eunuch saying, referred literally only to the first two types, men with a natural sexual defect and those who had received the dreadful punishment of emasculation. Underlying the third type, Filson thinks, is Jesus' "deliberate decision to refrain from marriage to be free to devote one's entire time to the cause of the Kingdom."[24] Gnostic scholar Elaine Pagels cites Jesus' teaching on eunuchs to show that he had compassion on the emasculated and others who were unmarried:

> Eunuchs, whom Jesus praised, were despised by rabbinic teachers for their sexual incapacity. Unmarried himself, Jesus praised the very persons most pitied and shunned in Jewish communities for their sexual incompleteness. . . . Jesus endorses—and exemplifies—a new possibility and one he says is even better: rejecting both marriage and procreation in favor of voluntary celibacy, for the sake of following him into the new age.[25]

Con

A preliminary consideration is whether the eunuch saying preserves what Jesus said, since it occurs only in one gospel and is not mentioned elsewhere in the New Testament. Finding the verse anomalous, some commentators question its authenticity. Robert Gundry makes a good case that it should be attributed to the Matthean redactor.[26] For purposes of this debate, however, we will assume that Matt 19:12 records a teaching of Jesus.

Johann Bengel, an outstanding early modern biblical exegete, coined the simple but profound epigram: a text without a context is merely a pretext (for the personal agenda of its user). When Jesus referred to a third type of eunuch, he used the term in an unprecedented manner. His meaning can only be found by relating the eunuch saying to the larger context of Matthew by means of literary and historical exegesis. The passage in which the saying is embedded emphasizes the positive values of marriage and children. Far from advocating a vow of permanent virginity, the context shows Jesus stressing permanence in marriage. Jesus would hardly have given a praiseworthy connotation to "eunuch," a term associated with a horrible mutilation, in a teaching that begins by commending the joining of sexual bodies.

The dialogue of Matt 19 begins with some Pharisees "testing" Jesus by asking, "Is it lawful for a man to divorce his wife for any cause?" According to the Torah, a husband could write "a divorce certificate" (literally an eviction get paper!) if he found "something objectionable" about his wife (Deut 24:1). At issue in Jesus' era was what types of conduct made a wife objectionable. Some rabbis argued that grounds for divorce included scolding a husband loud enough to be heard outside the home, spoiling food under preparation, going out with hair unbound, or the husband's finding someone else more beautiful.[27]

Jesus was addressing men of a culture in which divorce was exclusively a male prerogative, so ousting a wife whose behavior was deemed obnoxious could be accomplished without even a hearing before a judge. While a husband could break the marriage bond for trivial reasons and without a wife's consent, she could not divorce him even if he were irresponsible, cruel, lecherous, or otherwise abusive.

Before Jesus' ministry began, Herod Antipas had divorced a Nabatean princess in order to marry his brother's wife.[28] Jesus found the sanctity of marriage denigrated by the widespread flippant attitude toward divorce, extending from the Galilean ruler to the common people. Marital forgiveness for minor domestic offenses fell short of seven times, not to mention his "seventy times seven" standard (Matt 18:22). Jesus acknowledged the Roman practice that permitted either spouse to initiate a divorce, although he did not approve of that practice either. He taught, "Whoever divorces his wife and marries another commits adultery against her; and if she divorces her husband and marries another, she commits adultery" (Mark 10:11–12, NRSV).

Jesus encouraged mutual repentance in restoring dysfunctional marriages. In replying to the Pharisees, he reiterated what their scriptures stated was a purpose of the Creator, "the two shall become one flesh." Thinking that divorce law should be subordinated to the creation principle, he directed his interlocutors to the outlook on marriage contained in the Eden story. A man's bonding with his wife should replace the close ties he had with his parents (Gen 2:24). After pointing to the ideal of a permanent splicing, Jesus explained that Moses had allowed divorce legislation as a way of dealing with a moral malady. Jesus diagnosed the marriage-destroying disease as cardiosclerosis (Greek, *sklerocardia*), or hardening of the heart. When this condition persists in one or both spouses, legal controls for a sick marriage are needed. Eric Fuchs comments:

> Jesus does not criticize Moses, . . . but he does challenge the turn-about effected by Jewish doctors who raise a contingent law to the status of a norm in God's will. . . . Any repudiation of the wife by the husband is . . . a checkmate to God's plan, will, and promise. . . . Marriage is recognized as the place of man's and woman's apprehending of the promise and grace of God; . . . it can also signify (and more cruelly than in any other realm of human existence) the refusal to believe in the creative and recreative grace of love, a closing-in upon oneself in fear and covetousness—in brief, a refusal of the other.[29]

On hearing Jesus' emphasis on permanent commitment, his disciples were astounded by his radical teaching, even as they were by his teaching on the peril of wealth, also recorded in the same chapter of Matthew (19:25). They cynically quipped that the bond of marriage should be avoided if subsequent liberation from it is wrong. To this Jesus first replied that not all people can accept the fidelity ideal of no divorce or remarriage. He recognized that only some have the capacity for patience and striving toward reconciliation that he advocated. The issue here was not the indissolubility of marriage but whether one could live when abandoned and not remarry. Jesus then commented on two types of physical eunuchs and a spiritual type of "eunuch." He associated the third type, the celibacy of the de-yoked, with a shattering disability, not with a heroic ideal state. "The severity of his pronouncement," comments renowned biblical scholar Walter Wink, "is intended to prevent the wholesale dumping of ex-wives onto the streets."[30] Prostitution was then the usual survival practice resorted to by an ex-wife who had been cut off from the economic security of marriage.

Some ancient as well as contemporary gospel interpreters agree that Jesus' eunuch metaphor is unrelated to lifelong celibacy. It was figuratively used in the early church to justify the excommunication of unworthy "members" of the community in order to preserve the health of the rest.[31] Both Justin and Clement of Alexandria used the eunuch saying to demonstrate that Jesus did not sanction remarriage after divorce.[32] It reinforces what he had just stated, "What God has joined, let no one separate" (Matt 19:6).

Jesuit Quentin Quesnell, whose doctorate is from the Pontifical Biblical Institute in Rome, argues that the passage has nothing to do with priestly celibacy. Rather, Jesus asserts that husbands who cannot live by the Creator's requirement of marital fidelity should live in sexual continence after the separation. He concludes, "A man must in marriage take the risk of staking all he has and is on one person, becoming one flesh with her. . . . To continue this loyal and perfect love, even when the love is not returned, is effectively to make oneself a eunuch."[33] William Thompson, another Catholic exegete, agrees with Quesnell that "the 'eunuchs for the Kingdom' are those men who, although estranged from their wives for various reasons, will not remarry but will attempt to reunite with them and in this way remain faithful to their marriage covenant." Thompson suggests that Jesus may have personally been in such a situation.[34] To dramatize the stern obligation that marriage should place on husbands, Jesus used an unforgettable metaphor of self-castration for the kingdom of Heaven.

On examining the eunuch saying vis-à-vis the entire context of Matthew's gospel, Bruce Malina and Richard Rohrbaugh note that no interest is expressed in celibacy elsewhere. They think that the saying ought to be related to Matthew's community in which divorce in order to remarry was all too prevalent. A spouse who has been dishonored should strive to forgive the misconduct rather than seek divorce. Jesus commends spouses who patiently and chastely await the return of their prodigal partners. Malina and Rohrbaugh conclude, "Concern for reconciliation here fits in well with the moral teaching of Jesus throughout Matthew."[35] Anthony Saldarini also writes, "Matthew discourses on human sexual passions and opposes divorce in order to protect marriage, but does not encourage or praise celibacy as an ascetical practice."[36]

The first example of Matthew's treatment of Christian love pertains to the presumed sexual misconduct of Mary. "Her husband Joseph, being a just man and unwilling to expose her to public disgrace," decides to accept the child being carried by Mary as his own. In that episode, found only in Matthew's gospel, compassion replaces any impulse of revenge. Joseph's grace in a situation that he initially thinks is disgraceful is the gospel in microcosm. The mutual reconciliation of Joseph and Mary becomes the epiphany of God-with-us, Emmanuel (Matt 1:18–23). Also, in the passage immediately prior to Jesus' discussion of marriage and divorce, he teaches that God's forgiveness is withheld from the unforgiving (Matt 18:23–35). The eunuch saying's immediate context in Matthew 19 and in the larger context of the gospel indicates that it pertains to the till-death-do-us-part quality of true marriage. The thrust of the saying is that permanent marriage is sanctioned, not permanent celibacy.

The theme of steadfast love in spite of infidelity is at the core of the prophetic theology that Jesus admired (Hos 6:6; Matt 9:13; 12:7). After becoming reconciled with his adulterous spouse, Hosea thought of God as having a similar enduring affection for unfaithful Israel (Hos 1:2; 3:1). Likewise, Ezekiel articulated God's brokenheartedness over his precious bride Jerusalem, who brazenly prostituted herself to foreign lovers, and the divine forgiveness awaiting her return to him (Ezek 16). Isaiah also used the metaphor of God as the husband of wayward Israel. Her Spouse says, "In sudden anger for a moment I hid my face from you; but with everlasting love I will have compassion on you" (Isa 54:8). In imitation of God, spouses should attempt to overcome the painful estrangement that follows betrayed trust.

"Pray for those who abuse you," Jesus said, "For if you love only those who love you, what credit is that to you?" (Luke 6:28, 32). His moral imperative of *agape*, steadfast love when there may be no reciprocation, is exceedingly demanding. Openness to the return of the faithless, not abandonment, is the way of sacrificial love. William Countryman notes that this involves a rejection of patriarchal values: "Jesus demanded that the wife no longer be regarded as disposable (i.e., divorceable) property. Indeed, husband and wife were to be understood as human equals who now constitute one flesh."[37]

The Jesus Seminar has also shown that Jesus' cryptic aphorism on eunuchs was not intended to acknowledge that he was a celibate or to encourage others to take a vow of perpetual virginity. Over a six-year period, the Jesus Seminar, made up of dozens of biblical scholars from a variety of religious traditions, carefully examined each saying in the Gospels that is alleged to have been from Jesus. After cutting out from the eunuch passage "Let anyone accept this who can" as words that Jesus did not say, the Seminar ranked the saying about three types of eunuchs among the top fifth of those he probably uttered. Most of the Seminar fellows make the questionable judgment that the aphorism is separate from the context of teaching about marriage and divorce. They focus on the status of a literal eunuch rather than on a figurative eunuch in a disintegrated marriage:

> The saying may be understood as an attack on a male-dominated, patriarchal society in which male virility and parenthood were the exclusive norms. The true Israel consisted of priests, Levites, and full-blooded male Judeans, all of whom were capable of fathering children. Eunuchs made so by others and males born without testicles were not complete and so could not be counted among true Israelites and were therefore excluded from temple service. . . . If this saying goes back to Jesus, it is possible that he is undermining the depreciation of yet another marginal group, this time the eunuchs, who were subjected to segregation and devaluation, as were the poor, toll collectors, prostitutes, women generally, and children. . . . In any case, the sayings on castration should not be taken as Jesus' authorization for an ascetic lifestyle; his behavior suggests that he celebrated life by eating, drinking, and fraternizing freely with both women and men.[38]

In Israelite culture, to be a eunuch meant not only the loss of virility but also religious excommunication, because it contradicted God's will in creation. The Mosaic law excluded eunuchs from the priesthood (Lev 21:20) and ostracized "anyone whose testicles are crushed or whose penis is cut off" (Deut 23:1). Even a castrated animal was deemed unfit for cultic sacrifice (Lev 22:24). In the Jewish community during Jesus' century, Josephus asserted, "Shun eunuchs and avoid all dealing with those who have deprived themselves of their virility; . . . expel them as though they had committed infanticide."[39] Inflicting such treatment on oneself was so contemptible that Paul hurls at those determined to circumcise Gentile converts this hyperbole: "I wish those who disturb you would castrate themselves!" (Gal 5:12). Prima facie it is unlikely that Jesus took what was associated with a despicable condition and made it a laudatory term for describing the spiritually self-castrated. Jesus' attitude toward actual eunuchs may have paralleled his attitude toward lepers. Although the Torah required that lepers be segregated from the righteous and treated contemptuously (Lev 14), Jesus did not shun them. He touched such untouchables and treated them with compassion (Luke 17:11–19), but he did not advocate that his disciples imitate them.

The interpretation of the Jesus Seminar can be supported by a teaching of Isaiah, a prophet whom Jesus admired. Judean prophets were aware of the cruel practice among their kings, and also among foreign royalty, of castrating palace servants to make them safer for work in their harems (Isa 39:7; Jer 29:2). Some of Isaiah's description of a suffering servant can be appropriated to convey the rejection by the Jewish community of the eunuch: "He was despised and shunned by all; a man racked with pain and afflicted with infirmity, . . . one from whom people hid their faces" (Isa 53:3). The prophet announced that the Torah restriction was abolished: "Thus says the Lord: "No eunuch should say, 'I am just a barren tree.' The eunuchs who observe my sabbaths, who choose to do my will and cling to my covenant, will receive from me a name better than sons and daughters. I will give them a memorial in my own house and within my walls; I will give them an everlasting name that will not be cut off" (Isa 56:3–5).

2. Jesus adopted the celibate practice of a contemporary Jewish sect in Palestine.

Pro

A Jewish religious community called the Essenes was located at Qumran near the Dead Sea during the time of Jesus. A few scholars have argued that it was a monastic order and that he along with his disciples were associated with it.[40] George Buchanan, in his "Jesus and Other Monks" essay, argues that the Jesus band shared the Essene belief that the age to come would be composed only of celibate males.[41] Reginald Fuller, an eminent Anglican New Testament scholar, presumes that Jesus, like the members of the Qumran community, renounced marriage "to engage in the final battle between the children of light and the children of darkness."[42]

Con

The prevailing view of biblical scholars is that Jesus was not significantly influenced by the Essenes, who are not even mentioned in the

New Testament. Although Jesus as well as the Essenes accepted much of the Mosaic legislation, the dissimilarities between the two were greater than the similarities.[43] Also, the discoveries at Qumran and elsewhere of documents written by the Essenes indicate that the sect was composed of married persons who engaged in a cultic sexual abstinence of limited duration.[44] One Essene scroll refers to members of the community taking wives and fathering children.[45] In addition, female skeletons have been found in several cemeteries at Qumran, showing that women were not excluded. According to Linda Elder, "No published text from Qumran mandates celibacy."[46] Joseph Baumgarten writes, "Celibacy at Qumran was never made into a universal norm." Some abstained from sex some years beyond the beginning of puberty, but for most it was taken for granted that marriage was the norm for community life.[47] Only the secondary sources of Philo, Josephus, and Pliny—none of whom were members of the Essene community—state that celibacy was required by the Essenes.[48]

Jewish philosopher Philo told of another Jewish community that developed in the region of Alexandria during the first century before the Christian era. Called the Therapeutae, the cult combined asceticism with worship. Its philosophy was eclectic, the principal ingredients being Pythagoreanism, Platonism, and Stoicism. Celibacy was practiced by older spouses who had completed their procreative duties and wished to enhance religious purification.[49] Philo was heavily influenced by the asceticism of Greek culture. "In his enthusiasm for the systems of Plato and Pythagoras he surpassed all his contemporaries," noted ancient historian Eusebius.[50] He distorted the Torah's account by claiming that Moses abstained "for many a day" from sexual intercourse with his wife Zipporah in order to keep himself always in readiness to receive prophetic messages.[51] Philo also claimed that the animals on Noah's ark were temporarily celibate![52] The philosopher lived only in Egypt and there is no indication that his sexual outlook affected Palestinian Judaism; allusion to his writings is not found in ancient rabbinic or New Testament literature.

Celibacy was rejected both in theory and in practice in the traditions that influenced Jesus. Even the Nazirites, an Israelite sect noted for their temporary vows of abstinence from grape products, hair trimming, and corpse contact (Num 6), were not expected to refrain from coitus, as demonstrated in stories of Nazirite Samson, who was a lecher (Judg 13:7; 16:1, 4).

3. Jesus rebelled against his Jewish heritage in which marriage was expected of religious leaders.

Pro

Although Jesus was raised in a pious family of the Jewish community, some think he severed ties with Judaism as he grew up. Accordingly, he expressed his nonconformity to the Hebrew doctrine of creation by rejecting marriage for himself. The Vatican has asserted that it is fallacious to presume that Jesus was influenced by the prevailing outlook on sexuality of his Jewish community. Its semi-official journal stated: "Christ was anything but conditioned by the cultural and religious atmosphere of his time. . . . A 'married Christ' would not have made the marvel of virginity flower in the world."[53] That outlook is echoed by Catholic priest Peter Rinaldi, who claims that Jesus opposed what the Jews had established as the prerequisite for righteous adulthood: "There is not a shred of evidence in the New Testament or in the early Christian writers that can be seriously invoked to prove that Jesus could have been married. . . . Both by temperament and choice Jesus set his course against ancient tradition."[54] Another Catholic, Sidney Callahan, treats marriage as a cultural confinement from which Jesus, "an abnormal Outsider," rebelled: "As a feminist I think Jesus' celibacy was needed to break open the 'normal' bondage of women, marriage, and family life. . . . The holy family should be one where the mother is not dependent on the father and the father doesn't impose marriage and spouse on dependent children. Marriage at puberty isn't such a hot idea either. . . . We need time and loneliness and rebellion."[55]

Con

Rudolf Bultmann, one of the most influential New Testament interpreters of the twentieth century, thinks there is little biographical information about Jesus that is historically sound. Yet he declares, "It is at least clear that Jesus actually lived as a Jewish rabbi."[56] Rabbis were teachers associated with synagogues and were independent of priests who sacrificed in the one Jewish Temple in Jerusalem. A Mishnaic injunction states categorically, "An unmarried man may not be a rabbi."[57] Celibacy was not kosher in the Israelite religion, and Jesus grew up in that tradition. In the Gospels he was most commonly known as rabbi, but English translations often disguise that fact by rendering it "master" or "teacher."

Jerusalem scholar Schalom Ben-Chorin writes: "I am convinced that Jesus of Nazareth, like any rabbi in Israel, was married. His apostles and opponents would have mentioned it, if he had differed from the general custom." Ben-Chorin points out that we know nothing about the wives of Hillel, Shammai, Jesus, and many other notable men of that era and culture, but had they been unmarried, surely their adversaries would have pointed to their violation of sacred duty as a basis for criticism.[58] The fact that Jesus' marital status is a non-issue in the Gospels suggests that he conformed to cultural expectations in regard to marriage.

In the Hebrew patriarchy, it was the parents, especially the fathers, who were responsible for finding suitable mates for their children. Marriage continued to be more of a family choice than an individual one in Jesus' culture; arranged marriages were the norm during the second decade of life.[59] For ancient Jewish betrothals, "it was the word of the respective fathers rather than that of the parties themselves which gave binding validity to a promise of marriage, especially so as in many cases the parties themselves must have been minors."[60] Biblical sociologist Roland de Vaux states: "The parents took all the decisions when a marriage was being arranged. Neither the girl nor, often, the youth was consulted."[61] In Jesus' culture, Malina and Rohrbaugh assert, "Individuals really did not get married; rather families did. One family offered a male, the other a female. Their wedding stood for the wedding of the larger extended families."[62] If Jesus was usually obedient to his parents, as the New Testament states (Luke 2:51–52), then Joseph would have selected a suitable wife for him.

Reconstructing the basic features of Jesus' life necessitates using conjecture to fill in those years when beginning a family of one's own would customarily take place. Pertaining to his teens and twenties, about which there is no historical record, plausible reconstructions can be made that are based on what is known of the normative patterns of his culture. Catholic Jean Audet makes this argument from silence on the apostles' marital status:

> If the chance of her having a fever had not happened to bring Jesus to see Peter's mother-in-law, the gospel tradition would in fact have observed total silence on the disciples' marriage. Could we therefore conclude that not one of them was married? No, we could not. All we can say is this: the ideas and the customs of the time and place are enough to make it probable that most of the apostles were married; it is even quite possible that they all were, without exception.[63]

Had Audet followed his logic further, he would also have concluded that Jesus was probably not a celibate.

According to the Fourth Gospel, Jesus first "manifested his glory" by contributing to the conviviality of a wedding party (John 2:1–11). Donavan

Joyce believes that Jesus was the bridegroom in the Cana wedding and that it is "absolutely certain that Jesus was a married man."[64] Mormons have a similar view, and think that Mary, from nearby Nazareth, would not have been anxious about the refreshments becoming exhausted if she were not a hostess at a party for her son.[65]

4. Jesus was unwilling to share his severe lifestyle with a spouse.

Pro

Jesus was "more like a Cynic philosopher than anything else," according to Dominic Crossan. He thinks Jesus fit Epictetus's description of the celibate Cynic who freed himself from the entanglement of a wife and a home.[66] In a similar manner, Gerd Theissen believes that the Jesus group did not marry because they were like the Cynics who were contemptuous of wives, families, and possessions.[67]

Protestant biblical scholar Vernon McCasland thinks that Jesus did not want a mate to undergo the hardships he personally anticipated: "The daring role he assumed for himself had no place in it for a woman at his side. The uncertainty, the poverty, the danger, the implied final agony, were not the basis on which to found a marriage, to rear a family."[68] As a man of compassion, Jesus would not have asked a woman to marry someone who would have "no place to lay his head" (Matt 8:20).

Catholic biblical scholar Joseph Blenkinsopp suggests, "Jesus was celibate because he was too poor to marry."[69] It would have been unloving to a wife for him to have married, knowing the absence of living wages that would confront him as an unemployed craftsman. Similarly, religious journalist Louis Cassels writes, "Jesus chose a life of celibacy for a good and obvious reason; he could not support a wife and children while carrying on an unpaid itinerant ministry."[70]

Con

E. P. Sanders, a leading New Testament historian, argues that scholars such as Crossan "make an enormous mistake" in presuming that Jewish teachers in Galilee modeled themselves after Cynic philosophers rather than Israelite prophets.[71] During the era of Jesus, there is virtually no evidence that those philosophers were influential in Palestine.

How true to human experience is the notion that the celibate lives a more arduous life than those who live with the inevitable conflict of domestic situations and discharge their duties as spouse, parent, and in-law? A

Spanish folktale tells about a harried husband who, after hearing a preacher recount all the torments that Jesus endured, inquired if Jesus was married. On being told that he never had a wife, the married man concluded that Jesus could not have known the depth of suffering.[72] Achieving a permanent loving relationship may be as morally demanding for spouses as it is for a monk to muster the discipline to honor for life his vow to be sexually abstinent.

Those who speculate that Jesus voluntarily remained a bachelor because of his poverty as wandering teacher assume incorrectly that Jews did not marry early in life. He left the carpentry business and began to proclaim the gospel when he was "about thirty years old" (Luke 3:23), which would have been middle age in his culture. At the time when Jesus was likely to have married, poverty would probably not have been a problem. There is no evidence suggesting that construction workers in Galilee, a productive agricultural region, were not compensated enough to support a family. Since Joseph and Jesus had the same occupation, one should have been able to afford to marry as easily as the other. Meier judges that Jesus was probably no poorer than most of his fellow Nazarenes.[73]

The Jesus band was not involved in daily itinerations, so married life would not have been difficult to contemplate. For much of the time that he was a teacher in Galilee, Jesus settled in the fishing town of Capernaum. The earliest gospel refers to Jesus' "home" being there (Mark 2:1; 3:19).

5. Jesus remained virginal because sexual desire is defiling; a holy man must flee situations of temptation and sacrifice sexual gratification.

Pro

The author of the book of Hebrews states that Jesus "was tested in every respect as we are, yet without sin" (4:15). By equating sex with sin, some Christians take that New Testament affirmation as meaning that the sinless Jesus was tempted in every respect as we are, except for sex. Presumably, Jesus had only one of the two basic human drives. When he had hunger pangs in the wilderness testing area after his baptism, he resisted the food temptation by saying, "One does not live by bread alone" (Luke 4:4). But Jesus was so impervious to sexual temptation that the devil did not bother to attempt to charm him by offering him a voluptuous woman.

An anonymous Christian of the third century asserted that Jesus, like an ascetic Platonist, gratified only those sensual impulses that were necessary for individual survival: "Christ did not submit to discharging the sexual function, for regarding the desires of the flesh, he accepted some as necessary, while others, which were unnecessary, he did not submit to. For if the flesh were deprived of food, drink, and clothing, it would be destroyed; but being deprived of lawless desire, it suffers no harm."[74]

The distinguished twentieth-century Swiss Protestant theologian Emil Brunner, believing that all sex relations are shameful, relates his judgment to Jesus' life: "Man is not merely ashamed of the sexuality which is forbidden to him morally, but shame accompanies him even into the completely personal sex-relation in marriage, and indeed . . . the more spiritual his existence, the more is he aware of this. We cannot think of our Lord as married, although we are not in the least jarred by the fact that he ate and drank like the rest of mankind."[75]

Con

Jesus' saying pertaining to sexual desire should read, "You have heard the commandment, 'You shall not commit adultery,' but I say to you that anyone who looks longingly [*epithymia*] at another's wife has already committed adultery within" (Matt 5:27–28). *Epithymia* is usually mistranslated as "lust," which is associated with lechery. For example, Shakespeare describes lust as "savage, extreme, rude, cruel."[76] However, the Greek term is morally neutral, for Jesus tells his disciples, "I have fervently [*epithymia*] desired to eat this Passover with you" (Luke 22:15). In the Septuagint, *epithymein* was favorably used to refer to desiring one's beautiful wife and longing for God, but it is unfavorably used to refer to craving another person's spouse (Pss 45:11; 119:20; Exod 20:17).

In the saying under consideration from the Sermon on the Mount, *gune* was translated as "wife," with "of another" understood. The "Great Bible" of the English Renaissance properly translates *gune* as "another man's wife." Jesus interrelated two of the Ten Commandments: coveting a neighbor's spouse is the first step toward the act of adultery. He was in accord with his heritage in which there is no suggestion that the sexual impulse per se is immoral. Ancient Jewish teaching makes explicit that it is adulterous desire that is illicit:

> You are not to say that only he is called adulterer who uses his body in the act. We find Scripture saying that even he who visualizes himself in the act of adultery is called adulterer: "The eye of the adulterer also waits for the twilight, saying 'No eye will see me.'"[77]

Also, Rabbi Simeon said, "Even he who visualizes himself in the act of adultery is called an adulterer."[78]

On Matt 5:28, exegete Eugene Boring states: "This text does not deal with natural sexual desire and its associated fantasy, but with the intentional lustful look at the wife of another."[79] Regarding that saying of Jesus, David Mace has remarked:

> He obviously did not mean that a young man seeking a wife should experience no feelings of sexual desire as he contemplated an eligible young woman. Nor did he mean that the wholesome pleasure a man might feel in admiring a beautiful woman, or the delight with which a woman might look upon a fine specimen of manhood, was evil in itself. What he meant, surely, was that the best way in which we can all safeguard ourselves from unfaithfulness is to refuse to let the imagination dwell upon the thought of a sexual relationship which if it actually took place would violate a marriage, our own or another's.[80]

A second-century homily represents Peter as affirming that sexual desire is sanctioned when it is an urge to merge in holy wedlock:

> Lust has, by the will of God who created all things well, been made to arise within the living being, that led by it to intercourse, he may increase humanity, from a selection of which a multitude of superior beings arise who are fit for eternal life. But if it were not for lust, no one would trouble himself with intercourse with his wife; but now, for the sake of pleasure, and, as it were, gratifying himself, man carries out God's will. Now, if a man uses lust for lawful marriage, he does not act impiously; but if he rushes to adultery, he acts impiously, and he is punished because he makes a bad use of a good ordinance.[81]

Richard McBrien finds no conflict between the doctrine of the sinlessness of Jesus and his having sexual desires and temptations. Neither does the Catholic theologian find the possibility that Jesus engaged in sexual activities inconsistent with the Christian faith. McBrien comments: "Is it possible he was married? Yes, . . . and without any compromise of the church's historic faith in him as truly God and truly, truly human." [82]

Similarly, Protestant theologian Tom Driver asserts:

> It is not shocking, to me at least, to imagine Jesus moved to love according to the flesh. I cannot imagine a human tenderness, which the Gospels show to be characteristic of Jesus, that is not fed in some degree by the springs of passion. The human alternative to sexual tenderness is not asexual tenderness but sexual fear. Jesus lived in his body, as other men do. . . . The

absence of all comment in them about Jesus' sexuality cannot be taken to imply that he had no sexual feelings.[83]

In attitudes toward participation in earthly pleasures, the Semitic religions can be distinguished from Buddhism. Adolf Harnack, an acknowledged expert church historian, comments on Jesus' lifestyle: "It is certain that the disciples did not understand their master to be a world-shunning ascetic. . . . They did not send away their wives. . . . How differently things developed in Buddhism from the very start!"[84] Harnack was probably thinking of Siddhartha's permanent abandonment of his lovely wife and child in order to eschew worldly sensual pleasures. Both Buddha and Jesus advocated self-denial, but Jesus was not talking about sacrificing all sexual desires.

Jesus was not a recluse who preferred dwelling apart from the common people. He ate and drank with women and men in the villages he visited. The Gospels describe him as one with human passions like other humans and a fascination with children. Such qualities as love, joy, serenity, patience, humility, forgiveness, and faithful companionship—which he expressed in a fulsome manner—are also basic ingredients of the ideal marriage. Moreover, Jesus expressed no antipathy toward women or marital sexuality that might have motivated him to abstain from marriage. He described his lifestyle as being as different from that of wilderness-dweller John the Baptizer as a joyful wedding party is different from a gloomy funeral procession. Jesus indulged more than John in satisfying fleshly appetites, and some of his contemporaries made that behavior an excuse for slandering him as "a glutton and a drunkard" (Luke 7:31–34). Frequently he used connubial celebrations to illustrate the optimum life (Mark 2:19; Matt 22:1–14; Luke 14:7–11).

The common assumption that Jesus was a celibate is due, Clifford Howard thinks, "to the underlying Christian prejudice against the female as a source of defilement" that has been "ecclesiastically implanted."[85] Otherwise, Howard asks, why would the pious acknowledge that Jesus was subject to hunger, thirst, and weariness typical of humans while repelling as sacrilegious the notion that he engaged in sex?

Episcopalian priest Jeffery Cave said: "A married Jesus gives me some hope that intimacy and Christianity go together, that we are not meant to go through life denying some of the impulses in us which are most human. While some of us may choose to live alone, . . . a married Jesus teaches us that the friendship and devotion and loyalty, which can only come within the intimacy of human relationships, are all values worth striving for."[86]

6. Jesus abstained from marriage because he was preoccupied with a higher calling.

Pro

According to Luke, Jesus told his parents, "I must be about my Father's interests" (2:49), so he was determined even as a boy not to allow family matters to take priority. Because his divine vocation was all consuming, he had no time for a conjugal companion. Marital affection would have drained off vital energy that could better be used to fulfill his mission.

Reformed theologian Lewis Smedes believes that Jesus forsook one good for a greater good: "Jesus did not experience genital sex. . . . For Jesus, an urge toward sexual love would be in the same category as a temptation to take up fishing for a living. . . . Neither of these would be a temptation to do evil; both would be a temptation to turn away from his supreme vocation."[87] Catholic priest Gerard Sloyan explains Jesus' presumed unmarried status in this way: "In light of all we are told of his concentration on his mission . . . he did not have time for the demands of domestic life. His gypsy existence, the crowds, the never-ending requests for cures saw to that."[88] Tim Stafford also argues that being single matches up better with singleness of purpose:

> Consider Jesus. It is impossible to imagine a more single-minded person than he. Throughout his ministry he knew his business exactly. He could not be dissuaded from his agenda by the concerns of the crowds, the criticisms of the Pharisees, or the fears and hopes of his disciples. He "set his face" as he went toward Jerusalem to his own death. . . . But could Jesus have made these choices if he were married and had a family to care for? Perhaps; but certainly not so freely. . . . A single person can demonstrate with a remarkable clarity that he knows the reason he was created: to love and serve God and him only.[89]

Jesus separated from his Nazareth family in pursuit of his ministerial calling, and he recommended that his disciples free themselves from members of their households who might hinder them from following him. Pope Paul VI cites Luke in commending celibacy for holy people: "Jesus . . . promised a more than abundant recompense to anyone who should leave home, family, wife, and children for the sake of the kingdom of God."[90] Baptist theologian Harvey Cox claims that Jesus rejected marriage for himself and liberated himself from other kinship ties out of allegiance to a new kind of human community that goes beyond family bonds.[91]

Presenting a quite different argument, Protestant minister Richard Cromie speculates that Jesus remained a bachelor because of family responsibilities. Cromie presumes that Joseph died not long after Jesus came of age, making the eldest son the de facto family head. He remained unmarried and delayed leaving Nazareth until he was thirty in order to support and help rear his numerous siblings. Cromie believes that Jesus "captures the essential and sacrificing goodness of every son and daughter, who in choosing to remain at home to serve father or mother, younger brothers or sisters, gives up an individual married life in the process."[92]

German philosopher Friedrich Nietzsche believed that creative people find marital sexuality a fetter. Bachelor Nietzsche quotes with approval what the Buddha said on renouncing his wife and family, "Close and oppressive is life in a house, a place of impurity; to leave the house is freedom."[93] Similarly, Catholic professor John Engelche states, "Like the Buddha, Jesus found marriage quite incompatible with the demands of his life's work and mission. Each made the great renunciation: the Buddha after, the Christ before, marriage."[94] Letha Scanzoni and Nancy Hardesty think Jesus "must have ached to share love in the most intimate way" but he did not marry because he "saw real virtue in devoting one's life to God without the encumbrances of family."[95]

Confirmed bachelor Bernard Shaw presents a different point of view:

> The mere thought of Jesus as a married man is felt to be blasphemous by the most conventional believers; and even those of us to whom Jesus is no supernatural personage, but a prophet only as Mahomet was a prophet, feel that there was something more dignified in the bachelordom of Jesus than in the spectacle of Mahomet lying distracted on the floor of his harem whilst his wives stormed and squabbled and henpecked round him.

A married man, Shaw thought, is constricted by having to be an economic provider for his family. Marriage is "incompatible with both the contemplative and adventurous life." But for Shaw, being unmarried was not the same thing as being a celibate. Regarding Jesus, Shaw said, "He perceived that nobody could live the higher life unless money and sexual love were obtainable without sacrificing it." Shaw thought Roman Catholic priests were faithful to earliest Christianity in assuming that marital attachment is a kind of "slavery."[96]

Sherwin Bailey, an Anglican scholar, speaks of Jesus' "choice of the single life as a necessary condition for the fulfillment of his messianic vocation."[97] Geza Vermes, a Jewish scholar, thinks that Jesus was celibate after his baptism because he, like his contemporary Philo, associated sexual continence with the prophetic calling.[98] Edward Schillebeeckx, a Catholic theologian, asserts: "That whoever belongs to Jesus' group in a special way cannot do other than leave everything and give up married life is an authentic biblical fact. . . . In view of their joy on finding the 'hidden pearl,' some people cannot do other than live unmarried. This religious experience itself makes them unmarriageable, actually incapable of marriage; their heart is where their treasure is."[99]

Some Catholic leaders join some mystics of India in thinking that even moderate sexual experience makes it impossible to focus with profound clarity on God.[100] Jesus, whose religious commitment was greater than that of any other human, must have eschewed any diffusing sexual activity. John Paul II has given that position this tribute: "Virginity or celibacy . . . is that pearl of great price which is preferred to every other value no matter how great, and hence must be sought as the only definitive value."[101] The Pope appears to make celibacy an end rather than a means for achieving a goal. From his assessment, it would follow that only a celibate Jesus could attain his religious vocation.

Renaissance philosopher Francis Bacon said, "A single life doth well with churchmen, for charity will hardly water the ground when it must first fill a pool."[102] Similarly, Freud likened the psyche to a hydraulic system containing a limited quantity of energy; libidinous energy has to be shunted away from sexual outlets if higher cultural expressions are to be achieved. After pointing to the way in which celibate Francis of Assisi sublimated physical love into religious love, Freud commented: "The work of civilization has become increasingly the business of men. . . . What he employs for cultural aims he to a great extent withdraws from women and sexual life."[103] French scholar Ernest Renan also thought that Jesus' sexual impulses were sublimated into spiritual activity: "Jesus never married. All his power of loving was spent on what he considered his heavenly vocation."[104]

Con

Agreed, Jesus believed that family ties are not the be-all and end-all of life, and that his followers should sever bonds that are incompatible with religious devotion. On one occasion Jesus declared his independence from his Nazareth family when they were concerned about his sanity and safety after his gospel had provoked hostility in some Galilean villages. When they attempted to take him home, he announced that his strongest social ties were not with his biological family, but with his disciples. He showed fondness for friends traveling with him by saying: "Here are my mother and my brothers! Whoever does the will of God is my brother and sister and mother" (Mark 3:21, 34–35, NRSV). But this was not a disowning of his particular mother or siblings, because the New Testament indicates that Jesus continued to have ties with them (John 19:25; 1 Cor 9:5). In context, the saying means that when confronted with a conflict between following family advice and adhering to his spiritual convictions, he opted for the latter. Lawrence Marshall offers this explanation of Jesus' dilemma arising from strained kinship ties: "The reason of our Lord's breach with his family was that they were endeavoring to put a stop to his public ministry and were pronouncing it sheer madness on his part to carry on with it. Similarly, the Christian disciple is called upon to resist and even to renounce his family only if they seek to interfere with what he solemnly believes to be the will of God."[105]

Luke's Jesus was using hyperbole when he states that all his followers, not just his special group of disciples, must "hate" their parents, siblings, wives, and children (Luke 14:26). He found people so lethargic from routine religious practices that stark language was necessary to make them reassess their value priorities. In Matthew's parallel verse, the hyperbole is avoided; Jesus comments that parents and siblings (wives and children are not mentioned) should not be loved more than him (Matt 10:37). Judging from the full range of Jesus' teachings, he did not think that the love of God usually cut one off from family responsibilities. He asked a rich man if he had fulfilled, among others, the commandment to honor his parents (Mark 10:19). Jesus was critical of those who allowed a religious offering to take precedence over supporting their parents (Mark 7:9–13). Family obligations should be kept secondary; they need not rival giving allegiance to God.

Jesus' views on family life are analogous to his teaching that one cannot be devoted to both God and money (Matt 6:24). He did not mean that poverty was obligatory for discipleship, even though monks have given it that interpretation. Jesus approved of tax collector Zacchaeus's decisions to renounce extortion and to give away part of his wealth (Luke 19:8–9), but did not advise him to give up his livelihood. What Zacchaeus did abandon was his obsession with accumulating money as his main goal in life. In a parallel way, having a spouse is not incompatible with a religious vocation, but it is wrong to give him or her the ultimate priority.

Exegete Stuart Currie finds it instructive that Mark—the earliest gospel written—as well as Matthew and *Thomas,* do not include "wife" in the list of persons and things that Jesus' disciples are asked to leave (Mark 10:29–30; Matt 10:37; *Gospel of Thomas* 55, 101). Currie comments:

> Jesus was remembered to have set a high value upon marriage, confined though it is to this earthly scene; to have regarded it as constituted by a

resolution of commitment to leave father and mother and stick to one's spouse until separated by death; to have spoken about the cost of discipleship in terms of the possibility of leaving any of a list of kindred among whom "wife" is conspicuously absent. . . . This relationship of husband and wife constitutes so special a bond that it is not mentioned in the same breath with filial, sibling, and parental ties. . . . Jesus was ready to see in this form of commitment if not a model at least a figure of or analogy to the commitment of discipleship. . . . Marriage . . . combines not only the motif of permanence but also of a beginning requiring resolution and an involvement of the whole embodied person in a totality of sharing not equaled in other relationships. Children after all grow up and roles are reversed as the supported become supportive and then supporters. Sibling commitments are superseded by marriage.[106]

Freud, the psychiatrist most associated with the sublimation theory, also admitted its defectiveness: "An abstinent artist is scarcely conceivable. . . . The production of the artist is probably powerfully stimulated by his sexual experience. On the whole I have not gained the impression that sexual abstinence helps to shape energetic, self-reliant men of action, nor original thinkers, bold pioneers and reformers; far more often it produces 'good' weaklings who later become lost in the crowd."[107]

In a section entitled "A Contradiction in Freud's Theory of Culture," Wilhelm Reich says that his basic idea "that achievements result from sublimated sexual energy . . . is erroneous."[108] Also, Bacon undermined his advocacy of priestly celibacy by claiming that single men "are more cruel and hardhearted because their tenderness is not so oft called upon."[109]

Many religious leaders of various cultures have not found marriage to conflict with full-time devotion to God. Akiba, for example, a renowned ancient rabbi, gave credit to his wife for transforming him from an ignorant shepherd to a Torah scholar.[110] Contrary to Shaw's prejudiced view of Muhammad, the one wife with whom he spent most of his prophetic years spurred him on when he was doubtful of his religious calling. Wealthy Khadija gave her husband both psychological reassurance and material support. She was the first to be convinced of the genuineness of her husband's revelatory experiences, believing in him when he was not believing in himself.[111] After her death, Muhammad did have multiple wives during the last decade of his life, but there is no indication that they distracted him from his aim to banish idolatry from Arabia.[112]

Novelist Kingsley Amis thinks celibates are deluded when they believe they have renounced family responsibilities for the more demanding call of God. He maintains that the zenith and nadir of humanity are best disclosed in the person beset by the obligations of marriage. Had Jesus been celibate, he would have avoided what is for most people the most testing of all human experiences—close ties with spouse and children.[113] Unconditional love of profound depth is expressed by those who uphold their vows to be faithful "in plenty and in want, in joy and in sorrow, in sickness and in health."

Since God is the ground of all love, the notion that piety generally involves renouncing affection for individual humans is a gross misunderstanding of Christian theology. The Gospels do not suggest that Jesus' love of God was in any way lessened by his special love of particular men and women. Love is not like an exhaustible bottle of wine that diminishes in accord with the number imbibing; rather, it multiplies when used to nourish intimate as well as ultimate relationships. Marriage counselors Howard and Charlotte Clinebell consider a loving marriage to be an ideal opportunity for achieving "spiritual experiences which transcend the marriage relationship."[114] That in-depth encounter enables partners to discover that "God is love, and those who live in love live in God" (1 John 4:16). The Johannine passage contains another profound insight relevant to marriage, "Those who do not love one another whom they have seen are incapable of loving God whom they have not seen" (1 John 4:20). Karl Rahner, the distinguished Catholic theologian, has said: "It is downright erroneous to contend that the love of God as such and the love for one's fellow-humans as it is realized in marriage are in competition. This idea lies, however, at the basis of many apologies for evangelical virginity."[115]

7. Jesus was exclusively wed to his devotees.

Pro

In lieu of becoming an actual husband, Jesus opted for a surrogate marriage to his community of followers. Responding to being questioned as to why his disciples did not fast like the disciples of John the Baptizer, he asked, "Can the wedding guests fast while the bridegroom is with them?" (Mark 2:19). The first reason that Clement of Alexandria gives as to why Jesus did not engage in ordinary marriage is that "he had his own bride, the Church."[116] John Chrysostom, the most prominent bishop of Constantinople, thought of Jesus as a divine bridegroom; those who dedicate themselves to become priests have married him, so to marry an earthly woman involves deserting their first spouse and committing adultery.[117] Catholic Al Szews says it would be bigamy to be married both to the church and to a woman.[118] In recent decades, Schillebeeckx has defended this reason for a celibate Jesus: "He enters into a virginal marriage with his church, his bride."[119]

Theologian Paul Jewett states: "If Jesus was only and essentially a first-century Palestinian Jew, then in all likelihood he was married." But he embodied the kingdom of heaven, where there is no sexual congress between husband and wife. Jesus did not continue practices of the earthly kingdom because "he is the heavenly bridegroom who, though taken from his bride for a time, will return to celebrate his nuptial feast at the consummation of all things."[120]

Con

When Jesus referred to himself as a bridegroom, he was speaking as figuratively as when he called himself a shepherd (Mark 6:34). Moreover, the disciples are compared by Jesus to wedding guests, not to the bride. Jesus chose the wedding metaphor to point to the quality of his relationship with his disciples. In contrast to those who were associated with gloomy John the Baptizer, Jesus accentuated joy and love. Whereas John fasted, Jesus feasted (Mark 2:15–19).

8. Jesus believed that the angelic life should now be copied.

Pro

To the Sadducees, Jesus said: "People on earth marry, but those who are considered worthy of being raised from the dead will not marry; they cannot die anymore, because they are like angels" (Luke 20:34–36).

According to Jerome, Jesus' aim during his days in the flesh was to live the paradisiacal life of virginity and to enable holy men and women to "manifest themselves even in this life as angels."[121] Lucien Legrand claims that Jesus and many of his followers refrained from sexual activity because life as sexless heavenly spirits had already begun to stir in them.[122] Legrand, like Jerome, exhorted creatures of flesh to emulate discarnate angels. To engage in sex is to lower oneself to beastly copulation, whereas abstainers were assured of first-class citizenship in the heavenly kingdom.

Con

Jesus' response to a question from the Sadducees is unrelated to the practice of celibacy. How strangely incongruous that those who profess to follow the Incarnate One should attempt to imitate angels, who by nature are not incarnate.[123] Catholic philosopher Jacques Maritain, drawing on the medieval definition of "angel" as a bodiless mind, coined the term "angelism" to refer to futile attempts "to play the pure spirit" and detach oneself from the corporeal realm.[124]

Apropos here is the reflection of Kent Nerburn on the nature of our humanity:

> We are neither animals nor angels. We are something else—we are humans—part spiritual and part physical, and those two parts are combined into one. A true sexuality acknowledges both these dimensions and tries to embrace them both in the act of love. . . . Having sex is what the animals do. Achieving mystical union is what the angels do. We alone can make love, where the physical and the spiritual commingle in a single, joyous act.[125]

Jesus' teaching refers to his affirmation of a life after death—in contrast to the Sadducees, who rejected its possibility. He believed that resurrected humans are like angels in that they are incorporeal and neither reproduce nor die. According to the Talmud, there is no propagation in the world to come.[126] Clement of Alexandria wrote that anyone examining the biblical passage carefully would realize that Jesus was not denigrating marriage and exalting celibacy. Rather, he was criticizing those who assume that the afterlife would be simply an extension of life as now experienced, including marriage and propagation. Clement's point is that death, which necessitates reproduction, is not a quality of the immortal life, although it is intrinsic to the organic realm. By reductio ad absurdum logic, he argued that those who reject marriage on the claim that they are now living the nonphysical life of the resurrection should also abstain from eating and drinking.[127]

Jesus' reply to the Sadducees can more properly be used to encourage marriage in this life than to authorize celibacy. D. H. Lawrence comments: "We may well believe that in heaven there is no marrying or giving in marriage. All this has to be fulfilled here, and if it is not fulfilled here, it will never be fulfilled."[128]

Maurice Wiles speculates that the love and joy associated with earthly marriage will be extended in a heavenly realm:

> Marriage represents the deepest form of personal relationship, the highest form of social experience which is open to us in this life. Within the limitations of our finite, human experience such a relationship can only be shared with one other person at one time. But need such a limitation apply to the

life of heaven? Is it not more reasonable that the life of heaven should involve a going on from, rather than a drawing back from, the highest kind of personal relationship known to us? If this is so, the point of the saying of Jesus may be not that heaven involves a reversal of the words of God, "It is not good that man should be alone," but rather that a relationship which in this life necessarily involves exclusiveness finds in heaven an ultimate fulfillment in which the element of exclusiveness is done away.[129]

9. Jesus was too divine to marry.

Pro

Jesus, the only sinless man who ever lived according to Christian doctrine, would not have married a sinful woman. Philip Schaff, an eminent church historian, writes, "The Son of God and Savior of the world was too far above all the daughters of Eve to find an equal companion among them, and in any case cannot be conceived as holding such relations."[130] Even if the assumption is made that bride selection was primarily a parental responsibility, Mary and Joseph would not have followed the prevailing custom because they recognized Jesus' unique holiness.

Expositor Eric Krell argues that since God cannot be married, "anyone created in the image of God is never in need of another (opposite) sex." Jesus, as the last Adam, was distinguished as "male and female in one personality."[131] Hence, it is absurd to speak of that sexual whole as being attracted to a female. Sexual passion began when the first Adam fell and shattered the divine image.

Charles Feinberg, dean of the nondenominational Talbot Seminary, comments: "The idea of Jesus having sexual relations . . . challenges Christ's divinity and approximates blasphemy."[132] He was a perfect divine spirit, and marriage is not a part of the spirit world. David Schuyler, dean of Catholic Chaminade College, expresses a similar position: "Christ was not just a man, a member of a certain people and culture, subject to and following its normal pattern of life; He was the unique God-Man. . . . Christ presented to His followers the example of the ideal Son of God, undivided in heart, unmarried, and without earthly possessions."[133]

Con

Orthodox Christology affirms: "Jesus Christ . . . is complete both in deity and in human-ness, . . . with a rational mind and body. He is of the same reality as God as far as his deity is concerned and of the same reality as we are ourselves as far as his human-ness is concerned."[134] Marriage is not in conflict with his two natures, because the distinctiveness of each nature is conserved. Being "truly man" should not be identified with being a virgin for life.

After carefully reviewing the evidence for and against Jesus' alleged celibacy, Davis affirmed, "It is difficult to see that any inherent incompatibility between marriage and divine sonship excludes a married Jesus."[135] Canon Edwin Bennett claims that Jesus did not set aside his sexuality, because that is not something humans have but something humans are. Therefore, "when God became a human person, he did not change any of that. He is not a freak." The Episcopalian priest expands on the earthy implications of his position: "I would be very surprised if Jesus never masturbated, for example; every boy does." Also, as a down-to-earth divine person, "Jesus might have been married and had two kids."[136]

John Erskine, a distinguished American writer, suggests that Jesus had a wife and children prior to becoming a traveling teacher. He speculates that the wedlock might have become a deadlock, which was not inappropriate for his divine-human nature:

> It does not seem improbable that he did fall in love and had some experience of parenthood. . . . He understood women very well indeed, with the special understanding of a man who has been hurt by one of them. . . . I think he early met someone who charmed but who was unworthy, someone he idealized, and by whom he was cruelly disillusioned. . . . The Gospels indicate that Jesus had an extraordinary fondness for children, and a special understanding of the relation between father and son. It is evident that he exerted upon women of various temperaments a strong fascination. . . . The father of the prodigal son is not a portrait of Joseph, but the record of human yearning for a child. Whether these emotions in Jesus ever attached themselves to particular objects, the story does not say, but his character renders it for me utterly impossible that his youth and manhood could have been unmoved by warm, human emotions. . . . If he really took our nature upon him and was human, then he had our equipment of sex.[137]

The alleged New Testament evidence for Jesus' celibacy has been "weighed and found wanting." The gospel texts that celibate advocates have ripped from their contexts not only do not show that Jesus was a celibate but can more properly be used to show that he endorsed permanent marriage as being of penultimate value. The eunuch saying, if authentic, probably pertains to Jesus' sanctioning fidelity to a wayward spouse in hope of eventual mutual reconciliation, or possibly, it expresses his acceptance of men judged by his culture to be sexually irregular. His use of the bridegroom metaphor demonstrates his life-affirming general outlook and positive view of weddings. Jesus' response to the Sadducees explains that the resurrected life will surpass, but does not negate, earthly love between spouses.

His Sexual Orientation

Some who assume that Jesus was unmarried assume that he remained single because he had a homosexual personality orientation. Anglican bishop Hugh Montefiore suggested that Jesus was "not by nature the marrying sort," but being a continent homosexual would not have made him a sinner.[138] The bishop's comment was widely denounced, causing Blenkinsopp to perceive, "What irked many of his critics was not so much the suggestion that Jesus' nature may have contained more of the homosexual than the heterosexual but the inference that it contained any kind of sexuality at all." Blenkinsopp observes that even contemporary Christians tend to be "Docetists"—adhering to the earliest heresy, which denied the full humanity of Jesus—because of their revulsion to contemplating that he had sexual passion, which is a central drive of the human animal.[139] Bishop John Robinson, stimulated by his Anglican colleague, asked whether Jesus had a homosexual or a heterosexual tendency. He could have had either, Robinson acknowledged, even though the traditional answer has been that he had neither.[140]

John Boswell—a historian with a homosexual orientation—claims "the only persons with whom the Gospels suggest he [Jesus] had any special relationship were men, especially Saint John, who carefully describes himself throughout his gospel as the disciple whom Jesus loved."[141] Boswell agrees with Aelred, a medieval homosexual monk, who thought that Jesus displayed his homosexuality in allowing John "to recline on his breast as a sign of his special love."[142] Troy Perry, the founder of a gay denomination of Christians, also considers some of Jesus' behavior to be homosexually suggestive.[143] Perry notes that Jesus constantly associated himself with a group of male disciples and occasionally had bodily contact with them. The Synoptic Gospels state that he was kissed by a disciple in the garden of Gethsemane at night (Mark 14:45).

Tom Horner has written a book on homosexuality in the Bible that contains a chapter on Jesus' sexuality. He states: "Jesus' intimate group of disciples consisted of either single men or men who did not consider their marriage vows the first loyalty of their lives. And with these men, or at least with some of them, Jesus had a relationship that was unusually warm and intimate." While evidence is not sufficient to prove Jesus was gay, Horner thinks, yet "he was not the type of person who would have displayed any hostility toward those who might have had homosexual relationships." Jesus commended eunuchs, who, according to Horner, often assumed passive roles as homosexual partners.[144]

Historian Morton Smith discovered in 1958 at the Mar Saba monastery in Palestine a manuscript fragment suggesting that the second-century Carpocratian sect thought Jesus engaged in a homosexual tryst.[145] The Carpocratians were known for their "licentious" behavior and were considered heretical.[146] Clement of Alexandria alleged that they desecrated the Agape, the Christian love-feast, by extinguishing the lamps and having intercourse with anyone who pleased them.[147] The Carpocratians were aware of a scroll entitled the *Secret Gospel of Mark*, which associates Jesus' resurrection with male bonding. It states:

> The youth, looking upon him [Jesus] loved him and began to beseech him that he might be with him. And going out of the tomb they came into the house of the youth, for he was rich. After six days Jesus told him what to do and in the evening the youth comes to him wearing a linen cloth over his naked body. And he remained with him that night, for Jesus taught him the mystery of the kingdom of God.[148]

That youth might be identified with the one mentioned in Mark who slipped out of his linen cloth on being seized when Jesus was arrested in the garden of Gethsemane. He fled naked in the middle of the night and might have reappeared in a white robe several days later at the place where Jesus had been buried (Mark 14:51–52, 16:5). Perhaps the author of the Gospel of Mark was alluding to his own presence with Jesus in Jerusalem.

Some have speculated that Jesus might have been bisexual. Behavioral characteristics that many cultures label male or females were blended together in his personality.[151] The outstanding Catholic theologian Rosemary Ruether suggests:

> Jesus is not so much "feminine" or "masculine" as he is a figure that defies all such sex stereotyping. . . . He is an authority that overthrows conventional models of patriarchal, hierarchal, religious and political power systems; that champions women, the poor, the unwashed and outcasts, that rejects the power games of the male leadership classes. . . . Jesus' life shows close special friendships with both men and women that included physical

tenderness. . . . He could love both John and Mary Magdalene, physically embrace and be embraced by them, because first of all he knew them as friends, not as sexual objects.[150]

Methodist pastor James Conn portrays Jesus as a person who was neither married nor celibate: "I've always assumed Jesus' relationship with Mary Magdalene was hands-on stuff. And I have always been intrigued by the closeness between Jesus and his beloved disciple, John. John was apparently young and strong and handsome."[151] United Church of Christ minister Bill Johnson likewise thinks that Jesus expressed himself sexually with both women and men. He explains Jesus' bisexuality in this way: "As the gynandrous personification of Spirit in human flesh, Jesus was the paradigm of male/female Godliness fully experiencing life on this physical plane. . . . Men and women who intimately shared his earthly sojourn could well have been a significant lesbian/gay/bisexual community."[152]

Danish filmmaker Jens Thorsen tried to produce *The Many Faces of Jesus* in several European countries. Thorsen fantasized that Jesus engaged in sexual activity with various women and also enjoyed the companionship and sexual favors of John. Due to protests, the film has not been licensed for public screening.[153] *Corpus Christi*, a 1998 off-Broadway play by award-winning playwright Terrence McNally, depicts a contemporary Jesus as a homosexual who has sex with his apostles and is martyred by gay-bashers as "king of the queers."

Jesus had close companions of both sexes who accompanied him as he visited Palestinian villages, but having good friends does not imply having sexual relations with them. John reclined next to Jesus at the Last Supper, but reclining in a prone position on a cushion was the first-century custom in dining and should not be associated with sexual behavior. Likewise, Judas's kiss was the usual greeting exchanged by men in ancient Palestine (Gen 29:13; Exod 4:27; 2 Sam 14:33, etc.). Had Jesus been gay in a culture that treated homosexual liaisons as an "abomination" (Lev 20:13), one would expect to find some allusion to it in the Gospels.

After thoroughly reviewing the Carpocratians' suggestion that Jesus was gay, historical Jesus specialist Crossan dismisses the matter in this way: "I see no evidence that Jesus and the youth are engaged in anything shocking. And I prefer to let the Carpocratians alone in salivating over the incident."[154] Raymond Brown, in his definitive commentary on the narratives pertaining to Jesus' last week in Jerusalem, does not think the reference to the unclothed youth in Gethsemane should be associated with homosexual conduct. Brown finds in the account of the youth abandoning his garment on being grabbed no more than a desperate means of escaping capture.[155]

The case for a heterosexual Jesus is stronger, because that is the condition of almost all humans and was the only orientation sanctioned by the Jews. Sometime during the decade following Jesus' boyhood experience with his parents in the Jerusalem Temple, about which there is no historical record, Jesus probably married. Also, the likelihood of his having offspring would be similar to that of others in his culture. The absence of any mention of such family members may indicate that they, unlike Jesus' brother James, did not become a significant part of the early Christian community. The absence of Jesus' mention of daughters or sons in historical records could also have been due to infertility or to the children being among that large percent who did not survive infancy.

The inability to demonstrate fully that Jesus was married cannot be taken as proof that he was not. The Gospels, composed by "evangelists," are largely collections of sermon summaries used by the earliest Christian preachers, which only incidentally supply biographical information. The New Testament covers only a small fraction of the span of Jesus' life, so little can be stated about his life that goes beyond the realm of historical probability.

The absence of evidence is not the same as evidence of absence. The Gospels do not record that Jesus smiled or laughed, for example, but that silence gives no basis for inferring that he was never jovial. Also, it is invalid to conclude that Jesus was immune to infections just because there is no mention of his having been sick. Had he never smiled or had he always been in perfect health, those conditions, which deviate widely from the norm, would more likely have been remembered and recorded. Again, since nothing is recorded about Jesus' physical appearance, it was probably not extraordinary. Unlike Zacchaeus or Saul, who are described as exceptionally short or tall (Luke 19:3; 1 Sam 9:2), Jesus was probably of normal stature. Again, unlike John the Baptizer, who was clothed with camel's hair (Mark 1:6), Jesus' clothing was apparently not unusual.

A rather perverse example of the misuse of documentary silence has to do with Jesus' excretory functions. As with the records of most historical figures, there is mention in the Gospels of Jesus eating but not of his having bowel movements. Some second-century Christians, who wished to diminish Jesus' participation in animal functions and treat him as a supernatural figure, deduced, "Jesus ate and drank in a peculiar manner without the food passing out of his body."[156]

Again, due to the paucity of documentary sources, it cannot even be definitely asserted that Jesus received schooling in his hometown. Hence, to say that Jesus probably married or that he probably received some formal education is as strong a statement as can be made. Awareness of Hebrew marital mores and knowledge of how the Gospels were formed place the weight of the evidence mainly on the side of Jesus having been married. Although many have vested interests in stamping their authoritative imprimatur on a celibate Jesus, he probably had no responsibility for its development in the church.

Davis turns the silence argument around and uses it as his main reason for a married Jesus:

> If he [Jesus] had insisted upon celibacy it would have created a stir, a reaction which would have left some trace. So, the lack of mention of Jesus' marriage in the Gospels is a strong argument not against but for the hypothesis of marriage, because any practice or advocacy of voluntary celibacy would, in the Jewish context of the time, have been so unusual as to have attracted much attention and comment.[157]

The DaVinci Code, a novel by Dan Brown, is based in part on a legend that Mary Magdalene was pregnant when her husband Jesus was crucified. After fleeing to France, she gave birth to a daughter, from whom some European nobility were descended. Brown contends that Leonardo DaVinci accepted the legend as factual and painted Mary Magdalene in his *Last Supper* masterpiece as seated immediately to the right of Jesus. Since millions of copies of the book have been sold, a television special with Elizabeth Vargas investigated the historical basis for presuming Jesus had married. Vargas interviewed Karen King of Harvard Divinity School, an authority on *The Gospel of Philip,* a text that tells of Jesus often kissing Mary Magdalene, his sexual partner, causing his male companions to become jealous (*Gospel of Philip,* 63). Assuming that the ancient scroll, discovered in Egypt during the last century, may preserve an authentic tradition, King comments, "I think it's entirely plausible to think that Jesus may have been married. It was a normal practice for Jewish men. It would also be normal not to mention that he had a wife." The European aspects of the book are probably pure fiction.[158]

Episcopal bishop John Spong plausibly suggests

> that Mary Magdalene . . . was Jesus' wife, and that this record was suppressed but not annihilated by the Christian church before the Gospels came to be written. . . . By the turn of the first century there was in the life of the Christian church a clear need to remove Mary Magdalene, the flesh and blood woman who was at Jesus' side in life and in death, and to replace her with a sexless woman, the virgin mother.[159]

Spong muses, "Why is there still a continued sense, ranging from dis-ease to revulsion, that arises in us when we hear the suggestion that Jesus might have been married? I suggest that far more than any of us realize we are subconsciously victimized by the historic negativity toward women."[160] Theologian James Nelson likewise comments, "If we are offended at the thought that Jesus was ever inclined toward a fully sexual union, such offense might simply betray the suspicion that sex is unworthy of the Savior because it is unworthy of us. But we need not project our own alienation upon him."[161]

The Jesus Seminar, composed of scholars devoted to historical analysis, concluded: "The Fellows of the Seminar were overwhelmingly of the opinion that Jesus did not advocate celibacy. A majority of the Fellows doubted, in fact, that Jesus himself was celibate. They regard it as probable that he had a special relationship with at least one woman, Mary of Magdala."[162] But it is considerably more risky to attempt to identify whom Jesus married than to affirm that he married.

Notes

1. *Decree on the Ministry and Life of Priests*, 16.

2. John Paul II, *Letter to Priests*, April 9, 1979, 8.

3. Ignatius Hunt, "Celibacy in Scripture," *Celibacy: The Necessary Option* (ed. George Frein; New York: Herder, 1968), 129.

4. Alfons Stickler, *The Case for Clerical Celibacy* (San Francisco: Ignatius Press, 1995), 100.

5. Stanley Jaki, *Theology of Priestly Celibacy* (Front Royal, VA: Christendom, 1997), 34.

6. *New York Times*, March 25, 2002, A21.

7. David Gibson, *The Coming Catholic Church* (San Francisco: Harper, 2003), 248.

8. Helmut Thielicke, *The Ethics of Sex* (New York: Harper, 1964), 120.

9. Max Thurian, *Marriage and Celibacy* (London: SCM, 1959), 49.

10. *London Observer*, March 28, 1971, 25.

11. Uta Ranke-Heinemann, *Eunuchs for the Kingdom of Heaven* (New York: Penguin, 1990), 44.

12. *National Catholic Reporter*, April 12, 1996, 12.

13. *Expository Times* (August 1996): 334.

14. Helmut Lehman, ed., *Luther's Works* (Philadelphia: Fortress, 1957), 54: 1472.

15. Elisabeth Moltmann-Wendel, *The Women around Jesus* (London: SCM, 1982), 88.

16. Richard Langsdale, *The Sixth Jar* (New York: Vantage, 1973), 101, 115.

17. In modified form, this chapter contains excerpts from William Phipps, *The Sexuality of Jesus* (Cleveland: Pilgrim Press, 1996), 44–109. Used by permission.

18. B. Z. Goldberg, *Sex in Religion* (New York: Liveright, 1970), 345–49; Frederick Conybeare, *Russian Dissenters* (New York: Russell, 1962), 367–68.

19. William Phipps, *The Wisdom and Wit of Rabbi Jesus* (Louisville: Westminster/John Knox, 1993), 91.

20. Tertullian, *On Monogamy* 3.

21. Tertullian, *To His Wife* 6.

22. John Paul II, *Letter to Priests*, 8.

23. John Paul II, *The Theology of Marriage and Celibacy* (Boston: Daughters of St. Paul, 1986), 90, 102.

24. Floyd Filson, *A Commentary on the Gospel According to St. Matthew* (New York: Harper, 1960), 207.

25. Elaine Pagels, *Adam, Eve, and the Serpent* (New York: Random House, 1988), 14–16.

26. Robert Gundry, *Matthew: A Commentary* (Grand Rapids: Eerdmans, 1994), 381–82.

27. *Gittin* 9:10; *Ketuboth* 7:6.

28. Josephus, *Antiquities* 18:136.

29. Eric Fuchs, *Sexual Desire and Love* (New York: Seabury, 1983), 65.

30. Walter Wink, *Engaging the Powers* (Minneapolis: Fortress, 1992), 132.

31. Alan McNeile, *The Gospel according to St. Matthew* (London: Macmillan, 1915), 262.

32. Justin, *Apology* 1:15; Clement, *Miscellanies* 3:50.

33. Quentin Quesnell, "Made Themselves Eunuchs," *The Catholic Biblical Quarterly* (July 1968): 358.

34. William Thompson, *The Jesus Debate* (New York: Paulist Press, 1985), 162.

35. Bruce Malina and Richard Rohrbaugh, *Social-Science Commentary on the Synoptic Gospels* (Minneapolis: Fortress, 1992), 122.

36. Leof Vasage and Vincent Wimbush, eds., *Asceticism and the New Testament* (New York: Routledge, 1999), 21.

37. L. William Countryman, *Dirt, Greed, and Sex* (Philadelphia: Fortress, 1988), 188.

38. Robert Funk, ed., *The Five Gospels* (New York: Macmillan, 1993), 220–21.

39. Josephus, *Antiquities* 4:290.

40. Martin Larson, *The Essene Heritage* (New York: Philosophical Library, 1967), 172–74.

41. *Religion and Life* (Summer 1979): 136–39.

42. Reginald Fuller, "Matthew," *Harper's Bible Commentary* (ed. James Mays; San Francisco: Harper, 1988), 973.

43. James Charlesworth, *Jesus within Judaism* (New York: Doubleday, 1988), 58, 72–74; H. H. Rowley, *The Dead Sea Scrolls and the New Testament* (London: SPCK, 1957), 28–32.

44. *Damascus Document* 4:21; *Rule of the Congregation* 1:6–11; *War of the Sons of Light* 7:4–6.

45. *Damascus Document* 7:6–9.

46. Linda Elder, "The Woman Question and Female Ascetics Among Essenes," *Biblical Archaeologist* (December 1994): 225.

47. Lawrence Schiffman, ed., *Archaeology and History in the Dead Sea Scrolls* (Sheffield: JSOT Press, 1990), 20.

48. Philo, *Hypothetica* 11, 14; Josephus, *Wars* 2:120; Pliny the Elder, *Natural History* 5:15.

49. Philo, *On the Contemplative Life* 2–8.

50. Eusebius, *Church History* 2:4.

51. Philo, *Life of Moses* 2:68–69.

52. Philo, *Questions and Answers* 2:49.

53. *L'Osservate Romano,* March 10, 1971.

54. *New York Times,* January 29, 1971, 44.

55. Sidney Callahan, "Was Jesus Married?," *National Catholic Reporter,* December 25, 1970.

56. Rudolf Bultmann, *Jesus and the Word* (New York: Scribner, 1958), 58.

57. *Kiddushin* 4:13.

58. Schalom Ben-Chorin, *Bruder Jesus* (Munich: List, 1967), 128–29.

59. *Aboth* 5:21.

60. Ephraim Neufeld, *Ancient Hebrew Marriage Laws* (London: Longmans, 1944), 143.

61. Roland de Vaux, *Ancient Israel* (New York: McGraw-Hill, 1961), 29.

62. Malina and Rohrbaugh, *Social-Science Commentary,* 121.

63. Jean Audet, *Structures of Christian Priesthood* (New York: Macmillan, 1968), 41.

64. Donavan Joyce, *The Jesus Scroll* (New York: Signet, 1972), 78.

65. Ogdon Kraut, *Jesus Was Married* (Salt Lake City: Kraut, 1969), 10.

66. John Dominic Crossan, *Jesus* (San Francisco: Harper, 1994), v, 119, 121; Epictetus, *Discourses* 3:22.

67. Gerd Theissen, *The First Followers of Jesus* (London: SCM, 1978), 14–15.

68. Vernon McCasland, *The Pioneer of Our Faith* (New York: McGraw-Hill, 1964), 155.

69. Joseph Blenkinsopp, *Celibacy, Ministry, Church* (New York: Herder, 1968), 37.

70. Louis Cassels, *The Real Jesus* (New York: Doubleday, 1968), 77.

71. E. P. Sanders, "Jesus in Historical Context," *Theology Today* (October 1993): 430–31, 448.

72. F. Caballero, *Eli, la Espana treinta anos ha* (Leipzig: Brockhaus, 1881), 61.

73. John Meier, *The Marginal Jew* (New York: Doubleday, 1991), 1:282.

74. Pseudo-Justin, *On the Resurrection* 3.

75. Emil Brunner, *Man in Revolt* (New York: Scribner, 1939), 348.

76. Shakespeare, "Sonnet 129."

77. Job 24:15; *Pesikta Rabbati* 24:2.

78. *Leviticus Rabbah* 23:12.

79. Leander Keck, ed., *The New Interpreter's Bible* (Nashville: Abingdon, 1995), 8:191.

80. David Mace, *Whom God Hath Joined* (Philadelphia: Westminster, 1953), 30–31.

81. Clementine, *Homilies* 19.

82. Richard McBrien, *Catholicism* (San Francisco: Harper, 1994), 562–63; "Jesus, Mary, and DaVini," ABC-TV, November 3, 2003.

83. Tom Driver, "Sexuality and Jesus," *Union Seminary Quarterly Review* (March 1965): 240, 243.

84. Adolf Harnack, *What Is Christianity?* (New York: Harper, 1957), 83.

85. Clifford Howard, *Sex and Religion* (London: Williams & Norgate, 1925), 153.

86. Jeffery Cave, sermon, Manhattan's Church of the Epiphany, June 27, 1971.

87. Lewis Smedes, *Sex for Christians* (Grand Rapids: Eerdmans, 1976), 78.

88. Gerard Sloyan, *Jesus in Focus* (Mystic, CN: Twenty-Third Publications, 1983), 132.

89. Tim Stafford, *The Sexual Christian* (Wheaton, IL: Victor Books, 1989), 156–57.

90. Luke 14:26; 18:29–30; Paul VI, *Priestly Celibacy*, 22.

91. Harvey Cox, *The Seduction of the Spirit* (New York: Simon & Schuster, 1973), 230.

92. Richard Cromie, sermon, Southminister Presbyterian Church, Pittsburgh, January 25, 1976.

93. Friedrich Nietzsche, *Genealogy of Morals* (1887), 3:7.

94. *Honolulu Star-Bulletin*, November 14, 1970.

95. Letha Scanzoni and Nancy Hardesty, *All We're Meant to Be* (Waco: Word Books, 1974), 150–51.

96. Bernard Shaw, "Preface," *Androcles and the Lion, Complete Plays* (New York: Dodd, Mead, 1962), 5:387–92.

97. Sherwin Bailey, *Sexual Relation in Christian Thought* (New York: Harper, 1959), 10.

98. Geza Vermes, *Jesus the Jew* (London: Collins, 1973), 100–101.

99. Edward Schillebeeckx, *Celibacy* (New York: Sheed & Ward, 1968), 24–25.

100. Thomas Berry, *Religions of India* (New York: Bruce, 1971), 95–98, 197–201; Mircea Eliade, *Yoga* (Princeton: Princeton University Press, 1969), 49–50.

101. John Paul II, "The Apostolic Exhortation on the Family," *Origins,* December 24, 1981, 443.

102. Francis Bacon, *Of Marriage and Single Life* (1597).

103. Sigmund Freud, *Civilization and Its Discontents* (trans. James Strachey; New York: Norton, 1961), 56.

104. Ernest Renan, *Life of Jesus* (Boston: Little, Brown, 1899), 130.

105. Laurence Marshall, *The Challenge of New Testament Ethics* (London: Macmillan, 1960), 177.

106. Stuart Currie, "Sayings of Jesus on Marriage," *Austin Seminary Bulletin* (November 1971): 47–48.

107. Sigmund Freud, *Collected Papers* (trans. Joan Riviere; New York: Basic Books, 1959), 2:92.

108. Wilhelm Reich, *The Sexual Revolution* (New York: Simon & Schuster, 1974), 9–10.

109. Francis Bacon, *Of Marriage and Single Life.*

110. *Ketuboth* 63.

111. Alfred Guillaume, *The Life of Muhammad: A Translation of Ibn Ishaq's Sirat Rasul Allah* (Lahore: Oxford University Press, 1955), 106–7, 155.

112. William Phipps, *Muhammad and Jesus* (New York: Continuum, 1996), 57–70, 141.

113. William Purcell, ed., *The Resurrection* (Philadelphia: Westminster, 1966), 75.

114. Howard Clinebell and Charlotte Clinebell, *The Intimate Marriage* (New York: Harper, 1970), 185.

115. *Cross Currents* (Winter 1966): 110.

116. Clement of Alexandria, *Miscellanies* 3:49.

117. Chrysostom, *Letters to Theodore* 2:3.

118. *Milwaukee Journal Sentinel,* August 20, 2003, B1.

119. Schillebeeckx, *Celibacy,* 100.

120. Paul Jewett, *Man as Male and Female* (Grand Rapids: Eerdmans, 1975), 110–11.

121. Jerome, *Letters* 108:23.

122. Lucien Legrand, *The Biblical Doctrine of Virginity* (New York: Sheed, 1963), 43.

123. According to the satirist Voltaire, when the angel of annunciation appeared to Mary, she invited him to take a seat. Gabriel replied, "Je n'ais pas de quoi." Possessing neither bottom nor body, Gabriel was incapable of physical movement.

124. Jacques Maritain, *Moral Philosophy* (New York: Scribner, 1964), 454.

125. Kent Nerburn, *Letters to My Son* (San Rafael, CA: New World Library, 1993), 160.

126. *Berakot* 17a.

127. Clement, *Miscellanies* 3:48, 87.

128. D. H. Lawrence, *A Propos of Lady Chatterley's Lover* (London: Mandrake, 1930), 65.

129. Maurice Wiles, "Studies in Texts," *Theology* (December 1957): 501–2.

130. Philip Schaff, *History of the Christian Church* (New York: Scribner, 1914), 2:397.

131. Eric Krell, *Created in Our Image* (Milwaukee: Bible-Truths Expositors, 1970), 20–33.

132. *Los Angeles Herald Examiner,* November 21, 1970.

133. *Honolulu Star-Bulletin,* November 14, 1970.

134. Chalcedon Creed (451).

135. *London Observer,* March 28, 1971, 25.

136. *Religious News Service,* February 24, 1981, 3.

137. John Erskine, *The Human Life of Jesus* (New York: McClelland, 1945), 27–28.

138. Hugh Montefiore, *For God's Sake* (Philadelphia: Westminster, 1969), 182.

139. Blenkinsopp, *Celibacy, Ministry, Church,* 32–33.

140. John Robinson, *The Human Face of God* (Philadelphia: Westminster, 1973), 64.

141. John Boswell, *Christianity, Social Tolerance, and Homosexuality* (Chicago: University of Chicago Press, 1980), 115.

142. Ibid., 226; John 13:23.

143. Troy Perry and Charles Lucas, *The Lord Is My Shepherd and He Knows I'm Gay* (Los Angeles: Nash, 1972), 150.

144. Tom Horner, *Jonathan Loved David* (Philadelphia: Westminster, 1978), 122–24.

145. John Dominic Crossan, *Four Other Gospels* (Minneapolis: Winston, 1985), 91–111.

146. Irenaeus, *Against Heresies* 1:25:3.

147. Clement, *Miscellanies* 3:10.

148. Morton Smith, *Clement of Alexandria and A Secret Gospel of Mark* (Cambridge: Harvard University Press, 1973), 447.

149. William Phipps, *Genesis and Gender* (New York: Praeger), 78–86.

150. Rosemary Reuther, "The Sexuality of Jesus," *Christianity and Crisis* (May 29, 1978): 136–37.

151. Quoted in Malcolm Boyd, "The Sexuality of Jesus," *The Witness,* July 1991, 14.

152. Ibid., 14–15.

153. *The Christian Century* (October 27, 1976): 934–35.

154. Crossan, *Four Other Gospels,* 118.

155. Raymond Brown, *The Death of the Messiah* (New York: Doubleday, 1994), 1:303.

156. Quoted in Clement of Alexandria, *Miscellanies* 3:59.

157. *London Observer,* March 28, 1971, 25.

158. "Jesus, Mary, and DaVinci," ABC-TV, November 3, 2003.

159. John Spong, *Born of Women* (San Francisco: Harper, 1992), 197–98.

160. Ibid.

161. James Nelson, *Embodiment* (Minneapolis: Augsburg, 1978), 76.

162. Funk, *Five Gospels,* 220–21.26

Chapter 4

THE APOSTOLIC ERA

❦

Paul's Letters

Verses from the seventh chapter of Paul's first letter to the Corinthians are often quoted by those favoring obligatory priestly celibacy as clinching authority. In his *Holy Virginity* encyclical, Pius XII cites that chapter eleven times, far more than any other scriptural passage. About that chapter, biblical expositor Jean von Allmen observes, "Many warped interpretations of this chapter come from the fact that for centuries it has been scrutinized by celibates for whom marriage, not being their vocation, appears as a temptation and a fall."[1] This chapter will discuss what the apostle states in the letter and how it has been subsequently used not only for supporting but also for supplanting lifelong celibacy of church officers.

The prevailing translations of the opening verse of the seventh chapter have, because of the lack of proper punctuation, completely missed what Paul was trying to convey. Most English translations follow the King James Version in assuming Paul launched his discussion of marriage by declaring his basic outlook, "It is good for a man not to touch a woman." For example, the New Jerusalem Bible, with Catholic imprimatur, even adds an affirmation that is absent in the text, "Yes, it is a good thing for a man not to touch a woman." Latin church fathers mistakenly thought Paul, in his thesis sentence, was saying that even marital intercourse is bad.[2] Augustine exalts this assumed negativity toward sex and women by claiming that its source was "a voice from the clouds," meaning that it was the very word of God.[3] Subsequent interpreters of all of Paul's writings have commonly been disposed to treat the words of Paul as the direct word of God.

Because of the influence of celibate interpreters, virtually no one has doubted until the present generation that Paul was brashly stating his ascetic outlook on sexual intercourse at the outset of his consideration of the topic. Only recent translators have recognized that Paul was here—and elsewhere in this letter—quoting slogans that he will argue against (1 Cor 6:12; 8:1; 10:23). Unfortunately, quotations are not marked in Greek, but Paul indicates these by following them with his position, introduced by "but."

The opening sentences of the chapter under consideration should be translated: "Concerning the matters about which you wrote. You say, 'It is a good thing for a man not to have intercourse with a woman.' But because of sexual immorality, each man should have his own wife and each woman her own husband." The New Revised Standard Version, the Revised English Bible, and the Contemporary English Version now provide crucial quotation marks to distinguish Paul's outlook from that of an opposition group within the Corinthian community which advocated complete sexual abstinence.[4] The asceticism that Paul encountered in Corinth originated in pagan Greek philosophy and religion, which have been discussed here in Chapter 2. Church father Ambrosiaster, in his commentary on Paul's letters, attributed the condemnation of marriage quoted here to the perverse "pseudo-apostles" in Corinth to which Paul referred (2 Cor 11:13).[5] The cultural background of Paul's converts in that Greek city made it difficult for them to assimilate his radically different ethic.

Paul "rejects outright the extreme position he cites,"[6] and proceeds to explain why. He states that partners are equally obligated to surrender their bodies to one another for sexual satisfaction. He defends marital intercourse as both a right and a duty, "Do not withhold sexual intercourse from one another unless it is only temporary and by mutual agreement in order to spend time in prayer; but afterward resume relations so that Satan cannot tempt you because of a lack of self-control" (1 Cor 7:5). Jouette Bassler recognizes that the quoted position of some Corinthians "presents the issue of celibacy solely from the male perspective," while Paul's response "insists on the two-sidedness, the mutuality of sexual relations within marriage."[7]

"Even when Paul agrees to temporary periods of abstinence for special devotion to prayer, he does not present this with any enthusiasm but as a 'concession' to the preferences of the Corinthians."[8] That advice is in line with the Torah's assertion, in the form of a divine command, that a husband owes his wife her conjugal rights, and it echoes words attributed to a son of Jacob, "There is a time for having intercourse with one's wife and a time to abstain for the purpose of prayer" (Exod 21:10).[9] Jewish tradition permitted a husband who was preoccupied with religious matters to have an interlude from intercourse, with his wife's consent, for one or two weeks.[10] The Qur'an also declares the Semitic "mild sexual fasting" doctrine, because abstinence during daylight hours is expected during the holy month of Ramadan, and pilgrims to Mecca are to abstain while in the holy city.[11]

Centuries ago, Reformation scholar John Calvin perceptively grasped Paul's argument in this chapter:

> As far as we can gather from what Paul says, the Corinthians had become strongly influenced by the superstitious notion that virginity is an outstanding, almost an angelic virtue, so that they despised marriage as if it were something unclean. In order to get rid of this mistaken view, Paul teaches that each individual must know what his particular gift is; and in this connection must not try to do something he has not got the ability to do; for everybody is not called to the same state.[12]

Paul goes on to refer to himself as unmarried (*agamos*)—or, more precisely, "de-married"—meaning widower or divorcee; he distinguishes *agamos* from virgin (*parthenos*), which refers to a person of either gender who has not previously married (1 Cor 7:8, 11, 34). Methodius, a Greek patristic, assumes that Paul is stating here that he did not remarry after being widowed.[13] In encouraging others to choose his unusual option to remain single, Paul makes clear that he is not claiming celibacy to be superior to marriage. He affirms that both the celibate life and the conjugal life are "holy" (1 Cor 7:14, 34), and that the unmarried and the married states are equally a charisma, God's gift of grace. "God gives the gift of the single life to some, the gift of the married life to others," is the way one translator renders Paul's words in 1 Cor 7:7.[14] Even Jerome would have approved of that translation.[15] Pope John Paul II has corrected prior Catholic extolling of celibacy as a divine charisma at the expense of marriage. He cites the apostle who gave Christians the term charisma and its derivatives in European languages as his authority for saying that not only is celibacy a "gift of the Spirit," but that "a similar though different gift is contained in the vocation to true and faithful married love, directed toward procreation."[16] However, Paul never asserts that procreation is a purpose of marriage.

Luther states, "Paul counted himself among the unmarried and widowers, but it appears that he was married in his youth according to the custom of the Jews."[17] Modern scholars have reinforced Luther's conjecture by pointing out that Paul could not have become a leader in Judaism had he not been married. He had been a theologian of the Pharisees (Gal 1:14; Phil 3:3–6), and marriage was required for him to function in that capacity. Considering ancient lifespan averages, Paul was in midlife when he converted at about the age of forty. Jerome Murphy-O'Connor, in a thorough and scholarly account of Paul's life, states, "it is most probable that Paul had a wife" but that he was single during his Christian years.[18]

Some scholars suggest that Paul and his wife separated after he became a Christian. Theologian Edward Schillebeeckx conjectures: "Paul's own life of abstinence was not the celibacy of an unmarried man, or of a widower. In all probability it was the celibacy of a man who had either left his wife or had been left by her on his conversion."[19] Exegete Kenneth Foreman plausibly argues that Paul wrote from personal experience when, in a case of marital separation because of a non-Christian spouse, he gives this advice: "If a Christian man has a wife who is an unbeliever, and she is willing to live with him, he should not divorce her. And if a Christian woman has a husband who is an unbeliever, and he is willing to live with her, she should not divorce him. . . . But if the unbelieving partner wishes to separate, let it be so" (1 Cor 7:12–13, 15). Paul's counsel here, according to Foreman, suggests that his wife left him after he left Judaism; he felt constricted by "a marriage in which it had been impossible to be both a good husband and a good Christian missionary."[20] Had he found his wife, probably also from a rigid Pharisee family, unsympathetic toward his calling to be a Christian missionary?

Paul expressed his personal preference for continuing to be wifeless in his own existential situation, but in no way did he impose a celibacy rule on others. He was of the opinion that marriage was a distraction, not a defilement, perhaps in part because of his frequent travels. The apostle observes that those who marry will have troubles they might have avoided (1 Cor 7:28). When he says, "I wish that all of you were like me" (1 Cor 7:7), he is addressing everyone in the Corinthian church, not congregational leaders. Nowhere in the New Testament is a connection made between celibacy and clergy.

Surprisingly, Paul then passes on to the Corinthians a directive pertaining to marriage that he had received from traditions about Jesus, while admitting that no guidance had been transmitted from him pertaining to celibacy (1 Cor 7:10, 25). If Jesus were celibate and had given preference to the single state, why would Paul not have pointed to him as a model for celibacy? Catholic theologian Joan Timmerman regards Paul's admission that he could not cite Jesus to justify his celibate lifestyle to be a weighty argument from silence in favor of a married Jesus. She concludes that the tradition of Jesus' celibacy was not derived in Christianity from "biblical or theological sources authoritative in the early communities."[21]

Paul advises any who are betrothed and are "burning" with a sexual desire to marry because, as he repeats three times, "it is no sin" (1 Cor 7:9, 28, 36). For him, marital sexuality seems to be more of a therapeutic relief than a sharing partnership. Rather than criticize the apostle for discouraging the physical aspects of marriage, he can be more justifiably faulted for neglecting to deal sufficiently with its nonphysical qualities. In 1 Cor 7, which contains the apostle's fullest discussion of matrimony, nothing is said about marrying to intensify the joy of companionship outside the bedroom or to provide a loving environment for child nurture. Rather, Paul views marriage as a sexual safety valve that protects humans much as a fire extinguisher protects a home from burning. Since a convenient domestic remedy is available for those aflame with passion, a Christian should not rush out for illicit relief at a brothel (1 Cor 6:15–16). In writing to the Corinthians, the apostle gives attention to fleshly passion and to coital outlets but he inadequately integrates his central *agape* ethic with marital relationships. However, he is aware that marriage can be of such quality that the unbelieving partner becomes Christian (1 Cor 7:14).

Paul queries: "Do you have a wife? Do not seek to be free. Are you unmarried? Do not seek a wife. . . . A wife is bound to her husband as long as he lives. But if he dies, she is free to marry anyone she wishes, provided he is a Christian. However, in my opinion, she is happier as she is—and I think I also have God's Spirit" (1 Cor 7:27, 39–40). Why does Paul discourage marriage for those who had never married or remarriage for those whose spouses had died? When he wrote the Thessalonian and Corinthian letters, he was convinced that human history would be completed in his lifetime. He states that the archangel's last trumpet will soon sound and "we who are alive will be taken up into the clouds . . . to be with the Lord forever" (1 Thess 4:17; 1 Cor 15:51–52). That expectation is especially apparent in 1 Cor 7, Paul's most extensive discussion of marriage and celibacy. He thought he was living in the last years, as well as in the first years, of church history. Customary activities were shadowed by what he called "the impending crisis." In view of the brief span of time remaining, slaves should not concern themselves with becoming free, and those who are with or without spouses should not strive to alter their status (1 Cor 7:20–24, 26). Paul was not oriented toward producing and nurturing a future generation because he believed that the earthly kingdom would soon end. Celebrating, mourning, and buying a home also deserve little consideration because "the appointed time has grown short" (1 Cor 7:26–31). In his scholarly textbook on the apostle, Calvin Roetzel states Paul's main motivation for opting for remaining unspoused: "The eschatological crisis provided an important rationale for Paul's celibacy. . . . The practical issue of this cosmic emergency was clear to him. Entanglements should be avoided."[22]

Paul affirmed his preference for celibacy based on his mistaken timetable for the end of history. For almost two millennia, the apostle's error has been apparent. Did Jesus share Paul's view of the nearness of the end-time and consequently believe that their culture's marital requirement could be suspended? Many twentieth-century scholars thought Jesus was also motivated by the apocalyptic view that the end was just around the corner. For example, Susanne Heine portrayed the Jesus group as homeless, property-less, and spouseless because of their belief in an impending doomsday. She asked, "Is it worthwhile continuing to bring children into this world in order to hand them over to the suffering in which everything will soon come to an end?"[23] In contrast, a substantial majority of current American scholars specializing in the historical Jesus do not view him as a proclaimer of the imminent end of the world.[24] He declared that the reign of God had begun but had not fully arrived.

A comparison of Paul's later letters with his earlier ones suggests that his eschatological fervor cooled as he grew older. He gradually replaced an inaugurated eschatology for a futurist apocalypticism, and thus came in line with the outlook of Jesus himself.[25] During the final decade of his life, the apostle no longer expected an immediate reappearance of Christ. His emphasis shifted from awaiting a glorious theophany that would have transpired in the clouds after Christians became airborne, to an awareness of Jesus within the lives of Christians. "Christ in you, the hope of glory," Paul proclaims (Col 1:27). No longer did he consider the Christians of his day as composing the end-time community, for the coming of Christ in the church community was not the beginning of the end but the end of the beginning. In his earlier ministry he asked all Christians to consider becoming celibate, and he viewed marriage as little more than a means of licit sexual relief. But in his later writing celibacy is no longer mentioned and he admonishes, "Husbands, love your wives and never treat them harshly" (Col 3:19, NRSV). Recognizing the fluidity of Paul's thought as he struggled to understand the gospel, then transmitted orally, it is unfair to attempt to extract from 1 Corinthians his comprehensive and final position on marriage. He did not offer advice on celibacy as timeless moral truth but as a recommendation for a particular situation, when he wrongly presumed while on his mission in Greece that historical time was soon to end.

Partly separable from his eschatological reason for the single life, Paul also offered what he considered to be an abiding practical reason. He thought that the unmarried have fewer distractions and have more liberty to be consecrated Christians:

> An unmarried man is concerned with how to please the Lord. But a married man is concerned with worldly affairs; his aim is to please his wife, and his interests are divided. A woman who is not married and a girl who has never married is concerned with the Lord's work; their aim is to be holy in body and spirit. But a married woman is concerned with worldly affairs; her aim is to please her husband. (1 Cor 7:32–34)

In defending Catholic celibacy, Pius XII quoted the above passage along with Aquinas's opinion that marriage "keeps the soul from full abandon to the service of God."[26] He then makes this invidious comparison, "Virginity is more excellent than marriage chiefly because . . . it is a supremely effective means for devoting oneself wholly to the service of God, while the heart of married persons will always remain more or less 'divided.'"[27] Subsequently, also on the authority of Paul, Vatican II claimed that those who have the gift of celibacy "can more easily devote their entire selves to God alone with undivided heart."[28] The magisterium presumes that married Christians are pulled in two directions by having commitments to both Christ and a spouse. Because of this, they cannot succeed in loving God with their whole hearts.

Over against Paul and the Vatican, a case can be made that the concerns of most married Christians are not altogether worldly and that they have at least as much devotion to practicing the gospel as the unmarried. Where can one find a higher expression of unconditional love than in a couple whose lives are faithful to their wedding vows? Is not what Paul calls the "fruit of the Spirit," consisting of "love, joy, peace, patience, kindness, generosity, faithfulness, gentleness, and self-control" (Gal 5:22, NRSV), found at least as often in matrimony as in bachelorhood? Bearing and nurturing children provides opportunities for co-creating with God and for guiding spiritual development. Paul also failed to realize that the unmarried, as commonly as the married, may be selfish and materialistic. An anonymous fourth-century writer, critical of the apostle's assessment, comments, "We see virgins with their minds on the world and married people eager for the works of the Lord."[29]

Paul over-generalized when he claimed that a bachelor is more focused on pleasing God than a married man. From his study of Spanish priests, Manuel Galvez claimed, "all of them were obsessed by women."[30] His sample was too limited to apply to priests everywhere, but his conclusion appropriately offsets Paul's opposite judgment. Paul Dinter, when serving as Columbia University's Catholic chaplain, learned much about the lifestyle of his rabbinic colleague; this convinced him "that many of the arguments advanced by Catholic leaders about the rigors of the priest's life and the consequent need for celibacy look silly when compared with the religious commitment of the observant Orthodox Jewish husband."[31]

Schillebeeckx rejects the alleged rivalry between the love of God and the love of spouse: "In practice it can be easier for one person to arrive at a greater and more real and undivided love of God in marriage, whereas for someone else this only happens through an unmarried life." Schillebeeckx graciously uses Protestants to illustrate his point: "It can be seen from the history of married leaders throughout the churches of the Reformation that in most cases the marriage of ministers has in no way hindered their utter dedication to the [religious] community; on the contrary, in many cases it has furthered this."[32] Joseph Blenkinsopp, another Catholic professor, also criticizes the repeated claim that a celibate generally gives himself undividedly to his ministerial vocation:

> After having worked in both Catholic and Protestant theological seminaries I could not honestly conclude that students in the former are more available either for carrying out a local mission or for their own preparation for the ministry, acquiring the necessary academic and practical skills. In my experience married students in Protestant seminaries, even those with several children to look after, manage to get through just as much work, if not more, in the two or three years . . . as celibate Catholic students in the four years of their theological course of studies.[33]

Calvin acknowledged that he married in order to dedicate himself "more completely to the Lord, being more relieved from the worries of daily life."[34] Paradoxically, he renounced bachelorhood so that he would have more singularity in his Christian service. According to the biographer of Richard Mather, an early New England Calvinist, his wife "had taken off from her husband all secular cares, so that he wholly devoted himself to his study, and to sacred employments."[35]

Karl Rahner enthusiastically accepted celibacy for himself but he rejected the notion that living alone is more sacrificial and godly. He affirmed, "Any really Christian life involves abnegation and self-denial."[36] Priest Hans Kung corroborates that view: "Let no high-toned theological speculation becloud the fact that total surrender to God is just as possible for married people."[37] Irish Dominican Michael Commane testifies, "I don't believe for one minute that a priest's work is such that they would be unable to do it as well if they were married or had a family. There are of course priests who work hard, but from my experience, priests are not at the top when it comes to hard work."[38]

Most contemporary Catholic priests and their clientele do not accept Paul's argument that marriage distracts from serving God. In a scientific study of fifty clergy over a ten-year period, Julius Heuscher found that they are "unconvinced that the celibate life contributes to the effective performances of religious responsibilities."[39] Canadian sociologist Don Swenson devised an empirical test to discover if celibacy enables a person to be more undivided in religious performance. A comparison of seventy Catholic priests with a large group of evangelical ministers showed that "being a celibate did not make a significant difference to one's spiritual life." Swenson concludes, "In regards to one's devotional life and time for ministry, celibacy does not appear to matter."[40] When *U.S. Catholic* asked their readers to respond to this statement, "I don't believe a married priest can be anywhere as available and dedicated to his community as a celibate priest," 68 percent disagreed.[41]

To say that a priest can minister better if unmarried makes as much sense as to argue that unmarried pediatricians or marriage counselors are more capable than those with spouses and children because they can spend more time and concentration on their profession. Clergyman John Warner writes that if we believed Paul's "crazy idea" that celibacy is needed for vocational dedication, we would have only celibates for presidents, military officers, and the like.[42] Theologian Rosemary Ruether comments:

> Everyone has much the same needs for sleep, food, recreation, and companionship, whether one is single or married. . . . An analysis of what a parish priest actually does with his time each day, in contrast either with married ministers or professionals with demanding occupations, would quickly reveal the meaninglessness of this proposition of "full-time" ministry among the celibate. . . . The oft-stated view that by withdrawing from an exclusive relationship with one person, one is freeing oneself to love and be the father of everyone, rests on a very peculiar view of the psychology of human relationships. . . . One loves and serves only in real and concrete situations and commitments.[43]

Jeremy Taylor, an outstanding early Anglican bishop, similarly observes, "a married man may spend as much time in devotion as any virgins or widows do." "Though marriage hath cares," he said, "yet the single life hath desires which are more troublesome and more dangerous."[44] A former Catholic seminarian voices the forbidden fruit syndrome: "Celibacy, by its very prohibitions, guarantees a preoccupation with sexuality. You always want what you don't have or think you can't get."[45] Celibate Ignatius Hunt comments: "The unmarried person who is not happy in his state can be deeply concerned about the other sex and spend a great deal of time thinking over the situation, formulating plans of compromise and thus not only lack the time to be 'pleasing to God,' but in extreme cases lose all sight of pleasing God."[46]

Genuine historical information about Jesus and his disciples is best found in Paul's letters, because they were recorded decades before the Gospels were written. He mentions in passing that travel with wives was the standard practice of the apostles and Jesus' brothers (1 Cor 9:5). Only Paul mentions "the brothers of the Lord" having wives who accompanied them as Christian missionaries. Elsewhere he gives the name of one of those brothers, James, who was a Christian leader in Jerusalem (Gal 1:18–19). Second-century historian Hegesippus told about two grandsons of Jesus' brother Judas; they lived in the late first century and became church leaders.[47] Presumably Joseph arranged for the marriages of all of his sons. A plausible reason why Paul does not mention Jesus along with the others who traveled with their wives is that he was discussing an issue current to his own day, and was appealing to the practice of then itinerating missionaries. This earliest record of apostolic lifestyles shows that celibacy was not intrinsic to leaders of the church. In the culture of the early Christians, marriages were usually arranged at the time of puberty, so the personnel pattern for mission work when Paul was writing was probably the same as when the adult disciples traveled with Jesus to spread the gospel.

The gospel writers may not have intended to be silent with respect to the wives of those in Jesus' band. In some verses where "woman" is found in English versions, "wife" may be a better translation. *Gune* is the Greek word in the New Testament for designating, according to context, either "woman" or "wife," but it more often means "wife." Etymologically it is associated with one who gives birth (*gone*), a mother.[48] The New Revised Standard Version provides a more precise contextual translation at places in Paul's letters by changing "woman" of the King James Version to "wife" or "married woman" (1 Cor 11:3; Rom 7:2).

In Luke's gospel, *gune* is used in reference both to spouses of particular husbands (1:13; 3:19; 8:3; 14:20; 17:32; 20:28), and to women generally, unmarried or married (7:39; 8:2; 11:27; 13:11–12). A number of *gunai* itinerated with Jesus and "the Twelve" in order to provide for their needs (Luke 8:1–3). In view of the danger that a guardian would surely see in permitting a single daughter to live with men, it can be assumed that all of these women had married. Indeed, the very thought of a traveling ladies' aid society composed of virgins is so unfitting in first-century Palestine as to be ludicrous! Some of the women might have been widows but some were probably wives of the men with whom they camped. Mary Magdalene, the first named *gune,* may have been Jesus' wife.[49]

When on a training mission, the disciples traveled "two by two" and lodged in whatever accommodations they could find (Luke 10:1–7). Far from asking Peter and the others to become celibate, Jesus sent them out in pairs, which might well have been husband and wife teams.[50] Were these wives also present in a Jerusalem "upper room" after Jesus' crucifixion? Some textual authorities read *gunai* in Acts 1:14 as referring to the wives of the eleven disciples gathered there.[51] Codex Bezae, one of the ancient Greek manuscripts of the New Testament, includes "and children" with *gunai,* requiring the translation "with wives and children." That text may be the more accurate one here. It would be easier to understand why the celibate scribes of the New Testament would have removed "and children" from this sentence than to assume that they had added it.

If the *gunai* accompanying the disciples are recognized as wives in the opening of Luke's second volume of the beginnings of Christianity, then the same translation of *gunai* is needed in Luke 8:1–3. Therefore, it is plausible to assume that some wives were present in the band of Jesus from its inception; there is no reason for postulating a basic change in attitude toward female companionship before and after they witnessed Jesus' resurrection. Luke elsewhere uses the same "wives and children" words and states that Philip, a church officer and an evangelist, had children (Acts 21:5, 9).

A legend as ancient as the one that calls Peter the bishop of Rome claims that he had children and that his wife became the first woman martyr.[52] According to a "credible" tradition, his daughter was St. Petronilla, after whom a catacomb outside Rome was named.[53] When Peter was asked in John's gospel, "Do you love me more than these others?" (21:15), evidently Jesus was not suggesting that he abandon his wife and children.

The incidental reference to Peter's mother-in-law in the Gospels cannot be interpreted to mean that he was the only married disciple during the period of Jesus' public ministry (Mark 1:30). Since all of his disciples were subject to the traditional mores of their Jewish culture, those over twenty years of age when "called" were probably married. It is even possible that the wedding feast that Jesus attended in Cana was for one of them. Nathaniel was from Cana and the account of Jesus' visit with him comes immediately before the wedding episode (John 1:45–2:11; 21:2).

Why would the apostles travel with their wives? Their presence would both provide for the needs of their husbands and allay gossip. But also, wives could function as evangelistic copartners. According to Clement of Alexandria, an early church father, the apostles took them along "that they might be their fellow-ministers in dealing with housewives. It was through them that the Lord's teaching penetrated also the women's quarters without any scandal being aroused."[54] Paul referred to Priscilla and Aquila as "fellow workers in Christ Jesus" and jointly in charge of a church that met in their home (Rom 16:3; 1 Cor 16:19). Also, Paul named both Andronicus and Julia, who were probably husband and wife, "notable apostles" (Rom 16:7), even though some androcentric medieval scribe tried to perform a linguistic sex change operation and convert "Julia" to "Julius." One church father exclaimed with respect to her, "How great was the devotion of this woman, that she should be counted worthy of the title apostle!"[55]

When Paul acknowledges that he is an exception to the apostles in marital status, he also asserts his right to marry. He refers to individual human rights even though ancient cultures gave little consideration to what has become of fundamental importance in modern society. In the fourth century, Bishop Hilary of Poitier commented on Paul's reference to other apostles being married: "He does not put anything in the way of the right to marry."[56] Hilary, who was an eminent defender of orthodoxy and who became a Catholic saint, was married and had a daughter. Paul's position presaged Article 16 of the *Declaration of Human Rights of the United Nations*, which reads, "Men and women of full age, without any limitation due to race, nationality or religion, have the right to marry and to found a family." Paul maintained that an individual has the privilege of renouncing his or her own basic rights but not those of others. This judgment alone by an apostle should have kept subsequent church councils from enacting legislation that removed the right of clerics to marry.

Before the advent of critical biblical scholarship during the past two centuries, texts were often extracted and appealed to for scriptural authority without examining their historical or literary contexts. Verses in Paul's letters related to marriage illustrate this misuse of biblical literature. His advocacy of celibacy continues to be presented by the Catholic magisterium with disregard to the important contextual qualifications expressed in the Corinthian letter. The apostle's position needs to be weighed with these considerations in mind: a) he thought, wrongly, that the mortal era would soon end; b) he points out that he is giving his own opinion and not a teaching of Jesus; c) he is not discussing priestly celibacy; and d) he recognizes that other apostles are married, which was an appropriate expression of their human rights.

First Corinthians also contains other teachings that should have informed subsequent church practices. The letter reflects the nonhierarchical nature of the nascent church; a spirit of egalitarianism prevailed and the laity had no sheep complex. "Each is given the Spirit for the common good," Paul tells them (1 Cor 12:7). His advice for conducting a worship service resembles what might best be found now among Quakers or Pentecostals: "Each of you should contribute a hymn, some instruction, a revelation, an ecstatic utterance, or its interpretation" (1 Cor 14:26). Also, he gives the earliest historical account of what he calls the "Lord's Supper," but he says nothing about those who consecrate the Eucharist or about abstaining from sex for a period beforehand. Nowhere in the New Testament is there mention of any church officer administering the Eucharist. According to Richard McBrien, "Indeed, there is no compelling evidence that they presided when they were present, or that a chain of ordination from apostle to bishop to priest was required for presiding."[57]

Other New Testament Writings

Unlike the earliest Christians, the generation to follow no longer naively assumed that they were the last one before the judgment day. The exclamation "Lord, come!" (1 Cor 16:22) was bent into a question mark as the first century continued without another advent. The writings of Paul's disciples show that Christians had come to realize that secular society might long continue. Therefore, they returned to the default view of religious duty, which involved becoming married and having children. Salvation is even associated with childbearing (1 Tim 2:15). Catholic theologian Karl Schelkle points out that Paul recommended celibacy in writing the Corinthians so, in anticipation of Christ's immanent return, they could be free of every bond. But Schelkle finds a different message in the Ephesian letter: "If celibacy is the sign of the Church's expectation of her Lord, then one can and must say of marriage that it is the sign already present of the already realized union of Christ and the Church."[58]

The writer of Ephesians uses the same verb, *agapan*, to refer to conjugal affections as he does to divine-human relations, "Husbands love your wives as Christ loved the church and gave himself up for her" (Eph 5:25). The self-sacrificing and forgiving qualities of Christian love are best expressed in the tie between husband and wife. Human lovemaking, far from being antagonistic to religious devotion, is the closest analogy to Christ's love. Just as Jesus' giving was not a spiritual but a physical crucifixion, so this letter is not suggesting a sexless but a physical marriage. The writer describes the marital relation as a mutual subordination: "Be subject to one another out of reverence for Christ" (Eph 5:21). An interdependence is advocated in which each partner accepts and admires the superior gifts that the other contributes. Marriage with reciprocal responsibilities is described as the quintessence of human love, and it has a dignity that is radically different from that found in paganism.

Second-generation Christians pictured Jesus as the standard-setting cornerstone for the apostolic foundation and for the entire structure of the church community (Eph 2:20–21). Since we know that most of the apostles lived with spouses, the church in the latter part of the first century attempted to follow that established apostolic pattern. Consequently, centuries passed before clerics were expected to be celibate.

The only New Testament teaching directed particularly to church leaders is in letters addressed to pastors Timothy and Titus, who had been assistants of Paul. A letter to Timothy states that "everything created by God is good, and nothing is to be rejected, provided it is received with thanksgiving." Thus, anyone advocating abstinence from marriage and certain foods was denounced for betraying the Christian doctrine of creation (1 Tim 4:2–4). The letters affirm that successful marriage is a main criterion for choosing bishops, elders, and deacons for office. Each should be a "one-woman man" of irreproachable character, living with his spouse in monogamous fidelity.

The one-wife requirement should not be interpreted as a prohibition of digamy, the remarriage after the death of a spouse. The Pauline writer of the Pastoral Letters follows Paul, who permitted and in some cases recommended remarriage (1 Cor 7:7–8, 39; Rom 7:2–3). The remarriage of widows who are not elderly is encouraged in a letter to Timothy, and presumably, widowers would be similarly advised (1 Tim 5:14). Church leaders should have stable marriages whether or not they are digamists.

Also, a candidate for church office must show ability to govern his children, on the relevant assumption that the way a father relates to his family displays his talent for pastoral oversight of a church community (1 Tim 3:2, 5, 12; 5:14; Tit 1:6). As the New Testament indicates, Christians usually congregated in the homes of local church officers (Rom 16:5; 1 Cor 16:19; Phlm 2: Acts 20:20). When they broke bread together to give sustenance to their bodies, they also participated in the Lord's Supper (1 Cor 11:20–21). In that house-church situation, being a good husband and father would especially display an aptitude for the wider responsibility of ministering to "the household of faith" (Gal 6:10). Since the church community was viewed as the human family writ large, it is understandable that the affectionate designation "papa" (Italian), "pere" (French), "padre" (Spanish), or "father" for the parish leader later evolved.

Catholicism treats bishops as the successors of the apostles, even though bishops in the New Testament were not witnesses to Jesus' resurrection. The Vatican has virtually reversed the earliest qualification for the offices of bishop and elder, associating the ministry with celibacy rather than marriage. Some Protestants have gone to the opposite extreme and have made marriage compulsory for ministers. William Tyndale, the genius among English biblical translators, interpreted the Pastoral Letters to mean that church officers must be monogamists and display in their marriage the moral standards of Christianity. Pointing out that *episcopos* means overseer, he agreed with the author of the letters that commendable oversight of one's family is excellent preparation for congregational leadership. "People look as well unto the living as unto the preaching," Tyndale said, and they leave the church when they detect hypocrisy.[59]

Christians of the paleochurch were not interested in establishing a new priesthood. They had an antipathy toward Jewish priests and their Sadducaic party that had turned Jesus over to the Roman government for execution. Consequently, those who have the title "priest" in the New Testament belong to the old adversarial order, except for Jesus, who is frequently and ironically called a "high priest" (literally in Greek, a hierarch, *archi* + *hiereus*) by the anonymous author of the book of Hebrews. That author recognized that Jesus could not literally have been a priest, if for no other reason than that he was not from the priestly tribe of Levi (Heb 7:14). Jesus never offered animal sacrifices at the altar in the only Temple at Jerusalem, nor did he dress like a priest, live like a priest, or collect tithes like a priest. He is described in Hebrews as a holy sacrificer who is superior to the Levitical priests (8:1–6). Having attained a permanent sacerdotal role after his crucifixion, the immortal Jesus is both the bloody sacrifice and the sacred presenter of the offering to God (Heb 9:11–22). That unique, all-sufficient act by the heavenly hierarch was presumed to have ended, once and for all, the need for continual cultic performances by earthly hierarchs.

Writers of the Hebrew Bible viewed Israelites as "a priestly kingdom," who were consecrated for service to God (Exod 19:6; Isa 61:6). New Testament writers thought of Christians as carrying forward that role in an egalitarian manner (1 Pet 2:9; Rev 5:10). They are encouraged to form themselves "into a spiritual temple and be holy priests who offer spiritual sacrifices to God" (1 Pet 2:5). Having Jesus as their final mediator and symbolic sacrifice, they can dispense with functionaries who claim to have a special power of communication between the divine and human realms. Christians are urged to have personal boldness in searching for forgiveness and to eschew going through channels of priests or angels to obtain reconciliation with God. As there were no priests in the apostolic and early post-apostolic church, the early Christians recognized the priestly potential of all believers, so there was no priestly caste set apart and above others in the blessed community. Christians did not endorse either the ancient Hebrew or the current pagan idea of a dual standard of moral holiness in the community.

Instead of having a priest offer the butchered body of a domestic animal at an altar on behalf of a client, Paul begins a passage about moral conduct by pleading that Christians serve figuratively as their own priests and present directly their own living bodies as a holy offering to God (Rom 12:1). They should attempt to engage in self-giving similar to that of Jesus. Elsewhere that apostle described the individual Christian as dying and rising with Christ and thereby symbolically reenacting his crucifixion and resurrection (Rom 6:3–11). Paul also imaged the Christian as "a temple of the indwelling Holy Spirit" that s/he must keep clean for proper worship (1 Cor 6:19). In the letter of James, "religion that is pure and undefiled" is unrelated to rituals by religious professionals but is devoted to assisting those most in need (1:27).

In a convoluted manner, Catholicism has attempted to find precedents for its celibate priests in the intermediary-functioning priests of the Torah and in priest Jesus. Catholic Edward Peters offers this reason for Jesus' celibacy: "It was entirely in accord with Old Law tradition that the Redeemer, as priest and as warrior-king, should remain continent while offering sacrifice and waging war against sin-activities, which fill his entire life."[60] Robert Stern likewise writes:

> Jesus, the one Priest of the new dispensation, never married. . . . Celibacy was seen above all else as continence, and continence as an abstention from a necessarily polluting and profoundly worldly desire and behavior. The Hebrew priest, the pagan priest, and pre-eminently the Christian priest, needed to be a man of God, a man apart, a purified man; accordingly he had to renounce or abstain from sexual behavior.[61]

But Hebrew priests could only receive their office by inheritance from their priestly fathers, and they were required to marry so they could supply priests for posterity. Also, Jesus abrogated the purity laws of the old order (Mark 7:1–23), so purification rituals should not be associated with his work. Paul VI commendably recognized that no biblical basis exists for the ritual cleanliness argument that had been appealed to for many centuries to justify celibacy. But then, the Pope described Jesus as the first "Pontiff" of the church who "remained throughout his whole life in the state of celibacy." According to Paul VI, Jesus' celibacy was in some unspecified way associated with his being the mediator of a covenant between God and humankind, as stated in Heb 8:6.[62] The Pope showed no awareness that a celibate Jesus would be counter to the description of him in Hebrews. It affirms that Jesus "had to resemble his brothers in every respect" (Heb 2:17). This means that he confronted a wide sampling of human moral and spiritual testing, but did not succumb to conduct that transgressed God's will.

Oscar Cullmann discusses the importance of the assertions in Hebrews pertaining to Jesus. The distinguished Christologist observes that Christians have often not taken seriously statements that Jesus "learned obedience" through exposure to the same conditions as other humans:

> "We have not a high priest who is unable to sympathize with our weaknesses, but one who in every respect has been tempted as we are" (Heb. 4:15). The full significance of this description of Jesus humanity is rarely appreciated. . . . This statement of Hebrews, which thus goes beyond the Synoptic reports of Jesus' being tempted, is perhaps the boldest assertion of the completely human character of Jesus in the New Testament. It . . . casts a special light on the life of Jesus, leading us to consider aspects of his life with which we are not acquainted.[63]

Some comments in a New Testament letter attributed to Peter have relevance to the later development of church leadership by spouseless men. Wives and slaves are instructed to be obedient to their husbands and masters (1 Pet 2:18, 3:1). Showing an acceptance of the conventional notion that women were the pot in which the "seed" of her stronger husband could be planted and fertilized, the letter states that "woman is the weaker vessel" (1 Pet 3:7). This androcentric declaration indicates why women would be deprived of dignified roles in churches.

In the *Gospel of Thomas*, Peter is represented as saying to his fellow male disciples about Mary Magdalene and her gender, "Let Mary leave us, for women are not worthy of Life" (114). Another text of early Christianity puts these words into her mouth, "My Lord, you always grasp my understanding, but each time I come forward to give the correct interpretation of your words I am afraid of Peter, for he threatens me and hates our sex"

(*Pistis Sophia,* 72). Peter would not believe that Jesus would have granted a direct revelation to a woman.

Susan Haskins, in her magisterial study of Mary Magdalene, writes about women's status in the early church before a hierarchy of male deacons, priests, and bishops evolved:

> Peter's antagonism towards Mary Magdalen may reflect the historical ambivalence of the leaders of the orthodox community towards the participation of women in the Church. But by the end of the second century, the egalitarian principles defined in the New Testament, and adhered to in this context by St. Paul, had been discarded in favour of a return to the patriarchal system of Judaism which had preceded them.[64]

A verse from the last book of the New Testament has been interpreted as sanctioning perpetual virginity for holy men of the church. It reads, "These [144,000 men] who have kept their virginity and have not defiled themselves with women follow the Lamb wherever he goes" (Rev 14:4). Recognizing that "the Lamb of God" symbolizes Jesus, Augustine states, "Virgins follow the Lamb, because the flesh of the Lamb is also virginal. For he preserved it himself in his manhood what he did not take away from his mother in his conception and birth."[65] Aquinas agreed with Augustine that Rev 14:4 refers to male virgins who imitate Jesus in preserving their flesh from corruption.[66]

However, biblical commentators recognize that the verse under scrutiny, like everything in Revelation, is symbolic. The visionary who wrote that book was not intending to convey that the "redeemed" will consist exclusively of 144,000 virgins. "Virgins" should not be understood literally as men who do not "defile" themselves by engaging in sexual intercourse. Commentator George Caird writes about the treatment of "virgins" by the author of Revelation: "He is not disclosing in an unguarded moment his personal predilection for asceticism. . . . This is a symbol . . . for moral purity from the seductions of the great whore of Babylon [the persecuting Roman government]."[67] Elisabeth Schüssler Fiorenza maintains that everything pertaining to sex in this apocalypse "is metaphorical, signifying that these pure ones have not participated in the idolatry of the imperial cult."[68] Jesuit Jean D'Aragon notes: "The 144,000 whose foreheads bear the seal constitute the totality of the Christian people. . . . Virginity is a metaphor for fidelity to God."[69] The virgin metaphor pictures the church as a bride who has kept her purity for marriage to the Lamb (Rev 19:7; 21:2, 9), and has resisted "fornicating" by worshiping at the pagan altars of Rome.

An assertion of von Allmen encapsulates the discussion of this and the previous chapter, and provides a window through which to view the forthcoming chapters: "The New Testament knows nothing of the very considerable depreciation of marriage which the influence of an ascetic dualism is to introduce into the church."[70]

Notes

1. Jean von Allmen, *Pauline Teaching on Marriage* (London: Faith, 1963), 15.

2. Tertullian, *On Monogamy* 3; Jerome, *Against Jovinian* 1:7.

3. Augustine, *Confessions* 2:3; *On Marriage and Concupiscence* 1:16.

4. Those new translations have been informed by my exegesis: "Is Paul's Attitude Toward Sexual Relations Contained in 1 Cor. 7:1?" *New Testament Studies* (January 1982): 125–31.

5. *Corpus Scriptorum Ecclesiasticorum* 81:2:70.

6. Will Deming, *Paul on Marriage and Celibacy* (New York: Cambridge University Press, 1995), 218.

7. Carol Newsom and Sharon Ringe, eds. *The Women's Bible Commentary* (Louisville: Westminster/John Knox, 1992), 323.

8. Ibid., 323.

9. *Testament of Naphtali* 8:8.

10. *Ketuboth* 5:6.

11. Qur'an 73:6–8.

12. John Calvin, *The First Epistle of Paul the Apostle to the Corinthians* (Grand Rapids: Eerdmans, 1960), 11–12.

13. Methodius, *Symposium* 3:12.

14. Eugene H. Peterson, *The Message* (Colorado Springs: NavPress, 1993), 347.

15. Jerome, *Against Jovinian* 1:8.

16. John Paul II, *Letter to Priests* (April 9, 1979), 8.

17. Helmut Lehman, ed., *Luther's Works* (Philadelphia: Fortress, 1957), 54:353–54.

18. Jerome Murphy-O'Connor, *Paul: A Critical Life* (Oxford: Clarendon, 1996), 64.

19. Edward Schillebeeckx, *Marriage* (New York: Sheed, 1965), 128.

20. Kenneth Foreman, *The First Letter of Paul to the Corinthians* (Richmond: John Knox, 1961), 85.

21. Joan Timmerman, *Sexuality and Spiritual Growth* (New York: Crossroad, 1992), 29.

22. Calvin Roetzel, *Paul* (Columbia: University of South Carolina Press, 1998), 146.

23. Susanne Heine, *Women and Early Christianity* (Minneapolis: Augsburg, 1988), 67.

24. Marcus Borg, *Jesus in Contemporary Scholarship* (Valley Forge, PA: Trinity Press International, 1994), 7.

25. Gerd Theissen and Annette Merz, *The Historical Jesus* (Minneapolis: Fortress, 1996), 243–45.

26. Aquinas, *Summa Theologica* 2–2:186:4; Pius XII, *Holy Virginity* (1954), 20–21.

27. Pius XII, *Holy Virginity*, 24.

28. *Dogmatic Constitution on the Church*, 42.

29. Jacque Migne, ed., *Patrologia Latina* (Paris, 1879), 17:236.

30. Manuel Galvez, *Holy Wednesday* (New York: Appleton-Century, 1934), 135.

31. Paul Dinter, *The Other Side of the Altar* (New York: Farrar, 2003), 116.

32. Edward Schillebeeckx, *The Church with a Human Face* (New York: Crossroad, 1985), 246–47.

33. Joseph Blenkinsopp, *Celibacy, Ministry, Church* (New York: Herder, 1968), 44.

34. John Calvin, *Opera* (Brunswick, 1871), 10a:228.

35. Increase Mather, *The Life and Death of that Reverend Man of God, Mr. Richard Mather* (Cambridge, 1670), 25.

36. Karl Rahner, *Servants of the Lord* (New York: Herder, 1968), 165.

37. Hans Kung, ed., *Life in the Spirit* (New York: Sheed & Ward, 1967), 7.

38. *Irish Times*, April 30, 2002, 14.

39. Julius Hesher, *Comprehensive Psychiatry* (September 1972): 445.

40. Don Swenson, "Does Celibacy Make a Difference?," *Sociology of Religion* (Spring 1998): 37, 43.

41. *U.S. Catholic* (February 1999), 28.

42. *Charleston Gazette*, January 31, 2003, A5.

43. Rosemary Reuther, "The Ethic of Celibacy," *Commonweal*, February 2, 1973, 390, 394.

44. Jeremy Taylor, *Works* (London, 1928), 5:253.

45. Quoted in Joan Ohanneson, *And They Felt No Shame* (Minneapolis: Winston, 1983), 104.

46. George Frein, ed., *Celibacy: The Necessary Option* (New York: Herder, 1968), 133–34.

47. Eusebius, *Church History* 3:20.

48. Plato, *Cratylus* 414.

49. William Phipps, *The Sexuality of Jesus* (Cleveland: Pilgrim Press, 1996), 122–42.

50. Marcus Borg, ed., *Jesus at 2000* (Boulder: Westview, 1997), 39–40.

51. Kirsopp Lake and Henry Cadbury, *The Beginnings of Christianity* (Frederich Foakes-Jackson, ed.; London: Macmillan, 1933), 4:1, 11; Matthew Black,

ed., *Peake's Commentary on the Bible* (London: Nelson, 1962), 887; David Dockery, ed., *The New American Commentary* (Nashville: Broadman, 1992), 26:89.

52. Clement of Alexandria, *Miscellanies* 3:52; 7:63.

53. James Lees-Milne, *Saint Peter's* (Boston: Little, Brown, 1967), 14.

54. Clement, *Miscellanies* 3:53.

55. Chrysostom, *Sermons on Romans* 31.

56. Hilary, *Commentary on Psalms* 118:14.

57. Richard McBrien, *Catholicism* (San Francisco: Harper, 1994), 866–67.

58. Karl Schelkle, *Theology of the New Testament* (Collegeville, MN: Liturgical Press, 1970), 3:259.

59. William Tyndale, *The Obedience of a Christian Man* (London: Penguin, 2000), 86–87.

60. Edward Peters, "Sex and the Savior," *Catholic World* (March 1971), 322.

61. William Bassett and Peter Huizing, eds., *Celibacy in the Church* (New York: Herder, 1972), 81.

62. Paul VI, *Priestly Celibacy*, 6, 20–21.

63. Oscar Cullmann, *The Christology of the New Testament* (Philadelphia: Westminster, 1959), 95.

64. Susan Haskins, *Mary Magdalen* (New York: Harcourt, 1994), 42.

65. Augustine, *Holy Virginity* 27.

66. Aquinas, *Summa Theologica* 2–2:152:5.

67. Rev. 14:8; 17:5; George Caird, *A Commentary on the Revelation of St. John the Divine* (London: Black, 1966), 179.

68. Elisabeth Schüssler Fiorenza, *Revelation* (Minneapolis: Fortress, 1991), 88.

69. *The Jerome Biblical Commentary* (Englewood Cliffs, NJ: Prentice-Hall, 1968), 2:484.

70. Jean von Allmen, *A Companion to the Bible* (New York: Oxford, 1958), 256.

Chapter 5

THE PATRISTIC ERA

Movement toward Sexual Abstinence

The period of the "church fathers" is somewhat arbitrary in its span. For our discussion, it will extend from the second century "apologists" to Augustine, the most outstanding patristic. He died not long before the fall of the Roman Empire in 476, which ended the ancient period of history.

Two major events transpired in the latter part of the first Christian century that reoriented the moral perspective of the church. First, the martyrdoms of Peter and Paul at the beginning of the Roman persecution of the church resulted in Gentiles replacing the initial Jewish leadership. Second, Jerusalem, Christianity's original center, was razed. In the post-apostolic church, ethical standards began seeping in from Hellenistic customs and from philosophies fashionable in Roman cities where the church had been planted. Second-century Christians, nearly all Gentiles, had little historical knowledge of the Hebrew tradition or appreciation of the Jewish way of life.

In no area was there a more striking difference between the Hebraic and the Hellenistic social environments than in their outlook on sexuality. Eric Dodds calls the last period of ancient pagan philosophy the "age of anxiety" and gives it this description: "Contempt for the human condition and hatred of the body was a disease endemic in the entire culture of the period."[1] Although the Greeks have been associated with moderation—"nothing overmuch"—from Homer onward, a more extreme ethic was popular among many in the Greco-Roman culture who drew on the views of the Pythagoreans, Platonists, and Stoics. Plotinus, a leading Neoplatonist, held that the pure form of love "has no part in marriages."[2] Porphyry, a disciple of Plotinus, believed that virginity was the sine qua non of purity.[3]

Infant Christianity was orphaned before coming of age sexually, and the abrupt shift of the church's center of gravity to the Gentile world caused some radically different mores to be assimilated. Renowned historian Peter Brown tells of the consequences: "By 150 A.D., we stand at the beginning of an irreparable parting of the ways. The nature of the leadership acceptable in Judaism and that current in the Christian churches had begun to diverge precisely on the issue of marriage and continence."[4] Sorbonne philosopher Paul Ricoeur has also noted that the dominant dualism of the Gentile Mediterranean world infiltrated into Christianity and broke down the psychosomatic unity characteristic of the biblical view of humankind.[5]

During the first two centuries of the Christian era, there flourished among pagans an ascetic syncretism that is sometimes labeled Neopythagoreanism. Apollonius, Numenius, and Sextus were philosophers of that school. The celibate-teetotaler-vegetarian lifestyle of the celebrated Apollonius was influenced by both Greek philosophy and by religious practices he observed and appreciated while traveling in India.[6] Numenius claimed that Pythagoras soundly believed that the physical stuff from which the world is created is evil and opposed to God. For Numenius, individual salvation consisted in abandoning sexual activity in order to liberate the soul from passion.[7] Plutarch, writing about the same time as Numenius, mentioned certain philosophers who abstained from wine and women in order "to honor God by their continence."[8] Sextus approved of castration as a purity protector: "You may see men cutting off and casting away parts of their body in order that the rest may be strong; how much better to do this for the sake of chastity."[9]

A shift of theological outlook in post-apostolic Christianity left its ethic vulnerable to the impact of pagan asceticism. As we have seen, Paul believed early in his Christian career that he was living on a temporal isthmus between Jesus' resurrection and his coming at the end of history. With the fading of that eschatological expectation, many Gentile patristic interpreters of Paul assumed that he, like the ascetics of their culture, had favored the unattached life because it had permanent and intrinsic moral worth. That is distinctly different from viewing celibacy as a temporary expedient, as church historian Roland Bainton points out: "Paul's discouragement of new marriages because of the Lord's imminent return early lost its relevance since the Lord did not return. . . . But other reasons for disparagement crept in and replaced the eschatological. The second century was marked by an increasing prevalence of the Gnostic disparagement of life in the flesh and specifically of marriage."[10]

Although church leaders generally denounced those who believed that the flesh was so contaminating that a perfect Jesus could not have been fully incarnate, they absorbed much of the gnostic bloodless spiritualism. By the time the church was several centuries old, it was permanently scarred by the stance of Mediterranean cults and philosophies that found no sanctity, and much mischief, in the physical. As ethicist Morton Enslin sums up the situation: "Christianity did not make the world ascetic; rather the world in which Christianity found itself strove to make Christianity ascetic."[11]

The most notorious figure in second-century Christianity was Marcion, who identified sex with evil matter. Clement of Alexandria reported: "Nature is regarded by the Marcionites as evil because it was created out of evil matter. . . . Because they do not wish to fill the world made by the Creator-God, they abstain from marriage."[12] Tertullian, the earliest Latin patristic, elaborated on the way Marcion's major writing was aimed at severing Christianity from its Hebraic roots: "His Antitheses centers in this: the establishment of a diversity between the Old and New Testaments so that his own Christ may be separate from the rival Creator and from the law and the prophets."[13] Marcion discarded the Hebrew Scriptures and "circumcised the Gospel according to Luke, taking out everything written about the generation of the Lord."[14] He found fleshly desires repulsive, along with the resulting reproductive process. Since physical contact with a woman is defiling, his Jesus did not come from a fetus in the uterus. Marcion discards the birth, boyhood, and desert temptation traditions in Luke so as to have a divine Christ descend angel-like from heaven as a fully formed adult.[15] This arch-heretic was devoted to a deity masquerading as a man who was in no way conditioned by human impulses or by ethnic nurture.

Believing that the immortal soul could best be emancipated from its carnal dungeon by crushing erotic passion, Marcion imposed stringent sexual discipline on his followers.[16] He not only personally refrained from sexual relations with women but also prohibited marriage for all Christians.[17] Receiving the sacraments of Baptism and the Eucharist was limited to virgins, widows, and married couples "who agree together to repudiate marital consummation."[18]

Bishop Irenaeus traced Marcion's basic theology to the gnostic thought then popular in the Mediterranean world. Marcion's teacher was the gnostic

Cerdo, who had a doctrine of two gods—the inferior Creator and the good God of the Gospels.[19] Tertullian, while admitting the impact of Cerdo on Marcion, stated that he was also a "zealous student of Stoicism."[20] He may have been especially influenced by the most ascetic of the great Stoics, Epictetus, who lived a generation before Marcion near his birthplace in Asia Minor. Epictetus taught that the impulse to indulge in sensual love should be counteracted by an opposing discipline of renunciation.[21] Hippolytus accused Marcion of emulating Empedocles, an admirer of Pythagoras, who taught his disciples "to refrain from intercourse with women."[22] Clement traced Marcion's disdainful attitude toward conjugal relations to Athens. Clement quotes a speaker in Plato's *Republic* who refers to sexual passion in this way: "It is with greatest joy that I escaped from it—as if I had escaped from a wild and raging tyrant."[23] Clement concludes, "I have shown clearly enough that Marcion took from Plato the starting-point of his strange doctrines."[24]

With regard to people like Marcion, a second-century Christian sternly warned in a New Testament letter, "Many deceivers have gone out into the world, those who will not acknowledge the coming of Jesus Christ in the flesh; any such person is the deceiver and the antichrist!" (1 John 7). Marcion's influence on the nascent church was considerable, but in 144, he was excommunicated from the Christian community in Rome. Although orthodox Christianity rejected his extreme form of sexual asceticism, it did perpetuate celibacy for Christians who were presumed to be of a holier class.

Justin Martyr, who had been a teacher of Platonism and Pythagoreanism in the mid-second century, claimed, "philosophy is the greatest possession and most honorable before God to whom it leads us."[25] He shared with many pagan intellectuals of the Greco-Roman world the belief that sexual abstinence is prerequisite to sublime purity. Justin was against all conjugal sexuality apart from reproductive intentionality and pointed with pride to some Christians who renounced marriage and lived in perfect continence.[26] He told approvingly of a Christian youth who asked for government permission to have a surgeon emasculate him as a protection for bodily purity.[27]

Tatian learned from his teacher Justin to mix Christianity with Greek asceticism.[28] He was noted for his *Harmony of the Four Gospels* and for founding the Encratites (meaning "the continent ones"), who prohibited sexual intercourse, intoxicants, and meats.[29] Tatian taught that woman is entirely a creation of the devil, but man is only halfway so; above the waist he is a creation of God, but his belly and below is made by the devil.[30] Believing that sexual intercourse was an invention of the devil, he judged anyone who attempted to combine being married with being Christian as trying to serve two masters.[31]

The first claim that Jesus was a celibate came from Tatian. In his book *On Perfection according to the Savior*, he and his followers "proudly say that they are imitating the Lord who neither married nor had any possession in this world, boasting that they understand the Gospel better than anyone else."[32] In the third century, any assumption that Jesus married—such as is found in *The Gospel of Philip*—was squelched, and the speculation that he was perpetually virginal coagulated into unquestioned belief.

Tatian altered the text of the Gospels in order to entice Christians to worship a figure separated from Jewish heritage and fleshly associations.[33] By bending the meaning of the New Testament in a pernicious manner, he made it appear that "the price of eternal life is virginity."[34] Tatian's sexual asceticism was well publicized by his *Harmony of the Gospels*, which was one of the most widely used books in the church. Armed with Jesus as the paradigm of virginity, the Encratites spread widely, especially in Tatian's home region of Syria. Clement judged Tatian's views on marriage "blasphemous," but he was not considered a heretic in Syria.[35] The Encratites were so permeated with Hellenistic flesh-hatred that Hippolytus called them Cynics rather than Christians.[36]

The apocryphal New Testament illustrates the Encratite movement in third-century Christianity. In the guise of Apostle Thomas, Jesus appears to newlyweds as they enter their bridal chamber and offers them this counsel: "If you abandon this filthy intercourse, you become holy temples . . . and you will not acquire cares for life or for children, whose end is destruction. . . . Keep your souls pure, . . . waiting to receive that incorruptible and true marriage." The groom responds with gratitude for having been cured of conjugal disease and the bride is pleased that the shame of intercourse has been removed now that she is yoked to Jesus, her true husband (*Acts of Thomas* 12–15).

Minucius Felix, the first Latin defender of Christianity, was well read in the classics of pagan culture, as was his contemporary, Justin. Felix described the ascetic practice that was common in the patristic era: "Chaste in conversation and even more chaste in body, very many enjoy the perpetual virginity of a body undefiled. . . . Even lawful conjugal relations fill many of us with shame."[37] Catholic theologian Uta Ranke-Heinemann writes: "Christians did not invent reverence for virginity, which in no way comes from Jesus. Rather, Christians adapted themselves to their environment."[38] The social environment to which she refers was predominantly influenced by the body-hating ascetics among the Hellenistic philosophers.

In the early centuries of Gentile Christianity, sexual asceticism was applied with varying degrees of rigor. Just as there had been ascetic practices in paganism ranging from mild to wild, so in Christianity some leaders sanctioned copulation if motivated exclusively by desire for children, while others demanded celibacy of all church members. Since Christianity was competing with other salvation cults, the degree of sexual repression in a particular area was somewhat determined by the practice of its leading local rival. Christians sometimes tried to gain status by outdoing pagans at asceticism. Galen, a pagan physician of the late second century, commended Christians in Rome who conducted themselves like philosophers and "refrain from cohabiting all through their lives."[39]

Athenian Christian philosopher Athenagoras, who was influenced by Pythagoreanism and Stoicism, carried forward the ascetic ethic in the late second century. For him, the very thought of sexual pleasure was evil: "Among us are many men and women who have grown to old age without marrying, in the hope of being closer to God. If, then, to remain virgins and eunuchs brings us closer to God, while to indulge in wrong thoughts and passions drives us from him, we have all the more reason to avoid those acts, the very thought of which we flee from." Athenagoras claimed that Christians approved of sexual intercourse only when there was hope of procreating offspring: "Each of us thinks of the woman he has married as his wife only for the purpose of bearing children. For as the farmer casts his seed on the soil and awaits the harvest without sowing over it, so we limit the pleasure of intercourse to bearing children." He also condemned digamy, "He who severs himself from his first wife, even if she is dead, is an adulterer in disguise."[40] He was motivated more by a concern that the surviving spouse should mortify the flesh than by the sentimental thought that a husband should forever feel spliced to his deceased partner.

The ethic of Clement of Alexandria is an oasis amid the barren asceticism of the patristic era. He was disturbed by Christians who did not recognize that a couple cooperates in the holy work of creation when they obey God, who said, "Be fruitful."[41] In accord with the general biblical outlook, Clement viewed celibacy as an unmanly evasion of responsibility.[42] In the earliest criticism of Paul's judgment about the married being less able than the single to be undistracted in devotion to God, Clement asks rhetorically, "Is it not possible to live in harmony with God while seeking to please a wife and to give thanks to God? Is it not permitted also for both the married person and his partner to care for things of the Lord?"[43] Clement thought it was especially important for ministers to have a good marriage: "The apostle says that one should appoint bishops who by their oversight over their own house have learned to be in charge of the whole church. . . . Marriage is a way of salvation for all, priests, deacons, laity—if they use it correctly."[44] A third-century Syrian church manual also appeals to that New Testament standard as a criteria for selecting candidates: "It is required that the bishop be a man who has one wife . . . and has brought up his children to revere God."[45]

Clement's student Origen was the most influential theologian between Paul and Augustine. He had himself castrated because he thought Jesus had advised such and because he believed that the elimination of sexual functioning was the foremost of living sacrifices pleasing to God.[46] Eusebius states: "Origen did a thing that provided the fullest proof of a mind youthful and immature, but at the same time of faith and self-mastery. The saying 'There are eunuchs who made themselves eunuchs for the kingdom of heaven's sake' he took in an absurdly literal sense." Eusebius also records that young Origen was then teaching a class of mixed gender.[47] Perhaps his mutilation was an attempt to eliminate the troublesome excitement caused by interacting with some girls he was instructing. Edward Gibbon dryly comments: "The learned Origen judged it most prudent to disarm the tempter. . . . As it was his general practice to allegorize Scripture, it seems unfortunate that, in this instance only, he should have adopted the literal sense."[48]

Origen's belief that celibacy is more befitting of Christians was the opposite of Clement's belief, so his pupil accepted ideas on sexuality that were more pagan than Christian. Origen later deplored his eunuch state on realizing that his motivation for using the scalpel came from pagan Sextus.[49] Also, he may have interpreted the story of Jesus with the mythology of the Cybele-Attis cult in mind, because it was popular in Origen's day. Priests of mother-goddess Cybele castrated themselves to attain the perfection of Attis, her companion, who had done likewise. Pagan and Christian eunuchs probably did not realize that emasculating adults does not render them completely sexless; it destroys genital ability but not the libido produced in the brain. The human sex drive resides more between the ears than between the legs, so the psychological aspects of sexuality continue in adults who become eunuchs.

Origen introduced cultic taboos to separate as far as possible religious and sexual activities, thereby stifling conjugal joy. He admonished, "Whoever, after the conjugal act and the stain contracted by it, approaches boldly to receive the eucharistic bread, dishonors and profanes what is holy."[50] Origen argued that since some pagans abstain from sexual intercourse in order to worship idols, how much more should worshipers of the supreme God abstain.[51]

Pursuant to his concern that cultic functionaries avoid sexual defilement, Origen borrowed from paganism the concept of an ascetic priesthood.

Common among ancient Greeks was the precondition requirement of sexual abstinence before priests could enter into the designated sacred space. Origen also believed that continence was incumbent upon priests who serve the holy altar.[52] He spoke of "perfect priests" who "keep themselves in act and in thought in a state of virgin purity."[53] Origen thought that Christian priests should not express themselves sexually because, like Paul, their role is to father spiritual children.[54] The apostle had addressed converts in Galatia as "little children, whom I am begetting anew, until Christ be formed in you" (Gal 4:19).

In view of the prevailing pagan association of sacredness and sexlessness, nascent Christianity did well to withstand the sacerdotal system as long as it did. Church fathers did not use the Greek term for priest, *hiereus*, in connection with the Christian ministry until the time of Origen in the third century.[55] Church buildings had not been constructed until then, for at the end of the second century Minnicius Felix wrote, "We have no shrines and no altars."[56] Previously, the Eucharist had been administered without a priest officiating. Priests were now associated with buildings being consecrated for holy functions. Many generations of the faithful passed before a sacred class was set apart for altar rituals in basilicas adapted from the Roman court of law. During this period, the Eucharist was being profoundly transformed from a sacred participatory meal conducted by rank-and-file Christians in house-churches to a ritual sacrificial action conducted by priests for the laity in public buildings.

The church was beginning to ride roughshod over the "laity," a designation that comes from the Greek word *laos*, meaning "people." Earlier, a letter of Peter had addressed those who had been nobodies, "You are God's own *laos*, chosen to proclaim the virtues of him who has called you out of darkness into his amazing light" (1 Pet 2:9). Reflecting on the modern church, Catholic writer John Cornwell compares "the 98 percent of Catholic men and women who are neither priests, bishops, nor members of religious orders" to the original status of their forebears: "In the early days of Christianity the communities were led by 'lay' men and women who preached, taught, and celebrated the rituals of prayer and worship. It took at least two hundred years for the clerical caste to form and distinguish itself from the 'laity.' But in time the word 'laity' came to mean the . . . passive, unempowered, and unconsulted."[57]

⚬❦⚬

In Latin Christianity, the first designation of a Christian officer as *sacerdos*, priest, is credited to Tertullian, a contemporary of Origen.[58] That founding father of Latin orthodoxy praised those clergy who practiced sexual continence and thereby showed their preference "to be wedded to God."[59] The monogamous were at the base of his perfection pyramid and the virginal were at the top. "Virgin" rather than "celibate" (*caelibatus*) was the common term then for describing someone of either gender who lived by a vow of abstinence.

Tertullian was ambivalent toward the connubial bond. While rejecting Marcion's requirement of celibacy for church membership, he was as frigid toward marital coitus as he was fervent in his defense of the Christian's right to marry. He did not condemn sexual intercourse but he wondered why God had invented the sordid act![60] Tertullian rightly charged Marcion with being intoxicated by Greek attitudes toward sexual repression, yet he himself was also much influenced by them. He was embarrassed that pagans often did a better job of mortifying the flesh than Christians.[61] To stimulate Christians to at least match their competition, he reviewed some prominent Mediterranean practices of celibacy:

> We know about the Vestal Virgins, the virgins of Juno in a city of Achaia, those of Apollo at Delphi, of Athena and Artemis in certain other places. We know about others, also, who live a celibate life: the priests of that famous Egyptian bull [Serapis], for example, and those women who of their own accord leave their husbands and grow old in the service of the African Ceres, renouncing forever all contact with men, even the kisses of their own sons.[62]

In one treatise Tertullian followed Paul's understanding of *gune* in 1 Cor 9:5 by stating, "The apostles too were allowed to marry and take their wives with them."[63] But later Tertullian became more ascetic and reinterpreted New Testament verses according to his bias. In an effort to affirm the celibacy of the apostles, he recognized, as we have seen, that *gune* was an ambiguous term in the Greek New Testament that can have either the general meaning "woman" or the more specific meaning "wife," depending on the context. He perceived that both Paul and Luke refer to *gune* in connection with the apostles (1 Cor 9:5; Luke 8:1–3), and he assumed that in both passages they were simply female helpers who accompanied the unmarried men.[64] Tertullian plausibly argued that the *gunai* in the earlier Pauline record and the later gospel record had the same status, but there is little doubt that Paul was referring to wives. Although Clement of Alexandria, who knew Greek well, interpreted *gune* in 1 Cor. 9:5 to mean "wife,"[65] it was firmly believed from the third century onward that Jesus and his apostles were celibates. This happened even though the New Testament says nothing about a celibate Jesus and states that wives traveled with the apostles, including Peter, who was the "rock" on whom the church was built (1 Cor 9:5; Matt 16:18).

Tertullian was adamant that Christians should avoid digamy, arguing that they admit a single marriage even as they recognize a single God. He equated digamy with bigamy, saying, "it makes no difference whether a man has two wives simultaneously or successively." Those who remarry after the death of a spouse are castigated as "sensualists" who "find joy in things of the flesh." They are contrasted to the "spiritualists" who find pleasure in things of the Spirit.[66] Tertullian advised widowers who needed a housekeeper to take a spiritual wife with whom there would be no sexual intimacy. "It is pleasing to God," he wrote, "to have several such wives."[67] The spiritual marriage that Tertullian commended was occasionally found in the pagan culture. A man and a woman demonstrated their self-control by sharing house and bed but not genitals. Sextus advised the married to abandon conjugal intercourse in order to glorify God.[68] Neoplatonist Porphyry entered into a Platonic marriage with Marcell.[69]

Later such a relationship was practiced by Scuthin, an Irish monk, who became a saint. Girls would sleep on both sides of him every night; if there was any penile tumescence, he arose and jumped into a nearby tub of cold water.[70] It is difficult to imagine how this practice enabled Scuthin to concentrate more fully on service to God. Mahatma Gandhi similarly ceased having conjugal relations with the mother of his children for the last half of his life, and boasted of sleeping continently with naked girls.[71] As might be expected, ascetics who reported such sexual bravado did not easily persuade others.

Celibacy tends to breed misogyny, an unlovely spawn that has unofficially been propagated in Catholicism. Tertullian addressed women with this acid denunciation: "Do you not know that each of you is also an Eve? . . . You are the devil's door; you are the unsealer of that forbidden tree, you are the first deserter of the divine law, you are the one who persuaded him whom the devil was too weak to attack. How easily you destroyed man, the image of God! Because of the death which you brought upon us, even the Son of God had to die."[72]

Inadvertently, Tertullian portrayed women to be more powerful than the rival of God and puny males! His bigotry caused him to overlook that both women and men are made in the divine image according to Genesis. Had he deliberately tried, he could not have said more to oppose Jesus' respectful attitude toward women.

In spite of his jaundiced view of marriage, Tertullian had a wife whom he addressed in a letter. Historian James Brundage reports, "nearly every third-century Christian clergyman whose marital status is known seems to have been married."[73] But in the fourth century, "celibacy for clergy seemed to go hand-in-hand with a growing negativity about sex as such."[74] As Roman culture declined, churchmen more and more fled from the normal pattern of marriage.

The Council of Elvira, composed of nineteen Spanish bishops from the southern part of the Iberian Peninsula, made the first attempt around 310 to legislate a separation of the sacred from the sexual and thereby to establish a clerical elite. Almost half of the eighty-one canons it enacted pertain to sexual requirements, demonstrating the main way by which the Spanish church sought leadership control. For unmarried priests it decreed, "A bishop or any other cleric may have living with him only a sister or a virgin daughter dedicated to God; by no means shall he keep any woman unrelated to him."[75] Canon 33, the most famous, pertains to married priests: "Bishops, presbyters, deacons and all other clerics having a position in the ministry are ordered to abstain completely from their wives and not to have children. Whoever, in fact, does this, shall be expelled from the dignity of the clerical state." The council's severity is also found in Canon 18, which deals with what it calls a scandal: any cleric found guilty of engaging in sex will not be allowed to receive communion even before dying. Sexual transgression becomes the unforgivable sin and priests can achieve holiness only by refraining totally from conjugal intercourse.

Canon 38 of the Elvira Council permitted a layman, but not a digamist priest, to administer Baptism in extreme cases. Henry Lea states, "Although the church forbore to prohibit absolutely the repetition of matrimony among the laity, it yet, at an early though uncertain period, initiated the rule enforced on the *Flamen Dialis*, and rendered it obligatory on the priesthood."[76] The *Flamen Dialis* was the oldest and the most honored priestly order in Rome and its priests customarily married only once.[77] Several canons of the Council of Elvira pertain to flamen who converted to Christianity, so the Spanish church was obviously affected by the pagan culture of those priests. The pagan ban on priestly digamy encouraged church leaders to match its competition.[78] The New Testament standard that a church officer should have fidelity to his one wife was twisted to be a rule rejecting digamy. As has been shown, digamy was permitted by the earliest Christians, but polygamy and unfaithfulness to one's spouse was prohibited.

The Council of Elvira did not forbid married men to serve as priests, knowing that the church could not afford to disqualify most of her personnel, but tacit opposition was expressed toward Jesus' declaration, "What

God has joined, let no human separate" (Mark 10:9). The council provided no New Testament authority for any of its decrees, and its advocacy of asexual clerical marriages seemed oblivious to Jesus' saying that the married couple "shall be two in one flesh" (Mark 10:8). Nor was appeal made to church tradition; indeed, a new discipline was being inaugurated. Since the clergy were permitted to continue to live with their wives and since no bedroom purity squad was appointed, the enforcement of this harsh canon was possible only if a wife became pregnant. In his book on the council, patristic authority Samuel Laeuchli states, "It expresses the evolution toward a celibate priesthood, where the married priest was by definition always in the wrong."[79]

The attempted prohibition of marital sexuality at Elvira was a radical deviation from the Judeo-Christian religion. In Judaism, non-conjugal marriage was a contradiction in terms. According to the Torah, it was the husband's sacred duty to give his wife her marital rights (Exod 21:10). Regarding this, Marcus Cohn has stated, "The most important common obligation of the married couple is the performance of the marital act."[80] As we have seen, Paul introduced that Jewish custom into Christianity when he insisted that having sexual relations is the right and duty of all married couples (1 Cor 7:2–4).

The Elvira legislation made it appear that what gave Christianity a higher status than paganism was its more repressive sexual morality. The worthiness of clergy was measured by their ability to withstand one of the strongest forces of human nature and practice conjugal abstinence.[81] The aberrant mischief begun at Elvira has done much to shackle the church with the demeaning notion that any expression of sex is impure and dirty. Its judgment that women contaminate men of God has plagued Catholicism ever since. As a by-product of sexual repression of clerical men came a censuring of women for mourning overnight in a cemetery, having an abortion, "having anything to do with long-haired men or hairdressers," and receiving letters.[82]

In 325, celibacy was on the agenda of the highly significant first ecumenical Council of Nicea, where bishops from all over the Mediterranean area met near Constantinople. The perverted piety of self-gelding was so much a concern that the first canon of the council was to prohibit such emasculation. The prohibition was necessitated by what had occasionally been practiced by churchmen in the century following Origen.[83] For example, priest Leontius castrated himself so that he could continue to live intimately with a woman named Eustolia. Since the Syrian sired no children, he later became the bishop of Antioch.[84]

The third canon of the Nicene Council prohibited priests from living with anyone who was not related to them by marriage or blood. The problem had been described by Cyprian, a third-century bishop of Carthage. Virgins admitted embracing clergy and sharing their beds with them, yet they professed to live in pure communion. Cyprian urged that they marry rather than continue in what appeared to be scandalous conduct. Otherwise, he said, if these women do not pass an intact hymen inspection by midwives, they should be excommunicated and the involved clergy should be defrocked.[85]

The council also discussed whether a law should be enacted to prohibit clergy from having sex with their wives. Bishop Hosius of Cordova was probably the one who brought up this matter for consideration, for he had been involved in the Council of Elvira decision. Afterward he became an advisor to Emperor Constantine and encouraged him to convene the Council of Nicea, where Hosius presided. When the Spanish canon that prohibited a priest from having conjugal relations with his wife was considered for approval for the entire church, ancient historian Socrates alleges that a blind and celibate bishop from Egypt protested:

> Paphnutius having arisen in the midst of the assembly of bishops, earnestly entreated them not to impose so heavy a yoke upon the clergy, asserting that "marriage is honorable, and intercourse is pure" (Heb 13:4). . . . "For all men," said he, "cannot follow the discipline of strict continence;" . . . and he called chastity the intercourse of a husband with his wife.[86]

St. Paphnutius's view that the proposed stringent restriction was both contrary to the biblical ethic and to nature prevailed, perhaps because many of the bishops present were married.[87] Significantly, "chastity" was recognized as an appropriate a term for the married who avoid adultery as for the unmarried who avoid fornication.

Advocates of celibacy from the medieval era onward have doubted Socrates's treatment of Paphnutius because no other independent sources verify his testimony.[88] But other scholars find Socrates a reliable historian and accept his account of what transpired at Nicea.[89] The story is important, even if it expresses the outlook of Greek churches in the fifth century, because it appeals to a sound biblical reason for rejecting constraints on clerical marriage.

Some of the most outstanding bishops of the Eastern Church were married. Basil the Great thought that all the apostles had been married and he put them forward as role models for Christians in his time for whom celibacy was not attractive.[90] Athanasius, the eminent bishop of Alexandria, wrote approvingly in 355, "We know bishops who are fathers of children."[91] Historian Sozomen commented on Spyridon, a Cypriot bishop who was present at the Council of Nicea, "He was married and had children, yet was not on this account deficient in spiritual attainments."[92] Also in the fourth century, Asrug of Armenia, Antoninus of Ephesus, as well as Basil and Eulalius of Cappadocia were married and had children.[93] Basil became honored as a saint, as were his mother, wife, sister, and two of his brothers.[94] One brother was the outstanding theologian Gregory of Nyssa, who continued his marriage after becoming a bishop in 372. He became a saint in spite of his teaching that only those with unblemished virginity could attain perfection.[95]

Bishop Gregory of Nazianzus became converted to Christianity through his wife, who remained with him as long as he lived. They had two sons after he became bishop; both became bishops, and the younger Gregory became the patriarch of Constantinople. Historian Glen Olsen cites the elder Gregory as expressing the common opinion of this era, "Marriage is a legitimate and honorable condition; but still it belongs to the flesh; liberty from the flesh is a better condition by far."[96] He found deplorable the thought of a married priest touching him while he was being baptized: "That would be terrible if I were to be defiled at the instant I was purified!"[97]

In the late fourth century, Spanish archbishop Himerius solicited advice from the bishop of Rome pertaining to priests who were fathering children with their wives. Those priests had justified their conduct by pointing out that the Old Testament required priests to marry and procreate if possible. Pope Siricius's response began by judging priests who have sex with their wives as engaging in "crimes." He wanted to make the clerical celibacy decree of the local Elvira Council authoritative for the entire Western church. Eighty years after that council meeting, Siricius attempted to surround it with biblical sanctions:

> Why were the [Hebrew] priests ordered, during the year of their tour of duty, to live in the temple, away from their homes? Quite obviously so that they would not be able to have carnal knowledge of any woman, even their wives, and, thus, having a conscience radiating integrity, they could offer to God offerings worthy of his acceptance. Those men, once they had fulfilled

their time of service, were permitted to have marital intercourse for the sole purpose of ensuring their descent.[98]

Siricius's letter is precedent setting in that it is the first directive by a Roman bishop to an area outside his jurisdiction. He claimed that the sexual discipline pertaining to Hebrew priests was accepted and perfected in the New Testament. Since Christian priests offer sacrifices daily, compulsory continence has been extended for them from temporary to permanent. According to that pope's interpretation of a passage from the Ephesian letter, priests—by an "indissoluble law"—must perpetually be brides of Christ and "shine with the splendor of chastity . . . without stain or wrinkle" (Eph 5:27).

Siricius became the first pope to attempt to establish that hands fouled by spousal intercourse were unfit for handling the sacraments. He began an attack on holy matrimony that Roman pontiffs and church councils ever since have tried to defend. Another letter, a year later, reinforced his judgment that God only accepts worship led by sexually abstinent priests: "If lay people are asked to be continent so that their prayers are granted, all the more so a priest who should be ready at any moment, thanks to an immaculate purity, and not fearing the obligation of offering the sacrifice or baptizing. Were he soiled by carnal concupiscence [horniness] . . . with what shame, in what state of mind would he carry out his functions?"[99]

Evidence is lacking to support the premises of Siricius's argument. The Bible does not state that a Hebrew priest had a lengthy period of duty when he remained within the tabernacle precincts separated from his wife and children to avoid polluting the altar of sacrifice. Also, in Siricius's day, Christian tradition did not forbid priests to have sex on the day before Mass, nor was there a practice of administering the sacraments daily.[100]

In 386, Siricius's view on sexual abstinence for priests was reinforced by the Council of Rome, which declared, "intercourse is defilement" (*commixtio pollutio est*).[101] This treatment of clerical marriage exposes the beginning of what resulted centuries later in the division between Latin-speaking Christians in the Western Roman Empire and Greek-speaking Christians in what remained of the Eastern Roman Empire. Pertaining to the first general ban in Christianity on priests engaging in conjugal sex, reformer John Calvin sarcastically but accurately noted:

It was later than the apostles that men lit upon the remarkable piece of wisdom that the priests of the Lord are defiled if they have intercourse with their lawful wives. At last it went so far that Pope Siricius had no hesitation about calling marriage "an uncleanness of the flesh, in which no one can please God." What, then, will happen to the unfortunate apostles, who persisted in this impurity until their death?[102]

As we have seen, church leaders were more influenced by the abstinence required of priests in pagan cults in the Mediterranean area, than by the Hebrew priesthood that was wiped out with the fall of Jerusalem. Jewish novelist Herman Wouk has discerned that the Western notion of sexual intercourse somehow being intrinsically sinful "is the ghost of crushed paganism rising out of the marble of overthrown temples to Venus in the walls and floors of early Christian churches."[103] "The pagan view that had now been taken over by the Christians," Edward Schillebeeckx states, was rendered, "one does not approach the altar and the consecrated vessels 'with soiled hands.'"[104] But it would have been poor propaganda to have declared that rules of abstinence had been motivated by pagan competition. Moreover, as we have seen, this resurgence of stress on ritual purity reversed Jesus' abrogation of such.

Monasticism and Jerome

Responses to the crumbling pagan Roman culture include eremitism and monasticism. These solitude movements clearly established celibacy as the hallmark of the holier life. Previously, celibates had not separated from their communities, but now some of them believed that living amid married Christians was defiling. In the fourth century, Egyptian Christian Anthony launched the hermitic movement on a desert edge. Even there he was sorely tempted when "the wretched devil dared to masquerade as a woman by night." Athanasius tells us, in his adoring biography of Anthony, that he overcame sexual temptation by resisting all physical pleasures. He so renounced his natural impulses that even eating necessary food after fasting filled him with shame.[105] Thousands of Anthony's followers lived as hermits in the Natron Mountains. His powerful impact on subsequent Christian leaders was mainly due to what the revered Athanasius wrote about him. That account, as Dodds notes, resembles stories of ascetics such as Apollonius.[106]

Shortly after Anthony established eremitism, monasticism was inaugurated by Pachomius, who had been a priest in the Egyptian Serapis cult before his conversion to Christianity.[107] Unlike the hermits, who lived separately from one another in remote places, the monks formed communities wherever it was convenient. Flight from conventional society quickly reached epidemic proportions. At Oxyrhynchos in Egypt, for example, monks outnumbered laity and accommodations for thirty thousand celibates were constructed outside the city walls.[108] Female religious ceilbates in Egypt exceeded the number of monks.[109]

Christian monasticism had multiple fathers. Its practices bore a resemblance to those of the Egyptian Therapeutae sect, and this caused church historian Eusebius anachronistically to identify as Christian a community that had arisen prior to the beginning of Christianity.[110] To understand Christian monasticism, Henry Lea states, "we may look to Buddhism for the model on which the Church fashioned her institutions."[111] In his pioneering critical book on celibacy in church history, which Catholic theologian Peter De Rosa calls an objective and "masterly treatise,"[112] Lea shows parallels between Christian and Buddhist monasticism. Comparative religions specialist Geoffrey Parrinder also points to roots of sexual asceticism in the church: "Christian monasticism and glorification of celibacy and perpetual virginity is foreign to the general spirit of the Bible, and no doubt is an intrusion from Manichee or even Buddhist sources, which brought in a conflict of matter and spirit that is unhebrew."[113] There is no evidence that church leaders were aware of Indian religions until the beginning of the third century. Clement of Alexandria, the first Christian to mention Hinduism and Buddhism, claimed that they influenced Western asceticism.[114] He probably learned about features of those religions from his teacher Pantaenus, who had visited India.[115]

Christians became cognizant of Indian renunciation of the flesh mainly through the mediation of Manichaeism. Mani, a third-century Persian, visited India during his formative years and assimilated much of Buddhist monastic organization and morality into his syncretistic cult. His three fundamental prohibitions were against eating meat, harming plants or animals, and indulging in sexual intercourse.[116] Voobus, in his survey of Syrian asceticism, states that the principles of Manichaean monasticism were borrowed from Buddhism and were "by no means inspired by the spirit of the New Testament."[117] As Christian monasticism developed during the fourth century in the West, it was heavily indebted to Manichaeism, which had spread widely in the Mediterranean region.[118]

Going beyond moderating their natural impulses, Christian monks aimed at passionlessness (*apatheia*).[119] That highest ideal of Stoicism, which originated in Athens around 300 BCE, was a "powerful factor" in the evolution of Christian monasteries.[120] Monks assumed that accepting pain stoically was purer than pleasure, so much attention was given to ridding life of all fleshly satisfactions except those essential for individual survival. Nemesius, a Syrian monk-bishop of the fourth century, made this analysis: "Of the pleasures called bodily, some are both necessary and natural, and without them life would not be possible; for example, the pleasures of the table. . . . On the other hand, there are pleasures that are natural but not necessary, such as normal and legitimate marital intercourse. . . . Therefore a true man of God must pursue only the pleasures that are both necessary and natural."[121]

Nemesius credited Plato as the source of this ethical judgment.[122] Plato's distinction between necessary and unnecessary sensual activity had a profound impact on Christian asceticism. Thinking that copulation lowered humans to frenzied bestial passions, Plato vented his antipathy toward sexual desire by comparing it with the hot-blooded romping of an ignoble horse.[123]

The rigorous discipline of the ascetic has always had its defenders in various cultures, especially in India. Hinduism and Buddhism admire individuals who withdraw from the common amenities of society and live alone in a forest. They attempt to obliterate carnal appetites in order to purify the soul. Francesca Murphy, a theologian at Aberdeen University, champions an outlook that is prominent in religions originating in India: "Celibacy is a beautiful thing. A man without a woman is a person who has totally abandoned the world—and that is what religion is all about."[124]

Monasticism was soon duplicated throughout Eastern and Western Catholicism. Aphrahat, a monastic leader in Syria, was disturbed to realize that Judaism found celibacy offensive. In 344 he wrote, "I have heard from a Jewish man who insulted one of the brothers . . . by saying to him, 'You are impure you who do not marry women, but we are holy and better who procreate.'"[125] Not surprisingly, monasticism's widespread popularity caused a decline in population, and thus hastened the fall of the Roman Empire. According to historian Richard Lewinsohn, "Sexual abstinence did more than excess to bring the downfall of Rome."[126] Due to a life expectancy at birth of about twenty years in the Roman Empire, families needed to produce an average of at least five children to maintain a steady state population, but that was not at all the case.[127]

Even before celibacy movements were of significance, Caesar Augustus had legislation enacted that prohibited celibacy.[128] He and his successors had tried to eliminate the empire's problem of under-population by diminishing the amount of property that the childless could inherit.[129] But the first impact of Christianity on Roman law came in 320, when Constantine responded to monastic pressure by annulling that penalty. Indeed, the emperor reversed the earlier legislation by bestowing special honor on celibates similar to what had been given to the vestal virgins.[130] Welfare for the poor was not a priority for the new government, even though it presumably was upholding values championed by Jesus, but legislation was enacted to protect Christian priests, whether unmarried or married. In 357, special privilege was also extended in Roman law to clerical families when Constantius declared, "all clergymen should enjoy their wives and children, and servants of both sexes, and their children also, should be always exempt from tribute, and all public burdens."[131]

Christianity is like a river with Jesus at the headwater. The source contained "living water" that sprang up from the Hebrew soil where high valuation was given to sexual coupling and family life. The stream flowed from the Galilean hills and combined with other streams, receiving both enrichment and contamination. The Greek philosophical stream enabled a rational systematic theology to develop, but it also disparaged bodily functions. From the Tiber of Rome came a reverence for the vestal virgins and for the high priest of Jupiter, designated as *pontifex maximus*. From the Nile came monks whose constant fasting included abstaining from sex. By indirect meanderings, the Indus flowed by way of Mesopotamia and Egypt into Christianity, encouraging the sublimation of sexual energies. The river of church traditions became so mixed that some essential qualities of the original flow were lost. Catholics drank deeply from that stream, on the erroneous assumption that it was a pure runoff from the hills of Palestine. Whereas biblical prophets, from Moses to Jesus, were involved with the common life and the political cultures of their day, Christians came to value withdrawal from the structures of society more highly.

Monasticism brought with it a sharp dichotomy between the sacred and the secular vocations. Since only a minority of Christians refrained from marital relations, those who did began to acquire a reputation for superior sanctity. Eusebius, the bishop of Caesarea, explained the heavenly and earthly states of life, and retrojected into the teachings of Jesus the dual lifestyles:

> Two ways of life were . . . given by the law of Christ to his church. The one is above nature, and beyond common human living; it admits not marriage, childbearing, property nor the possession of wealth. Wholly and permanently separate from the common customary life of mankind, it devotes itself to the service of God alone in its wealth of heavenly love! Those who enter on this course appear to die to the life of mortals, to bear with them nothing earthly but their body, and in mind and spirit to have passed to heaven. . . . Such then is the perfect form of the Christian life. . . . It is fitting that those in the priesthood and occupied in the service of God should abstain from the intercourse of marriage.

Eusebius called the marital way a "secondary grade of piety" and considered it fit only for the profane Christian. Sexual expression is incompatible with the function of clerics, "It is fitting that those who have been conse-crated and who have taken on the task of serving God abstain from rela-tions with their wives."[132] Catholic historian Richard McBrien writes about a change that came with the first Christian emperor:

> The Edict of Constantine in the early fourth century established Christian-ity as the state religion and conferred authority and privileges upon the clergy, thereby introducing a sharp division between clergy and laity and constituting the clergy as a special caste within the Church. This division would be accentuated in the Middle Ages with the development of the dis-tinction between the *ordo clericorum* and the *ordo laicorum,* the former devoted to higher things of the spirit and the latter devoted to lower things of the flesh.[133]

Brundage describes those clerics who, at this time, made sexual repres-sion a cardinal virtue:

> Rejecting carnal pleasures and the usual social expectation that every free person would marry and reproduce, Christian ascetics dedicated themselves to total sexual abstinence. In place of children and family life, ascetics exalted the importance of virginity.... Monks and hermits frequently looked down on married persons as spiritually inferior to those who sacri-ficed sexual pleasure in order to gain spiritual merit.[134]

The dichotomy imposed by these Christian ascetics between first and second-class citizens in the kingdom of God had an abiding impact.

Jerome needs to be examined carefully because, as Lea has observed, no churchman has done more to exalt celibacy as the only acceptable lifestyle for those in a religious vocation.[135] He certainly is the most virulent cham-pion of virginity's superiority to marriage. As a young man, Jerome fled to a desert in Syria to separate himself from beautiful prostitutes who had cap-tivated him.[136] There he realized that he had freed his body from Roman brothels but not his mind. He later recalled his hermit years "as a prison house where my only companions were scorpions and wild beasts," but imaginary companions obsessed him: "When I was living in the desolate, lonely desert, parched by the burning sun, how often did I fancy myself among the pleasures of Rome! . . . Again and again I found myself in the midst of dancing girls. My face was pale and my frame chilled with fasting, yet my mind was burning with desire and the fires of lust kept bubbling up before me when my flesh was as good as dead."[137] Jerome's mental images of Roman entertainment were derived from firsthand experience: "I extol virginity to the skies, not because I myself possess it, but because, not possessing it, I admire it all the more."[138]

In the letter that tells of his desert fantasies, Jerome reflects on the eunuch remedy to his problem. He allegorizes a psalm beatitude that contains a savage cry for revenge toward Judah's Babylonian captors, "Blessed is the man who smashes your little ones against a rock" (Ps 137:9): "When I see a woman and am filled with desire, if I do not at once cut off that sinful desire and take hold of it, as it were, by the foot and dash it against a rock until sensual passion abates, it will be too late afterwards when the smoldering fire has burst into flame. Happy the man who puts the knife instantly to sinful passion and smashes it against a rock! Now the Rock is Christ."[139]

"Little ones" is interpreted by Jerome as a euphemism for testicles. He writes further: "Some people may be eunuchs from necessity; I am one of free will. . . . [As the Bible says,] 'There is a time to cast away stones.'" (Eccl 3:5)[140] Clearly Jerome became at least a mental eunuch, and probably he used a scalpel on himself while in the desert. He commended pagan Greeks who castrated themselves, "The high priests of Athens to this day emasculate themselves."[141]

Jerome returned to Rome in 382 to become secretary and spokesperson for Pope Damasus, a bishop's son. To secure his position as pope he had hired thugs to eliminate his opposition, and 137 were massacred.[142] But he was later canonized a saint, perhaps because of the poems and essays that he, or his ghostwriter Jerome, wrote on virginity.[143] The aged pope depended on Jerome for biblical interpretations and commissioned him to translate the Bible into Latin.[144] Jerome included Damasus in his book *On Illustrious Men*. Because of the flattery he had given Damasus and the reciprocated patronage, Jerome thought he might become the next bishop of Rome. Regarding the popularity that he once had in Rome, he bragged: "Almost everyone concurred in judging me worthy of the highest office in the Church. My words were always on the lips of Damasus, of blessed memory. Men called me saintly, humble, and eloquent."[145]

But Jerome was not accepted as the successor to Damasus, so he returned to western Asia to live in Bethlehem. He attracted Paula, a widow, to come to live with him there and use her great wealth to build a monastery. Jerome kept up a correspondence with other aristocratic widows, advising them not to remarry. He followed Tertullian in recalling approvingly what Dido, the legendary founder of Carthage, did after the death of her husband. To avoid remarriage when the king of Libya wanted her to be his queen, she committed suicide by throwing herself on her husband's funeral pyre. In contrast to Paul advising widows that "it is better to marry than to burn" with passion (1 Cor 7:9), Jerome said he considered it better "to burn than to marry."[146] Will Deming, an authority on early Christian sexuality, uses Jerome's punny account of Dido to illustrate the "seachange in Christian thinking on marriage and celibacy" between Paul and subsequent churchmen.[147]

Jerome condemned the practice of spiritual marriage with *agapetae* (darlings), which had persisted since the time of Cyprian, because he found such arrangements too dangerous:

> I blush to speak of it, it is so shocking: yet, though sad it is true. How comes this plague of *agapetae* to be in the church? Whence come these unwedded wives, these novel concubines, these harlots, so I will call them, though they are one-man women? One house holds them, and one chamber. They often occupy the same bed, and yet they call us suspicious if we fancy anything wrong. . . . Both alike profess to have but one object, to find spiritual consolation . . . but their real aim is to indulge in carnal intercourse. It is on such that Solomon in the book of Proverbs heaps his scorn. "Can a man take fire in his bosom," he says, "and his clothes not be burned?" (6:27)[148]

By blocking erotic satisfactions, Jerome only increased his preoccupation with sex. He wrote a young woman whom he had never seen: "Your dress is purposely slit to show white flesh beneath. . . . You wear stays to keep your breasts in place, and a tight girdle closely confines your chest. . . . Your shawl sometimes drops so as to leave bare your curvatures, and then it hastily hides what it intentionally revealed."[149] Just as a man on an austere diet may focus more on tempting cuisine than a man who is regularly satisfied with modest and wholesome meals, so the sex-starved monk wrote about his sensual fantasies.

Jerome implored earthly virgins to remain sexually inactive in order to get a head start on paradise.[150] Marriage is earthbound, providing a social institution for surviving the present age, but celibacy foreshadows heaven for "those who are found worthy to attain that other world." Through austerities, celibates can imitate Jesus, who quenched the flame of passion, "and while in the body live as though out of it."[151] Jerome wrote, "Christ in the flesh is a virgin; in the spirit he is once married."[152] He asked Eustochium, Paula's virgin daughter and Bethlehem convent head, to think of her relationship with Jesus as similar to that of the bride to the groom in the erotic Song of Songs: "Always allow the Bridegroom to play with you within. Do you pray? You speak to the Bridegroom. Do you read? He speaks to you. When sleep overtakes you, he will come from behind and put his hand through the hole of the door, and your heart shall be moved for him" (5:4).[153]

Presuming that virginity was prerequisite to the saintly life, Jerome injected his bias into the Vulgate. In 1 Cor 9:5, he selected the Latin term *mulier* (woman) rather than *uxor* (wife) for translating *gune*. This makes it appear that the apostles were accompanied on their journeys not by wives but by female servants. Consequently, the Douay version, which relies on the Vulgate and has for centuries been the standard translation for English-speaking Catholics, provides a footnote stating that "wife" is an erroneous translation. But the Jerusalem Bible reads, "Have we not . . . every right to be accompanied by a Christian wife, like the other apostles, like the brothers of the Lord, and like Cephas [Aramaic for "Peter"]?" Modern exegetes consider the latter translation (by Catholics) to be accurate. Actually, in quoting 1 Cor 9:5, Jerome was as inconsistent as Tertullian had been. They both rendered *gune* as *uxor* once, but changed their translation in later diatribes. In order to support their defense of celibacy, they maintained that the apostles, both during their years with Jesus and afterward when they represented him as missionaries, traveled with "holy women" who provided for them.[154]

While in Bethlehem, Jerome read an essay by a monk named Jovinian, who, while having no personal desire to marry, boldly argued that marriage was as virtuous as virginity. Like Jerome, he had undergone rigorous mortification but he came to realize that hermits engaging in such activities were in no way superior to other Christians. He demonstrated that certain fanatical celibates had wrongly attempted to use the Bible to prove that their lifestyle was the holier way to live. Jovinian warned celibate priests against being proud of retaining their virginity, and he found married priests of equal worth. He argued that celibacy was not more meritorious because there is "one reward in the kingdom of heaven for all who have kept their baptismal vow."[155]

Jovinian's writings have not survived but it is possible to recover some of his biblical interpretations in the invective of Jerome, even though that adversary judged them "nauseating trash."[156] Jovinian argued that Abraham and Sarah, Simeon and Anna, and the many other married holy women and men of the Bible were on a par with any celibates in the Christian tradition. Moreover, the Song of Songs tells of the holiness of earthy weddings and the expression of sexual desire.[157] Jovinian rejected the allegorical counterfeit of Origen and Jerome who attempted to show that sexual abstinence was the theme of the songs, a rendering diametrically opposite to the literal meaning.[158] The lyrics were probably collected to be sung at wedding celebrations.[159] To demonstrate that the married state is no less excellent than the single state, Jovinian cited Jesus' commending the Eden story about man and woman being joined into "one flesh" and his going to Cana to participate in marriage festivities.[160] He also pointed out that Paul had stated that the other apostles were married. Those who exalt virginity over marriage, Jovinian charged, are unwittingly endorsing a doctrine of Manichaeism.[161]

Jerome attacked Jovinian's biblical exposition with the harshest vituperation ever written by a "saint." "All sexual intercourse is unclean" was Jerome's leitmotif.[162] He retrojected his celibacy ideal into the Bible, beginning with its opening chapter. He noticed that God's declaration of the goodness of his created acts was omitted only on the second day of the creation week. Since the number two signified marriage for Jerome, he concluded that the creation account subtly conveys that marriage is not good. Adam and Eve remained virgins as long as they were in paradise; they married after they were cast out. In order to maintain this stance, Jerome shifts the verse about Adam cleaving to Eve and the two becoming one flesh to after they leave paradise.[163]

Jerome and his celibate followers believed that all the major characters of the Old and New Testament were celibates unless they were explicitly associated with spouses and/or children. Elijah among the prophets and John among the apostles were the "virgins" most frequently praised, even though the Bible does not indicate that either was celibate. Jerome ranked John higher than the first pope because of his alleged virginity.[164] If Peter had known better, Jerome contended, he would never have married before meeting Jesus, but on becoming a disciple he cast aside his fishnet and his wife.[165] Others commended as having the supposed highest good of virginity were Miriam, Joshua, Elisha, Jeremiah, and Daniel in the Old Testament. John the Baptizer, Barnabas, Timothy, Paul, and all the other apostles—except Peter—were also held to be virgins. Jerome would have declared other outstanding personalities—such as the Hebrew patriarchs, Moses, Deborah, Samuel, David, Solomon, Josiah, Job, Isaiah, and Ezekiel—to be virgins if there had not been a scriptural remark about a spouse or a child who belonged to that person. He asserts that God honored celibate Joshua more than married Moses by permitting him rather than his mentor to enter the Promised Land before his death.[166]

One of Jerome's influential scriptural fabrications pertains to Jesus' parable that tells of farm soil bringing forth three different yields: a hundredfold, sixty, and thirty (Mark 4:8). According to Jerome, these represent three classes of Christians, from greatest to least: consecrated virgins, chaste widows, and pious spouses. Thirty connotes matrimony, because the Roman numeral XXX symbolizes the kissing and interlocking of husband and wife.[167] They reluctantly engage in the dirty work of sex to keep the human species from expiring. For Jerome, the primary positive purpose of marriage was the production of virgins, without which a celibate system could not survive.[168] Just as lovely pearls come from ugly oyster shells, so virgins come from shameful coitus; or, to change the figure, marriage is the goose that lays the golden egg of virginity.[169]

Jerome noted that Paul instructed his followers to "pray always" (1 Thess 5:17). "If we are to pray always," Jerome reasoned, "we must never be in the bondage of wedlock, for as often as I render my wife her due I incapacitate myself for prayer."[170] He applied this hypothetical reasoning to the clergy: "A priest must always pray, so he must be released from the duties of marriage." The ministerial vocation should not be forbidden to the man who has married, but he should be a coital abstainer after ordination. Indeed, a man who generates children with his wife after becoming a bishop should be condemned as an adulterer.[171]

After becoming aware of Jerome's denunciations, Siricius excommunicated Jovinian for the crime of heresy in 389. Satisfied, Jerome explained, "Jovinian has been condemned because he has dared to set matrimony on an equality with perpetual chastity."[172] Jovinian fled to Milan after being driven out of Rome, but Ambrose convened bishops of that region to excommunicate him again.[173] In opposing Jovinian, the bishop of Milan made the preposterous claim that Jesus declared the superiority of virginity by choosing to have a virgin for his mother.[174] Augustine called Jovinian a "monster" who "spreads poison," but admitted that he "was so influential in Rome that even some nuns, whose virginity was above all suspicion, decided to marry."[175] "Jovinian was scourged with a leaded thong and exiled to the rock of Boa, on the coast of Dalmatia, while his followers were hunted down, deported, and scattered among the savage islands of the Adriatic."[176]

Benedictine Stanley Jaki, a Templeton Prize recipient, praises Jerome for his refutation of Jovinian's attempt to abolish "a difference of dignity between the virginal and the marital status." In Jaki's opinion, Jerome valiantly defended "a hierarchy of states of sanctity."[177] But Carmelite priest Allan Budzin gives Jovinian an overdue positive assessment in his essay on the maligned Christian: "For Jovinian, the unity of the Church is constituted fundamentally by the one sacrament of baptism that Christians of diverse vocations have all equally received. In this regard, Jovinian's doctrine is remarkably consonant with the teaching of St. Paul. . . . [Jovinian] rejected an implicit caste structure in which virgins were considered superior to married Christians."[178]

Richard Sipe compares two Italian Catholics who challenged church doctrine:

> The condemnation of Jovinian in regard to sexuality, marriage, and celibacy was as misguided as the condemnation of Galileo for his espousal of heliocentrism. Both condemnations by church officials have been detrimental to the credibility of the church and its legitimate role as a teaching authority. The former, however, has proved far more disastrous in terms of personal and cultural suffering.[179]

Jerome was also offended by the nerve of Helvidius, a scholarly contemporary who like Jovinian contended that marital sexuality was as holy as virginal abstinence. Jesus' mother was cited as proof, because the New Testament suggests that she had a number of normal pregnancies (Mark 6:3). Helvidius pointed out that Jesus is called Mary's "first-born" (*prototokos*), while Luke uses another Greek term (*monogenes*) to refer to a person who procreates only one child (Luke 2:7, 7:12, 8:42).[180] Jerome believed that Joseph of Nazareth vowed to be a celibate husband and lived in total abstinence with Mary. He rejected the claim of a second-century apocryphal gospel that Joseph was a widower with children by his former marriage. He was sure that Joseph was a lifelong virgin and that consequently Jesus did not have even step-siblings; the brothers and sisters of Jesus who are referred to in the Gospels were really cousins![181]

Priest Vigilantius visited Jerome and other celibates in Bethlehem, and then monks in Egypt. When he returned to Gaul "not only did he deny the necessity of celibacy, but he pronounced it to be the fertile source of impurity."[182] Unfortunately, his writings have been lost, so we know of him only through the polemic against him by his acrimonious Bethlehem host. Vigilantius criticized the exaggerated emphasis on virginity, pointing out that humanity would perish if all remained virgins. He thought it best to resist sexual temptation in secular society rather than to retreat to the desert to live as a monk.[183] Jerome knew of hundreds of bishops who shared Vigilantius's outlook.[184] Like Jovinian earlier, his popularity alarmed the hierarchy, who treated him as a heretic. After those courageous dissenters of the church establishment were denounced, Lea notes, centuries would pass before there was another protest against celibacy.[185]

In Catholic tradition, Jerome has been respected as an authoritative interpreter of the Bible even though he manipulated the text when it clashed with his prejudices.[186] But most Catholics have regarded him as not only an excellent Latin translator but as a great exegete. *The Jerome Biblical Commentary* editors refer to him as "the foremost Scripture scholar among the Church Fathers, a pioneer in biblical criticism."[187] But far from establishing sound principles for biblical interpretation, Jerome's perverse treatments lend credence to the old saw of cynics that anything can be proved by shrewd students of scripture.

Augustine's Anti-Sex Theology

Augustine, whose lifespan (354–430) coincided with the precipitous decline in the power of the ancient Roman Empire, has been the most influential Christian leader during the millennia that separate the biblical era from the present day. An examination of relevant aspects of his life and thought is imperative for comprehending sexuality in the Christian tradition. He surpassed even Jerome in molding the prevailing sin-sex syndrome that has affected billions of churchgoers over the centuries. Thanks to his *Confessions*, the first introspective autobiography in history, much is known about his struggles.

A Roman public bath in North Africa was where Augustine first confronted his virility and realized how others would view it. His father proudly announced to his wife—later known as St. Monica—that their son had had an erection at the bath and should soon be supplying them with grandchildren. But both Augustine and his pious mother were distraught by the incident.[188] As a teenager he prayed, "Give me chastity and continence, but not yet."[189] For nine years, Augustine immersed himself in anti-sex Manichaeism even while living with a common-law wife in Carthage. He claimed that his twelve-year relationship with her lacked only the official sanction of marriage, and they had a son named Adeodatus (God-given).[190] After the three went to Italy, accompanied by Monica, she insisted that he cast off his unnamed companion, who had the social role of a concubine. Augustine obeyed his domineering mother and sent the woman away, while keeping their son. He confessed when they separated, "My heart which clung to her was torn and wounded till it bled," while she swore everlasting faithfulness to him.[191] Although Augustine was consumed with avoiding sexual sin when he wrote about this in his *Confessions*, he seems to have overlooked the sin of this abandonment, which from the gospel perspective was the greatest one of his life. Monica, recognizing that her son was determined to have sexual gratification, selected a potential wife for him, one-third his age, from an acceptable social class. But the ten-year-old girl lacked two years of being of marriageable age, so Augustine took a mistress for the interim.

While in Milan, where Augustine went to teach, he was attracted to its cathedral by Bishop Ambrose's ascetic sermons. Peter Brown provides a scholarly treatment of the thought of that major Latin theologian:

> The absence of sexual desire in the circumstances of Christ's own conception and in Christ's own human flesh was not, for Ambrose, simply a prodigy, incapable of imitation by others. Rather, Christ's sexless birth and unstirred body acted as a bridge between the present, fallen state of the human body and its future, glorious transformation at the Resurrection. Christ's flesh was a magnetically attractive token of human nature as it should be. A body "unscarred" by the double taint of a sexual origin and of sexual impulses stood for human flesh as it should be.[192]

Ambrose's belief that married priests are "foul in heart and body" is reflected in his response to one of them who thought he should have the privilege of the marital bed on days when he was not celebrating the Eucharist. Appealing to scripture for an authoritative response, Ambrose stated that it is not enough to avoid sex only on days when the sacrament is being celebrated, because the Israelites at Mount Sinai "had to be purified two or three days beforehand, so as to come clean to the sacrifice" (Exod 19:10). Regarding Ambrose's outlook, Catholic professor Eugene Bianchi writes:

> Ask pope, pastor, or parishioner to spend three minutes joyfully imagining how Jesus Christ would make love to his wife. If their reactions would be as negative as I suppose they would, what does this tell us about the locus of the problem? Why would such a healthy musing seem downright sacrilegious? Because St. Ambrose's gut feeling is still very much abroad: "The ministerial office must be kept pure and unspotted, and must not be defiled by coitus."[193]

Ambrose's teachings, along with Athanasius's *Life of Anthony*, contributed significantly to Augustine's dramatic conversion experience. Shortly after the bishop baptized him, he became a priest. He could have been ordained after marrying his fiancée, but he resolved to give up sexual intercourse forever. He prayed, "Thou converted me to Thee, so that I sought neither a wife nor any ambitions for this world."[194] Like a transformed alcoholic, Augustine shifted from sexual addiction to complete abstinence and came to view even mild sexual thought as a product of the devil's workshop. After opting for celibacy, he returned to Algeria, where he soon became the bishop of Hippo and established a monastery for himself and his friends. Frederik Van der Meer tells how he treated the opposite sex there: "No woman might set a foot over the threshold of his house. No woman might speak to him except in the presence of some other person and outside his reception room. He did not even make an exception for his own elder sister."[195]

Augustine's scheme of sin and salvation begins with Adam's inability to keep his penis from rising. Like an ass rebelling against training, it does not respond to its owner's commands.[196] The bishop found that the penis seems to have a mind of its own and can be awake when the rest of the body is asleep. He exclaimed, "Sometimes it refuses to act when the mind wills, while often it acts against its will!"[197] Except for the urinary function of that organ, it acts involuntarily and is unresponsive to rational control as a result of the originating sin of Adam and Eve.[198] The rambunctious private parts of Adam's offspring are proof that they have been conceived in iniquity and therefore are normally destined for infernal torment.[199] According to Augustine, our indecent genitals or "pudenda" (from Latin "to be ashamed") remind us that sexual desire is a shame as well as a sin.[200] As evidence of its shamefulness, he used the common compulsion to cover genitals in public and to seek privacy when copulating even when married.[201]

Augustine believed that God effected in Mary a unique exception to the rest of humanity by miraculously enabling her to become fertilized without receiving the contaminated semen that Adam transmitted.[202] To avoid any suggestion of passionate sexual arousal in Mary, Augustine fancifully told of an ear impregnation by Gabriel.[203] The superlatively pure Jesus could not have had sexual desire and therefore, unlike ordinary humans, there was no reason for him to blush.[204] The lustless Savior rescues some who otherwise would receive their just damnation.

Those few whom God elects show their appreciation by attempting to imitate the alleged lifestyles of Jesus and his mother. Virgins Mary and Jesus are exemplars for women and men of the holier way of life. Augustine followed his mentor Ambrose, who had said, "By Mary's example all are summoned to the cult of virginity."[205] According to Augustine, her example was exceeded only by that of Jesus: "We are to contemplate in Christ himself the chief instruction and pattern of virginal purity."[206] Jesus and Mary became "the real foundation of religious virginity." Schillebeeckx states: "Praise of virginity became to an ever greater extent the praise of the virgin Mary; she is virginity already embodied."[207]

The abiding influence of Jerome, Ambrose, and Augustine is displayed in Elizabeth Abbott's erroneous judgment, "Celibacy is at Christianity's core, the story of a divine infant miraculously born to a human, virgin mother."[208] But Jesus' alleged virginal conception was at the periphery of the gospel and is not mentioned by Jesus or his apostles. His criterion of moral conduct is contained in his parable of the last judgment: assisting the needy is essential but sexual behavior is not mentioned (Matt 25:35–36). The nativity story is best interpreted as a normal conception of Mary in which Jesus is described poetically as having both divine and human father.[209]

Augustine was among the first to equate "original sin" with sexual desire.[210] From Adam onward, as Augustine interpreted the Bible, lust (*concupiscentia*) has been a "disease" congenitally transmitted in the semen, so infants are sinful "by contagion and not by decision."[211] The evil sexual impulse inherent in parents is passed to offspring in the same physiological way as children inherit the skin pigmentation of their parents.[212] The doctrine of a historical "fall of mankind," precipitated by the disobedience of Adam and Eve that left humans with an inborn irreparable depravity, is not found in the Bible. The notion of a plunge into the abyss of damnation by a primal couple who had defaced the "image of God" was introduced afterward.[213] Augustine's doctrine did much to attract guilt-stricken individuals to monasteries and nunneries.

From Manichaeism, Augustine adopted the notion that the first humans had no sexual desire until they were overwhelmed by evil lust. Some of his contemporaries charged that his outlook on sex was what Mani would have favored, and many modern scholars agree.[214] Also woven into the fabric of Augustine's thought was the Stoic ideal of passionlessness. He admired Cicero, who wrote, "Sensual pleasure is quite unworthy of the dignity of man; . . . we ought to despise it and cast it from us."[215]

Augustine believed that consecrated virginity was the closest approximation in earthly society to ideal morality. If virtuous Israelites had lived after the advent of Jesus, he hypothesized, "they would have immediately made themselves eunuchs for the kingdom of heaven's sake."[216] Appealing to a Hebrew saying about "a time to embrace, and a time to refrain from embracing" (Eccl 3:5), he stated that the sexual indulgence that was hallowed in the old dispensation is no longer acceptable for latter-day Christian saints.[217] Augustine was untroubled by the fact that celibate Christians cannot reproduce themselves; he cheerfully accepted the prospect that human history would quickly end if everyone took his advice. To renounce sexual intercourse entirely would hasten the coming of the perfected city of God.[218]

Near the end of his life, Augustine had a significant controversy with Julian, bishop of Eclanum, over the relationship of sex to Christian theology. Julian was an Italian bishop's son and was married to a bishop's daughter. He argued that sexual desire was a neutral energy that became sinful only when the individual chose to express it in illicit extramarital behavior.[209] Augustine's doctrine of infant sinfulness was, in Julian's opinion, a slander against God.[220] He also found it repugnant because it destroyed the sanctity of marriage. Julian held that withhn marriage the sexual impulse could perform the work of God, and therefore passion for one's own spouse was commendable.[221] Sexual desire should no more be condemned because of obscene excesses than hunger should be condemned because of gluttony.[222] Julian daringly asserted that Jesus had sexual desires and yet his nature was not sinful.[223] In responding to Julian, Augustine came close to reversing New Testament doctrine: "If Christ had had in his nature sexual desire, which is not good, he would not have healed it in ours."[224]

Julian, whom Augustine regarded as a smart but detestable heretic, was deposed and exiled because of his audacious challenge to the sexual asceticism of his era. He went to live in Syria with Theodore of Mopsuestia, who shared his Christology; as a result, the Council of Constantinople in 553 condemned Theodore's teaching. He was charged with the "blasphemous" view that Christ was "vexed by the sufferings of the soul and the desires of the flesh."[225] Unfortunately the works of Julian are no longer extant and his ideas can only be known through the writings of his opponents. Even then, one needs to read Latin to ferret out his teachings, because Augustine's *Unfinished Work against Julian* has not been published in English. It is reported that in one of his books Julian mocked the "puerile" views of Jerome, which were so arbitrary that "the reader can scarcely refrain from laughing."[226] In spite of the overwhelming historical impact of Augustine, most Christians today would probably prefer Julian's balanced sexual outlook.

Consider, for example, Augustine's bizarre comments on the purpose of woman's creation. Reflecting his satisfaction with monastic life, he claims that procreation is the only reason she is needed: "If woman is not made for man as a help in rearing children, what sort of a help is she? If it was to work with him in tilling the land . . . surely a man would have been a lot better for that. The same goes for consolation when loneliness is a burden. How much more pleasant for life and conversation when two male friends dwell together than when man and woman dwell together."[227]

What legacy has Augustine's anti-sex theology and ethics had in history? Coming as it did at the beginning of Western monasticism, it appealed to those celibates who would provide future ecclesiastical leadership. Ethicist Paul Lehmann comments on Augustine's treatise *On Marriage and Concupiscence*:

It is at once the basis for and the most succinct statement of the ethical teachings of the Roman Catholic church concerning sex. If one wants to know why the Roman Catholic church holds that the chief and decisive end of marriage is procreation, that divorce and birth control are inadmissible, and that continence is the ideal of sexual self-discipline, the reasons are all given by the bishop of Hippo in his discussion of marriage.[228]

For the Hebrews the originating sin was disobedience to God's will, but for Augustine it was sexual expression. Catholic psychotherapist Sile states, "That judgment has pretty well penetrated all of church teaching on human sexuality even to the present day, even when it is explicitly denied."[229] Sepe, who taught classes in sexuality at Catholic seminaries, recognizes that "Augustine's understanding about sex and celibacy has been decisive theoretically and practically for all of Western Christianity."[230] The dynamics of celibacy can be traced to this Augustinian eduation: "sexual pleasure = women = evil."[231] Historian of Christian sexuality Sherwin Bailey points out that Augustine's impact has been felt far beyond Catholicaism, "Augustine must bear no small measure of responsibility for the insinuation into our culture of the idea, still widely current, that Christianity regards sexuality as something peculiarly tainted with evil."[232]

Augustine set the pattern for the Christian conscience that has prevailed for nearly sixteen centuries by his virtual e1uating of sexual desire (libido) with sin. By way of separating Augustine's views on sexuality from those of the apostolic church, historian Vern Bullough states, "What we call Christian attitudes toward sex are really Augustinian attitudes."[233] Likewise, Reay Tannahill points out that what modern culture understands by "sin" comes more from the teachings of Jerome and Augustine than from Jesus. Jason Berry states a consequence of this in Catholicism, "Augustine's symbiosis of sex and sin gave a supremacy to the celibate state of life and fortified the power of an unmarried male hierarchy in the governance of the church."[234] According to Augustine, "only the celibate could hope to achieve the state of grace that had existed in the Garden of Eden."[235]

Rudolf Bultmann shows how far the patristics deviated from the outlook of the founder of their religion: "Jesus desires no asceticism; he requires only the strength for sacrifice. As little as he repudiates property as such does he reject marriage or demand sexual asceticism. The ideal of virginity . . . is entirely foreign to Jesus; he required only purity and the sanctity of marriage."[236] Likewise, Homes Dudden has written:

Jesus nowhere teaches . . . that the gratification of the natural cravings is fraught with sin. He does not recommend men to treat their bodies with contempt. He does not suggest that flight from the world and disengagement from physical conditions is sanctification. He does not say that those who, for duty's sake, renounce the world, are on a higher spiritual level than those who do their duty in the world. He does not hint that the only way of avoiding sin lies in an austere renunciation of all those things from which an occasion of sin might arise. . . . He never implied that the married attain a lower grade of perfection than the continent.[237]

Notes

1. Eric Dodds, *Pagan and Christian in an Age of Anxiety* (New York: Norton, 1970), 35; see H. W. Smyth, ed., *Harvard Essays on Classical Subjects* (Cambridge: Harvard University Press, 1912), 136.

2. Plotinus, *Enneads* 3:5:2.

3. Porphyry, *On Abstinence* 4:20.

4. Peter Brown, *The Body and Society* (New York: Columbia University Press, 1988), 61.

5. *Cross Currents* (Spring 1964): 135.

6. Philostratus, *Apollonius of Tyana* 1:2, 13; 6:10; 8:7.

7. Kenneth Guthrie, *Numenius of Apamea* (London: Bell, 1917), 97, 133.

8. Plutarch, *On the Control of Anger* 464b.

9. Henry Chadwick, *The Sentences of Sextus* (Cambridge: University Press, 1959), 138.

10. Roland Bainton, *What Christianity Says about Sex, Love, and Marriage* (New York: Association Press, 1957), 25.

11. Morton Enslin, *The Ethics of Paul* (New York: Harper, 1930), 180.

12. Clement, *Miscellanies* 3:12.

13. Tertullian, *Against Marcion* 4:6.

14. Ibid., 27:2.

15. Ibid., 4:7.

16. Ibid., 4:24.

17. Ibid., 4:7.

18. Ibid., 4:24, 29, 34.

19. Irenaeus, *Against Heresies* 1:27.

20. Tertullian, *Against Marcion* 4:6; *Prescription against Heretics* 30.

21. Epictetus, *Discourses* 3:12, 24.

22. Hippolytus, *The Refutation of All Heresies* 7:17.

23. Plato, *Republic* 329.

24. Clement, *Miscellanies* 3:18, 21.

25. Justin, *Dialogue with Trypho* 2.

26. Justin, *Apology* 1:29.

27. Ibid., 2:2.

28. Martin Elze, *Tatian und Seine Theologie* (Gottingen: Vandenhoeck, 1960), 61–68.

29. Origen, *On Prayer* 24:5; Eusebius, *Church History* 4:29; Irenaeus, *Against Heresies* 1:28.

30. Epiphanius, *Against Heresies* 45:2.

31. Clement, *Miscellanies* 3:12, 80–81.

32. Ibid., 3:49, 81.

33. Theodoret, *Treatise on Heresies* 3:12, 81.

34. Arthur Voobus, *Celibacy, a Requirement for Admission to Baptism in the Early Syrian Church* (Stockholm: Estonian Society, 1951), 17–19.

35. Arthur Voobus, *History of Asceticism in the Syrian Orient* (Louvain: Corpus Scriptorum Christianorum Orientalium, 1958), 1:37.

36. Hippolytus, *The Refutation of All Heresies* 8:13.

37. Minucius Felix, *Octavius* 31:5.

38. Uta Ranke-Heinemann, *Eunuchs for the Kingdom of Heaven* (New York: Doubleday, 1990), 47–48.

39. Richard Walzer, *Galen on Jews and Christians* (London: Oxford, 1949), 65.

40. Athenagoras, *A Plea Regarding Christians* 33.

41. Clement, *Miscellanies* 3:66, 84; *The Instructor* 2:83.

42. Clement, *Miscellanies* 2:23.

43. Ibid., 3:88.

44. Ibid., 3:79, 90.

45. *Didascalia Apostolorum* 4.

46. Origen, *Sermons on Romans* 9.

47. Eusebius, *Church History* 6:8.

48. Edward Gibbon, *Decline and Fall of the Roman Empire* (1776), 15:4.

49. Origen, *Sermons on Matthew* 15:1–3.

50. Origen, *Ezekiel Selections* 7.

51. Origen, *Commentary on 1 Corinthians* 7:5.

52. Origen, *Sermons on Leviticus* 1:6.

53. Origen, *Against Celsus* 7:48.

54. Origen, *Sermons on Leviticus* 6.

55. Leonard Elliott-Binns, *The Beginnings of Western Christendom* (London: Lutterworth, 1948), 329.

56. Minicius Felix, *Octavius* 32:1.

57. John Cornwell, *Breaking Faith* (New York: Viking, 2001), 176–77.

58. Tertullian, *On Baptism* 17.

59. Tertullian, *An Exhortation on Chastity* 13.

60. Tertullian, *On Monogamy* 3.

61. Ibid., 17.

62. Tertullian, *An Exhortation on Chastity* 13.

63. Ibid., 8.

64. Tertullian, *On Monogamy* 8.

65. Clement, *Miscellanies* 3:53.

66. Tertullian, *On Monogamy* 1, 4.

67. Tertullian, *An Exhortation on Chastity* 12; *On Monogamy* 16.

68. Sextus, *Sentences* 230.

69. Edward Wynne-Tyson, ed., *Porphyry* (London: Centaur, 1965), 7.

70. Robert Zacks, *History Laid Bare* (New York: Harper, 1994), 41.

71. Ved Mehta, *Mahatma Gandhi* (New York: Penguin), 194–204.

72. Tertullian, *On the Apparel of Women* 1:1.

73. James Brundage, *Law, Sex, and Christian Society in Medieval Europe* (Chicago: University of Chicago Press, 1987), 69.

74. Lisa Cahill, *Sex, Gender, and Christian Ethics* (New York: Cambridge, 1996), 173.

75. Samuel Laeuchli, *Power and Sexuality: The Emergence of Canon Law at the Synod of Elvira* (Philadelphia: Temple University Press, 1972), Canon 27.

76. Henry Lea, *History of Sacerdotal Celibacy in the Christian Church* (London: Watts, 1932), 18.

77. Aulus Gellias, *Attic Nights* 10:15.

78. Tertullian, *An Exhortation on Chastity* 13; Jerome, *Against Jovinian* 1:49.

79. Laeuchli, *Power and Sexuality,* 96.

80. "Marriage," *The Universal Jewish Encyclopedia* (New York: Ktav, 1948).

81. Laeuchli, *Power and Sexuality,* 90.

82. Canons 35, 63, 67, 81.

83. Dodds, *Pagan and Christian,* 32–33.

84. Theodoret, *Church History* 2:19; Socrates, *Church History* 2:26.

85. Cyprian, *Letters* 4.

86. Socrates, *Church History* 1:11.

87. Ibid., 5:22.

88. Christian Cochini, *Apostolic Origins of Priestly Celibacy* (San Francisco: Ignatius Press, 1990), 195–200; Stefan Heid, *Celibacy in the Early Church* (San Francisco: Ignatius Press, 2000), 18.

89. Lea, *History,* 36–37; Henry Percival, ed., *The Seven Ecumenical Councils* (Grand Rapids: Eerdmans, 1976), 51–52, "Paphnutius," *New Catholic Encyclopedia* (New York: McGraw-Hill, 1966).

90. Basil, *On Renunciation of the World* 1.

91. Athanasius, *To Bishop Dracontius* 9.

92. Sozomen, *Church History* 1:11.

93. Cochini, *Apostolic Origins,* 92–93.

94. *Butler's Lives of the Saints* (Collegeville, MN: Liturgical Press, 1995), 1:13.

95. Gregory of Nyssa, *On Virginity* 2.

96. Glen Olsen, *Christian Marriage* (New York: Crossroad, 2001), 103.

97. Gregory of Nazianzus, *Logos* 4:26.

98. Cochini, *Apostolic Origins,* 9.

99. Ibid., 11.

100. Daniel Callam, "Clerical Continence in the Fourth Century," *Theological Studies* (March 1980): 26.

101. Cochini, *Apostolic Origins,* 14–15.

102. John Calvin, *The First Epistle of Paul the Apostle to the Corinthians* (Grand Rapids: Eerdmans, 1960), 12.

103. Herman Wouk, *This Is My God* (New York: Doubleday, 1959), 155.

104. Edward Schillebeeckx, *The Church with a Human Face* (New York: Crossroad, 1985), 244.

105. Athanasius, *Life of Anthony* 5:45.

106. Dodds, *Pagan and Christian,* 30–31.

107. Philip Schaff, *History of the Christian Church* (New York: Scribner, 1910), 2:390–91.

108. Hans Lietzmann, *A History of the Early Church* (London: Lutterworth, 1953), 4:148.

109. Patricia Wittberg, *The Rise and Decline of Catholic Religious Orders* (Albany: SUNY, 1994), 32.

110. Eusebius, *Church History* 2:17.

111. Lea, *History,* 71.

112. Peter De Rosa, *Vicars of Christ* (New York: Crown, 1988), 397.

113. Geoffrey Parrinder, *Upanishads, Gita, and Bible* (New York: Harper, 1972), 54.

114. Clement, *Miscellanies* 1:71.

115. Eusebius, *Church History* 5:10–11.

116. Augustine, *On the Morals of the Manichaeans* 10.

117. Voobus, *History of Asceticism,* 1:114, 168.

118. William Phipps, "Did Ancient Indian Celibacy Influence Christianity?" *Studies in Religion* (July 1974): 45–49.

119. Palladius, *Lausaic History* 8:4; 48:3.

120. Herbert Workman, *The Evolution of the Monastic Ideal* (London: Epworth, 1913), 37.

121. Nemesius, *On the Nature of Man* 18:37.

122. Plato, *Republic* 559.

123. Plato, *Phaedrus* 250, 253.

124. *Scotland Sunday Herald,* April 21, 2002, 11.

125. Aphrahat, *Demonstrations* 18:12.

126. Richard Lewinsohn, *A History of Sexual Customs* (New York: Harper, 1958), 101.

127. *Harvard Studies in Classical Philology* (1982): 248–50.

128. Cicero, *Laws* 3:3:7.

129. Suetonius, *Augustus* 89:2; Tacitus, *Annals* 3:25.

130. Sozomen, *Church History* 1:9.

131. Clyde Pharr, ed., *The Theodosian Code* (Princeton: University Press, 1952), 8:16; 16:2.

132. Eusebius, *The Proof of the Gospel* 1:8–9, 4:10.

133. Richard McBrien, *Catholicism* (San Francisco: Harper, 1994), 859.

134. Brundage, *Law, Sex, and Christian Society*, 79.

135. Lea, *History*, 10.

136. Jerome, *Against Vigilantius* 16.

137. Jerome, *Letters* 22:7.

138. Ibid., 48:20.

139. Jerome, *Sermons* 48; *Letters* 22:6.

140. Jerome, *Letters* 22:6, 19.

141. Jerome, *Against Jovinian* 1:49.

142. Ammianus Marcellinus, *History* 27:3:12–13.

143. Jerome, *Letters* 2:22.

144. John Kelly, *Jerome* (New York: Harper, 1975), 34.

145. Jerome, *Letters* 45:3.

146. Tertullian, *An Exhortation on Chastity* 13; Jerome, *Against Jovinian* 1:43.

147. Will Deming, *Paul on Marriage and Celibacy* (New York: Cambridge, 1995), 225.

148. Jerome, *Letters* 22:14.

149. Ibid., 117:7.

150. Jerome, *Against Jovinian* 1:36.

151. Jerome, *Letters* 108:23.

152. Jerome, *Against Jovinian* 1:16.

153. Jerome, *Letters* 22:25.

154. Jerome, *Letters* 22:20; *Against Jovinian* 1:26.

155. Jerome, *Against Jovinian* 1:3.

156. Ibid., 1:4.

157. Ibid., 1:30.

158. William Phipps, "The Plight of the Song of Songs," *Journal of the American Academy of Religion* (March 1974): 95–100.

159. Otto Eissfeldt, *The Old Testament* (New York: Harper, 1965), 89.

160. Jerome, *Against Jovinian* 1:5, 40.

161. Augustine, *On Marriage and Concupiscence* 2:38.

162. Jerome, *Against Jovinian* 1:20.

163. Ibid., 1:16.

164. Ibid., 1:26.

165. Jerome, *Letters* 118:4.

166. Jerome, *Against Jovinian* 1:22.

167. Jerome, *Letters* 48:2; 123:9.

168. Jerome, *Against Jovinian* 1:3.

169. Jerome, *Letters* 22:20.

170. Ibid., 48:15.

171. Jerome, *Against Jovinian* 1:34.

172. Jerome, *Letters* 48:2.

173. Ambrose, *To Siricius* 44.

174. Jacque Migne, ed., *Patrologia Latina* (Paris, 1879), 16:1124.

175. Augustine, *Retractions* 48.

176. Lea, *History,* 49.

177. Stanley Jaki, *Theology of Priestly Celibacy* (Front Royal, VA: Christendom Press, 1997), 91.

178. *Toronto Journal of Theology* (Spring 1988): 55–56.

179. Richard Sipe, *Sex, Priests, and Power* (New York: Brunner, 1995), 192–93.

180. Jerome, *Against Helvidius* 8.

181. Jerome, *Against Helvidius* 14, 17, 21.

182. Lea, *History,* 50.

183. Jerome, *Against Vigilantius* 15–16.

184. Jerome, *Letters* 69:2.

185. Lea, *History,* 51–52.

186. William Phipps, *Influential Theologians on Wo/Man* (Washington: University Press of America, 1980), 37–55.

187. Raymond Brown et al., *The Jerome Biblical Commentary* (Englewood Cliffs, NJ: Prentice-Hall, 1968), xx.

188. Augustine, *Confessions* 2:6.

189. Ibid., 8:17.

190. Ibid., 6:22.

191. Ibid., 6:25.

192. Brown, *Body and Society,* 351.

193. *National Catholic Reporter,* September 13, 1974, 8; Ambrose, *Duties of the Clergy* 1:258.

194. Augustine, *Confessions* 8:30.

195. Frederik van der Meer, *Augustine the Bishop* (London: Sheed, 1961), 215.

196. Augustine, *City of God* 14:19.

197. Augustine, *On Marrage and Concupiscence* 1:7.

198. Ibid., 2:53.

199. Augustine, *Sermons* 151:5; Peter Brown, *Augustine of Hippo* (Berkeley: University of California Press, 1969), 388–96.

200. Augustine, *City of God* 14:17–18.

201. Augustine, *On Marriage and Concupiscence* 1:24; *Incomplete Work against Julian* 3:67.

202. Augustine, *On Marriage and Concupiscence* 2:14.

203. Augustine, *On the Birth of the Lord* 121.

204. Augustine, *Against Julian* 5:8, 15; *Against the Pelagians* 1:33.

205. Ambrose, *On Educating Virgins* 5:36.

206. Augustine, *Of Holy Virginity* 35.

207. Edward Schillebeeckx, *Celibacy* (New York: Sheed & Ward, 1968), 56–57.

208. Elizabeth Abbott, *A History of Celibacy* (Cambridge: Da Capo, 2001), 17.

209. William Phipps, *The Sexuality of Jesus* (Cleveland: Pilgrim Press, 1996), 17–32.

210. Norman Williams, *The Ideas of the Fall and of Original Sin* (London: Longmans, 1927), 366.

211. Augustine, *Unfinished Work against Julian* 4:98.

212. Augustine, *Against Julian* 5:14.

213. William Phipps, *Genesis and Gender* (New York: Praeger, 1989), 9–14, 51–66.

214. Augustine, *On Marriage and Concupiscence* 2:7, 35; Roy Battenhouse, ed., *A Companion to the Study of St. Augustine* (New York: Oxford, 1955), 384; Adolf Harnack, *History of Dogma* (London: Williams, 1898), 5:219; Paul Tillich, *A History of Christian Thought* (New York: Harper, 1968), 106; Brown, *Augustine*, 394.

215. Cicero, *On Offices* 1:30; Brown, *Augustine*, 50, 300.

216. Augustine, *On Christian Doctrine* 3:8.

217. Augustine, *On Marriage and Concupiscence* 1:14–15.

218. Augustine, *The Good of Marriage* 10.

219. Augustine, *Incomplete Work against Julian* 4:39–41.

220. Ibid., 1:48.

221. Augustine, *Against Julian* 5:9, 15.

222. Ibid., 4:14.

223. Augustine, *Incomplete Work against Julian* 4:45–64.

224. Augustine, *Against Julian* 5:15.

225. John MacArthur, *Chalcedon* (London: SPCK, 1931), 18.

226. Brown, *Augustine*, 383.

227. Augustine, *The Literal Meaning of Genesis* 8:5.

228. Battenhouse, *Companion to the Study of Augustine*, 221.

229. Sipe, *Sex, Priests, and Power*, 164.

230. Ibid., 88.

231. Ibid., 108.

232. D. Sherwin Bailey, *Sexual Relation in Christian Thought* (New York: Harper, 1959), 59.

233. Vern Bullough, *Sexual Practices and the Medieval Church* (Buffalo: Prometheus, 1982), xi.

234. Jason Berry, *Lead Us Not into Temptation* (New York: Doubleday, 1992), 179.

235. Reay Tannehill, *Sex in History* (New York: Stein, 1980) 138, 142.

236. Rudolf Bultmann, *Jesus and the Word* (New York: Scribner, 1958), 99.

237. "Asceticism," *A Dictionary of Christ and the Gospels* (Edinburgh: Clark, 1908).

Chapter 6

THE MEDIEVAL ERA

֍

Historians disagree on the length of the Middle Ages, but this chapter will trace the development of celibacy in the church during the millennium from the fall of Rome at the end of the ancient era to the Renaissance and Reformation at the beginning of the modern era. Relative to the marriage of church leaders, the Greek-speaking Christians remained closer to the practice of the early church during this time, so their tradition will be examined first. Attention will then be given to the ratcheting up by the Vatican of celibacy requirements for Latin-speaking priests, which played a large part in the separation in 1054 of Roman Catholicism from Eastern Orthodoxy. Following this, an examination will be made of the increase in debauchery that ensued in the centuries after the Vatican annulled the marriages of all priests.

Roman-Byzantine Schism over Clerical Marriage

The archbishops of the Eastern Mediterranean did not accept the pope's demand that both married and unmarried priests be sexually continent. Writing in fifth century, Byzantine historian Socrates reports: "In the East all clergy practice sexual abstinence as they wish and even the bishops do it only if they want to, without being under the constraint of a law. Many among them have had children from their legitimate wives while they were bishops."[1]

Syrian church rules, published in the late fourth century as *Apostolic Constitutions*, suspended—or even deposed—any bishop, priest, or deacon who deserted his wife "under the pretense of piety."[2] They also state that any cleric "blasphemously misrepresents God's work of creation" who abstains from marriage, meat, or wine "out of abhorrence, forgetting that all things are exceedingly good, and that God made man male and female." Anyone having such an outlook is told to mend his ways or be deposed from office and expelled from the church.[3] While those rules were not written by apostles, they express faithfully, as we have seen, views found in the Pastoral Letters of the New Testament. In 420, a decree by the emperor in Constantinople confirmed the church ruling that priests should not separate from their wives, thereby protecting the marriage rights of clergy spouses.[4]

The Syrian church manual also continued the Jewish practice of arranged marriage for pubescent offspring: "Fathers: . . . at the time when your children are of marriageable age, join them in wedlock and settle them together, lest in the heat and fervor of their age their course of life become dissolute, and you be required to give an account by the Lord God in the day of judgment."[5] Parents desired early marriage to maximize progeny for their extended family as well as to prevent illicit sex among young adults. A line of John Milton's *Paradise Lost* shows that the latter purpose continued to be praised by Christians: "Hail wedded love. . . . By thee adulterous lust was driven from men."[6]

In the fourth century Synesius, on being elected bishop of the North African diocese of Cyrene, expressed his disdain for spouse abandonment that some were advocating for the episcopate. He wrote Theophilus, the bishop of Alexandria who had officiated at his wedding, that he would not accept episcopal consecration if it required ceasing normal relations with his wife and with the three small sons they had already produced: "God, the law, and the anointed hand of Theophilus have given me a wife. I declare openly that I do not intend to be separated from her, nor to live with her in secret, like an adulterer. Separation would be contrary to love, clandestine relations would be unlawful. I hope and pray to have lots of children with her."[7]

Historian Elizabeth Abbott comments on this cleric's integrity, "Synesius categorically refused to stoop to the subterfuge of so many of his colleagues: skirt the issue, protect their jobs, swear false vows of celibacy, then contrive [with his wife], in unpriestly stealth, to creep into her bed at night."[8] The record does not state whether Synesius was appointed bishop under the conditions he laid down.

Justinian, a sixth-century emperor of the Byzantine Empire in the eastern Mediterranean area, ruled that church law would have the force of imperial law. Intensified was the enforcement of the rule that clerics who marry after ordination will not only be dismissed from the priesthood but their children will be declared illegitimate. A married man without children could be considered for the office of bishop, but only if he separated from his wife.[9]

In 692, the Eastern Council of Trullo that met in Constantinople officially approved the prevailing practice of permitting the ordination of married men for the diaconate and the priesthood. Their conjugal rights could be exercised except on days when they were performing religious services. When a wife died, remarriage was prohibited. Sexual continence was required of both bishops and monks, so a cleric aspiring to become a hierarch usually did not marry. The Trullo Council made explicit the deviations of Roman Catholicism from the traditions of the early church that the Eastern church wanted to avoid:

> In the Church of Rome the rule was established that candidates, before receiving ordination as deacon or priest, make a public promise not to have relations any more with their wives; we, conforming ourselves to the . . . apostolic discipline, want the legitimate marriages of consecrated men to remain in effect. . . . To demand that a deacon or priest abstain from relations with his wife would insult marriage, which was instituted by God and blessed by his presence, while the voice of the Gospel calls to us: "Let no man put asunder those whom God has united," and the Apostle [Paul] teaches: . . . "Are you tied to a wife by the bonds of marriage? Then do not seek to break them."[10]

The Trullo decisions, with little change, have continued ever since to be the rule for Eastern Orthodoxy and also, due to a 1596 agreement, for churches of the Eastern Rite in union with Rome. The Armenian, Maronite, Melkite, and Romanian churches are among those in this group. About one-third of the Byzantium churches have pledged allegiance to Rome while retaining their married priesthood tradition.

Thus, in Eastern Orthodoxy, married men have always been permitted to become priests, and most of them have integrated marriage into their consecrated life. Demetrios Constantelos explains the outlook of the leaders of his denomination: "They prefer parish priests to be married as a means of preventing moral failures and scandals in the Church, even though they realize that marriage does not necessarily solve the sexual problem. . . . The married priest who has learned responsibility and awareness of his obligations [in caring for his own family] may prove to be much more effective in his ministry."[11]

Meanwhile, the evolution of the office of bishop was affecting Rome's celibacy requirements. In the apostolic era, a bishop was not a prominent figure. The first Christian use of the term is in the opening of the Philippian letter, where Paul indicates that more than one bishop (*episcopos*) was in the small church in Philippi, a city in Greece. In the New Testament, "bishop" was a designation used interchangeably with "elder" (*presbuteros*) (Acts 20:17, 28; Titus 1:5–7). They appear to have had local oversight responsibilities in a congregation similar to the role Jewish elders had in a synagogue. In the second century, the terms bishop and elder were no longer synonyms, because one bishop presided over the elders and deacons in a congregation. The third century brought an extension of power, with one bishop assuming jurisdiction over a group of churches, called a diocese. The elders then began to function as intermediaries between deity and worshiper; this shift is reflected in the English contraction of the Greek term *presbuteros* into "priest."

In the fourth century, the hierarchial movement was increased by the establishment of five "metropolitan" bishops in the capitals of prominent Roman provinces. Archbishops at Jerusalem, Antioch, Rome, Alexandria, and Constantinople were recognized as rulers over all bishops, priests, deacons, and lay members. The final move toward autocracy was in the fifth century when Leo, the archbishop of Rome, claimed authority over all the other archbishops. He adopted the power structure of the pagan Roman chief priest and applied the *pontifex maximus* title to himself. Accordingly, Father (pope or papa in Latin) Leo's successors have been called the Supreme Pontiff. There is some truth in Thomas Hobbes's jibe, "The Papacy is not other than the Ghost of the deceased Roman Empire, sitting crowned upon the grave thereof."[12] The archbishops of the four areas of the eastern Mediterranean have never accepted the audacious claim of the pope in Rome to be the authoritative Vicar of Christ over the whole church.

Leo I, one of the two popes to be designated by Roman Catholics as Great, declared in 445 that all levels of the clergy, even the subdiaconate, should be celibate. Pertaining to married priests, he stated, "In order for their union to change from carnal to spiritual, they must, without sending away their wives, live with them as if they did not have them, so that conjugal love be safeguarded and nuptial activity be ended."[13] The pope commended Joseph of Nazareth as the exemplar for married clerics, because he showed "they should not give up their wives but should live together in wedded love, without the acts of love."[14]

In the sixth century, Benedict established a monastery at Monte Cassino in Italy that was to have a great impact for the next thousand years. Unlike the monastic life found in the deserts of the eastern Mediterranean, he developed a discipline that was closely connected with the church's hierarchy. Benedict's rule required monks to sleep clothed, "girdled with belts or cords," in separate beds of a common dormitory where a lamp burned throughout the night.[15] That sexual discipline, when faithfully carried out, was viewed by the brothers as a form of daily crucifixion. Exposed here is the first evidence that homosexual craving was a by-product of regulations pertaining to monastic celibacy. To further protect against homoerotic behavior, the Benedictines discouraged bathing because it involved exposing the naked body, making it more alluring. An aphorism of Nietzsche is apropos in considering Benedict and his followers, "Saints—It is the most sensual men who have to flee from women and torment their body."[16]

In living a saintly life, Benedict had to struggle to keep a lid on his id:

> He was seized with an unusually violent temptation. The evil spirit recalled to his mind a woman he had once seen, and before he realized it his emotions were carrying him away. . . . Just then he noticed a thick patch of nettles and briers next to him. Throwing his garment aside, he flung himself naked into the sharp thorns and stinging nettles. There he rolled and tossed until his whole body was in pain and covered with blood. Yet once he had conquered pleasure through suffering, his torn and bleeding skin served to drain off the poison of temptation from his body.[17]

Seven centuries later, Francis of Assisi had an experience similar to Benedict's, perhaps stimulated by his lifelong companion Clare. While at the Sartiano hermitage he had "a most grievous temptation of lust" and beat himself with his tunic rope, exclaiming, "There, brother ass!" This being an ineffective remedy, he resorted to a more desperate effort to cool his overheated libido. An early biographer states, "Seeing that, in spite of scourging himself, the temptation did not leave him, though he had colored all his members with weals, he opened the cell, went out into the garden and plunged naked into deep snow."[18] Those expressions of masochism were probably driven by the desperate desire to circumvent masturbation.

Medieval monks treated voluntary semen emission as a cardinal sin of commission. One of their handbooks required three years of penance for clerical masturbators; by comparison, seven days' penance was assigned to violators of the Decalogue's commandment against stealing.[19] Some monastic masturbators felt guilty of murder, much as devout Catholics now regard aborting a conceptus. The medieval culture claimed that a homunculus, a tiny human being, was contained in the semen that the masturbator had thrust out to die.

Gregory I, a great-grandson of Pope Felix III and a great-great-grandson of Felix II, was later honored as a saint because of his piety and given the rare title "Great." In replacing martyrdom with celibacy as the ultimate witness to Christ, he said, "Though we bend not the neck to the sword, yet with a spiritual weapon we slay fleshly desires in our hearts."[20] Methodius, bishop of Olympus, had earlier claimed that virgins, "not bearing the pains of the body for a little moment of time but enduring them through all their life," imitate Jesus better than martyrs did during the era when the Christians were persecuted. He glibly believed that the celibate necessarily suffers more than the married person and that "archvirgin" Jesus, who carried the most painful burden possible, must have been a life-long virgin.[21] The association of celibacy with martyrdom has persisted over the centuries;[22] the "red martyrdom" involving blood shedding was said to have been replaced by the "white martyrdom" of semen spilling.[23]

Gregory told of a priest who carried out the church's insistence that he "love his wife like a sister and flee from her like an enemy." When he was dying, his wife bent over his bed to detect if he was still breathing. Her close presence triggered erotic inflammation and "in great fervor of spirit he burst out saying, 'Get away, woman; take away the straw; there is fire left!'"[24] That deathbed scene suggests that, for some, abstinence makes the heart grow fonder.

Century after century church councils met to make pronouncements related to celibacy. The agenda usually included restating the demand for clerical sexual abstinence.[25] In 742, a council called by Boniface, archbishop of Mainz, decreed that anyone marrying after becoming a priest, or not sexually abstinent if already married, or living with a concubine if unmarried should be severely whipped and imprisoned for two years.[26] In spite of such threats, married clerics appear to have responded about as faithfully to requirements of abstinence as the laity now comply with papal castigations over the use of artificial contraception. Accordingly, St. Boniface informed Pope Zacharias that some priests had several concubines at once and that some in such relationships became bishops.[27] Bishop Ratherius of Verona tried to enforce the celibacy requirement but acknowledged that if he were to dismiss unchaste priests in his diocese no one would be left to administer the sacraments except their sons, and if he observed rules against bastards, even they would be excluded.[28]

A canon enacted in the ninth century attempted to correct a rectory abuse, "Priests and deacons are not permitted to share the same bed and the same room with their wives, lest they fall under suspicion of carnal relations."[29] Also, the Council of Nantes directed, "The cleric should not even allow mother, sister, or aunt to live with him in the house, because horrible acts of incest have already taken place." In 888, another church court ruled, "Clerics may have no females whatsoever in their house, since some have gone astray even with their own sisters."[30] "Such pronouncements suggest how much misery many people have suffered from the unfortunate practice of coercing priests into celibacy," Uta Ranke-Heinemann comments.[31] In 867, Eastern patriarch Photius, at a council in Constantinople, charged Pope Nicholas with heresy for having a celibate priesthood.

Historians estimate that there have been some forty married popes, many of whom continued their marriage after election to the highest church office.[32] This means that more than a quarter of those occupying the chair of espoused Peter during the church's first millennium were married. Most of the bishops of Rome during the patristic era were probably married, although there is a paucity of biographical data to confirm this. Ninth-century Hadrian II was the last married pope; his daughter was raped, and was murdered along with her mother during his reign.[33] The son of fourth-century Pope Anastasius I became Pope Innocent I; likewise, the son of sixth-century Pope Hormisdas became Pope Silverius, and all four were canonized as saints.[34] Indeed, a high percentage of all popes who have become official saints were married, even though most of the canonized saints are alleged to have been virgins. Also, a number of popes in the first millennium of the church were sons of priests. Among them were St. Damasus I, St. Boniface I, St. Felix III, Anastasius II, St. Agapitus I, Theodore I, Marinus I, Boniface VI (twice defrocked for immorality), and John XV.[35]

In his scholarly essay on celibacy in the church, Charles Frazee writes, "The great majority of clergymen in the West from Gregory the Great [sixth century] to the tenth century were married men."[36] In the first millennium of Christianity no effective church-wide restraints were imposed on the clergy with respect to being married, and clerical marriage was "openly defended" as late as the tenth century.[37] Edward Schillebeeckx, a leading Catholic theologian, adds:

> The Eastern and Western Churches of the first ten centuries never thought of making celibacy a condition of entering the ministry: both married and unmarried men were welcome as ministers. From the fourth century on, church law, which was at that time new, contained a *lex continentiae* . . . forbidding sexual intercourse during the night before communicating the

Eucharist. . . . [When] the Western churches began to celebrate the Eucharist daily, in practice this abstinence became a permanent condition for married priests.[38]

As the frequency of married popes diminished, papal sexual scandals increased. A story was told of how Sixtus III, when placed on trial for seducing a nun, defended himself by reminding the court of Jesus' non-condemning response to a woman caught in adultery. Lea comments, "Whether it were intended to be regarded as a confession, or as a sarcasm on the prelates around him, whom he thus challenged to cast the first stone, the tale, whether true or false, is symptomatic of the time that gave it birth."[39] Sixtus later became canonized as a saint, perhaps because of the good reputation he acquired by having a chastity essay attributed to him that "barely admits that married people can earn eternal life."[40]

In the tenth century, Sergius III had a child by Marozia, a teenager whom he seduced in the Lateran Palace. She had contempt for John X, a succeeding pope, whose mistress, Theodora, was her mother and the wife of the ruler who enthroned him. Marozia connived to have John X imprisoned and, after his death there, she was responsible eventually for having her firstborn elected as John XI at age twenty.[41] Marozia also lived to see her sixteen-year-old grandson become Pope John XII. Edward Gibbon wryly comments, "The bastard son, the grandson, and the great-grandson of Marozia, a rare genealogy, were seated in the chair of St. Peter."[42]

Pornocracy was operative during John XII's reign inasmuch as "powerful dirty harlots" governed papal decisions.[43] At the Synod of Rome in 963, he was charged with turning his papal residence into a brothel, and Emperor Otto I reproached him for committing incest with his sisters. Also, "his rapes of virgins and widows had deterred the female pilgrims from visiting the tomb of St. Peter, lest, in the devout act, they should be violated by his successor."[44] Lea concludes that tenth-century Catholicism "rendered matrimony more objectionable than concubinage or licentiousness."[45] A century later Benedict IX was elected pope when he was a child; medieval chroniclers state that by the age of fourteen he had already exceeded the profligacy of his predecessors and that he "feasted on immorality" throughout his life.[46] Those popes, whom Cardinal Baronius calls "less apostles than apostates," affected those who looked to Rome for moral guidance.

In his classic *History of European Morals*, William Lecky comments:

It is a popular illusion, which is especially common among writers who have little direct knowledge of the middle ages, that the atrocious immorality of monasteries, in the century before the Reformation, was a new fact, and that the ages when the faith of men was undisturbed, were ages of great moral purity. In fact, it appears from the uniform testimony of the ecclesiastical writers, that the ecclesiastical immorality of the eighth and three following centuries was little if at all less outrageous than in any other period, while the Papacy, during almost the whole of the tenth century, was held by men of infamous lives.[47]

Papal Attempts to Put Asunder Espoused Clerics

In the eleventh century, sons of married priests of St. Paul's Church in London inherited their father's position.[48] Because of such practices, Benedict VIII advocated celibacy law modifications that would protect the church's large landholdings. He and subsequent pontiffs wanted to increase the subjugation of married priests by diminishing their family loyalty and by prohibiting their children from inheriting property.[49] Benedict persuaded King Henry II to proscribe in the imperial code the bestowing of legacies to such children so that the church coffers would not be reduced.

In 1049, at the Synod of Mainz, Pope Leo IX condemned "the evil of clerical marriage." He ruled that the *damnabiles feminae*, meaning priests' wives, were to be seized and sold into slavery.[50] In 1054, the Pope sent Cardinal Humbert to Constantinople to improve relations with the Eastern sector of the church. However, the alienation was compounded by Humbert's denouncing while there the practice of allowing priests to marry. He said: "Young husbands, just now exhausted from carnal lust, serve the altar. And immediately afterward they again embrace their wives with hands that have been hallowed by the immaculate Body of Christ. That is not the mark of a true faith, but an invention of Satan."[51] Humbert excommunicated his host, Patriarch Michael, and he reciprocated by excommunicating Latin church leaders for permitting irregularities such as prohibiting the marriage of priests. The tragic split between Eastern and Western Catholicism dates from that year, and it has never been healed.

In the medieval era, homosexual conduct was included in judgments against clerics (Rom 1:22–27). The early church had considered it a perversion of nature, even though no comment of Jesus about homosexuality was recorded in the Gospels.[52] Only after Christianity became the state religion was it punished severely. Believing that "crimes against nature are responsible for famines, earthquakes, and plagues," Emperor Justinian in 533 decreed death for the practice of homosexuality, even when consenting adults were involved.[53]

Peter Damian, an Italian monastery abbot and a cardinal, wrote the *Book of Gomorrah* in 1049 against clerics who stimulate semen emissions, whether it involves one person masturbating or partners engaging in homosexual activity. The English translation of that polemic is included in *The Fathers of the Church* series as a letter to Leo IX. Damian invented the term *sodomia* to damn gays,[54] because the pagan city of Sodom—along with Gomorrah—by the Dead Sea were repeatedly associated in the Bible with depravity and divine destruction. The word, as Damian used it, ranged in meaning from individual or mutual masturbation to anal penetration of men or beasts. "Sodomy" became the common term Christians used to refer to such "unnatural" practices until the term "homosexual" was introduced eight centuries later. The detail Damian provided about gay conduct suggests that he might have had homoerotic tendencies himself.[55] He found that gay priests confessed to one another this "worst of crimes" to avoid being punished for their behavior. Attempting to obtain repentance through fright, Damian wrote, "For a momentary pleasure experienced at the moment of ejaculation, a punishment will follow that will not end for thousands of years."[56] He unsuccessfully attempted to involve Leo IX (both became Catholic saints) in punishing sodomites harshly. The pope thought that conviction of posterior penetration, but not of occasional masturbation, should be grounds for removing clerics from office.[57]

Damian reported to Pope Nicholas II, "I have wanted to place locks on priests' loins and restraints of continence upon their genitals."[58] Reference is here to chastity belts that the zealot thought would constrain men regardless of their sexual orientation. He observed that sexually active heterosexual priests are punished but "silent tolerance" is extended to the "epidemic" of bishops engaged in the same conduct. Such bishops should be deposed because by touching women's private parts with holy hands they have been condemned by Jesus who said, "Do not give what is holy to dogs" (Matt 7:6).[59] Damian attempted to add further biblical denunciation to his vitriol by labeling bishops who lived with their wives "Nicolaitans." That term was dredged up from biblical verses that referred to a group of despised fornicators (Rev 2:14–15), about whom nothing more is known. With no basis, Damian attributed to one of the first deacons false teaching that all clergy ought to marry:

> O unhappy bishop, have you no fear that as you wallow in the mire of impurity, you have become guilty of the heresy of the Nicolaitans? It was Nicolas, one of those whom the Apostle Peter had ordained deacons, who boldly taught that clerics of every rank should be married. . . . The voice of God spoke of this crime through the angel of the Church at Ephesus: "You hate the practices of the Nicolaitans, as I do" (Rev 2:6; Acts 6:5).[60]

Damian's tirade against the wives and concubines of priests exposes his misogyny: "You furious vipers, by the ardor of your ungovernable lust you cut off your lovers from Christ, who is head of the clergy. . . . By the lure of your charms and your pretty faces you tear unfaithful men from the service of the holy altar. . . . You suck the blood of miserable, unwary men, so that you might fill them with your lethal poison."[61]

A bishop of Turin, who had allowed the "obscene" practice of clerical marriage in his diocese, was reminded by Damian that clerics "are bound to hold themselves aloof from all associations involving physical love." Recalling that Leo IX had made women who had been living with priests in Rome "slaves of the Lateran palace," Damian believed that justice demands that every bishop enslave women in their dioceses who are living with priests.[62]

Following the pattern of earlier eleventh-century popes, Nicholas attempted to stop laity from receiving the sacraments from married priests, which precipitated a rebuff from an Italian bishop: "Ulric insists that the canons must now make it clear that clerical marriage is not only tolerated but is legal. . . . He argued well from scripture and the [Church] Fathers . . . that when celibacy is imposed, priests . . . will seek sexual release wherever they can find it, 'forcing themselves on their fathers' wives, not abhorring the embraces of other men or even of animals.'"[63] In Germany at this time, the tenaciousness of clerical marriage also withstood much of the destructive efforts of the church. In Hamburg, for example, "Bishop Libentius ordered the wives of all his canons to leave town . . . [but] the ladies promptly resettled in nearby villages, where their husbands continued to visit them."[64]

One of the most powerful medieval leaders was a monk named Hildebrand, who rigidly enforced celibacy when he was a Benedictine abbot. He insisted that monks live in a common dormitory that provided surveillance for purity violators.[65] In 1073, when he became Pope Gregory VII, he used his monastic zeal to tighten up on the practice of celibacy throughout Catholicism:

The themes that dominate Gregory VII's remarks about sex are purity and cleanliness. Virtually everything he said about the subject rests on the assumption that sex is dirty and unclean, that those who indulge in it are defiled by the experience, and they must be cleansed before they can participate in Christian worship. . . . The equation of sex with defilement and sexual abstinence with purity seems to explain Gregory's repeated admonitions to layfolk to boycott Masses said by married or concubinary priests. . . . Clearly sexual purity was for Gregory at the very core of Christian morality.[66]

Gregory realized that his control over the church could be more effective if he could tear priests away from the clutches of their wives. Lecky describes the way in which Gregory pursued "the destruction of priestly marriage . . . with the most untiring resolution":

> Finding that his appeals to the ecclesiastical authorities and to the civil rulers were insufficient, he boldly turned to the people, exhorted them, in defiance of all Church traditions, to withdraw their obedience from married priests, and kindled among them a fierce fanaticism of asceticism, which speedily produced a fierce persecution of the offending pastors. Their wives, in immense numbers, were driven forth with hatred and with scorn.[67]

Terrence Sweeney tells of the effectiveness of his bedroom crusade:

> Though Pope Gregory VII's unsparing and relentless efforts to assure a continent clergy were the most far-reaching and effective to date, his efforts, if contemporary descriptions are to be believed, left in his wake a married clergy, some of whom were reduced to poverty and homelessness; others mutilated and publicly paraded through the streets; still others submitted to torture, imprisonment and lingering death—and many of the wives of clergy mocked, abused, and shamed, some of them driven to madness, others found dead in their beds of suicide.[68]

Siding with the German revolt, King Henry IV, head of the Holy Roman Empire, assembled bishops in Worms who audaciously attempted to depose Gregory. One reason they gave for this action was that "his association with a woman was a scandalous outrage for the whole Christian world."[69] In retaliation, Gregory gathered a council at the Lateran in 1076 and had Henry excommunicated. The king, recognizing that some in his realm wanted a new emperor, became frightened over his future and made a pilgrimage to Italy in search of reconciliation with the alleged "keeper of the keys" to the pearly gates. In 1077 he knelt barefooted in a penitent's garb outside the castle of Canossa, forced by Gregory to literally cool his heels in the snow before being received by him. After begging for forgiveness and pledging loyalty to Christ's Vicar, Henry was granted absolution. Gregory set the stage for his successors to wield the greatest secular and sacred control in the history of the papacy. His office was similar to that of

Augustus Caesar who, by assuming the role of *pontifex maximus,* had united religious and governmental authority. Papal supremacy over national rulers made Gregory's reformers a formidable force in smashing those who were lax in adhering to the Vatican's standards.

In spite of Gregory's power, his demand that priests abandon their wives in order to celebrate Mass with holy hands was strongly resisted. Some bold Italian bishops gathered in Pavia in 1076 to condemn the pope because his rejection of marriage for priests had resulted in increased clerical sexual immorality.[70] In Germany, implementing Gregorian reforms incurred heavy resistance. A Dominican of Strasbourg reported that Gregory saw many infant skulls taken out of a pond near a nunnery and was chagrined on realizing that his demand for celibacy had contributed to such slaughter.[71] "Centuries of imposed celibacy had not inhibited the erotic drives of monks or nuns, and underground passageways were known to connect some monasteries and nunneries."[72]

When St. Altmann, bishop of Passau, tried to bring his clergy into compliance, they attacked him and, assisted by imperial troops, drove him out of his diocese.[73] Archbishop Siegfrid of Mainz also attempted to enforce Gregory's crackdown on espoused priests but, when his obstinate clergy threatened to kill him, he permitted their lifestyle to continue. The pope then excommunicated him and suspended four French bishops who similarly disobeyed his orders.[74] His harsh penalties provoked an angry response:

> The clergy protested in the most energetic terms that they would rather abandon their calling than their wives; they denounced Gregory as a madman and a heretic, who expected to compel men to live as angels, and who in his folly, while denying natural affection its accustomed and proper gratification, would open the door to indiscriminate licentiousness; and they tauntingly asked where . . . he expected to find the angels who were to replace them.[75]

Gregory's motto appears to have been, "Make war, not love," because his expression of power was more divisive than unifying. Eager to lead the first crusade to the Holy Land, this pope—later to be canonized as saint—preached from a favorite text, "Cursed is he who keeps back his sword from bloodshed" (Jer 48:10).[76] Richard Sipe finds it understandable that strident celibacy demands came during the same era as the crusades, because both sprang out of male aggression.[77] Urban II, another papal theocrat, tried to match Gregory in enforcing celibacy regulations, but was unsuccessful in his crusade against sex. Urban was more satisfied with the "holy" war that he launched against Muslims. His crusaders conquered Jerusalem, giving him immediate acclaim but lasting infamy. A millennium later, filmmaker Peter Mullan commented on those crusading popes: "The Church's obsession with celibacy is perverse. . . . No war has come about because of people making love. But plenty of wars have come about through people deciding that their faith is better than another's."[78]

In her scholarly study of eleventh-century celibacy, Anne Barstow writes, "Despite six hundred years of decrees, canons, and increasingly harsh penalties, the Latin clergy still did, more or less illegally, what their Greek counterparts were encouraged to do by law—they lived with their wives and raised families."[79] But she acknowledges that the attack on clerical marriages did have profound effect:

> Celibacy was one of the keynotes of papal power. The popes most absolutist about papal primacy . . . were the popes most insistent on clerical celibacy. . . . Thus was formed one of the most powerful and enduring "men's clubs" that history has recorded. . . . The most revolutionary and lasting legacy of the Gregorians was the monasticizing of the clergy. . . . This change contributed to the papacy's control over its personnel which it needed to assume the predominant place in the European world, a role which it filled magnificently for two centuries. . . . Once set aside and above the rest of society, not only by function but by life-long vows, the clergy became "a race apart."[80]

In the early twelfth century, two of the brightest stars in the constellation of medieval philosophical churchmen became a study of contrasts in the relentless movement toward the ideal of an asexual priesthood. Anselm, the archbishop of Canterbury, excommunicated married priests, confiscated their property, and enslaved their wives.[81] He is remembered for his deft theological argumentation, not for his upholding of church policies on celibacy. His French contemporary Peter Abelard shared his brilliance but not his outlook on sex. His love affair, the most famous of the era, ended in tragedy because of celibacy requirements. Young Abelard, already a successful teacher, tutored Heloise while living in the home of Fulbert, a canon at Notre Dame cathedral. Fulbert was probably the father of the highly intelligent girl, but he called her his niece to avoid scandal.

In his *Story of Calamities*, Abelard told of their flaming passion:

> Her studies allowed us to withdraw in private, as love desired, and then with our books open before us, more words of love than of our reading

passed between us, and more kissing than teaching. My hands strayed oftener to her bosom than to the pages; love drew our eyes to look on each other more than reading kept them on our texts. . . . Our desires left no stage of love-making untried, and if love could devise something new, we welcomed it.[82]

Their romance stimulated Abelard to compose love songs that were also sung by his many students. Heloise soon became pregnant and, to keep the affair secret, she left Paris to give birth to their child. For Abelard's sake, she did not want to marry him, preferring "love to wedlock and freedom to chains." She realized that becoming publicly wedded to him would have ended his chances for advancement in the church, which was the only place for professorial employment. Lea shows how this liaison illustrates the denigration of marriage that resulted from the church's demand that clerics be bachelors:

> Heloise recognised that while the fact of his openly keeping a mistress, and acknowledging Astrolabius as his illegitimate son, would be no bar to his preferment, and would leave open to him a career equal to the dreams of his ambition, yet to admit that he had sanctified their love by marriage, and had repaired, as far as possible, the wrong which he had conmitted, would ruin his prospects for ever. From a worldly point of view it was better for him, as a Churchman, to have the reputation of shameless immorality than that of a loving and pious husband; and this was so evidently a matter of course that she willingly sacrificed everything, and practised every deceit, that he might be considered a reckless libertine.[83]

But Abelard persuaded Heloise to agree to a secret wedding to make amends for "living in sin." However, news spread of their clandestine marriage, so he sent her off to a nunnery to take up the veil. He visited her convent and made love with her in a hallowed place "dedicated to the most holy Virgin."[84] Indignant over the lovers' hypocrisy, one night Fulbert and his friends entered the room where Abelard was sleeping and left him castrated. Humiliated by this revenge, the eunuch joined a monastery where he continued to engage in educational work. He no longer had empathy for those who could not control their sexual drive and was disgusted to find it common for his fellow monks to have children as well as concubines.

Abelard and Heloise continued to exchange letters in which she confessed that her devotion to God had not eclipsed her love for him. He urged her to sublimate her affection for him and enjoy the intimacy to which she was entitled as the bride of Christ: "You were previously the wife of a poor mortal and now are raised to the bed of the King of kings. . . . You who have been led by the King of heaven himself into his chamber and rest in his embrace, and with the door always shut are wholly given up to him."[85] Abelard claimed after his castration that he, unlike the Apostle Paul, was relieved of his "thorn in the flesh."[86] Yet Abelard was the only scholar of his era who rejected Augustine's view that sexual urges were sinful because mankind had inherited contaminated genes from the fallen Adam.[87] Abelard inquired, "If cohabitation with a wife and the enjoyment of pleasant things were allowed us in Paradise from the first day of our creation without guilt being incurred, who may argue that these things are now sinful, provided only that we do not exceed the limits of our permission?"[88]

St. Bernard of Clairvaux despised Abelard, condemning him as a heretic for not regarding sexual pleasure as intrinsically evil. In his sermons, Bernard attempted to denature the Song of Songs by converting to an ode to perpetual virginity what was composed as a tribute to the holiness of sensual lovemaking and marital sexuality.[89] In the spirit of St. Gregory VII, who substituted hatred for blocked love, Bernard recruited men for the Second Crusade by proclaiming, "Let the cry of Jeremiah reverberate through Christendom, 'Cursed be he that withholdeth his sword from blood.'"[90]

Schillebeeckx clarifies the marital situation of priests during the medieval era: "The Latin church until the twelfth century allowed its clerics to be married, but required them to practice complete continence. Because of this psychologically abnormal situation, the law of continence remained . . . a dead letter."[91] In 1123, bishops assembled in Rome for the first General Council of the Latin Catholic Church, known as Lateran I, and issued a draconian edict concerning clerical celibacy. Peter De Rosa, a Catholic scholar, describes it: "A thousand prelates decreed that clerical marriages should be broken up and the spouses made to do penance because these marriages were invalid. . . . This teaching was new; it went against centuries of tradition. . . . No more than other Councils did the First Lateran alter priests' behaviour."[92] In 1139, Innocent II gathered some five hundred bishops for Lateran II to deal again with clerical sexual conduct. He declared, "Since priests are supposed to be God's temples, vessels of the Lord and sanctuaries of the Holy Spirit, . . . it offends their dignity to lie in the conjugal bed and live in impurity."[93] Both councils were more concerned to take away the marriage liberty than the sexual liberty of priests.

Subsequently, women who cohabited with priests, even in a committed relationship, had no rights, and children of the furtive liaisons were stigmatized as bastards.

The ban against priestly marriage was not prompted mainly by concern for moral reform or theological correctness but for power and money. Ex-Jesuit Eugene Bianchi, after pointing to these underlying but unpublicized historical reasons for mandatory celibacy, accurately says, "Arguments about a celibate Jesus or about special dedication are largely theological smoke and mirrors."[94] Hierarchs can exercise tighter control over bachelor clergy who have no family responsibilities. Also, the medieval church received income from their massive real estate holdings and was eager to use it for cathedral constructions that were getting underway. The pontiffs shrewdly counted spouses and children of priests as economic liabilities were they to be accepted as legitimate. As has continually been the case, bachelors are low-maintenance personnel and can be easily transferred at little cost. But uxorious clerics need more provisions than single priests, so church offerings are expended in part to support their families, and indirectly to pass on legacies to them. Understandably, priests have thought of this as a legitimate use of donations they have assisted in collecting.

Along with an increased determination to keep priests from marrying came an expansion of the place of homosexuals in the medieval church. John Boswell, an authority on homosexual history, shows that the ban on clerical marriage was accompanied by more tolerance toward gay practice. He states, "The approach to sexuality adopted by early twelfth-century theologians effectively 'decriminalized' homosexual relations altogether." Perhaps the church realized that "gay priests would be more willing than heterosexual ones to enforce prohibitions against clerical marriage."[95] In medieval Spain, the Inquisition burned adult homosexuals but gay clergy were shown leniency.[96] Sociologist David Greenberg observes: "Homosexual relationships did not result in progeny, and therefore did not threaten the preservation of church property. . . . The more the church suppressed priestly marriage and concubinage, the stronger must have been the homosexual drive it aroused within its ranks."[97] Several medieval popes were accused of engaging in various debaucheries with men and boys.[98]

Even though clerical marriage had been nullified in the strongest terms, it continued to be widely practiced. Making rules and enforcing them are quite different, as Americans know from the short history of the temperance amendment to the U.S. Constitution. Halfhearted enforcement continually accompanies laws that prohibit indulgences that most people find acceptable in moderation. "When the Bishop of Paris told his priests that they must give up their wives and children, they drove him from the church with jeers and blows, and he found it necessary to take refuge with the royal family in order to escape the wrath of his outraged clerics."[99] Also, during the reign of Alexander III, seventeen concubines were banished from the Vatican chambers in a single day but they soon sneaked back into the cathedral precincts. That pope privately opposed mandatory celibacy but he appeared vigorous in prosecuting offenders in public.[100]

In 1171, when monk Clarembald was selected to become abbot at Canterbury, it was known that the "venerable patriarch had seventeen bastards in one village." Lea is surprised "that a man whose profligacy was so openly and shamelessly defiant could be elected to the highest place in the oldest and most honoured religious community in England."[101] De Rosa tells more about the twelfth-century situation in the English church:

> When, at Rome's bidding, bishops got tougher, many priests indulged in incest, or felt that, being deprived of lawful wives, they were entitled to their mistresses. . . . [A cardinal sent to restore celibacy] gathered the senior clerics together and, during Mass, bitterly denounced the clergy's evil ways. So magnificent was his oration that the priests gave a banquet in his honour. The cardinal, wisely leaving them to their revels, retired for the night. Not long afterwards, representatives of the English clergy crashed into his room to find the cardinal was not saying his prayers. On the contrary, in the most glorious Chaucerian tradition, he was abed in the arms of a woman, without his vestments on, or, as a contemporary wrote, "naked to his finger-nails." . . . Having toasted the prelate of the Scarlet Skin and the "fayre ladye" beside him on the pillow, the intruders left him in peace for the night.[102]

This account of sexual celebration by a professed celibate brings to mind an apocryphal story about a monastic scribe in medieval Oxford. He was in anguish after checking the original Latin manuscript of an ancient clergy manual on the accuracy of a sentence in the marriage section. He found that, due to a mistranslation over the centuries, *celebratus* was being copied as "Celibates (not celebraters) perform the Eucharist."

De Rosa reports on a remarkable practice during the medieval era in a London parish: "It provided a brothel exclusively for priests and friars. Only men with a tonsure, the shaven circle representing Christ's crown of thorns, were admitted." Ironically, the tonsure mark on the crown of clerics' heads had been introduced at ordination rites to represent worldly renunciation and to aid in identifying those who morally stray from the fold. English laymen who were disgusted by such licentious celebrations suggested that castration would be a more appropriate mark of ordination![103] De Rosa comments further:

> Priests, without the discipline of the bond of matrimony, became almost completely promiscuous. . . . Concubines were actually the least harmful method of restraining the priests' appetites. . . . Impeccable Catholic sources, papal documents, letters of reforming saints, all paint the same depressing picture. . . . Bishops, in every sense the fathers of their people, kept harems and the few brave souls who tried to enforce the discipline risked being poisoned or beaten to death. Alexander IV, in a Bull dated 1259, bemoans the fact that the laity were not reformed but corrupted by the clergy.[104]

Clerical concubinage was more the de facto rule than the exception throughout western Europe during the century following the Lateran celibacy mandate.[105] In concubinage, relationships were relatively stable, akin to what has been described as "common law marriage." Usually the woman was of a lower social class than the man. Unlike prostitution, those liaisons lessened promiscuity among participants; they were not merely for pleasure to the man and payment to the woman.

> Concubinage was tolerated by the Church and . . . might in fact be considered the functional equivalent of marriage. . . . From [twelfth-century canonist] Gratian onwards the prevailing view maintained that the fact of habitual cohabitation and the existence of marital affection constituted a marriage. . . . In the law of Justinian marital affection was the sole requisite condition for constituting a marriage—dowry, ceremonies, and the rest were mere adjuncts. . . . Clerical concubinage was frequently and openly practiced virtually throughout the medieval period.[106]

A clerical poet in the thirteenth century raged against Innocent III's efforts to enforce the law of celibacy:

> Innocent? No sweetheart he,
> He's just as deadly as can be!
> Our Lord decreed we should have wives;
> Our Pope demurs—and spoils our lives.
>
> Priests who lack a girl to cherish
> Won't be mindful lest they perish.

They will take whom'er they find
Married, single—never mind![107]

Thomas Aquinas, who was educated by the Benedictines before joining the Dominicans, became the main pillar of medieval orthodoxy. Honored by Catholics ever since his thirteenth century as a saint and "the angelic doctor," he differed little from Augustine in his sexual outlook. Both damned marriage with faint praise by making invidious comparisons of its lower good to the higher good of virginity. They believed that marriage was a concession to human weakness and that the curse of sexual desire had been perpetuated throughout history from the aboriginal disobedient Adam and Eve. The virginal monk's sexual experiences were so limited that he could only quote Augustine's judgment, "I feel that nothing so casts down the manly mind from its heights as the fondling of women and those bodily contacts which belong to the married state."[108] Aquinas added that, by contrast, the celibate life is "unseared by the heat of sexual desire that is experienced in achieving the greatest bodily pleasure, conjugal intercourse."[109] As C. S. Lewis observes, "According to the medieval view passionate love itself was wicked, and did not cease to be wicked if the object of it were your wife."[110]

Aquinas followed Aristotle in thinking that the entire individual essence for human reproduction was in the ejaculate, so the gravest sexual sins occur when semen is not planted in a woman, who is defined as a body for procreation. In his hierarchy of sins, he ranks "every emission of semen in such a way that generation cannot follow" as nearly as heinous as homicide.[111] Masturbation, defined as "provoking orgasm to obtain sexual pleasure, without carnal union," along with homosexual acts and zoophilia, are classified as "sins against nature." Fornication, adultery, rape, and incest are a lesser offense because pregnancy is a possible outcome.[112] This explains why, from the medieval era onward, masturbation has continually caused morbid feelings of guilt among Catholics. Previously, in the biblical era, the attitude toward masturbation was literally laissez faire, meaning not hands off by humans but let nature act without legal restrictions.[113] It was then treated with benign indifference and was not even given a name, but hysteria over its practice grew from the medieval era until the twentieth century.

Aquinas condoned prostitution in order to diminish horniness that might otherwise stimulate more serious sexual sins. He wrote: "Those who are in authority rightly tolerate certain evils lest . . . certain greater evils be incurred. Thus Augustine says, 'If you do away with prostitutes the world will be convulsed with lust.'"[114] Aquinas compared prostitution to a sewer that conveys filth away from respectable ladies and gentlemen. Just as a palace would be foul without a sewer system, so a city without a brothel would be polluted by unnatural lusts.[115] Overlooking the Bible's condemnation of prostitution (Deut 22:21; 1 Cor 6:15), he thought it was less wicked to use a whore as an instrument for relieving genital pressure than to use one's own hand. Prostitution in monasteries might not have been so common had sexual relief by masturbation been judged acceptable. Siring bastards was deemed less reprehensible than indulging in genital self-stimulation. Even though lifelong virginity is against the procreation aspect of natural law, for Aquinas it was the crowning sexual virtue.[116] "Perpetual continence is required for perfect piety," he declared. "Sexual union hinders the mind from giving itself wholly to the service of God. . . . That is why Jovinian, who put marriage on the same level as virginity, was condemned."[117]

Misogyny underlies Aquinas's notions of priestly celibacy. From his favorite pagan, Aristotle, he borrowed this definition, "The female is a defective male." He accepted the philosopher's view that nature always wants to produce a male, so a woman is a man gone wrong.[118] Males are naturally superior to females, Aquinas believed, in mind, body, and will.[119] In woman, the sexual appetite predominates, while in man, more stable rational qualities are found. Woman was invented to play a passive role in generation.[120] Because of her nature and purpose, "man is the beginning and end of woman, just as God is the beginning and end of every creature."[121] In Aquinas's opinion, a woman is in some ways inferior to a male slave: "Woman is in subjection according to the law of nature, but a slave is not."[122]

James Brundage, in his thoroughly documented study of medieval sexual behavior, states:

> Clerical concubinage and fornication remained persistent problems throughout the fourteenth century, and priests seem to have lived with their female companions almost as openly and as often as had their eleventh-century predecessors. The chief difference was that . . . these unions were no longer legitimized as marriages, and so clerical couples lived in sin, under threat of suspension and deposition if a vigilant archdeacon or a reforming bishop should find them out. Not all bishops took great pains to ferret out such cases, since some of them were doing much as their priests did: Bishop

Henry of Gelders at Liege, to take a flagrant example, boasted that he had sired fourteen sons in twenty-two months [and more than sixty children altogether]. . . . In Norway and Sweden during the early fourteenth century large numbers of the clergy were themselves illegitimate sons of priests.[123]

But the admissions of Henry, the Belgium bishop, exceeded what the church could tolerate, and he was deposed by the pope "for deflowering virgins and other mighty deeds."[124]

In fifteenth-century England, "the Catholic clergy often felt that although celibacy might require them not to marry, it did not oblige them to renounce sex." A fine was imposed for siring bastards, but the clergy paid much less than the laity. Priests in Wales decided after a religious revival to separate from their concubines, but their bishop prohibited this after calculating the revenue he would lose from concubinage fines.[125] A London notary estimated that less than a third of the clergy were sexually abstinent and that he had written during his career a thousand dispensations to allow the sons of priests to become ordained.[126] Throughout the church "at the end of the fifteenth century, the great majority of priests were living with concubines."[127]

In a church history text heavily supported with source material, Johann Gieseler writes, "In no century had there been so many decrees passed against the concubinage of the clergy as in the 15th; yet in none were complaints so common of their incontinence (which in Italy degenerated into unnatural vices). . . . It was openly said that nothing could remedy these evils but to allow the marriage of priests."[128] In 1429, the Council of Paris assessed the moral malaise: "On account of the crime of concubinage, with which multitudes of the clergy and monks are inflicted, the Church of God and the whole clergy are held in derision, abomination, and dishonor among all nations; and that abominable crime has so prevailed in the House of God that Christians do not now consider mere fornication a mortal sin."[129] At the 1440 Council of Basel, the bishop of Lubeck supported the judgment of a physician who "argued that clerical celibacy should be abandoned in theory because it had long since been disregarded in practice."[130]

Chancellor Gerson, a spokesperson of the Council of Constance that met during this period, argued that clerical incontinency did not violate celibacy, but marriage did.[131] A citizen of Constance recorded that hundreds of prostitutes visited the German city to sell their services while the council was in session.[132] Council entertainment also included watching Czech reform leader Jan Hus burn at the stake and condemning John Wyclif, who had exposed the apostasy of Rome to English commoners by his Bible translations. Wyclif and his Lollard followers taught that God deemed marriage, not celibacy, as best for priests.[133] Scholar-priest Hus was much influenced by Wyclif. When on trial before the Council, he pointed out that marriage of priests had not been prohibited for the first thousand years of Christianity. He then asked: "Has not God himself instituted marriage as a means to satisfy the craving for love in all men? . . . Is not he, who becomes a priest also made of flesh and blood? . . . I hold this to be the seed of iniquity and the root of all evil, the fact that the priest does not marry. . . . He turns to the other sex, baits those who have husbands, lures those who are widows or those who are simple maidens." After those words, Hus's defense was halted because prelates began to chant loudly, "Burn him."[134]

In the late Middle Ages, some popes continued to have personal difficulty in abiding by their own law of celibacy. Clement VI was charged with sexual immorality,[135] and Pius II's letters to his mistress show that "he was convinced that to defraud nature of her rights was absolute insanity."[136] They were followed by Innocent VIII, called the honest pontiff because he was the first to openly acknowledge his illegitimate children and not call them his nephews and nieces. He used the power of his office to marry them into wealthy families; the aim of one son was to carry off papal treasures. Innocent named his thirteen-year-old grandson a cardinal.[137]

At the end of the fifteenth century, Alexander VI had children by several mistresses both before and after he became pope. "The great object of his schemes was to heap honors and riches on his five illegitimate children, and especially on his favorite Caesar Borgia,"[138] who was made cardinal when he was nineteen. Although without peer among popes in moral degeneracy, he supported the controversial doctrine of the immaculate conception of the mother of Jesus.[139] Bishop Johann Burchard, who kept a diary of events in Alexander's life, describes in a 1501 entry a banquet in a Vatican chamber where the pope, his son Caesar, and his daughter Lucretta were among those attending. Fifty prostitutes entertained them by dancing naked and crawling between candles placed on the floor: the orgy ended with an award to the person who could perform the most sex acts with them.[140] Burchard's unimpeachable history demonstrates that at one time the Vatican was a veritable grande bordello.

Alexander VI was followed by Julius II, who had several illegitimate children when he was cardinal. He is noted for beginning a new cathedral in Rome but he also helped to spread a new disease that had been named syphilis. Subsequently, Medici bastard Clement VII became pope, and he was succeeded by Paul III, whose sister had been a mistress of Alexander VI. Paul had fathered several children after becoming a priest, and on becoming pope he appointed two of his teenage grandsons as cardinals. He was succeeded by Julius III, who had a sexual liaison with an adolescent pickup who was then made a cardinal.[141] Attention has been given to the sexual conduct of popes because those lower in the religious pyramid often took their cues from the behavior they observed at the apex.

The situation at the end of the medieval period rivaled any previous century in sexual iniquities across the ranks of the priesthood. "The laity were glad to secure their families in any way from the attacks of priestly lust, and favored, or even furthered, the permanent connexion of their priests with concubines. Thus it happened that in many countries, such connexions were openly suffered amongst those whose holiness was . . . supposed to be sullied by wedlock."[142] One town in Switzerland required a new priest to have a concubine to protect the wives of parishioners.[143] A Swiss bishop levied a fine for each child born to a priest. Judging from the fines collected in his diocese during 1522, some 1,875 babies were born of clerical liaisons. At that time, Bishop Hugo von Landenberg of Constance also collected large fines for the 1,500 children of priests born there annually.[144] Understandably, *pfaffenkind* (priest's child) became the German word for bastard.[145]

In his sexual history, Gordon Taylor comments on medieval Catholicism:

> In the eyes of the Church, for a priest to marry was a worse crime than to keep a mistress, and to keep a mistress was worse than to engage in random fornication—a judgment which completely reverses secular conceptions of morality, which attach importance to the quality and durability of personal relationships. . . . The simple clergy found it difficult to accept this scale of values, and frequently settled down to permanent relationships. . . . For this they were periodically expelled from their livings and the women driven out or seized by the Church.[146]

Much of medieval church history reads like a casebook in abnormal psychology. James Cleugh has shown that clergy frequently obtained their sexual pleasure by masochism and sadism. The thesis of his lengthy disclosures is that "the remarkable proliferation of sexual perversions among the clergy of the Christian Middle Ages, especially the monks, from flagellation and sodomy to bestiality, was directly due to the senseless enforcement of celibacy."[147] Gordon Taylor, after presenting pathetic cases of sexual aberrations in medieval cloisters, concludes: "The Church's code of repression produced, throughout Western Europe, over a period of four or five centuries, an outbreak of mass psychosis for which there are few parallels in history. . . . While the Church claims that repressive measures were required because of the immorality of the times, it seems more probable that, in reality, the immorality of the times was the result of the pressures."[148]

Pathological sexuality was also associated with belief in and persecution of witches. In 1484, Innocent VIII issued a bull commending misogynistic witch-hunters Heinrich Kramer and James Sprenger. He addressed them as "dear sons" and delegated the "Professors of Theology" to carry out an inquisition. In that pursuit, they wrote *The Hammer of Witches* and used the pope's bull as the book's preface. The authors were obsessed with demons, who they alleged took the form of women in order to engage men in sexual orgies. Kramer and Sprenger were inspired by Aquinas, a fellow Dominican, who told how demons take semen from men they have seduced and insert it into licentious women, causing them to bear monsters.[149] *The Hammer* fabricates this etymology, "Femina comes from Fe (faith) and Minus (less), since she is ever weaker to hold and preserve the faith." Moreover: "All wickedness is but little [compared] to the wickedness of women. . . . They are feebler both in mind and body. . . . She is more carnal than a man; . . . the mouth of the womb is never satisfied. . . . Ambitious women . . . are more hot to satisfy their filthy lusts."[150] For centuries, *The Hammer* was used as a guide in the Inquisition and as a text in Catholic seminaries. Geoffrey Simons perceptively surmises, "It is highly likely that the search for witches represented no more than the repressed sexuality of a celibate priesthood."[151]

In his *Canterbury Tales,* Geoffrey Chaucer described an adulterous friar as a sample of clergy who succumbed to the immorality of his medieval era. Reflecting on the effect of hierarchs on their subordinates, the bard asked, "If gold rusts, what shall iron do?" But he recognized that distinct from the "shitty shepherds" among the Lord's flock were some genuine priests. One such person was his "parson," who taught "Christ's own love . . . but first he followed it himself."[152]

Desiderius Erasmus, the fifteenth-century Dutch harbinger of the Protestant Reformation, was another priest that Chaucer would have admired. He was born to a priest, so his quip that priests are called "fathers" because of their propagation achievements was personally appropriate. He became an eloquent and constructive protester against priestly celibacy, reporting the flagrant lechery and increased illegitimacy that resulted from the requirement. As a youth he experienced the monastic life, but came to believe that chastity was less in danger outside the cloister. Erasmus thought the Apostle Paul was justifiably unmarried because his mission "was difficult to combine with matrimony," but he observed, "we live in an age when moral integrity is nowhere better exemplified than in marriage." The wordsmith penned this ode to matrimony:

> I would like to see permission given to priests and monks to marry, especially when there is such a horde of priests among whom chastity is rare. How much better to make concubines into wives and openly acknowledge the partners now held in infamy! How much better to have children to love and rear religiously, as legitimate offspring of whom there is no need to be ashamed and who in turn will honor their sires! I think that bishops would long since have given this permission if they did not derive more income from the taxes on concubines than they could reap from wives. . . . Why refrain from that which God institutes, nature sanctions, reason persuades, divine and human laws approve, the consent of all nations endorses and to which the highest examples exhort? . . . You are bound to friends in affection. How much more to a wife in the highest love, with union of the body, the bond of the sacrament and the sharing of your goods! . . . Nothing is more safe, felicitous, tranquil, pleasant and lovable than marriage.[153]

Erasmus's outlook was despised by Catholic officialdom and consequently his *Encomium of Marriage* was condemned and burned in 1525.

"The problem of clerical fornication remained endemic throughout the Middle Ages."[154] Lecky comments: "The writers of the middle ages are full of accounts of nunneries that were like brothels, of the vast multitude of infanticides within their walls, and of that inveterate prevalence of incest among the clergy, which rendered it necessary again and again to issue the most stringent enactments that priests should not be permitted to live with their mothers or sisters."[155]

Generally speaking, the nadir of wholesome sexuality in church history came during the medieval era, sometimes ironically designated as the "age of faith." For example, Vatican officials castrated boys who had been trained for the Sistine choir, enabling them to continue to sing falsetto after pubescence. That inhumane practice continued until the twentieth century, when female sopranos were at last considered worthy to sing on the premises of the Vatican.[156] Arguably there has been less sexual abuse in the modern era of Christendom than during the period when the church was the dominant European power.

Notes

1. Socrates, *Church History* 5:22.

2. *Apostolic Constitutions* 8:6.

3. Ibid., 8:51.

4. Clyde Pharr, ed., *The Theodosian Code* (Princeton: University Press, 1952), 1:16.

5. *Apostolic Constitutions* 4:11.

6. John Milton, *Paradise Lost* 4:750–53.

7. Jacques Migne, ed., *Patrologia Graeca* (Paris, 1864), 66:1484.

8. Elizabeth Abbott, *A History of Celibacy* (Cambridge: Da Capo, 2001), 108.

9. *Code of Justinian* 1:3:44, 47.

10. Council of Trullo, Canon 13.

11. William Bassett and Peter Huizing, eds., *Celibacy in the Church* (New York: Herder, 1972), 36–37.

12. Thomas Hobbes, *Leviathan* (1651), 4:47.

13. Leo I, *To Bishop Rusticus* 3.

14. "Celibacy, History of," *New Catholic Encyclopedia* (New York: McGraw-Hill, 1966).

15. *Rule of St. Benedict* 22.

16. Nietzsche, *Daybreak* (1881), 294.

17. Gregory I, *Dialogues* 2:2.

18. Thomas of Celano, *Lives of St. Francis of Assisi* 2:116.

19. John McNeill and Helena Gamer, eds., *Medieval Handbooks of Penance* (New York: Octagon, 1965), 113, 253.

20. Gregory I, *Sermons on the Gospel* 1:3.

21. Methodius, *Symposium* 1:4; 7:3.

22. Pius XII, *Holy Virginity*, 49.

23. Paul Dinter, *The Other Side of the Altar* (New York: Farrar, 2003), 66.

24. Gregory, *Dialogues* 4:11.

25. Christian Cochini, *Apostolic Origins of Priestly Celibacy* (San Francisco: Ignatius Press, 1990), 255–416.

26. Henry Lea, *History of Sacerdotal Celibacy* (London: Watts, 1932), 102.

27. James Brundage, *Law, Sex, and Christian Society in Medieval Europe* (Chicago: University of Chicago Press, 1987), 151.

28. William Lecky, *History of European Morals* (New York: Appleton, 1870), 2:349; Lea, *History*, 118.

29. Council of Orleans, Canon 17.

30. Council of Mainz, Canon 10.

31. Uta Ranke-Heinemann, *Eunuchs for the Kingdom of Heaven* (New York: Doubleday, 1990), 123.

32. George Frein, ed., *Celibacy: The Necessary Option* (New York: Herder, 1968), 50.

33. John Kelly, *The Oxford Dictionary of Popes* (New York: Oxford University Press, 1986), 109.

34. Ibid., 37, 52.

35. Ibid., 32, 40, 46, 49, 58, 73, 111, 115, 133.

36. Charles Frazee, "Celibacy," *Church History* (June 1972): 158.

37. Johann Gieseler, *Textbook of Ecclesiastical History* (Philadelphia: Carey, 1836), 2:113.

38. Edward Schillebeeckx, *Ministry* (New York: Crossroad, 1981), 85.

39. Lea, *History*, 60.

40. Ibid., 27.

41. "Marozia," *New Catholic Encyclopedia*.

42. Edward Gibbon, *The Decline and Fall of the Roman Empire* (1776), 49:2.

43. Cardinal Baronius, *Ecclesiastical Annals* (Antwerp, 1618), 10:629.

44. Gibbon, *Decline and Fall*, 49:2

45. Lea, *History*, 115.

46. Kelly, *Oxford Dictionary of Popes*, 126–27; Peter De Rosa, *Vicars of Christ* (New York: Crown, 1988), 5–54.

47. Lecky, *History of European Morals*, 2:349.

48. Ranke-Heinemann, *Eunuchs for the Kingdom of Heaven*, 160.

49. Edward Schillebeeckx, *Celibacy* (New York: Sheed & Ward, 1968), 61–62.

50. "Celibacy, History of," *New Catholic Encyclopedia*.

51. Ranke-Heinemann, *Eunuchs for the Kingdom of Heaven*, 107.

52. William Phipps, "Paul on 'Unnatural' Sex," *Currents in Theology and Mission* (April 2002): 128–31.

53. Justinian, *Novellae* 77; *Institutes* 4:18:4.

54. Mark Jordan, *The Invention of Sodomy in Christian Theology* (Chicago: University of Chicago Press, 1997), 29.

55. William Jordan et al., eds., *Order and Innovation in the Middle Ages* (Princeton: Princeton University Press, 1976), 333–34.

56. Peter Damian, *Letters* (Washington, DC: Catholic University, 1969–92), 31:10, 22, 67.

57. Ibid., 31:4.

58. Ibid., 61:2.

59. Ibid., 61:4, 12.

60. Ibid., 61:13.

61. Ibid., 112:34–36.

62. Ibid., 112:2, 5, 37.

63. Anne Barstow, *Married Priests and the Reforming Papacy* (New York: Mellen, 1982), 108–9, 112.

64. Brundage, *Law, Sex, and Christian Society*, 218.

65. Barstow, *Married Priests,* 57.

66. James Brundage, *Sex, Law and Marriage in the Middle Ages* (Chicago: University of Chicago Press, 1993), 4:71.

67. Lecky, *History of European Morals,* 2:352.

68. Terrance Sweeney, *A Church Divided* (Buffalo: Prometheus, 1992), 93.

69. Hans Kung, ed., *Life in the Spirit* (New York: Sheed & Ward, 1967), 137.

70. Barstow, *Married Priests,* 72.

71. Robert Burton, *The Anatomy of Melancholy* (New York: Tutor, 1938), 811.

72. Franz Alexander and Sheldon Selesnick, *The History of Psychiatry* (New York: Harper, 1966), 67.

73. Lea, *History,* 187–88.

74. Barstow, *Married Priests,* 72.

75. Lea, *History,* 185–86.

76. Colin Morris, *The Papal Monarchy* (New York: Oxford, 1989), 110.

77. Richard Sipe, *Sex, Priests, and Power* (New York: Brunner, 1995), 177–80.

78. *The Scotsman,* February 1, 2003, 5.

79. Barstow, *Married Priests,* 45.

80. Ibid., 180–81, 190–91.

81. Synod of London (1108), Canon 10.

82. *The Letters of Abelard and Heloise* (London: Penguin, 1974), 67–68.

83. Lea, *History,* 223.

84. *Letters of Abelard and Heloise,* 146.

85. Ibid., 138, 142.

86. 2 Cor 12:7–8; *Letters of Abelard and Heloise,* 148.

87. D. E. Luscombe, *Peter Abelard's Ethics* (Oxford: Clarendon, 1971), 12–15, 20–25.

88. Abelard, *Know Thyself* 3.

89. William Phipps, *Recovering Biblical Sensuousness* (Philadelphia: Westminster, 1975), 53–56.

90. Ailbe Luddy, *Life and Teaching of St. Bernard* (Dublin: Gill, 1937), 528.

91. Schillebeeckx, *Celibacy,* 42.

92. De Rosa, *Vicars of Christ,* 408.

93. Ranke-Heinemann, *Eunuchs for the Kingdom of Heaven,* 110.

94. *National Catholic Reporter,* August 27, 1993, 23.

95. John Boswell, *Christianity, Social Tolerance, and Homosexuality* (Chicago: University of Chicago Press, 1980), 217, 227.

96. Brian Moynahan, *The Faith* (New York: Doubleday, 2002), 450.

97. David Greenberg, *The Construction of Homosexuality* (Chicago: University of Chicago Press, 1988), 288.

98. Mark Jordan, *The Silence of Sodom* (Chicago: University of Chicago Press, 2000), 117–18.

99. Brundage, *Law, Sex, and Christian Society*, 221.

100. Ibid., 342.

101. Lea, *History*, 234–35.

102. De Rosa, *Vicars of Christ*, 412; Lea, *History*, 232–33.

103. De Rosa, *Vicars of Christ*, 413.

104. Ibid., 409–10.

105. Brundage, *Law, Sex, and Christian Society*, 404.

106. Brundage, *Sex, Law and Marriage in the Middle Ages*, 7:4–5, 9.

107. Brundage, *Law, Sex, and Christian Society*, 402.

108. Aquinas, *Summa Theologica* 2–2:151:3; Augustine, *Soliloquies* 1:10.

109. Aquinas, *Summa Theologica* 2–2:152:1.

110. C. S. Lewis, *The Allegory of Love* (London: Oxford, 1936), 14.

111. Aquinas, *Summa contra Gentiles* 3:122.

112. Aquinas, *Summa Theologica* 2–2:154.

113. William Phipps, "Masturbation: Vice or Virtue?" *Journal of Religion and Health* (October 1977): 183–94.

114. Aquinas, *Summa Theologica* 2–2:10:11; Augustine, *De Ordine* 2:4:12.

115. Aquinas, *Opuscula* 16:14.

116. Aquinas, *Summa Theologica* 2–2:152:5.

117. Ibid., 2–2:186:4.

118. Aristotle, *On Generation of Animals* 2:3; Aquinas, *Summa Theologica* 1:92:1.

119. Aquinas, *Summa Theologica* 3:81:3.

120. Ibid., 1:92:1.

121. Ibid., 1:94:4.

122. Ibid., 3:39:3.

123. Brundage, *Law, Sex, and Christian Society*, 474.

124. De Rosa, *Vicars of Christ*, 417.

125. H. Maynard Smith, *Pre-Reformation England* (London: Macmillan, 1938), 46, 48.

126. Brundage, *Law, Sex, and Christian Society*, 537.

127. Eric Fuchs, *Sexual Desire and Love* (New York: Seabury, 1983), 135.

128. Gieseler, *Textbook of Ecclesiastical History*, 3:279, 282.

129. Council of Paris, Preamble to Canon 23.

130. Brundage, *Law, Sex, and Christian Society*, 538.

131. Gieseler, *Textbook of Ecclesiastical History*, 3:282.

132. John Mundy and Kennerly Woody, eds., *The Council of Constance* (New York: Columbia University Press, 1961), 190.

133. James Gairdner, *Lollardry and the Reformation in England* (New York: Franklin, 1908), 1:48.

134. Beda von Berchem, ed., *The Trial of Hus* (New York: Granville, 1930), 57–58.

135. Kelly, *Oxford Dictionary of Popes*, 221.

136. Voltaire, "Clergy," *Philosophical Dictionary* (1764).

137. F. L. Glaser, ed., *Pope Alexander VI and His Court* (New York: Brown, 1921), xiii; Kelly, *Oxford Dictionary of Popes*, 252.

138. Gieseler, *Textbook of Ecclesiastical History*, 3:236–38.

139. Kenneth Latourette, *A History of Christianity* (London: Eyre, 1954), 638–39.

140. Glaser, *Pope Alexander VI*, 154–55.

141. Kelly, *Oxford Dictionary of Popes*, 256, 259, 261, 263.

142. Gieseler, *Textbook of Ecclesiastical History*, 3:83–84.

143. Lea, *History*, 299.

144. Ranke-Heinemann, *Eunuchs for the Kingdom of Heaven*, 115.

145. Lea, *History*, 285.

146. Gordon Taylor, *Sex in History* (New York: Harper, 1973), 69.

147. James Cleugh, *Love Locked Out* (New York: Crown, 1964), 298.

148. Gordon Taylor, *Sex in History* (New York: Harper, 1973), 49–50.

149. Aquinas, *Summa Theologica* 1:51:3, 6.

150. Heinrich Kramer and James Sprenger, *The Hammer of Witches* (New York: Dover, 1971), 43–47.

151. Geoffrey Simons, *Sex and Superstition* (New York: Barnes & Noble, 1973), 110.

152. Geoffrey Chaucer, *The Canterbury Tales*, Prologue, 500, 527–28.

153. Roland Bainton, *Erasmus of Christendom* (New York: Scribner, 1969), 49–50.

154. "Celibacy: Christian," in William Johnson, ed., *Encyclopedia of Monasticism* (Chicago: Fitzroy Deaborn, 2000).

155. Lecky, *History of European Morals*, 2:351.

156. Ranke-Heinemann, *Eunuchs for the Kingdom of Heaven*, 134–35; Abbott, *History of Celibacy*, 333.

Chapter 7
FROM LUTHER TO PAUL VI

꧁✦꧂

The Anti-Celibate Protestants

In the sixteenth century, the Protestant Reformation arose in no small part as an attempt to de-escalate the lengthy medieval crusade against marriage for those in sacred vocations. Issues pertaining to celibacy were important subjects for the Reformers, who wholeheartedly endorsed marriage for all people, even though they respected the voluntary choice of bachelorhood for the few with a preference for it.

In 1521, Lutheran Andreas Karlstadt, who lived in the German university town of Wittenberg, was the first Protestant to write a tract attacking celibacy. He recognized that the main reason for the tradition was the desire of the Catholic hierarchy to increase revenues and power over the clergy. Celibacy, he claimed, encouraged masturbation and homosexual behavior.[1] A year later, also at Wittenberg, Franciscan Johann Eberlin wrote of his dilemma:

> So I am caught. I cannot be without a wife. If I am not permitted to have a wife, then I am forced to lead publicly a disgraceful life, which damages my soul and honor and leads other people, who are offended by me, to damnation. How can I preach about chastity and unchastity, adultery and depravity, when my whore comes openly to church and my bastards sit right in front of me? How shall I conduct Mass in this state?[2]

Martin Luther, like Gregory VII, had been a German monk, but in contrast to that pope, he thought that morals could be improved by strengthening marriage. He helped give Protestants their name by protesting against the medieval requirement of mandatory celibacy for clerics that Gregorian reforms had brought in. Luther cited his authority for contending that clerical marriage is superior to celibacy: "On our side we have Scripture, the Church Fathers, ancient Church laws and even papal precedent. We'll stick to that. They have the contrary statements of a few Fathers, recent canons and their own mischief."[3] He admitted it was a sin for him to have renounced the lifelong celibacy vow he made on entering an Augustinian monastery, but he believed that it was more sinful not to have obeyed God's commandment to honor his father, who did not want his son to become a monk.[4]

According to Luther, Jesus discouraged celibacy; moreover, "a vow of chastity is diametrically opposed to the Gospel."[5] With regard to a New Testament passage that associates the prohibition of marriage with the "doctrines of demons" (1 Tim 4:1–3), Luther declared: "It is the devil who has forbidden the marriage of priests and has set up monastic orders. . . . The pope's regulations about chastity have hardly produced a single priest in a thousand who has observed chastity in public, not to speak of the unchastity that is practiced in private." Luther tersely commented: "Christ wants a minister of the Word to have a wife, but the pope does not. You can see which of them has the spirit of demons."[6] Forbidding clerical marriage by "the Roman See has . . . caused the Greek Church to separate, and discord, sin, shame, and scandal were increased no end. . . . My advice is . . . leave every man free to marry or not to marry."[7] Luther pointed out that a letter to Timothy encourages widows to remarry if they are less than sixty years old, because their sexual desires may still be strong and scandal may be avoided (1 Tim 5:9–14). Using this as a guideline, Luther wryly suggests that sixty for women and seventy or eighty for men [today's equivalent of ninety and one hundred] is an appropriate age for permitting a vow of celibacy![8]

Luther judged the New Testament's "divine ordinance" that a church officer should be "the husband of one wife" to have more validity than Vatican celibacy regulations. In discussing the matter, he charged, "The pope has as many concubines as Solomon had."[9] Luther later recognized that the success of his reform movement was due in large part to disgust by faithful church members toward the hypocrisy that clerical "celibates" of his day expressed by their actions.[10]

Finding celibacy contrary to natural impulse, Luther appealed to the lives of some renowned saints to illustrate that the renunciation of marriage tended more to inflame than to suppress desire. He observed: "When he was quite old Augustine still complained about nocturnal pollutions. When he was goaded by desire Jerome beat his breast with stones but was unable to drive the girl out of his heart. Francis made snowballs and Benedict lay down on thorns."[11]

According to Luther, sexual indulgence between a man and woman who are closely associated is virtually inevitable. Therefore, he wrote, to allow the priest to have a woman as housekeeper—as the pope permits—but not to allow them to marry "is just like putting straw and fire together and forbidding them to smoke or burn!"[12] He also realized that men consort with prostitutes when deprived of wives.[13] These comments lend some credence to the rumors regarding Luther's incontinence prior to his public renunciation of his priestly vows in his fifth decade of life.[14] In 1525, Luther married Katherine von Bora, a former nun, saying he was doing this to please his father, to spite the pope, and to vex the devil. He often called her "my lord," and was satisfied throughout the rest of his life with his wife as well as with their six children.[15]

Luther was especially irked by the Catholic claim that priests are morally excellent because they do not marry. Even if the boast that Catholic clergy are sexually abstinent were universally true, he disliked the invidious comparison of celibacy with marriage. As Luther read the Gospels, all humans are sinners but the married couple is no more imperfect than the clergy. All Christians are challenged to become holy, and not just a special celibate class. Luther moved away from the medieval sacred-secular split in vocations by raising the status of men and women laity. To the Reformer, the cobbler who mends the sole of the pope's shoe is pursuing his calling just as much as the pope who prays for the soul of the cobbler. Following the New Testament, Luther avoided calling Christian leaders "priests" and recognized that Peter designated the entire church membership as "a holy priesthood" (1 Pet 2:5):

> Every baptized Christian is a priest already, not by appointment or ordination from the pope or any other man but because Christ Himself has begotten him as a priest and has given birth to him in Baptism. . . . The pope has usurped the term "priest" for his anointed and tonsured hordes. By this means they have separated themselves from the ordinary Christians and have called themselves uniquely the "clergy of God."[16]

"Pastor," a metaphor from the fields of ordinary rural folk, became Luther's designation for ordained congregational leaders because the title connotes more accessibility to the "flock" apart from the church altar. By contrast, Joseph Blenkinsopp says:

Being celibate may actually constitute a serious impediment to the priest's or minister's availability. . . . The vital requirement of pastoral visitation is either drastically curtailed or even done away with for fear of the celibate priest finding himself in a compromising situation or coming under suspicion . . . [The clergy becomes] essentially a sacristy-based corps dispensing the sacraments to those who care to come to the ecclesiastical filling-station.[17]

Luther's denunciation of celibate vows had an immediate impact, causing a mass exodus from German monasteries. He was accused of being like the "heretical" monk Jovinian, who denied that virginity was a higher state than matrimony, and who convinced many celibates that they should marry. In 1525, Luther was the last of the Wittenberg professors to marry, but on entering that estate, he fully expressed his impulses. He rejected a Neopythagorean saying that Jerome had quoted approvingly, "He who loves too ardently his own wife is an adulterer." Luther retorted, "No man can commit adultery with his own wife unless he did not think of her as his wife or did not touch her as his wife."[18]

The Reformer's connubial relations provoked an international response: "Luther's marriage . . . was central to Catholic attacks on Protestant morality. The assertion that widespread dissemination of a religion preached by a married monk would lead to equally widespread immorality was a vital feature of the Catholic response. . . . God had allowed such a marriage [according to twice-married St. Thomas More] in order to reveal the full shame of the sin of man."[19] But not all Catholic leaders were opposed to clerical marriage. Advocates at that time included such influential persons as Emperor Charles V and the French cardinal of Lorraine.

The sex lives of clergy in Switzerland were changed when Lutheran reforms swept into that country. Ulrich Zwingli, who began his career as a Catholic priest in Zurich, admitted siring at least one child with his concubine, Anna Reinhard. Such conduct should not be considered gross, he explained, since he had abided by his principle not to seduce a virgin or a nun.[20] Like most clergy liaisons of his time, Zwingli's relationship with Anna took on the quality of faithful partnership, and after becoming Protestants they were publicly married. The acceptance of clerics' weddings in Protestant communities legitimized both the marriages and the children, who could now respectably be called sons and daughters.

John Calvin studied to become a Catholic scholar in France but became convinced of the truth of Lutheran thought. Fearing persecution from leaders of his Catholic-dominated nation, he fled to Switzerland and settled in Geneva for most of the rest of his life. He criticized the inconsistency of medieval doctrine that made sexual desire the seat of sin while exalting to a holy communion sexual consummation in marriage. Catholics, he said, "affirm that in the sacrament the grace of the Holy Spirit is conferred," while condemning sexual intercourse as "pollution and carnal filth." They bar priests from marriage and "deny that the Holy Spirit is ever present in copulation."[21] In his Genesis commentary, Calvin also spoke of the error of Christians "who think that woman was formed only for the sake of propagation." He found Jerome especially irksome in his use of flaming rhetoric to urge Christians to "cut down the tree of marriage with the ax of virginity."[22] Calvin thought the main purpose of marriage was social, not generative, and that spouses should also be companions in activities outside of the bedroom. He revived an emphasis of biblical ethics in writing that "conjugal intercourse is a thing that is pure, honorable, and holy."[23]

Calvin was convinced that the prohibition of clerical marriage violated the wholesome biblical endorsement of marriage for religious leaders. Commenting on the history of priestly celibacy, he charged, "The forbidding of marriage to priests came about by an impious tyranny not only against God's Word but also against all equity." In his prefatory address to King Francis of France, Calvin pointed out that the Council of Nicea agreed with participant Paphnutius that clergy marriages should be permitted and that chastity included cohabitation with one's spouse.

Catholics responded by affirming that they honored marriage for most Christians and that the celibacy law prohibited marriage for only a few. To refute that defense, Calvin provided an analogy, "It is as if a tyrant should contend that a law is not unjust when only a part of a city is oppressed with its injustice!" He added: "Freedom of bishops to be married existed both under the apostles and for some centuries afterward. The apostles themselves, and those pastors of prime authority who followed in their place, used this freedom without any difficulty."[24] Calvin found his own marriage fulfilling in spite of his children dying as infants. When his wife died, he wrote: "I have been bereaved of the best companion of my life. . . . As long as she lived she was the faithful helper of my ministry."[25]

Calvin condoned Christians remaining sexually abstinent in special circumstances but he thought they should view celibacy as a gift that usually has a temporary duration: "Let no man long for celibacy unless he can live without a wife [in chastity]. . . . Let every man abstain from marriage only so long as he is fit to observe celibacy. If his power to tame lust fails him, let him recognize that the Lord has now imposed the necessity of marriage upon him."[26] William Bouwsma states, "Sexual irregularities of Catholic clergy seemed to him in some degree excusable because celibacy, being contrary to nature, leads to acts against nature."[27] Calvin observed, "Experience shows how much better it would have been never to have imposed this yoke upon priests, than to shut them up in a furnace of lust, to burn with a perpetual flame."[28]

Along with other sixteenth-century Reformers, Calvin described how celibacy "has not only deprived the church of good and fit pastors, but has also brought in a sink of iniquities and has cast many souls into the abyss of despair."[29] He expressed indignation over the practices of many clerics in the church in which he was reared: "Disgraceful lusts rage amongst them, so that hardly one in ten lives chastely; and in monasteries, the least of the evils is ordinary fornication. . . . We disapprove of the tyrannical law about celibacy, chiefly for two reasons. First, they ["papists"] pretend that it is meritorious worship before God; and secondly, by rashness in vowing, they plunge souls into destruction."[30]

As a graduate student I lived in the sixteenth-century cathedral town of St. Andrews, where David Beaton, the most elevated prelate of Scottish history, lived on the eve of the Reformation. The many children of the "carnal cardinal," as John Knox slurred him, are officially described in post-Reformation records as "bastards of the Archbishop of St. Andrews." I became aware that the "whoremongering" higher clergy did much to trigger Calvinist Knox's takeover of Scotland's religious life. Historian Ian Cowan explains: "Celibacy had been reluctantly accepted by the [Scottish] church in the eleventh and twelfth centuries but had been seldom practiced. If there had been moral outrage it related to the bishops . . . with their many mistresses rather than to the humble parish priest with his loyal housekeeper who also shared his bed and bore his children."[31]

The treatment of celibacy by Charles Hodge, the most influential nineteenth-century American Calvinist theologian, well represents the Protestant appeal to biblical authority, church history, and human experience:

> The doctrine which degrades marriage by making it a less holy state, has its foundation in Manicheism or Gnosticism. It assumes that evil is essentially connected with matter; that sin has its seat and source in the body; that holiness is attainable only through asceticism and neglecting the body. . . . Our Lord more than once quotes and enforces the original law given in Gen. 2:24, that a man shall "leave his father and his mother, and shall cleave unto his wife, and they shall be one flesh." . . . It is thus taught that the marriage relation is the most intimate and sacred that can exist on

earth, to which all other human relations must be sacrificed. We accordingly find that from the beginning, with rare exceptions, patriarchs, prophets, apostles, confessors, and martyrs, have been married men.... The teaching of Scripture as to the sanctity of marriage is confirmed by the experience of the world. It is only in the marriage state that some of the purest, most disinterested, and most elevated principles of our nature are called into exercise. All that concerns filial piety, and parental and especially maternal affection, depends on marriage for its very existence.... It is in the bosom of the family that there is a constant call for acts of kindness, of self-denial, of forbearance, and of love.... There has been no more prolific source of evil to the church than the unscriptural notion of the special virtue of virginity and the enforced celibacy of the clergy and monastic vows, to which that notion has given rise.[32]

Henry VIII of England was a strong defender of priestly celibacy even though he was a sequential polygamist with six wives. He had severed ties with Rome because his divorce request was rejected by Paul III, who had multiple mistresses rather than wives. The king had his parliament pass this statute: "Priests, after the order of priesthood received, as afore, may not marry, by the law of God."[33] Thomas Cranmer, archbishop of Canterbury, shipped his second wife back to her original home in Germany after an English priest was hanged for not abandoning his wife. But in 1549, shortly after Protestant Edward VI replaced his deceased father, Parliament legalized clerical marriage. Four years later, Edward was succeeded by a fierce Catholic, Queen Mary, who demanded that married priests abandon their wives. After her death in 1558, the next English monarch, Elizabeth I, realized that she must accept married priests even though the virgin queen disapproved of the practice. On being introduced to the archbishop of Canterbury's spouse, she said, "Mistress I may not call you. Madame I will not call you." Since priests at that time tended to marry servants who had been their concubines when marriage was prohibited, the queen's curtness may have reflected her disdain for the woman's low class.[34]

By 1563, Anglicans had arrived at a different understanding of God's law: "Bishops, priests, and deacons are not commanded by God's law either to vow the estate of a single life, or to abstain from marriage. Therefore it is lawful for them, as for all other Christian men, to marry at their own discretion, as they shall judge the same to serve better to godliness." Episcopalians have been bound ever since by that Article 32 of their creed. Many Anglicans continued to favor voluntary celibacy, as extolled in a couplet of seventeenth-century Bishop Thomas Ken, "A virgin priest the altar best attends, / Our Lord this state commands not, but commends."[35]

John Donne, the famous early Anglican poet and preacher, gave exquisite expression to the Protestant view of clerical marriage.[36] "Roman Catholics," he asserted, "injure the whole state of Christianity when they oppose marriage and chastity, as though they were incompatible."[37] The Eden story demonstrates, Donne affirmed, that "God loves couples" and that matrimony is preferable to the single state.[38] In another sermon he describes women's place of dignity, "To make them Gods is ungodly, and to make them Devils is devillish; to make them Mistresses is unmanly, and to make them servants is unnoble; to make them as God made them, wives, is godly and manly too."[39]

Donne analyzed the virtue of virginity:

> The extreams are, in Excesse, to violate it before marriage; in Defect, not to marry. . . . Avarice is the greatest deadly sin next Pride; it takes more pleasure in hoording treasure than in making use of it. . . . Virginity ever kept, is a vice far worse than Avarice, it will neither let the possessor nor others take benefit by it, nor can it be bequeathed to any: with long keeping it decayes and withers, and becomes corrupt and nothing worth. . . . The name of Virgin shal be exchanged for a farre more honorable name, A Wife.[40]

Donne labeled monastic enthusiasts, such as Jerome, "semi-heretiks" because of their undervaluation of marriage.[41] Ascetic mortification of the flesh is, he held, an offense to the Son of God who was pleased to assume the human body.[42] Donne faulted ascetics for misunderstanding the mutual relation of soul and body:

> Consider that man is not a soule alone, but a body too; . . . he is not sent into this world to live out of it, but to live in it. . . . Though we must love God with all our soule, yet it is not with our soule alone; our body also must testifie and express our love, not onely in a reverentiall humiliation thereof . . . but the discharge of our bodily duties, and the sociable offices of our callings, towards one another; not to run away from that Service of God by hiding our selves in a superstitious Monastery.[43]

The Counter-Reformation

After the Protestant Reformers and depreciated celibacy, the Catholic Church was troubled by the popular results. Consequently, Paul III assembled the Council of Trent in northern Italy to condemn the Protestant Reformation and to improve clerical morality. The Council received a report that 96 percent of Bavarian priests had concubines or clandestine wives.[44] An Austrian inspector in 1563 found a typical monastery to be composed of nine monks, seven concubines, two "wives," and eight children.[45] In 1542, Archbishop Albrecht of Brandenburg admitted to a papal representative that all his priests were living in concubinage, but they would become Lutherans if he tried to do something about it.[46] Bavarian Duke Albrecht V and German Emperor Ferdinand, both ardent Catholics, advocated the abrogation of clerical celibacy. But the bishops believed that the best means for eliminating sexual immorality was to apply more sanctions to canon laws than their medieval counterparts had enacted. Pius IV, the "father of three natural children,"[47] presided over the council at the end of its eighteen years of sessions. In 1563, he made this harsh declaration: "If anyone says that it is not better and more godly to remain in virginity or celibacy than to marry, let him be accursed."[48] That inferiority of marriage decree, along with a reaffirmation that clerics cannot validly contract marriage, became the definitive position of Roman Catholicism for the next four centuries.

From his probe of Vatican documents, Peter De Rosa explains the Tridentine understanding of celibacy:

> The conservatives at Trent . . . said that without celibacy the pope would be nothing more than the Bishop of Rome. In brief, the papal system would collapse without the unqualified allegiance of the clergy; celibacy alone could guarantee that sort of allegiance. Celibacy, on Trent's own admission, was not and never was primarily a matter of chastity but of control. Clergy are the worker bees that enable the hive to function. Far from being first and foremost a way of serving God in freedom, Trent said it was a way of serving the institution through compulsion. Once a priest was ordained, he was a prisoner of the system. If he proved disloyal, he was unable to function even as a normal human being by marrying. . . . So, strangely, celibacy, which had to a large degree provoked the Reformation, now became the standard-bearer of the Catholic Counter-Reformation, the proof that Catholicism was not going to yield an inch to Protestants.[49]

To suppress secret marriages, the council decreed that weddings be conducted in the presence of a priest and two witnesses, and that permanent public records be made of them. Throughout the ancient era, marriage was entered into without a priest's blessing or a state license. All that was needed was an exchange of consent by a couple and, for those with close family ties, parental approval as well as dowry arrangements. To make the community aware of their new status, a wedding party usually followed to which friends were invited. The mutual pledge was then sealed by the honeymoon consummation.

In the medieval era, marriage had been elevated to a glorious church rite, largely due to anti-sex militant Jerome's mistranslating of *mysterion*. He followed the Ephesian letter writer's quotation of the Genesis definition of marriage as "two in one flesh" with the declaration that this is a *sacramentum* (Gen 2:24; Eph 5:31–32). Consequently, marriage is the only one of Catholicism's seven sacraments that is recognized by that name in the Latin New Testament. However, in spite of that classification, the church continued to view marriage as little more than a non-licentious way of reproducing humankind. Protestants had limited sacraments to the two initiated by Jesus, Baptism and the Eucharist; they thought of marriage as having been a sacred act from the creation of the first humans onward.

The Council of Trent did nothing to raise the status of women. In the seventeenth century, French priest Pierre de la Font wrote, "The apostles rightly found it too difficult and onerous to have to keep a woman by one's side; . . . hence it was more tolerable to resist the natural inclinations that lead to marriage than to make oneself constantly suffer the mad and outlandish behavior of a woman." And Jesuit Antoine Vieira warned:

> Of all the miseries that overcome us, all bodily hardships, spiritual vices, all these woes of today and of eternity, these grievous consequences of original sin, what is the primary cause? A woman, a wife, and not an adulteress. . . . All the sorrows, diseases, private and public disasters, plagues, famines, wars . . . can only have their prime source in the disobedience of woman, who was given to man by God Himself.[50]

Attempts by inquisitors to root out clerical sodomists after Trent were not very effective:

> In Seville, where sodomy prosecutions were left to civil authority, a Jesuit active as prison chaplain between 1578 and 1616 noted the high incidence of sodomy in the religious orders and the diocesan priesthood. He reports the view that Jesuits rarely sin with women because they can so easily find partners among their students or novices. . . . One priest is accused of murdering boys in the religious house so that they could not inform against him—a charge he continued to deny even when he confessed to have sexual relations with eleven young men. . . . Members of religious orders were often protected by their superiors . . . in prosecutions of sodomy.[51]

❦

Beginning with Lateran IV in 1215, confession to a priest was required at least once a year. In the centuries to follow, the practice increased and became an effective means of controlling parishioners. After the Council of Trent's crackdown on the lax discipline of priests, efforts were made to remove scandal from the confessional. To curtail sexual abuse on the premises of the church, the confessional box with a partition between priest and kneeling penitent was introduced. But that did little to stop the exchanging of absolution for sexual favors, as Henry Lea has amply documented.[52]

Stephen Haliczer's archival research also details the way in which the penance sacrament was profaned during and after individual confessions. The Inquisition prosecuted cases of misconduct by priests from 1561 to 1820 but failed to halt the rising levels of sexual solicitation. In Spain Haliczer found the names of thousands of men in holy orders who were accused of such behavior;[53] the number of those who were involved but never accused is impossible to estimate. Usually an aggrieved penitent recognized the futility of bringing charges against a soliciting priest because there was usually no witness, and church courts tended to side with the word of a holy man rather than with a woman or boy who brought testimony of unchaste activity.

Confessors sometimes engaged in prurient inquiry designed primarily for satisfying their own need for sexual excitement.[54] A woman was often prone to confide more in her priest than in her mother or husband about repressed desires. A nineteenth-century confessor published standard questions asked of women, which included: "Have you desired to commit fornication or adultery, and how often?" "Have you ever endeavored to excite your own passions?"[55] Haliczer attributes this abusive treatment of penitents to a "revolt against celibacy on the part of many members of the clergy." The more the hierarchy attempted to reform parish priests the worse the situation became:

> The demands of celibacy proved too great for many priests, and with ordinary sexual and social outlets having been largely circumscribed, the confessional was left as the only place where they could make contact with women and talk with them personally and intimately. By sharply repressing the sexual activity of the clergy and placing their moral conduct under the control of episcopal officials, and by insisting that priests demand an exact and detailed accounting of sins, the Church itself had created the objective conditions for solicitation in the confessional.[56]

Priests approached Voltaire in hopes that he would confess and receive absolution before he died while holding views they deemed blasphemous. The story is told that when one confessor visited him, Voltaire asked him for his biblical authority to serve in that capacity. In response, the priest trotted out the proof text, "Confess your sins to one another" (Jas 5:16). Convinced by the citation, Voltaire proceeded to disclose many sins. After the priest gave absolution and started to leave, Voltaire reminded him that they had only completed half of the New Testament injunction. The satirist admitted that he had confessed his sins in order to learn about the priest's sins that were likely more intriguing. Voltaire accurately understood that confession was initially intended to be a two-way interchange between Christians. But the sacrament of penance, judging from the penitential manuals, had become focused on confessors listening to sexual peccadilloes and had viewed it as a mutually humbling occasion for sharing remorse for wrongdoing. Voltaire may have fancied that he would hear a priest's confession along the lines of his amorous story in *Candide*. That novel tells of a pretty boy who becomes, as a Jesuit novice, engaged in "the most tender friendship" with his superior. Later he is discovered naked in a Turkish steam bath with a Muslim.[57]

Edward Beecher, a nineteenth-century Protestant minister, expressed with some compassion the dilemma that the confessional poses for Catholic priests:

> These unhappy men, thus condemned through life to contend with those powerful impulses which God has implanted in their breasts, are . . . deliberately, remorselessly, and constantly thrust into the very centre of the fiery furnace of temptation. This is done by requiring them to hear the confessions of all their flock, in which, of course, are included those of females of all ages. . . . They are required by their theological teachers and text books to make the most minute examinations as to the thoughts, imaginations, desires, and acts of every female who comes to confessional. . . . Satanic ingenuity could not devise a system better adapted to corrupt and debase the clerical body.[58]

A nineteenth-century researcher noted that Catholics excommunicate those who express creedal deviations, but "when confessors seduce their female penitents in confession, it is only necessary that she should change her confessor! The confessor, on the other hand, is not censurable in any degree, unless he falls oftener than 'three or four times a month.'"[59] William Hogan, who served as a priest in Ireland as well as in America and became a chaplain for the New York legislature in the nineteenth century, exposed the "woman-trap" confessional: "Every nun has a confessor [and] . . . there is scarcely one of them who has not been herself debauched by her confessor. . . . Every confessor has a concubine, and there are very few of them who have not several." Hogan claimed that the three priests he worked with in Albany fathered at least sixty children, many by married women. They heard confession in the sacristy, a room back of the altar that could be locked to protect the Eucharist elements stored there. But priests also locked the room from within so they could engage with impunity in seductions after confessions.[60]

Mark Twain reported another account of confessional-related scandals based on what he was told by a Carmelite who had resigned his church position in 1872 to marry:

> The confessional's chief amusement has been seduction—in all the ages of the Church. Pere Hyacinth testifies that of a hundred priests confessed by him, ninety-nine had used the confessional effectively for the seduction of married women and young girls. One priest confessed that of nine hundred girls and women who he had served as father confessor in his time, none had escaped his lecherous embrace but three elderly and the homely. The official list of questions which the priest is required to ask will overmasteringly excite any woman who is not a paralytic.[61]

Priestly pederasty was practiced in the Victorian era but, like all matters pertaining to sexuality, it was usually mentioned in hushed tones, if at all. Even so, *The Priest and the Acolyte* was published in 1894 about a curate's seduction of a pubescent boy. The confessional became the site for his homoerotic incitation and performance. The priest idealizes his passion in terms of "reverence" toward the beloved boy. In discussing that story and similar Victorian ones in *Decadence and Catholicism*, Ellis Hanson responds to those who cannot understand why gay men become priests, "The real question ought to be why straight men become priests." He points to such appealing factors for gays as "public trust and respect, freedom from the social pressure to marry, opportunities for intimacy with boys, passionate friendship and cohabitation with likeminded men." Hanson shows how the Catholic priesthood is "one of the most attractive occupations available to men who love boys." He finds it ironical that "the Roman Catholic Church may well be the world's most homophobic institution, but it also may well be the world's largest employer of lesbians and gay men."[62]

⊚⧫⊚

Latin American priests have long been noted for their sexual activity, and the Vatican was able to ferret out this information in 1899: "Of 18,000 priests, 3,000 were living in regular wedlock, 4,000 in concubinage with their so-called housekeepers, and some 1,500 in relations more or less open with women of doubtful reputation."[63] On a visit to Mexico around 1850, Hogan interviewed priests who described fellow priests as "chaste" who provided for their children and concubines with whom they had lived for years. One such priest in Veracruz with a good reputation "kept three sisters, the eldest not over 25, and had children by each of them." Hogan also told of hospitals in Paris, Madrid, and Dublin attached to convents where maternity care was given to nuns and other women impregnated by priests. He recommended such facilities for American cities so there would be fewer strangled infants and abortions of fetuses sired by priests.[64] American priests were involved in comparatively fewer such scandals at that time, which Lea attributes to Catholics being kept in line by "antagonistic Churches" surrounding them in the predominantly Protestant nation.[65]

A novel about priestly seductions written in Portugal in 1875 has become the basis for the most popular film ever made in Mexico. *The Crime of Father Amaro*, released in 2003, depicts realistically practices that have continued in many Latino communities. A bishop assigns an idealistic seminary graduate to a mentor who preaches about the virtue of celibacy while carrying on an affair with a businesswoman. The new priest's carnal cravings arise on hearing her daughter's steamy confession, and consensual sex follows. Young Amaro is subsequently condemned—not for being unchaste, but for preaching and practicing Jesus' gospel to the poor.

Cardinal James Gibbons, a distinguished nineteenth-century American, perverted the biblical treatment of sexuality by asserting that Jesus chose his mother and his apostles based on their virginity. Moreover, after ascending on high, he selected a large band of virgin angels to surround his throne. That amazing distortion concluded, "Not only did our Lord thus manifest while on earth a marked predilection for virgins, but he exhibits the same preference for them in heaven."[66] According to the New Testament, as we have noted, most of the apostles were married and church officers were expected to marry, but that does not prevent the *New Catholic Encyclopedia* from falsely asserting that "many of the early clergy practiced celibacy by choice, after the example of Christ and most of the apostles."[67]

❧

Many Christians in the modern era have treated earthly passion and divine love as polar concepts because they view Christianity through the distorting lens of Augustine. Prominent nineteenth-century historian Jacob Burckhardt wrote: "Sensual enjoyment is a direct contradiction of Christianity. . . . Asceticism and its complete realization in the monastic life is the New Testament taken literally."[68] Jesuit Wilhelm Bertrams defended celibacy by affirming, "it is more precious to give all one's love to God than to share it with a human being."[69] A similar dichotomy was made by the celebrated Søren Kierkegaard, a rare Lutheran celibate. Believing that divine and human loves are exclusive, he entered in his journal, "Every time we see celibacy from love of God we see an effort to comply with God's intention."[70] He suppressed his ardent desire to marry his fiancée and remained a celibate.[71] In explaining why he opted for the single status, Kierkegaard gave this rationale: "To love God a man must give up all egoism, and first and foremost the potentiated egoism of the propagation of the species, the giving of life. . . . So God wishes to have celibacy because he wishes to be loved."[72]

Kierkegaard approved of Luther's rejection of a marital distinction between clergy and laity. But he applied the doctrine of the priesthood of all believers in this manner: "It is not that the priest should be unmarried, but that the Christian should be unmarried."[73] Kierkegaard, like Marcion, thought that Christians should oppose marriage because it is designed to continue normal worldly activities.[74] He appealed to the alleged celibacy of Jesus as his ultimate support: "Christianity recommends the single state, which the Pattern exemplifies. . . . I am unable to comprehend how it can occur to any man to unite being a Christian with being married."[75]

Viewing Kierkegaard's proposition, "to love God is to hate what is human," Jewish philosopher Martin Buber calls it a desecration of the biblical ethic.[76] Moreover, Kierkegaard's celibacy advocacy could be catastrophic to the church if her membership took his zealotry seriously. Only non-Christians would be left if celibacy were the modus operandi for the "priesthood of all believers." For several centuries a consensus had been developing that Kant's categorical imperative of universality is basic to morality. It involves each person asking what would be the outcome if everyone were to do what he or she has in mind. If the moral agent cannot give the green light for all to act in a generally similar way, then it is not right for that person to engage in the action. To reject the family structure that has evolved for mammals to reproduce and nurture their kind appears to be unethical by the Kantian rule—even though Kant himself chose life-long bachelorhood.

In a major twentieth-century theological book entitled *Agape and Eros,* Lutheran bishop Anders Nygren followed Kierkegaard in postulating, without biblical warrant, a fundamental opposition between human passion and divine love.[77] Russian writer Leo Tolstoy also expressed a viewpoint similar to that of Kierkegaard, "Sexual love, marriage, is a service of self, and consequently in any case an obstacle to the service of God and man, and therefore from a Christian point of view a fall, a sin."[78]

In the first half of the twentieth century, policies and practices pertaining to celibacy in the church were unchanged. Emmett McLoughlin, who became one of the most effective of all priests in helping to improve the health of the poor of all races, tells about his twelve years in a California seminary after World War I. His Franciscan superior instructed him, "You must always remember that all women are vicious and malicious." All mail that he received or sent was examined to see if any affection was expressed from or to a girl, all of whom were untouchables. To crush carnal desires he accepted without complaint this discipline:

> There hangs, inside the door of each cell or bedroom, a scourge or whip. It is made of several strands of heavy cord, each knotted at the end. Each Monday, Wednesday, and Friday evening at 5:45 o'clock we closed the doors of our cells; to the chant of the "Miserere" we disrobed and "scourged our flesh to bring it into submission." The Superior patrolled the corridors to listen to the sounds of beating—the assurance of compliance.[79]

McLoughlin observed that in spite of that training, or because of it, illicit indulgences abounded: "No priest who has heard priests' confessions and has any respect for the truth will deny that sexual affairs are extremely common among the clergy. The principal concern of the hierarchy seems to be that priests should keep such cases quiet and refrain from marriage."[80] Edward Henriques, a Catholic priest who became an Episcopal priest, draws on his experience for this similar insight:

> Is it not significant that canon law imposes no punishment whatever upon such extra-parochial diversions as clerical fornication, adultery, sodomy, flagrant promiscuity, or any other form of sexual aberration, nor even for continued and prolonged concubinage, but only for "committing" matrimony? . . .

The law of celibacy has engendered more sexual deviation, more promiscuity, than it has ever fostered virtue.[81]

In 1918, the celibacy law was given this reformulation, "Clerics in major orders may not marry and they are bound by the obligation of chastity to the extent that sinning against it constitutes a sacrilege."[82] Yet the twentieth-century drive toward recovering the long lost outlook on clerical sexuality of early Christianity was beginning with the lower Catholic clergy. In 1920, some Czechoslovakian priests audaciously attacked the Vatican in an effort to express their right to marry. They were turned back by this countercharge of Pope Benedict XV:

> The Latin church owes its flourishing vitality . . . to the celibacy of the clergy. . . . Never will the Holy See in any way even lighten or mitigate the obligation of this holy and salutary law of clerical celibacy, not to speak of abolishing it. We also deny . . . that the innovations of a "democratic" character for whom introduction into ecclesiastical discipline some are agitating, can ever be approved by the Holy See.[83]

Recognizing that church leaders through most of Christian history are the cultural equivalent to the Pharisees of Jesus' day, it may not be overly presumptive to imagine him expressing indignation over the celibacy law by saying, "Woe to you popes, you load men with intolerable burdens and will not lift a finger to lighten the load" (Luke 11:46). Other scriptural words may also be germane that were originally spoken in response to church leaders who wished to add requirements that were counter to the gospel of grace. Peter asked the Jerusalem church, "Why do you provoke God by imposing on these Christians a burden that neither we nor our ancestors have been able to bear?" (Acts 15:10).

Pius XI, in encouraging priests to diminish living as humans, quoted in a 1935 encyclical the first words attributed to Jesus, which were spoken to his parents when he was growing in divine and human wisdom (Luke 2:49, 52): "Since God is spirit, it is only fitting that he who consecrates to God's service should in some ways free himself from his body. . . . Ought he not to be obliged to live as far as possible like a pure spirit? The priest who ought to be entirely 'about the Lord's business,' ought he not to be entirely detached from earthly things, so that his life be lived entirely in heaven?"[84]

Papal decrees from the fourth century until the mid-twentieth century have used laws in the Bible pertaining to Hebrew priests to ground sexual abstinence for priests. Pius XI informed his priests that they were nobly following the Levitical priests, citing Lev 8:33–35 to prove that those priests were sexually abstinent before performing sacred functions. Actually, there is no explicit reference to sexual abstinence in those verses. Moreover, since all Hebrew priests were required to marry (Lev 21:13–15), it is absurd to appeal to them in buttressing a doctrine of perpetual priestly celibacy. In the same encyclical, Pius also appealed to Cicero's reference to sexual abstinence among pagan Roman priests. Pagan practices are the only honest historical ground on which to establish sacerdotal celibacy. Pius XII was the last pope to attempt to connect celibacy with Levitical laws of purity.[85] Priests sully the sacrament, he believed, if they touch the elements on the Eucharist table with hands that have fondled impure sex organs.

In a 1954 encyclical, Pius XII quoted approvingly words addressed to virgins by Cyprian, a third-century church father: "What we shall be, you have already begun to be. You already possess in this world the glory of the resurrection; you pass through the world without suffering its contagion. In preserving virginal chastity, you are the equals of the angels of God."[86] The pope also stated: "Virginity . . . is a state superior to that of matrimony. But . . . this superiority does not in any way decrease the beauty and grandeur of married life."[87] Pius XII invidiously compared the values of married couples to those of holy virgins:

> Their hearts are divided between love of God and love of their spouse, and beset by gnawing cares, and so by reason of the duties of their married state they can hardly be free to contemplate the divine. . . . Persons who desire to consecrate themselves to God's service embrace the state of virginity as a liberation, in order to be more entirely at God's disposition and devoted to the good of their neighbor. . . . Holy virginity surpasses marriage in excellence.[88]

Marriage, unlike virginity, is a sacramental state in Catholicism, but higher value has incoherently been placed on celibacy. Kenneth Woodward comments on the absence of happily married Christians among the saints: "No one has ever been beatified or canonized precisely for being an exemplary Christian spouse."[89] Richard McBrien similarly observes that most officially recognized saints are celibate even though "there have been far more married people than monks and virgins who have been luminous examples of Christain discipleship." He asks, "If the great majority of recognized saints had never expressed love for another human being in sexual intimacy, or if they manifested a disdain and contempt for such intimacy, what message would that send to the world and to the Church regarding the sanctity of marriage and the sacramental and cocreative character of human sexuality?"[90]

Seminaries were a Tridentine product that changed little from the six-teenth to the twentieth century. As ecclesiologist McBrien points out, they encouraged "an academic and spiritual formation for priests in isolation from the ordinary workday world of the rest of the People of God."[91] Richard Ginder, a seminarian in the mid-twentieth century, testified that he and his fellow seminarians lived in a monastic environment and were "unbelieveably innocent about sex." He has written about the "psychologi-cal castration" that was involved in accepting the papal demand to become spiritual eunuchs, "The seminarian swears before witnesses and signs his oath averring that he is a completely free agent, that he is fully aware of what he is doing and of its nature, and that he forever renounces marriage and all use of sex, 'so help me God and these his holy Gospels on which I rest my hand.'"[92]

A priest testifies to the "brainwashing" he received:

Like the typical candidate for the priesthood, I entered the seminary at the age of 14. For the next 12 years I was isolated from the world. . . . I was instructed to avoid the company of young women, never to be alone with one, never to have a date. . . . People speak about such young men as mak-ing a free, deliberate, solemn promise. But how could we be said to be free when we knew virtually nothing about love, marriage, the conjugal life or the joys of parenthood?[93]

Those seminary students were usually directed toward ideals of the holy order before coming to psychosexual maturity and before recogniz-ing fully its price in never loving a woman physically or fathering chil-dren. They pledged lifelong sexual abstinence, having had virtually no sex education or opportunities to recognize their sexual identities. Kenneth Mitchell, director of religion and psychiatry at the Menninger Founda-tion, has focused on problems arising with most adolescents on the priest-hood track: "It is impossible to make meaningful decisions about the intimate sharing of your physical or psychological self with another person when you have not yet discovered what or who your self is."[94] Mitchell stated that his opinion was influenced by Eric Erikson, the eminent psy-chiatrist, who placed the intimacy phase of development at about the age of thirty.

Leo Lehmann, who has worked with fellow priests on several conti-nents, has also written of the unhealthy psychological effects of mandatory clerical celibacy: "Its victims have to confess that, far from freeing them from the sexual urge, it actually breeds a very ferment of impurity in the mind. It is the boast of the Roman Catholic Church that priestly celibacy makes its clergy something more than men—that it makes them supernatural, almost angelic. The simple people readily believe this. In truth it makes them something less than men."[95]

Catholics have traditionally emphasized separating boys with an interest in the priesthood from girls before their tempestuous teens. Boys were enrolled in seminary boarding schools near the age of puberty, where they remained until ordination about a dozen years later. "Familiarity breeds attempts and children" appears to have been the warning of seminary administrators. Sex instruction consisted of slogans such as "Beware of Punch and Judy" (a.k.a., "booze and broads"), either of which can be debilitating. Through much of the twentieth century, Otto Weininger's book *Sex and Character* was influential in Catholic seminaries.[96] He claims that Jesus, by being celibate, emancipated himself from women.[97] Weininger speaks of "woman's incapacity for truth," and how she "is a liar by nature."[98] "However degraded a man may be, he is immeasurable above the most superior woman."[99] Polly Blue writes: "Priestly celibacy . . . seems, to many of us, to draw an improbably large number of men who actively and passionately dislike women and are happiest in a world that claims a divine right to contain and exclude them."[100]

When everlasting virginity is the goal of training, sexual ignorance is assumed to be its best protector. Consequently, inductees customarily leave cloistered seminaries unprepared to cope with the temptations from which they have been sheltered and can be easily overwhelmed by a natural yearning for physical intimacy. Lea described the unintended results of such seminaries:

> The Church . . . turns loose young men, at the age when the passions are the strongest, trained in the seminary and unused to female companionship, to occupy a position in which they are brought into the closest and most dangerous relations with women who regard them as beings gifted with supernatural powers and holding in their hands the keys of heaven and hell. Whatever may have been the ardour with which the vows were taken, the youth thus exposed to temptations hitherto unknown finds his virtue rudely assailed when in the confessional female lips repeat to him the story of lustful longings, and he recognises in himself instincts and passions which are only the stronger by reason of their . . . repression.[101]

Vatican II and Aftermath

Following Pius XII, John XXIII (1958–65) opened windows of the Catholic Church to let renewing winds of the Spirit and modern culture blow through. He recognized that "the celibacy injunction . . . is written in erasable Latin, not carved in granite."[102] Just as Pope Siricius was the first to attempt to impose celibacy by simply writing a letter to another bishop in the fourth century, so another pope could as easily discard it. That is the advantage of a church in which the rule is from the top down. In 1963, he admitted to French philosopher Etienne Gilson that the law was not a divine imperative but a matter of church discipline that could be changed or eliminated:

> The thought of those young priests who bear so bravely the burden of ecclesiastical celibacy causes me constant suffering. . . . It often seems . . . as if voices were demanding that the Church free them from this burden. . . . Ecclesiastical celibacy is not a dogma. The Scriptures do not impose it. It is even easy to effect the change. I take up a pen, I sign a decree, and, the next day, priests who wish to may get married.[103]

Pope John disclosed that he was not ready to issue such a decree but he anticipated that celibacy would be debated by the more than 2,500 bishops and cardinals he had assembled in 1962 from around the globe for the Second Vatican Council. He informed them, "Human beings have the right to choose freely the state of life which they prefer, and therefore the right to set up a family, with equal rights and duties for man and woman, and also the right to follow a vocation to the priesthood or the religious life."[104] The pope charged the council with the need for "todaying" (*aggiornamento*) church institutions, but he died after the first session and before any revolutionary changes in celibacy were effected. Hans Kung believes that the implication of the liberal pontiff's expression on human rights would have been carried out and celibacy would have been made voluntary had he lived to the end of Vatican II.[105]

Vatican II did follow Aquinas and John XXIII and recognize that celibacy is not essential to priesthood.[106] It declared that perpetual sexual abstinence

> is not demanded by the very nature of the priesthood, as is evident from the practice of the primitive Church and from the tradition of the Eastern Churches. In these Churches, in addition to all bishops and those others

who by a gift of grace choose to observe celibacy, there also exist married priests of outstanding merit. While this most sacred Synod recommends ecclesiastical celibacy, it in no way intends to change the different discipline which lawfully prevails in the Eastern Churches. It lovingly exhorts all those who have received the priesthood after marriage to persevere in their sacred vocation, and continue to spend their lives fully and generously for the flock committed to them.[107]

Several thousand Roman Catholic priests—belonging to the Eastern Rite in countries such as Lebanon, Iraq, Syria, India, Hungary, Slovakia, and the Ukraine—marry with the approval of the Vatican. More than 90 percent of Ukrainian priests marry. Nestorians in those countries allow priests to marry after ordination as well as before. Married priests in the Eastern Rite are treated as neither second-rate nor as less holy. Indeed, they are among the few priests who are able to receive all seven sacraments of the church during their lifetimes. Americans know little about these priests because they were banned from serving in the United States by a 1929 Vatican decree.

But then, after finding praiseworthy Eastern married priests, the Vatican II document goes on to uphold the traditional celibacy requirement: "In the Latin Church, it was imposed by law on all who were to be promoted to sacred orders. This legislation, to the extent that it concerns those who are destined for the priesthood, this most holy Synod again approves and confirms." An unfounded assurance is given, "Perfect continence . . . is never denied to those who ask."[108]

As we have seen, the basic justification for celibacy before Vatican II was that holy men would be defiled if they touched a woman's genitals. It was presumed that Hebrew priests had the same purity requirement and that it was continued for Christian priests, but this base reason was omitted from the council's rationale. Dropping the tie with ritual cleanliness may have been due to the influence of Dutch Dominican Edward Schillebeeckx, who made plain to the Vatican II bishops who had invited him to speak that the office of priest had wrongly developed. In the New Testament, he explained, the church was the priestly people of God but its leaders were not priests. Moreover, the Levitical ceremonial cleanliness rules were not in line with the gospel because Jesus had rejected the purity laws of Judaism, including those pertaining to menstrual impurity. The notion that wives are contaminants and destructive to priestly sanctity is alien to original Christianity.[109] Accordingly, a commentary on the updated canon laws published in 2000 states: "Untenable motives for celibacy—arising from notions of cultic purity or from a subliminal deprecation of the body and of sexuality—are avoided, motives still commonly mentioned until quite recently in official documents."[110]

Beginning with Vatican II, the eunuch verse from Matthew's gospel has been officially cited as the main rationale for celibacy. Several of its documents refer to the verse as the first reason for priestly celibacy.[111] Vatican II has also continued the traditional claim that celibate priests are "a vivid sign of that future world . . . in which the children of the resurrection will neither marry nor take wives."[112] Accordingly, more than half of American bishops agreed with this statement, "The primary reason for celibacy is that it witnesses to the future life with God."[113]

Only a small beginning was made by Vatican II to correct the damage done by curtailing clerical marriage, beginning with the first Latin Church council in the fourth century and continuing for sixteen centuries. In the context of discussing Christian marriage, Vatican II exhorted seminarians to recognize "the superiority of virginity consecrated to Christ" as they "attach themselves to God by a total gift of body and soul."[114] Celibates are declared to be more perfectly bonded to Christ.[115]

The traditional Catholic view of marriage as primarily for progeny is by no means completely dissipated in the Vatican II pronouncements. For example, "It is not good for man to be alone" belongs to the Eden story context that gives companionship, not procreation, as the reason for marriage. But Vatican II interprets the Genesis verse to mean "children are really the supreme gift of marriage," a view that expresses the deficient understanding of Ambrose and Augustine.[116]

But Vatican II recognized that in marriage a man and a woman should "experience the meaning of their oneness and attain to it with growing perfection day by day,"[117] and that holy lives could be lived apart from a commitment to celibacy:

> Married couples and Christian parents should follow their own proper path to holiness by faithful love, sustaining one another in grace throughout the entire length of their lives. . . . By such lives, they signify and share in that very love with which Christ loved His Bride and because of which He delivered Himself up on her behalf. A like example, but one given in a different way, is that offered by widows and single people, who are able to make great contributions toward holiness and apostolic endeavor in the Church.[118]

That stance would have great effect on Catholics in the generation following the council. As Peter Steinfels observes: "The status that celibacy once enjoyed as the model of holiness, to be routinely required of every parish priest and Eucharistic minister, is simply incompatible with the church's currently affirmed Catholic humanism. If the church wants to restore celibacy to their former status, there is really only one practical way to do it: demote marriage to the second-class standing it once had."[119]

Vatican II especially affected nuns because their status as saintly virtuosi was nullified by the recognition that sacred vocations should be associated with all who have been baptized. The council declared that the laity are also equally "called to the fullness of the Christian life and to the perfection of charity."[120] For eighteen centuries, Catholics held that "only vowed members of religious orders could achieve true spiritual perfection."[121] When nuns could no longer contemplate their exalted ecclesiastical status, little was left to make their office appealing—material benefits were miserable and assignments were often demeaning. Since the sisters would continue to be excluded from the priesthood even if celibate, thousands of convents were emptied.

John XXIII sped up the procedure for approving priests who wished to leave their ecclesiastical duties, usually to marry. As a result the curia was overwhelmed with petitions for honorable discharges, and 46,302 dispensations were granted between 1963 and 1983.[122]

It is estimated that at least as many resigned from the active ministry to marry who never made a time-consuming request to the Vatican, or who left after the request was refused. There have been approximately 100,000 priests worldwide whose vocation has been abruptly wrecked, mainly by the celibacy issue. David Rice states dramatically, "Pope John's dream of a Church renewed has shattered into one hundred thousand pieces, each of those pieces a priest who left his ministry, which is almost a quarter of all the active priests in the world."[123]

Those formal dispensations have been called "laicization," meaning the reduction of a priest to the status of a layman. But the Council of Trent had made it clear that priesthood is permanent by enacting this unequivocal canon law, "If anyone would say that a validly ordained priest of the New Testament can become a layman, let him be condemned."[124] Also, supreme Catholic scholar Aquinas stated, "No ecclesiastical prelate can make . . . a priest not a priest, even though the prelate may for some particular cause prohibit the exercise of sacred orders."[125] Media references to "former" priests display ignorance of Catholic doctrine, which bestows on priests an ontological state that remains forever. During the ordination ritual the candidate lies prostrate on a cathedral floor before rising to receive "the laying on of hands" and the bishop's pronouncement, "Thou art a priest forever." That sentence from the Bible was used to describe Melchizedek, a Canaanite priest-king (Gen 14:18; Ps 110:4). Ordination remains valid even after a bishop has dismissed a priest from his work in the institutional church.

In order to circumvent the indissolubility of both ordination and marriage according to canon law, the church has devised duplicitous legal fictions to permit priests and spouses to break their commitments. They must apply for annulment and confess that their ordination or marriage was invalid. But many priests are reluctant to declare that their service to the church was not genuine, even as spouses with children find it untruthful and humiliating to state that they have been illegitimately living in sin in order to be approved for separation—what secular law calls divorce.

Paul VI, who presided over the last session of Vatican II in 1965, lacked his immediate predecessor's openness to changing ecclesiastical law. Catholicism's movement from Tridentine rigidity toward modernity and renewal reverted to sexual regressiveness. Recognizing that some bishops wanted to put celibacy on the council's agenda, he made a preemptive strike by removing it as an item for discussion. The pope informed the council members: "It is not opportune to debate publicly this topic which requires the greatest prudence, and is so important. Our intention is not only to preserve this ancient law as far as possible, but to strengthen its observance."[126] Garry Wills comments, "He turned even the Council's bishops into intellectual eunuchs when he said that they could not question the celibacy ordinances."[127] Finding the topic too delicate for consideration, the pope did not even avail himself of information from researchers as to the nature of its current problems.

More than 99 percent of the 2,254 sheep-like council bishops followed their papal shepherd and voted for the status quo on celibacy. But one protestor, Cardinal Saigh of Antioch, wrote the pope a personal letter in which he candidly said: "The priesthood must not be sacrificed to celibacy, but celibacy to the priesthood. . . . It is useless to close our eyes to this problem or consider it taboo. Your Holiness knows very well that truths on which silence is maintained turn to poison."[128]

Eugene Kennedy, a psychological therapist of priests, employs medical metaphors to express the pope's response to the chronic illness caused by celibacy:

Apparently concerned that the world's bishops might attempt diagnosis and treatment of this unhealed sexual wound, Paul VI judged it to be inoperable, sewed up the incision, and sent the patient back to his uncomfortable existence. . . . Long before the U.S. Armed Forces, the official Church sponsored a "Don't ask, don't tell" policy regarding the sexual behavior of priests. They would rather not look at the wound than admit either that it existed or their inability to heal it.[129]

In 1967, Paul VI issued *Priestly Celibacy*, in which "the golden law of sacred celibacy" is hailed as "a brilliant jewel" undiminished in value over time. The intransigent tone of the encyclical shattered the widespread expectation of major reform after Vatican II, and it triggered an exodus of more than one thousand priests annually. The pope's lauding of celibacy as the crown jewel of the church was right in one respect; its decimating of the priesthood was most costly. There was nearly a forty-fold increase in the annual resignation rate for diocesan priests in the United States during the five years immediately after Vatican II compared with the two decades before. Most of that enormous increase was due to the desire of heterosexuals to marry.[130] Catholics became the only major religious group worldwide having serious problems in retaining an adequate supply of clergy.

Richard Schoenherr observed that generally it was not the case that the inferior priests left and the superior ones stayed:

> The losses sustained by the Church in terms of numbers are indeed great, but the loss in terms of quality may prove to be an equally important consideration. . . . In our national study of American priests we discovered that among those who left or are planning to leave there are higher proportions of more mature, better educated, more open and younger men than among those who were remaining in the active ministry.[131]

Paul VI focused on the large majority who remained, saying that "there are still today in God's holy Church, in every part of the world where she exercises her beneficent influence, great numbers of her ministers—subdeacons, deacons, priests, and bishops—who are living their life of voluntary and consecrated celibacy in the most exemplary way."[132] But psychiatrist Joseph English and Colman McCarthy, having studied the development of Catholic priests, expose the involuntary nature of priestly celibacy:

> The vocation to the priesthood and the vocation to celibacy are not the same, although the Church still markets them as a package deal. What happens, then, is that often a man accepts both the priesthood and celibacy consciously, but subconsciously he rejects celibacy. He might hate it, in fact, but because he loves serving as a priest, he will attempt to endure celibacy.

Spiritually, he thinks that he is yielding on a low plane to gain on a higher one. But psychologically, he is not. He lives on both planes simultaneously; and he is on a collision course with the two unresolved tensions within. Unless a young man about to be ordained is absolutely sold on the idea of celibacy and is as aware as possible of his own emotional and sexual needs, he is self-deceiving to become a priest. . . . There is no end-all solution to this agony of enforced celibacy, outside of a papal decree changing the rule.[133]

Prelates have long defended obligatory celibacy by claiming that those contemplating the priesthood choose it freely. Church law asserts: "For a person to be ordained, he must enjoy the requisite freedom. It is absolutely wrong to compel anyone, in any way or for any reason whatsoever, to receive orders or to turn away from orders anyone who is canonically suitable."[134] To that unequivocal statement Terrance Sweeney responds, "Rectors of seminaries the world over will admit that many seminarians promise celibacy, not as a spontaneous and full-hearted choice, but only because it is required for the priesthood."[135] He argues that it is wrong to bar any adults from marrying whenever the call to that state of life arises, for that is implied by this canon law, "All Christ's faithful have the right to immunity from any kind of coercion in choosing a state of life."[136]

It stretches the meaning of "voluntary" to say that a young man who is called to sacred orders is not coerced into making the demanded celibacy commitment. Some celibates point out that although there is a sense in which they were not forced to commit themselves to celibacy, freedom was largely lacking because it was a requirement for ordination. Charles Long tells of the forced option he faced, "During my seminary days . . . I had clearly decided what most young priests, I think, decide: that celibacy is not per se a good, but rather a necessary burden, a *conditio sine qua non* for entering the priesthood."[137] Many of those contemplating a career as a priest view the law of celibacy as more of an occupational hazard with which they must contend than as a liberating discipline they want to uphold.

Vatican II referred to "the inalienable human right to marry and beget children."[138] In accord with this, Paul VI succinctly asserted, "Where the inalienable right to marriage and procreation is lacking, human dignity has ceased to exist."[139] John O'Brien comments, "I believe His Holiness has aptly expressed in the briefest compass the most cogent and convincing argument for making clerical celibacy optional."[140] If a right is "inalienable," then no institution can morally abrogate it, whether it be in "the pursuit of happiness" or in the pursuit of a permanent partner at any stage of life. Paul VI was reinforcing a declaration made in papal encyclicals sent out in 1890 and 1930, "No human law can deprive man of the natural and original right to marry."[141] Since the church has always called the celibacy law a human law, it is surprising that three popes did not recognize the invalidity of a law that infringes on the privilege of priests to marry. Yet the church has continued to enforce Canon Law 1072, which trenchantly rules, "A marriage is invalid when attempted by clerics in sacred orders."

Prelates who have established canon law do not appear to have given priority to coherence of policy. Paul VI dealt with inconsistencies in his celibacy arguments by appealing to "higher logic." On the one hand, he stated that Jesus raised matrimony "to the dignity of a sacrament and of a mysterious symbol of his own union with the Church." On the other hand, the pope asserted that the priest, in rejecting marriage for himself, "takes on the likeness of Christ most perfectly, even in the love with which the eternal Priest has loved the Church His Body." So, is the love of Christ for his church best expressed in non-sacramental celibacy or in sacramental marriage?[142]

The celibacy affirmations of Paul VI amazed Anthony Padovano, who has a theology doctorate from Rome. He reasoned, "To declare that celibacy is a sign of total dedication implies that marriage is less. Was Peter not totally dedicated to Christ?" Padovano then questioned if the pope really accepts the doctrine of the incarnation of God in Christ: "To teach . . . that priests are more perfect the more they are removed from flesh and blood is a form of Gnosticism. . . . Should we not conclude that God should have become an angelic spirit to lead us rather than a human being? Would the priesthood fare better if it were made up of angels rather than people?"[143] Padovano found Paul VI typical of Christians who are unprepared to accept a Jesus who is like us in sexuality, even though the New Testament asserts that as we "share flesh and blood, he too shared the same things. . . . For clearly he did not come to help angels. . . . Therefore he had to become like his brothers in every respect so that he might be a merciful and faithful high priest" (Heb 2:14, 16–17).

The encyclical of Paul VI reviewed the argument about following the purity standard of Hebrew priests, but admitted that this argument was bankrupt. Recognition was tacitly given that what had been put forward by the papacy for sixteen centuries as a major reason for requiring celibacy cannot be grounded in the outlook of the early church. Following Vatican II, the pope's principal justification for priestly celibacy was Jesus' approval of the eunuch, to which four references are made. Yet, as we have seen, Christian scholars, beginning in the second century, have demonstrated its irrelevance to the issue, especially since the eunuch saying is addressed to individuals and not to a priestly group. Wills perceives: "This is the main text the Pope relies on to establish a scriptural basis for priestly celibacy. . . .

New Testament passages are twisted, omitted, extended, distorted, perverted to make them mean whatever the Pope wants them to mean."[144] No reference is made to the Apostle Paul's assertion of his right to marry or to his indication that the rest of the apostles and the Lord's brothers have exercised that apostolic prerogative (1 Cor 9:5). The pope gave preference to a saying of Jesus of questionable authenticity but disregarded a verse in Paul's letter that is undoubtedly apostolic.

Even though Paul VI recognized that contracting marriage before ordination has been acceptable for priests in the Eastern churches, he declared that the Holy Spirit has "supernaturally" caused the two branches of Catholicism to be different.[145] But he made no attempt to address why the Holy Spirit has acted inconsistently. The encyclical also made the astounding assertion that "the cause of the decrease in vocations to the priesthood is . . . the fact that individuals and families have lost their sense of God and of all that is holy."[146] Shifting the blame from the Vatican to the victims is a self-serving and unhelpful ploy.

Paul VI did not heed the pragmatic counsel that Catholic scholar Karl Rahner gave Vatican II, "If in practice you cannot obtain a sufficient number of priests in a given cultural setting without relinquishing celibacy, then the church must suspend the law of celibacy."[147] In his essay criticizing the pope's pontificating on celibacy, Catholic scholar Peter Riga reinforces Rahner's judgment: "There is only tragedy for the modern Church in that she is both losing and failing to attract the best men for the service of God's holy people. It is a question to be investigated by the whole Church and a consensus must be reached. This consensus cannot be attained if, in an encyclical on the subject, all are called upon now to keep silent because 'Peter has spoken.'"[148]

John O'Brien, the distinguished Notre Dame theology professor-priest, in response to Paul VI's encyclicals on celibacy and natural but not artificial birth control (often ridiculed as "Vatican roulette"), asked:

> Can anyone believe that if the majority of its priests and prelates, and particularly the pope, were married—as was the case with practically all the apostles and disciples—the Roman Church would not now be recommending something vastly more effective than the unreliable rhythm method for the regulation of births? Bachelors are seriously handicapped in trying to deal with a problem completely outside their range of experience. "Can a blind man lead a blind man? Will they not both fall into a pit?"[149]

Paul VI displayed his faithfulness to the sexual tradition of Catholicism in other ways. In 1970, he restored a rite that had not been practiced for the past millennium called "Consecrated to a Life of Virginity for Women Living in the World." The ceremony involves a simulated wedding between a virgin bride and Jesus. As of 2003, some fifteen hundred virgins have taken that vow of perpetual sexual abstinence while working at secular jobs.[150]

Also, Pope Paul was in accord with medieval theology in believing that sexual desire is always sinful. Following Aquinas, who implied that Jesus did not experience erections and never masturbated,[151] the Pope unhesitatingly pronounced masturbation "an intrinsically and seriously disordered act," linking it to "original sin" and to "loss of a sense of God."[152] Yet his declaration was an improvement on *The Dictionary of Moral Theology,* a 1962 Catholic publication that compounds reprehensible doctrine with a lie about the Bible. It states: "Direct voluntary pollution is properly called masturbation. . . . In the Holy Scriptures it is condemned as a sin which excludes a person from the Kingdom of Heaven."[153] Biblical interpreters have frequently confused Onan's unsanctioned coitus interruptus with masturbation (Gen 38:9). Celibate interpreters have attempted to give a masturbation identification to the enigmatic "thorn in the flesh" affliction that tormented Paul, which was provoked by an "angel of Satan" (2 Cor 12:7).[154] Paul VI's declaration admits that the Bible, which denounces sins galore, does not explicitly refer to masturbation. The Vatican's ban on masturbation, as well as on contraception, has been driven by the presumption that every seminal discharge should be potentially directed toward ovum fertilization.

Archbishop Joseph Bernardin, then president of the U.S. Conference of Catholic Bishops, welcomed the papal statement on masturbation as a fundamental proclamation of values.[155] A 1970s survey shows that more than half of American bishops agreed with this statement, "In most cases, deliberate masturbation is a mortal sin."[156] The discomfort level was especially increased for celibates who recognized that a mortal sin can result in eternal damnation if they were to die without repenting and confessing it. When a student asked one Catholic bishop why masturbation is a mortal sin, he was given this quaint reply, "If it wasn't men wouldn't get married and father children."[157]

In 1970, after years of intense discussion, Dutch priests by a 93 to 2 vote adopted a resolution that obligatory celibacy "must be abolished."[158] Cardinal Alfrink conveyed the opinion to the Vatican but found there no openness to consider the subject. Also that year, the admired Bishop James Shannon of Minnesota married and pleaded with Paul VI that he stop the "hemorrhaging" of the body of Christ by eliminating the man-made rule requiring priests to be bachelors.[159] In 1971, the National Federation of

Priests' Councils voted 193 to 18 to petition "that the choice between celibacy and marriage for priests now active in the ministry be allowed and the change begin immediately." But Catholicism is a rigid autocracy, so outcries from the overwhelming majority of American priests have been ineffective in causing the Vatican to reconsider its policy.

The ascetic Paul VI was in character in deciding that the third-century patron of passionate love would no longer be honored. During his reign, the Vatican dropped St. Valentine's Day as a time of official celebration. According to medieval legend, the Italian saint helped to unite lovers who were in difficult circumstances. Chaucer described it as a day when birds choose their mates, so it had become a day consecrated to romantic song and amorous action. Given all the Catholics with harsh passions who have been made and remain saints, some of whom have contributed to establishing the law of celibacy, was the removal of the popular St. Valentine from the church's calendar due to his encouragement of sexual passion?

But the celibacy requirement continued to have more to do with patriarchal power than with passionate sex. Charles Frazee concluded his historical treatment of priestly celibacy by reflecting on its persistence: "More enlightened attitudes towards sexuality and marriage have destroyed the primitive connection between sexual abstinence and ritual purity. . . . [But] popes and bishops generally resist change, still fearing that a married priesthood would diminish their power, an opinion which they have in common with their twelfth-century predecessors."[160]

Schoenherr concurred and provided a sociological perspective on the power structure of the Church:

> From a management point of view, it is in the best interests of the administrative subsystem of the Church, namely, the Pope and the bishops, to want to maintain the discipline of celibacy because . . . the restriction on marriage for priests creates a well-disciplined and easily controlled group of religious professionals who are ready to carry out Church responsibilities without being restricted by family duties.[161]

Notes

1. Andreas Karlstadt, *De Coelibatu* (Wittenberg, 1521), A4.

2. Peter Dykema and Heike Oberman, eds., *Anticlericalism* (Leiden: Brill, 1993), 456.

3. Luther's preface to Steffan Kligebeyl's *Von Priester Ehe* (Wittenberg, 1528).

4. Helmut Lehmann, ed., *Luther's Works* (Philadelphia: Muhlenberg, 1959), 44:248.

5. James Atkinson, ed., *Luther's Works* (Philadelphia: Fortress, 1966), 44:262.

6. Lehmann, *Luther's Works*, 36:260-61.

7. Atkinson, *Luther's Works*, 44:176.

8. Lehmann, *Luther's Works*, 36:388.

9. Titus 1:6; Jaroslav Pelikan, ed., *Luther's Works* (Saint Louis: Concordia, 1956–68), 29:18.

10. Pelikan, *Luther's Works*, 26:458–59.

11. Lehmann, *Luther's Works*, 54:3777.

12. Atkinson, *Luther's Works*, 44:178.

13. D. Martin, *Luthers Werke* (Weimar, 1891), 12:94.

14. Richard Friedenthal, *Luther* (New York: Harcourt, 1970), 432–33.

15. Roland Bainton, *Here I Stand* (New York: Mentor, 1955), 225–29.

16. Pelikan, *Luther's Works*, 13:329.

17. Joseph Blenkinsopp, *Celibacy, Ministry, Church* (New York: Herder, 1968), 43.

18. Hilton Oswald, ed., *Luther's Works* (St. Louis: Concordia, 1973), 28:13.

19. Bruce Gordon, ed., *Protestant History and Identity in Sixteenth-Century Europe* (Brookfield, VT: Ashgate, 1996), 1:143.

20. Ulrich Zwingli, *Samtliche Werke* (Berlin: Schwetschke, 1905), 7:110.

21. John Calvin, *Institutes of the Christian Religion* (1559), 2:1:9; 4:19:36.

22. Jerome, *Letters* 123:13.

23. John Calvin, *The First Epistle of Paul the Apostle to the Corinthians* (Grand Rapids: Eerdmans, 1960), 11.

24. Calvin, *Institutes*, 4:12:23–27.

25. William Bouwsma, *John Calvin* (New York: Oxford, 1988), 23.

26. Calvin, *Institutes*, 2:8:43.

27. Bouwsma, *Calvin*, 60.

28. John Calvin, *Theological Treatises* (Philadelphia: Westminster, 1954), 212.

29. Calvin, *Institutes*, 4:12:23.

30. John Calvin, *Commentaries on the Epistles to Timothy, Titus, and Philemon* (Grand Rapids: Eerdmans, 1948), 131–33.

31. Ian Cowan, *The Scottish Reformation* (New York: St. Martin's, 1982), 70.

32. Charles Hodge, *Systematic Theology* (New York: Scribner, 1895), 3:369–71.

33. *Statutes of the Realm*, Six Articles Act, 14.

34. George Frein, ed., *Celibacy: The Necessary Option* (New York: Herder, 1968), 87–88.

35. Thomas Ken, *Edmund*, 9:129–30.

36. William Phipps, *Influential Theologians on Wo/man* (Washington, DC: University Press of America, 1980), 109–29.

37. Evelyn Simpson and George Potter, eds., *The Sermons of John Donne* (Berkeley: University of California Press, 1952–62), 2:340.

38. Ibid., 8:94.

39. Ibid., 3:242.

40. Robert Hillyer, ed., *The Complete Poetry and Selected Prose of John Donne* (New York: 1941), 286–87.

41. Simpson and Potter, *Sermons*, 8:102.

42. Ibid., 6:266, 270.

43. Ibid., 7:104.

44. Council of Trent (1562), 8:622.

45. Hans Kung, ed., *Life in the Spirit* (New York: Sheed & Ward, 1967), 141.

46. Uta Ranke-Heinemann, *Eunuchs for the Kingdom of Heaven* (New York: Penguin, 1990), 113.

47. Kelly, *Oxford Dictionary of Popes*, 266.

48. Council of Trent, 24:9.

49. Peter De Rosa, *Vicars of Christ* (New York: Crown, 1988), 420–21.

50. Jean Delumeau, *Sin and Fear* (New York: St. Martin's, 1990), 433.

51. Mark Jordan, *The Silence of Sodom* (Chicago: University of Chicago Press, 2000), 126–27.

52. Henry Lea, *History of Sacerdotal Celibacy* (London: Watts, 1932), 496–99.

53. Stephen Haliczer, *Sexuality in the Confessional* (New York: Oxford, 1996), 86.

54. Ibid., 114, 118–19.

55. William Hogan, *Auricular Confession* (Hartford: Andrus, 1853), 293.

56. Haliczer, *Sexuality in the Confessional*, 207.

57. Voltaire, *Candide* (trans. Peter Gay; New York: St. Martin's, 1963), 121, 275.

58. Edward Beecher, *Papal Conspiracy Exposed* (New York: Dodd, 1855), 150–51.

59. *Romanism as Revealed by Its Own Writers* (New York: Delisser, 1859), 37.

60. Hogan, *Auricular Confession*, 247, 268–69.

61. Mark Twain, *Letter from the Earth* (1909; Greenwich: Fawcett, 1962), 53.

62. Ellis Hanson, *Decadence and Catholicism* (Cambridge: Harvard University Press, 1997), 26, 297.

63. Lea, *History*, 561–62.

64. Hogan, *Auricular Confession*, 270, 283.

65. Lea, *History*, 560.

66. James Gibbons, *The Faith of Our Fathers* (Baltimore: Murphy, 1895), 456.

67. "Celibacy, Canon Law of," *New Catholic Encyclopedia* (New York: McGraw-Hill, 1966).

68. Jacob Burckhardt, *On History and Historians* (New York: Harper, 1965), 37–38.

69. Wilhelm Bertrams, *The Celibacy of the Priest* (Westminster, MD: Newman, 1963), 21.

70. Ronald Smith, ed., *Søren Kierkegaard: The Last Years Journal* (New York: Harper, 1965), 93.

71. Peter Rohde, *Søren Kierkegaard* (New York: Humanities Press, 1963), 69–70.

72. Smith, *Søren Kierkegaard: The Last Years Journal*, 266–67.

73. Ibid., 119.

74. Ibid., 77–79, 171.

75. Soren Kierkegaard, *Attack upon Christendom* (Boston: Beacon, 1956), 213.

76. Martin Buber, *Between Man and Man* (London: Kegan, 1947), 51–52.

77. William Phipps, *Recovering Biblical Sensuousness* (Philadelphia: Westminster, 1975), 99–109.

78. Almer Maude, *The Life of Tolstoy* (London: Oxford, 1965), 2:271.

79. Emmett McLoughlin, *People's Padre* (Boston: Beacon, 1954), 9, 17, 19.

80. Ibid., 93–94.

81. James Colaianni, ed., *Married Priests and Married Nuns* (New York: McGraw-Hill, 1968), 147.

82. *Code of Canon Law*, 132.

83. Benedict XV, address, December 16, 1920.

84. Pius XI, *The Catholic Priesthood*, 12.

85. Pius XII, *On Holy Virginity* (1954), 23.

86. Cyprian, *On the Dress of Virgins* 22; Pius XII, *On Holy Virginity*, 29.

87. Pius XII, *Address to Young Women*, July 13, 1958.

88. Pius XII, *On Holy Virginity*, 20, 24.

89. Kenneth Woodward, *Making Saints* (New York: Simon & Schuster, 1990), 344.

90. Richard McBrien, *Lives of the Saints* (San Francisco: Harper, 2001), 13–14.

91. Richard McBrien, *Catholicism* (San Francisco: Harper, 1994), 637–38.

92. Richard Ginder, *Binding with Briars* (Englewood Cliffs, NJ: Prentice-Hall, 1975), 45–46.

93. *Christian Century* (April 8, 1970): 417.

94. *Journal of Pastoral Care* (December 1970): 218.

95. Leo Lehmann, *The Soul of a Priest* (New York: Agora, 1933), 122.

96. Richard Sipe, *Sex, Priests, and Power* (New York: Brunner, 1995), 171.

97. Otto Weininger, *Sex and Character* (New York: Putnam, 1906), 328–29, 346–48.

98. Ibid., 268.

99. Ibid., 252.

100. Linda Harcombe, ed., *Sex and God* (New York: Routledge, 1987), 58.

101. Lea, *History*, 560.

102. *National Catholic Reporter,* May 12, 1995, 21.

103. *Commonweal,* May 15, 1964, 223.

104. John XXIII, *Peace on Earth* (April 10, 1963), 1.

105. *Washington Post,* September 30, 1989, C1.

106. Aquinas stated that priestly celibacy is not essentially connected by God with Holy Orders, so the law can be reversed at any time by church authority (*Summa Theologica* 2–2:88:11).

107. *Decree on the Ministry and Life of Priests,* 16.

108. Ibid.

109. Robert Schreiter, ed., *The Schillebeeckx Reader* (New York: Crossroad, 1984), 234.

110. *New Commentary on the Code of Canon Law* (New York: Paulist Press, 2000), 357.

111. *Decree on Priestly Formation,* 10; *Decree on the Ministry and Life of Priests,* 16; *Decree on the Appropriate Renewal of the Religious Life,* 12.

112. *Decree on the Ministry and Life of Priests,* 16.

113. Andrew Greeley, *The Catholic Priest in the United States* (Washington, DC: Catholic Conference, 1972), 241.

114. *Decree on Priestly Formation,* 10.

115. *Dogmatic Constitution on the Church,* 44.

116. *Pastoral Constitution on the Church in the Modern World,* 50; Ambrose, *On Paradise* 10:47; Augustine, *Against Julian* 2:20.

117. *Pastoral Constitution on the Church,* 48.

118. *Dogmatic Constitution on the Church,* 41.

119. Peter Steinfels, *A People Adrift* (New York: Simon & Schuster, 2003), 330.

120. Ibid., 31–40.

121. Patricia Wittberg, *The Rise and Fall of Catholic Religious Orders* (New York: SUNY, 1994), 214.

122. *CORPUS Reports* (September 1986).

123. David Rice, *Shattered Vows* (New York: Morrow, 1990), 10.

124. Council of Trent, 23:4:4.

125. Aquinas, *Summa Theologica* 2–2:88:11.

126. Peter Hebblethwaite, *Paul VI* (New York: Paulist Press, 1993), 441.

127. Garry Wills, *Papal Sin* (New York: Doubleday, 2000), 128.

128. *Christian Century* (April 8, 1970): 418.

129. Eugene Kennedy, *The Unhealed Wound* (New York: St. Martin's, 2001), 121, 123.

130. William Bassett and Peter Huizing, eds., *Celibacy in the Church* (New York: Herder, 1972), 135–36.

131. Ibid., 138–39.

132. Paul VI, *Priestly Celibacy,* 13.

133. Frein, *Celibacy*, 158.

134. *Code of Canon Law*, 1026.

135. Terrance Sweeney, *A Church Divided* (Buffalo: Prometheus, 1992), 102.

136. *Code of Canon Law*, 219.

137. Colaianni, *Married Priests and Married Nuns*, 180–81.

138. *Pastoral Constitution on the Church in the Modern World*, 87.

139. Paul VI, *The Development of the People*, 37.

140. Frein, *Celibacy*, 24.

141. Leo XIII, *Rerum Novarum*; Pius XI, *Casti Connubii*.

142. Paul VI, *Priestly Celibacy*, 20, 26.

143. *CORPUS Reports* (July 1995): 11.

144. Wills, *Papal Sin*, 197.

145. Paul VI, *Priestly Celibacy*, 38.

146. Ibid., 62.

147. *National Catholic Reporter*, May 12, 1995, 21.

148. Colaianni, *Married Priests and Married Nuns*, 92.

149. Matt 15:14; *Christian Century* (April 8, 1970): 416.

150. *New York Times*, April 26, 2003, B6.

151. Aquinas, *Summa Theologica* 3:15:2.

152. Paul VI, *Declaration on Sexual Ethics* (1975), 9.

153. "Onanism," *Dictionary of Moral Theology* (Westminster, MD: Newman, 1962).

154. Richard Sipe, *A Secret World* (New York: Brunner, 1990), 285.

155. *New York Times*, January 16, 1976, 10.

156. Andrew Greeley, *The Catholic Priest in the United States* (Washington, DC: Catholic Conference, 1972), 99.

157. Elinor Burkett and Frank Brune, *A Gospel of Shame* (New York: Harper, 2002), 53.

158. *Christian Century* (April 8, 1970): 418.

159. Ibid., 415.

160. *Church History* (June 1972): 167.

161. Bassett and Huizing, *Celibacy*, 139.

Chapter 8

THE CONTEMPORARY ERA

꧁⚜꧂

John Paul II's Intransigence

A national study commissioned by American bishops found in 1970 that most clergy expected significant change in the law of celibacy to occur before 1980. They were embarrassed to learn "that four-fifths of the priests in the country believed that married men should be ordained priests and that priests who had left the active ministry to marry should be permitted to return."[1] The priests who were surveyed did not anticipate that a pope even more conservative on celibacy than Paul VI would not only succeed him but would also have one of the longest tenures in the history of the papacy. John Paul I, elected to follow Paul VI, would probably have been more open to change, but he died a month after assuming office in 1978.

John Paul II has been a reformer in some important ways, but a reactionary in the sphere of sexuality. Even before becoming pope, Polish Cardinal Wyszynski recorded his strong advocacy of celibacy.[2] As pope he has stated that he "does not wish to leave any doubts in the mind of anyone regarding the Church's firm will to maintain the law that demands perpetual and freely chosen celibacy for present and future candidates for priestly ordination in the Latin rite."[3] His take on the celibacy law is like Mesopotamian kings' view of the "law of the Medes and Persians that cannot be revoked" (Dan 6:8; Esth 1:19), although he did not declare it infallible.

No pope has appealed more to the New Testament for proof texts to buttress Catholic doctrines than John Paul. In unison with Paul VI, he uses the eunuch text from Matthew's gospel as his exhibit A for defending celibacy. Catholic theologian Uta Ranke-Heinemann notes, as we have seen, that the eunuch text's literary context shows that Jesus was defending the "voluntary renunciation of remarriage" in a divorce situation. Moreover, she says: "Jesus . . . did not say anything at all about celibacy. He simply corrected, to his disciples' horror, the biases of a polygamous society contemptuous of women, and sketched an ideal image of marital unity."[4]

John Paul has also appealed to other New Testament passages that traditionally have been cited as authority for the celibacy doctrine of Latin Catholicism. From the discussion of Jesus with Jerusalem priests (Mark 12:18–27), he extrapolates, "Celibacy is an anticipation of the future resurrection when people will no longer marry."[5] Also, the pope follows Origen in using a metaphor of Paul as a basis for this claim: "The priest, by renouncing fatherhood proper to married men, seeks another fatherhood and, as it were, even another motherhood, recalling the words of the apostle about the children whom he begets in suffering. These are children of his spirit . . . more numerous than an ordinary human family can embrace."[6] But no Pauline exegete interprets the verse in the Galatian letter to which the pope alludes (4:19) as having any connection with celibacy.

The extent of John Paul's asceticism is displayed in his belief in the inherent evil of sexual desire. Championing the view of Jerome, he states: "Adultery in the heart is committed not only because man looks in this [lustful] way at a woman who is not his wife. . . . Even if he looked in this way at the woman who is his wife, he could likewise commit the adultery in his heart."[7] Jerome had interpreted Jesus' saying about lustful looking being tantamount to committing adultery (Matt 5:28) to mean that he was denouncing sexual longing even by spouses for one another.[8] But, as we have seen, Jesus was referring to lusting after someone else's spouse.

A new catechism, containing the definitive statement of Catholic doctrine, reinforces John Paul's archaic teachings pertaining to sexuality and reaffirms the claim that a pope has "full, supreme and universal power, which he can exercise with complete liberty."[9] John Paul has been reluctant to appoint any priest to the office of bishop who has questioned papal policies on celibacy, on male priests only, and on birth control. In 1993, the pope implored the faithful to cease taking issue with the church's teaching on ordination requirements and to give it "full and unconditional assent."[10]

The church's guardian of correct ideas, the Congregation for the Doctrine of the Faith, aims at stifling dissent. In 1990, with the pope's approval, it prohibited public disagreement even on such non-infallible church teachings as celibacy and contraception. Kowtowing to papal expectations, a global synod composed of hundreds of bishops met in Rome that year and strongly reaffirmed the priestly celibacy requirement.[11] Hendrick Hertzberg perceives, "Like the Church's rejection of contraception, . . . mandatory priestly celibacy is increasingly driving a wedge between the hierarchy and the laity, with priests themselves caught in the middle."[12]

When Brazilian Cardinal Arno requested that John Paul II reconsider the celibacy law in 1985, he watched as the pope ripped apart his letter.[13] Even so, five years later, Brazilian Cardinal Lorscheider reported that the pope had permitted the ordination of two married men to serve a remote region with a severe priest shortage on condition that they refrain from having any sexual intimacy with their wives.[14]

Diocese Problems

From 1975 to 2003, Catholic membership in the United States increased from about 49 to 63 million, averaging an additional half-million per year. This gain has been largely due to Hispanic immigration. The birth rate for Catholic couples is now less than two, the same as for non-Catholics, and the number of baptisms has dropped. That growth is not reflected in the size of worshiping congregations, because "in 1972, 49 percent of Catholics reported attending church weekly, in 2000 a mere 26 percent did."[15]

Even though church membership is up, hundreds of priests leave annually and are not replaced. The percentage of their decrease is about the same as the membership increase since 1970. On the basis of their meticulously documented *Full Pews and Empty Altars*, Richard Schoenherr and Lawrence Young projected that the American Catholic priesthood engaged in active ministry will plunge from 35,000 to about 21,000 between 1966 and 2005, a 40 percent reduction.[16] Subsequently, Young projected a clergy decline of about 46 percent between 1966 and 2015,[17] which is reinforced by 441 ordinations in 2003 in comparison to 994 in 1965. Also in 2003, 5,499 brothers were in religious orders, less than half the 1965 number. Diocesan resignations and retirements more than double the number of ordinations; consequently, the median age of those remaining has risen to above sixty years. The graying of American priests is clear—more are over seventy-five than under forty, and many more are over ninety than under thirty.[18] In the archdiocese of San Antonio most priests are over sixty and only 5 percent are in their thirties.[19]

The 1,269 to 1 ratio of parishioners to diocesan priests in 1965 has increased to 2,165 to 1 in 2003, which includes not only the active but the many retired priests. During that same period, parishes without resident priests have grown more than five times, from 549 to 3,040.[20] One U.S. survey, taken in 1983, showed that 94 percent of priests and nuns gave as the reason for defecting their inability to live within their celibacy vows.[21] Catholic University sociologist Dean Hoge, who has carefully investigated why dozens of priests have resigned within five years of ordination, found that about one-quarter of them left in the 1990s because of being in love with a woman, an additional quarter left because the celibacy requirement caused them to feel "lonely and unappreciated," and about one-tenth left because they wanted an "open, long-term relationship" with a man.[22]

Gathering figures from a number of sources, Elizabeth Abbott writes:

> Some priests simply endure, with loneliness their overriding companion. Many cheat and take lovers they either disguise as housekeepers or friends or flaunt as mistresses. Other find the struggle intolerable and finally leave. . . . Since Vatican II, over one hundred thousand have joined the exodus, . . . nearly one-quarter of the world's working priests. In the United States, 42 percent of priests leave within twenty-five years of their ordination, which translates into the bleak statistic that half of American priests under the age of sixty have already gone.[23]

At the same time, seminary enrollment has declined drastically. "Bare, ruined choirs" is the way numerous seminaries now appear, for many have closed and others operate on a much-diminished scale. In 1985 there were 71,000 candidates for the Catholic priesthood worldwide, a 40 percent decline over three decades.[24] Stimulated by the hope of church renewal by Vatican II, seminary attendance peaked in the United States at 8,325 in 1965, but in 2003 there were 3,414—a 59 percent drop. In 1966, 20,129 boys were on a pre-seminary track, but in 1994 there were 1,229—a 94 percent drop.[25] "Quigley Seminary [in Chicago], the largest high school seminary in America, has 200 students. But if present trends continue, only four or five from its graduating class will survive to ordination." In 1993, each of the dozen seminarians who graduated there and became ordained cost $375,000.[26]

Along with the decrease in quantity, the leadership ability of those now entering training for the priesthood is recognized by church officials to be lower than a generation ago. "Most men who survive to ordination these days rate high on the conformity scale."[27] The statement illustrates that seminaries are being less selective in admitting those with good potential.

Eagerness by the church to accept as many unmarried men as they can garner has resulted in accepting some whose abilities and lifestyles are unlikely to match the roles they are expected to fill.

Previously the attractiveness of a celibate priesthood "had much to do with the anti-world, anti-body, anti-sexuality spirituality and a two-class understanding of holiness."[28] The present precipitous drop in the number of young men entering the priesthood is principally caused by their awareness that marriage can be fully as holy as celibacy. Those who might otherwise be attracted to the ministerial vocation find little reason for committing themselves to lifelong celibacy. From his 1980s research on causes of the priest shortage, Hoge concludes, "As a rough estimate, the number of young Catholic men who would be seriously interested in the priesthood under the conditions of optional celibacy would increase fourfold or more from the present level."[29] Similarly, Andrew Greeley—personally a happy and wealthy celibate—opines about American Catholicism:

> The numerical decline of the priesthood . . . does not seem to be properly attributable to a spiritual decline among young Catholics, a very considerable proportion of whom are interested in social and religious problems and even (10%) would be willing to consider a life of dedication to the Church. A change in the requirement of priestly celibacy would probably lead to the ordination of fifteen hundred more priests a year than are now being ordained.[30]

Hoge and Greeley supply empirical data that Paul VI lacked or disregarded when he declared, "It is simply not possible to believe that the abolition of ecclesiastical celibacy would considerably increase the number of priestly vocations."[31] One faithful follower of John Paul has given this explanation, "The lack of priests is a token of all those unborn children who might have had a priestly vocation had they not been deprived of life through the epidemic of contraception."[32]

Catholics in positions of power are reluctant to treat the underlying cause of the clerical exodus. Priest James Sullivan, in his article entitled "Don't Give the Priest Shortage the Silent Treatment," tells about the Vatican's persistence in stifling debate over making changes pertaining to celibacy and the consequent timidity of bishops in dealing with the issue.[33] Their inaction is not due to unawareness of what is causing the shortage of priests. In 1988 the Office of American Bishops circulated a document on the morale of priests that acknowledged, "Every study or commentary done on the priesthood and shortage of vocations mentions sexuality, and specifically mandatory celibacy, as a major reason a) for leaving the priesthood

b) for shortage of vocations and c) for loneliness and personal unhappiness of those who stay."[34]

Priest organizations in a number of states have followed the lead of more than 160 daring priests in the Milwaukee archdiocese who in 2003 openly petitioned Wilton Gregory, president of the U.S. Conference of Catholic Bishops, for the acceptance of married men into the priesthood as a way of responding to the acute problem of priests becoming an endangered species. He responded as dismissively as his Vatican boss has done, saying he saw no need for "fostering another review of the topic."[35] Gregory doubted that "a change in the discipline of clerical celibacy would necessarily bring about an increase in the numbers of candidates for priesthood" inasmuch as some Christian denominations with married ministers, such as the Lutherans and Presbyterians, are suffering from clergy shortages.[36] Gregory was misinformed because the Protestant denominations he named, as well as others, have an oversupply of clergy.[37] A number of Protestant denominations have had a precipitous drop in members, but not in ministers, over the past generation. The Association of Theological Schools, which accredits most North American seminaries, reports enrollment increases during the past decade of slightly more than 10 percent. If the 22 percent of those seminaries that are devoted to training students for a celibate priesthood are factored out, the increase among non-Catholics would be even higher.[38]

Because of compulsory celibacy, priests are a dying breed not only in the United States but worldwide, even in predominantly Catholic nations. Jesuit Jan Kerkhofs, in a 1970s study, found that "for every one hundred priests resigned or died, Holland had eight replacements, Belgium fifteen, Germany thirty-four, France seventeen, Italy fifty, Ireland forty-five, Spain thirty-five, and Portugal ten."[39] Sociologists project a 70 percent decline in the number of active diocesan priests in Spain, from 6,454 in 1966 to 1,910 in 2005, and identify celibacy as a main cause.[40] A study in 2000 of Catholic priests in *Britain Catholic* predicted that half of them will die in a decade. No longer can American Catholics easily recruit priests from Ireland to fill its ranks, because annual ordinations there plummeted from 259 in 1970 to 43 in 2000.[41] Central Europe is confronted with a similar problem. In her article "On the Verge of Ideological Mutiny," Cathleen Falsani stated that in 1995 "half of Austria's one million Catholics petitioned the Vatican to lift the ban on married and women priests."[42]

In the Southern Hemisphere, the paucity of priests is also pronounced. Adrian Hastings, a notable Catholic missionary for forty years, reports that because of the celibacy constriction "the vast majority of Catholic Africans are being deprived of any sort of regular Eucharist."[43] Between 1965 and

1985, there was a 55 percent drop in the proportion of African priests relative to the Catholic population. In Brazil, the world's largest Catholic nation, the ratio of priests to Catholic laypersons is one for every 7,000, and more than 50,000 congregations are unable to hold Sunday Mass. One-quarter of the priests in Brazil have left the church to marry. Many South American Catholics are converting to other Christian faiths, especially Pentecostalism, in part due to the lack of priests, who have the exclusive right to consecrate the bread and wine of Holy Communion. Also, many of the traditionally Catholic Hispanic population in America are either converting to the Pentecostal faith or dropping out of church membership, in part because of the lack of Catholic priests.

Catholic priests generally agree with non-Catholics on biblical issues pertaining to clerical celibacy. As James Coriden puts it, "They are simply not persuaded that the Gospel is more effectively proclaimed, the people better served and their own lives more truly Christlike because of a universal regulation against marriage."[44] Jesuit John Carmody is convinced that Catholicism's ban on clerical marriage has "no basis in Scripture, tradition, or theological understanding" and is therefore an "unfounded restriction of basic human rights." Moreover, this perversion of the gospel has brought an "excess of coldness, rigidity, and neurosis among today's clergy."[45] Paul Southgate comments on the usual plight that confronts parish priests like himself after ordination: "Taught that his celibacy will help him to share the very condition of Christ, who had nowhere to lay his head, he is sent to live as the sole occupant of a roomy house, where he must learn to combat selfishness and loneliness. This does nothing to dispel the idea of religion as eccentric, private, individualistic, and yes, in our day, suspicious."[46]

Recognizing the negative impact mandatory celibacy is having upon recruitment, Southgate asks, "Can it be justified when half the world's billion Catholics have only rare access to the Eucharist, which is the heart of their worship, and to the sacraments of reconciliation and anointing of the sick, which only priests are allowed to administer?"[47] Codified in the Middle Ages was the regulation that only priests could perform the miracle of the Mass. Indispensable pastoral service has been abandoned for approximately half of the Catholic parishes around the globe who have no resident priest by refusing to allow women or married men to fill that role.

Priest Paul Dinter comments on the demoralizing malaise of his church: "Mandatory celibacy . . . discourages openness and accountability and encourages the clergy to ignore or cover up for activity that would besmirch the priesthood. The establishment seeks to sustain its ideal of heroic celibacy behind a facade of denial."[48] Kennedy adds: "Only as the once intensely isolated Catholic culture opened itself, through the expanded educational opportunities . . . did the controls on celibacy begin to falter. You cannot allow sunshine into a once shuttered institution without stimulating what is healthy in those dwelling within. And you cannot let fresh air in without exposing the decay of centuries."[49]

In 1971, Kennedy was asked by American bishops to investigate personality characteristics of American priests. He and Victor Heckler found that more than half of their sample of priests showed immaturity due to arrested development. They gave this diagnosis: "Their difficulties are precisely those you would expect if you took a group of young men, sent them to special schools, virtually eliminated their contact with women, and then put them to work in circumstances that continued to reinforce all-male living in a socially restricted public religious role."[50] Moreover, Kennedy estimates that at least 80 percent of those who leave the priesthood come from the top third of priests who were profiled as being more mature.[51]

Sexual dysfunction is abetted by seminarians being instructed never to fall in love. To protect from that shameful descent, a former seminarian recalled being told by his spiritual director: "If you are tempted by a woman, think of her as your mother or sister to stem your concupiscence. If that doesn't work, imagine yourself lusting after the Blessed Mother."[52] Minneapolis priest Harvey Egan tells of his seminary preparation: "The world was an enemy, the flesh a danger. We lived like monks deep in a quiet cloister and starved our cultural interests, social concerns and sensual appetites. . . . Sexuality was a muddled and rarely mentioned subject."[53]

Dinter, who has closely observed priests in various residences, writes:

> A priest's resentment of celibacy usually does not emerge full-blown until some years after he is ordained. Then, not surprisingly, a sexual awakening, though delayed or repressed for years, can emerge at least as energetically as, if not more than, it erupts in a horny teenager. If a priest's self-discovery is coupled with strong sexual attraction—often akin to a first crush—he will find ways both to entertain and to justify his desires. For the ideal that he has of himself as a self-giving, generous, other-directed person dedicated to serving God does not shrivel up and die when he feels overwhelmed by recrudescent sexual desire.[54]

Thomas Keneally tells of how his irrepressible desire for physical intimacy during six years in a sterile seminary environment resulted in a nervous breakdown. He discovered, "Sexuality is always there—the more assiduously repressed, the more likely to cause psychic mayhem."[55] Human maturity is difficult enough to achieve without the celibacy barrier. A former priest who is now a psychotherapist testifies: "Maturing goes far beyond sexuality, to responsibility in thinking about someone else, to sharing your life. I twice carried my wife, unconscious and bleeding to death, into the hospital (it was during those weeks after a birth). I carried my own son into the hospital after a seizure."[56]

Richard Gardner, a child psychiatry professor at Columbia, asserts that the church is misguided in believing it can fashion asexual beings in seminaries. Some youth who become priesthood candidates are sexually troubled and expect the seminary to impede their compulsions. While confirmed in communities where sexual issues are averted, they deceive themselves into thinking that they can cope with sexual temptation. Then, when as priest they are exposed to wayward youth of both sexes, alter servers, and choir boys, they find themselves "in situations where sexual hormones are likely to cascade."[57] Because of the failure in recruiting youth to Catholic seminaries, students enrolled now are significantly older, which inadvertently solves much of the past sexual immaturity problems. In 2002,[57] percent of seminarians were over thirty years of age.[58]

In 1992, a Gallup survey found that 70 percent of American Catholics supported allowing priests to marry and continue functioning as priests, up from 58 percent in 1983.[59] When surveyed again in 1998, 80 percent thought that celibacy should be a matter of individual decision and not a requirement imposed by the church.[60] Also, "the National Opinion Research Center conducted a nationwise survey which indicated that 79 percent of Catholics would prefer a married priest as their pastor."[61] Clinical psychologist Sheila Murphy, on the basis of hundreds of male and female celibate respondents, found that 90 percent of them believe celibacy should be optional.[62] A 1994 scientific survey of 1,800 active American and Canadian Catholics revealed that support for the priestly celibacy requirement is less than one-third generally and less than one-fourth of those under fifty. The survey also showed that priests receive little support from their communities toward fulfilling their celibacy pledge because most of their parishioners do not favor the requirement.[63]

Schoenherr found thirty American bishops were courageous enough to indicate in Catholic publications from 1989 through 1992 their approval of the ordination of married men. Moreover, he found twenty-one bishops in ten foreign countries who also publicly expressed their approval. Schoenherr observes, "Growing minorities of bishops and the majority of theologians, priests, and laypersons agree that both celibacy and marriage should be permitted in the priesthood."[64]

Catholics on other continents also tend to favor optional celibacy. Eighty percent of Swiss Catholics think that priestly celibacy should no longer be required,[65] survey data from other nations are not easily obtained. In 1998, an Indonesian bishop reminded John Paul II that for three decades Indonesian Catholics have requested the ordination of married men to relieve the critical shortage of priests.[66] David Rice has visited in homes of hundreds of married priests and celibates on several continents. What impressed him was the joyousness, caringness, and piety practiced by ousted priests and the virtual absence of unloving families. "In sum it would seem that being a priest makes a man a better husband, and being a husband makes him a better priest." By contrast, Rice gives many examples of "priests who use their Roman collars as tomcats use their meows, to charm all the women they can and lure them to bed—and use their collars a second time around, to break the relationship or evade their responsibilities."[67] False celibates communicate nonverbally to their congregations that hypocrisy is an acceptable modus operandi when confronting anything that is personally unacceptable.

The costly integrity of priests who have exchanged their black clerical collars for golden wedding bands stands out when compared with priests who are living a lie. Richard Sipe describes the double lives of furtive priests, "They have a woman in another town, or have affairs or relationships with a man—or in the worst cases, relationships with children." But priests who marry are more likely to have "a desire for honesty" that impels them to "sacrifice the security of the priesthood."[68] Edward Schillebeeckx comments on the unemployed priests in Holland: "Most of these married priests at heart want to continue their priestly apostolate. They can do even less than Christian 'laity'; as far as the Church is concerned (and in some countries in social terms as well), they are shunted off into a siding, treated as lepers."[69] Some local churches do not permit them to engage even in non-sacramental work.

The thousands of married Catholic priests may now outnumber the active parish priests. Some twenty thousand priests in America have been forced out of the public ministry by marrying, and several thousand of them would like to help relieve the shortage that has resulted. "Celibacy Is the Issue" (CITI), a national organization for married priests, lists hundreds of them in *God's Yellow Pages* available for performing baptisms, anointing, and weddings in homes. Louise Haggett, the founder of CITI, reports that married priests are assisting the 70 percent of Catholics who are not regular in church attendance; in 2002 they conducted 2,500 weddings and hundreds of funerals.[70] Many other married priests who would eagerly respond to a call to active duty belong to CORPUS, an acronym for "Corps of Reserved Priests United for Service," which is organized in several dozen countries.

Some priests have attempted to follow a middle path between celibacy and marriage. They recognize that the church encourages everyone to love fellow humans while condemning genital sexuality for priests. Pius XII and his confidante, Sister Pasqualina, might exemplify such a relationship. That beautiful German nun became his housekeeper in the 1920s when he was on a Munich assignment. The rumor spread that "the nuncio had cast more than priestly eyes on her." After he returned to Italy, she lived in the Vatican with him and joined him for a voyage to America. Later she took care of his needs in the papal quarters, and their affective bond lasted until she was expelled from the Vatican on the day he died.[71]

Does a priest have liberty to indulge in intimate friendship with a woman or a man? Dominican Donald Goergen, in his book on this topic, discusses such relationships by celibates. His major premise is that "a rejection of the sensual is just as much a deviation from the life of virtue as is making the sensual the end of life itself."[72] From that proposition he argues that it is not sinful for a celibate to obtain relief by masturbating or by passionate kissing and intimate "holding," just so long as sexual intercourse is avoided.[73] For example, a Jesuit tells about his long-term relationship with a nun: "Although we don't have sexual intercourse, we do express our love physically and feel guilty about it."[74] Goergen is also positive toward homosexual activity, since that involves no combining of genitals.[75]

Raymond Hedin illustrates what Goergen advocates by telling about the life as a priest of his Catholic seminary classmate. During his first years in a parish, he recalled learning from a seminary professor this bit of Augustinian wisdom, "After you're ordained, your prick isn't going to know that you're a celibate." Before recognizing that he could be intimate without being sexual in a relationship, he expressed his delayed adolescence, "He experimented with every variety of sexual activity he could muster:

homosexual as well as heterosexual, with friends, strangers, bar mates, prostitutes."[76] A priest-psychologist has "insisted that no one should remain within the priesthood who is not capable of conducting an intimate but 'non-genital' . . . relationship with a woman or a man."[77] "Bed sharing, which might or might not lead to arousal and genital activity, seems to have become the halfway house of clerical desire."[78]

At best this stopgap method for obtaining affection provides a less than ideal accommodation to the church's requirement of an unmarried priesthood. Understandably, clerics who feel trapped in a celibacy commitment may behave in this manner in order to tolerate continuance in their vocation. Sipe has reviewed these experimentations along the slippery middle slope, which he estimates involve about 10 percent of priests. He comments, "Regardless of whatever the unconscious factors are that motivate two people who share a conscious ideal of celibacy to initiate a close 'meaningful' relationship that has neither sex nor marriage as its goal, the result is inevitable psychic conflict when they find themselves in a mutually inclusive affectionate bond." He commends the healthier outlook of Frank Bonnike, the former president of the National Federation of Priests' Councils, who wrote about his plans to marry a former nun, "Once I discovered myself closer to God because of Janet, I knew I could not just be open with Him about our relationship, but that I had to be open about it before people, too."[79]

Clandestine sexual intercourse is the more likely outcome of clerics who engage in intimate friendships. Murphy, who has worked sympathetically with "vowed celibates," prepared and administered a questionnaire to a sampling of several hundred middle-aged celibates of North American Catholicism. Since pledging to be celibate, 62 percent of the men and 49 percent of the women admitted sexual behavior (not identified by some as genital expression). One-third in her sample had so rationalized their conduct that they believed "it is possible for some people to be sexually active and committed celibates at the same time." A large majority of professed celibates who are sexually active did not want their religious superiors to become aware of their behavior. Her study showed that a craving for "forbidden fruit" sometimes increases when sex is repressed.[80]

Based on his studying and counseling more than 1,500 American Catholic priests over the past generation, Sipe estimates that 10 percent of them enthusiastically embrace the idea of celibacy. One priest, after a long career in the church, observed: "I never met one priest who delighted in his celibacy or spoke of it as a privilege or a blessing. . . . [Most priests] struggle year in and out repressing their heterosexuality or homosexuality."[81] Yet, as James Martin states: "There is no reason to believe that homosexual priests are any less likely to keep their promises of celibacy than heterosexual ones."[82] According to Sipe, 40 percent reluctantly stick by the celibacy rule, and half are occasionally sexually active. Approximately 20 percent of priests are involved at any one time in heterosexual relationships.

In *A Secret World*, Sipe writes of a young parish worker who was distressed by a curate's advances. When Sipe encouraged her to report this to her pastor, she replied, "I can't do that; he's involved with my mother." Sipe knows of some fifty women who have had abortions after being impregnated by priests, who usually were the sexual pursuers. Fearful of being dismissed from employment, the priests often insisted on pregnancy terminations and have sometimes paid for them. The celibacy deception is continued at all costs because the power of priests comes from "a system that pretends that all of them are sexually virginal."[83] Sipe comments on the deceit of these priests, "They really do not believe that the rules which apply to others—or even about which they preach—apply to them. At the same time, their demandingness does not lend itself to a mutuality that fosters relationships."[84] Such priests do not view the chasm between preachment and practice as hypocrisy, because self-deception is the first step along the path of dissemblance.

Cathy Finnegan-Grenier has counseled with some 2,500 women who have been sexually involved with priests, about thirty of whom have had children by them. Some have had abortions and others have contemplated suicide. Some of these priests marry with a bishop's tacit approval so long as they keep up the celibacy charade.[85]

Some apologists for celibacy have compared it to marriage in that both occasionally lapse into immorality. Violators of pledges of chastity can be found among both the celibate and the married. Celibacy defenders argue that since no one suggests that the marriage institution should be discarded because of the unfaithful conduct and divorces of many who had publicly vowed to be faithful "till death do us part," so the law of celibacy should not be removed because of the misbehavior of some celibates. But it is a poor analogy to compare violations of something unnatural and recognized to be nonessential to the priesthood with something natural and universally recognized as necessary for maximizing human intimacy and nurture.

Even though many Catholic priests in America frequently violate the celibacy rule, their sexual liaisons are less than half of what is usually found in other cultures.[86] One study reveals that half the priests in the Philippines have "a lasting relationship with a woman and the communities they serve accept this fact without difficulty."[87] Cardinal Jaime Sin of Manila has condoned the situation since his priests pretend to be celibate and apparently do not use condoms. Church offerings are small in the Philippines because parishioners know that much of it goes to support the large illicit families of the clergy.[88] One Filipino bishop responded to a woman who came to him for confession and for advice on how to end an affair with another reverend father by giving her his apartment key and gifts of food that parishioners had left as offerings. Knowledge of that errant celibate came from his jilted previous mistress.[89] When Sin threatened to suspend Monsignor Nico Bautista if he did not cease publicly advocating that marriage ought to be optional for priests, he retorted, "Even Bishop Yalung who fathered two children was not defrocked."[90]

In Europe, Cardinal Jean Danielou, the influential Jesuit theologian at Vatican II, died in a Parisian whorehouse.[91] A young and sanguine Polish priest, who lives in a nation where there is both a widespread flaunting of the celibacy requirement and an adoration of their Polish pope who strives to enforce it, rationalizes why he does not let the rule impose constraints on his behavior: "Compulsory celibacy is just a human law. Everyone knows it's going to change eventually. So why should our lives be spoiled by something that's going to change in twenty years?"[92]

Jesuit sociologist Joseph Fichter learned that one-third of German Catholic priests are having short- or long-term sexual relations with women. While some are in loving partnerships, the kept women are subjected to social ostracism. To avoid suspension by their bishops, priests must make it appear that they have not fathered any offspring even when savvy parishioners know about the affairs and express a willingness to raise the illegitimate children.[93] Fichter's data on priestly fornication suggests little moral improvement since the sixteenth century among German priests. Peter Canisius, the first German Jesuit, found that 90 percent of them were living in concubinage.[94] In a 1984 survey by the Cologne archdiocese, clergy were asked if they believed that "a certain number of priests are only celibate outwardly but, hidden from public view, they evade celibacy through numerous compromises." "Yes" was the response of 88 precent of the priests who belonged to a monastic order and of 74 percent of the diocesan priests.[95]

Italians clerics joke about *scrupulosi Americani* who take their celibacy pledge seriously, in comparison to priests in other continents who live more openly with paramours as well as with wives and children. Currently, around two-thirds of the native Brazilian priests and four-fifths of the local priests in Peru are intimately involved with women.[96] Abbott writes about the "surreptitiously uncelibate priests" in Latin America:

> The Church's position on celibacy blatantly ignores cultural realities, specifically traditional perceptions of celibacy. Peru is an excellent case in point. Life in the Andes centers around the notion of the *pareja*, the couple, and a man's authority is based on his having a family. Celibacy is neither understood nor respected. Responsible men are supposed to have families and support them. The idea of a celibate Peruvian leader is an oxymoron.[97]

African philosopher John Mbiti describes the general way in which celibacy is viewed on his continent: "Marriage is the focus of existence . . . a rhythm of life in which everyone must participate. . . . He who does not . . . is a curse to the community, he is a rebel and a law-breaker, he is not only abnormal, but 'underhuman.'"[98] Adrian Hastings documents that in the Congo, the nation with the largest number of dioceses in Africa, most of the clergy voted in favor of rejecting mandatory celibacy. They stated: "Marriage for the Congolese priest will not be a devaluation of the priesthood, but a fulfillment of the ancestral priesthood within the Christian priesthood. In fact, according to African tradition, it is the father of the family who presides over the liturgy and is the intermediary, not only between living and dead, but also between men and God."[99] In 1307, Pope Clement V permitted priests in a missionary area to marry, even after ordination, but his action established no precedent for the Southern Hemisphere.[100] Historian Philip Jenkins attributes the decline of the Catholic Church in Kongo, which had developed along the lower Congo River in the sixteenth and seventeenth centuries, in large part to the Vatican's unwillingness to accept a married native clergy as it had done in eastern Europe and western Asia. He calls this "one of the greatest wasted opportunities in the story of African Christianity."[101] Bishops from the Southern Hemisphere planned to insist at Vatican I that clerical celibacy be made optional. The reason the council was never reconvened after being interrupted by the Franco-Prussian War in 1870 may have been due to the Vatican's dermination to avoid the issue.[102]

Since the unmarried African has little status, few priests are being ordained there in proportion to Catholic membership. To relieve the acute shortage of pastors, Africans strongly requested that Vatican II approve the ordination of married priests. Cardinal Josh Malula of Congo informed Paul VI that celibacy was causing a crisis among his people, but the pope summarily rejected his urgent plea. In 1993, Cardinal Polycarp Pengo of Tanzania pleaded with the Vatican that priests be permitted to marry, explaining, "Failure to procreate continues to be one of the greatest misfortunes in society that can befall an African man or woman."[103] Local priests who have fathered children by various women are commonplace in the Congo.[104] One journal reports that as many as half of the priests are having affairs, but many of the liaisons are actually long-termed quasi-marriages.[105]

Medical missionary Mary O'Donohue states, "Celibacy in the African context means a priest does not get married but does not mean he does not have children." She reports that a women's group in Malawi was dismissed by a bishop after it complained that diocesan priests had impregnated twenty-nine sisters. There, as elsewhere, priests sometimes insist on abortions for sisters who are carrying their babies.[106] Faithful to the Vatican, African bishops do not permit the use of condoms,[107] so their unprotected priests become infected by AIDS and spread it to others. Many Africans believe that having intercourse with a virgin will cure the disease. Many African priests, fearful of the AIDS epidemic, are replacing their use of prostitutes with safer outlets. Reliable reports tell of nuns and Catholic schoolgirls being exploited by priests.

In 2001, when Zambian archbishop Emmanuel Milingo married, he received considerable acceptance in his own nation.[108] He was part of a mass wedding conducted in New York by ex-con and self-designated second messiah Sun Myung Moon, who had selected for him a much younger Korean bride, Maria Sung. But then he was summoned to the Vatican and confined until he capitulated to the pope. When Milingo left the bosom of his bride to return to the bosom of the church, his wife went on a hunger strike to protest being ditched. Milingo was then restored to his position in Africa, while Sung vowed never to love another man.[109]

Rice provides this devastating evaluation of what he has found in many nations:

> "By their fruits you shall know them," Jesus said, and the fruits of compulsory celibacy are those thousands of men leading double lives, thousands of women leading destroyed lives, thousands of children spurned by their ordained fathers, to say nothing of the priestly walking wounded, the psychiatric cases, the alcoholics and the workaholics, the gray lonely faces that witness to the wretched lives of so many priests.[110]

Eastern Orthodoxy spokesman Demetrios Constantelos is hopeful that his church will make marriage an option for priests throughout life, recognizing that "any change to allow marriage after ordination, a second marriage for a widowed priest or a married bishop, would be in full accord with the faith and practice of the Church in Apostolic times and in the first seven centuries of our era."[111] By demanding that marriage be done before ordination, Orthodox seminarians sometimes quickly find a willing woman to wed after completing their training without either party having time to discern if the match is likely to provide permanent compatiblity. Over 90 percent of Greek Orthodox priests in America are married and only rarely do they resign.

⊙╬⊙

After Vatican II, many heterosexually oriented priests left the priesthood to marry. The resulting situation "has dramatically changed the gay/ straight ratio and contributed to the disproportionate number of priests with homosexual orientation."[112] Sipe estimates that 30 percent of American priests are homosexually oriented, and that half of that group are sexually active.[113] He predicts that if the current trend continues, a majority of priests will be homosexuals by the year 2010.[114] Jason Berry judges, on the basis of the eighteen gay clerics he interviewed in 1987, that the majority of the younger generation are gay.[115] A survey of 101 American gay priests shows that those ordained after 1981 say that seminaries are 70 percent gay; those ordained before 1960 remember seminaries as having been about 50 percent gay.[116] In writing about the "predominantly homosexualized clergy" in the Catholic Church of America, Richard Hasselbach estimates that "among the clergy under the age of sixty, it is well in excess of 50 percent."[117] According to a 2002 survey, between one-third and one-half of Roman Catholic priests are homosexual.[118] Gay Catholic clergy probably compose the largest group of closeted professionals in the world.

The trend toward an increase of homosexuals in Catholic seminaries and rectories in North American is undeniable, but those percentages may be inflated. According to a survey in 2002 of more than 1850 priests, 15 percent identify themselves as homosexual.[119] That datum should be interpreted with a recognition of the tendency to deny unacceptable behavior. The proportion of gays in the European priesthood appears to be similar to that of the United States, and the phenomenon is "prevalent" in Italy.[120] In some places a dominant subculture has developed among homosexual priests that has caused some heterosexuals to feel marginalized.

In the United States, the percentage of gays in the priesthood appears to be between two and ten times that of the general male population. In 1948, the pioneering research of Alfred Kinsey found that about 4 percent of American males engage exclusively in homosexual behavior throughout their lives.[121] The best subsequent scientific study was done in 1992 with a sample of 3,500 American men. Interviews showed that about 3 percent of them think of themselves as homosexual or bisexual and about 7 percent have had sexual contact with a male partner since puberty.[122]

The large number of gay clerics may help to explain an increase in tolerance of homosexuality among American Catholics. *Newsweek* finds that 61 percent of non-Catholics oppose same-sex marriages, compared with 47 percent of Catholics.[123] Reporter Peter Steinfels states: "I have never encountered the visceral reaction to homosexuals among Catholic leaders that I have often encountered among evangelicals. Efforts to 'convert' gay and lesbian individuals to heterosexuality enjoy little support among Catholics."[124]

In a halting manner, Catholics are beginning to make a crucial distinction, unknown in past eras, between sexual orientation and sexual activity. Many homosexually as well as heterosexually oriented clerics are lifelong virgins. The 1994 edition of their catechism stated that gays "do not choose their homosexual condition." Implicit in that statement is an acknowledgement that genetic predisposition and early childhood environment contribute significantly toward one's sexual orientation. If that condition is received from God's natural creation or from infant nurture, individual choice is not possible. But the 2000 edition of the catechism has deleted the affirmation that homosexuality is not a matter of choice and reverts to the traditional doctrine that the homosexual condition is a perversion, "This inclination . . . is objectively disordered."[125]

Regardless of contemporary psychological theory, the Vatican continues in its time warp with regard to homosexuals. In 2002, John Paul II's spokesman stated that the ordination of priests with homosexual orientation should be considered invalid.[126] Vatican official Andrew Baker writes that men with homosexual orientation are inherently unsuitable for holy ordination because they are prone to "substance abuse, sexual addition, and depression." Moreover, the priesthood involves no sacrifice for the homosexual in renouncing having a family of his own, and a celibate gay priest "cannot redirect his inclination" toward the church as Christ's bride.[127]

Presuming that homosexuals have no civil right to permanent bonding, the Vatican has declared, "There are absolutely no grounds for considering homosexual unions to be in any way similar or even remotely analogous to God's plan for marriage and family." Recognizing that same-sex unions cannot produce new life, committed as well as casual gay conduct is condemned as "gravely immoral." Catholics in government positions are told that homosexuals and heterosexuals should not be treated as equals under the law.[128] Whereas the Apostle Paul said to heterosexuals that it is better to have lasting exclusive sexual partnership than burn with passion,

Catholics say to homosexuals that it is better to burn than to have such a relationship.

Institutional homosexuality affects both priests and prisoners. The exclusively male seminaries and monasteries unwittingly encourage its residents to satisfy their carnal cravings with males in their dormitories. "At times the situation rather than the core sexual orientation of the priest dictates his sexual choice."[129] British writer Brian Sewell compares the situation of celibates and prisoners, where most men are not homosexual in orientation: "It is probable that in all wholly closed male groups, homosexual activity is to some extent inevitable and, where it is not mutually willing, that there is some element of erotic excitement in the exercise of power and compulsion."[130]

Sexual histories frequently show that those who cannot be near to someone from the gender they would prefer to love seek affection from a person from the gender they are near. Among humans as well as among many animal species, in situations where a member of the opposite sex is unavailable for sexual activity, a member of the same sex may be substituted.[131] One priest told Rice of his change from his seminary and missionary years when he wantonly indulged in sex with men: "When I married, I resumed a normal heterosexual life. I have a son and two beautiful daughters now, and I've never looked back. My biggest regret is that I did not start heterosexual life earlier than I did."[132] Likewise, the prisoner with an essentially heterosexual orientation who is confined to a penitentiary often adjusts to same-sex outlets because the opposite sex is not available. When released from this forced sexual isolation, he or she will return to a heterosexual choice of lover.

Steinfels thinks that the priesthood is probably not attracting more gays, but fewer heterosexuals because the latter have come to recognize that marriage can be an authentic path to holiness.[133] McBrien writes: "The ordained priesthood is attractive to certain people precisely because it excludes marriage. To put it plainly: as long as the Church requires celibacy for the ordained priesthood, the priesthood will always pose a particular attraction for gay men who are otherwise not drawn to ministry." The priesthood gives "occupational respectability and freedom from social suspicion."[134]

Ellis Hanson does not think people should find it difficult to understand why gays become priests, because "the real question ought to be why straight men become priests." He points to such appealing factors as "public trust and respect, freedom from the social pressure to marry, opportunities . . . for cohabitation with likeminded men."[135] The priestly brotherhood provides the homosexually oriented person not only prestige but other advantages: power, guaranteed employment, health care, and retirement benefits. Employment for most people tends to be precarious, especially for gays who have come out, but gays who remain closeted in the priesthood have an economic security for life that may not be found in other professions. Required for these benefits is the appearance of celibacy.

Donald Cozzens, a former seminary rector, learned from his experience with homosexuals that it is imperative for the Vatican to review "the closed system of legislated celibacy." He observes:

> Celibacy is, in effect, optimal for gay priests. Only the integrity of the gay priest, who is free to travel and vacation with another man, sustains his life of celibacy. Celibacy . . . is impossible to enforce for the priest who is gay. . . . Examples of the shadow side of gay clerical life abound; reports of priests at gay bars . . . and the sex ring scandal uncovered at Canadian orphanages run by religious orders. . . . The perpetrators live in a closed, all male system of privilege, exemption, and secrecy that drives sexuality underground, where it easily becomes twisted.[136]

Ironically, the Catholic priesthood serves as a magnet for gays in spite of the church's strong tradition of homophobia. Paul VI called homosexual acts "a serious depravity" and stated that "the propensity itself is to be judged objectively disordered."[137] Accordingly, Cardinal Anthony Bevilacqua of Philadelphia has asserted that men with homosexual orientation are not suitable for the priesthood, even if they are not sexually active.[138] Jesuit John McNeil, who had published *The Church and the Homosexual*, was expelled from his order after he criticized the Vatican's declaration that the homosexual inclination itself was evil. Charles Curran, an eminent moral theologian at Catholic University, was dismissed by orders from the Vatican in 1986, in part because he argued that stable homosexual unions were preferable to multiple unloving and unsafe liaisons.

The homosexual act is classified as a mortal sin in Catholicism because it "cannot fulfill the procreative purpose of the sexual facility" and therefore "runs contrary to a very important goal of human nature."[139] Andrew Sullivan, a devout gay Catholic, exposes a cruel inconsistency: "Homosexuals are informed that they are born that way, but no sexual intimacy is permissible, because it cannot lead to procreation. But the infertile are married every day; postmenopausal spouses are allowed active sex lives."[140] Another irony is that Catholicism extols celibacy, which likewise is non-procreative.

Advancement in the priesthood sometimes comes by providing sexual relief to the more senior priests and bishops. For example, one gay American bishop, now a cardinal, would entertain young priests at his country home. Since he always had one less guest bed than the number invited, he picked one from the group to share his bed.[141] In 1993, an investigation of a seminary in California disclosed that 12 of the 44 priests had been sexually active with their teenage students.[142]

Secrecy and silence is so much a part of the modus operandi of prelates' personal lives that knowledge of their sexual activities rarely comes to light. Some have thought that Paul VI had a gay lover before becoming pope, but no proof has been given for the claim.[143] Cardinal Francis Spellman is among the most eminent prelates who are known to have been gay. John Cooney's biography of the New York archbishop, entitled *The American Pope*, contains a testimony from a reliable priest about an affair he had with Spellman. Based on such evidence, Cooney writes:

> For years rumors abounded about Cardinal Spellman being a homosexual. As a result, many felt—and continue to feel—that Spellman the public moralist may well have been a contradiction of the man of the flesh. Numerous priests and others interviewed took his homosexuality for granted. Others within the Church and outside have steadfastly dismissed such claims.[144]

Sipe writes about stories he heard while studying in Rome pertaining to Spellman's years at the Vatican, when he had trysts with monsignors at afternoon teas in their apartments. He suggests that friendships established then may have helped Spellman become the Vatican's secretariat of state. Sipe explains why he comments on the private life of prelates: "The important issue is not any particular churchman's sexual practice, but the fact that sexual activity that is proscribed by Church teaching and disavowed by professors of celibacy can take place at the highest levels of power."[145]

While recognizing from his experience as a priest that many gay priests are good pastors, Hasselbach is disturbed by the institutional hypocrisy: "The church condemns the homosexual lifestyle; at the same time it turns a blind eye on rampant clerical homosexuality as long as the relationship doesn't become embarrassing."[146] Gay men tend to be less attracted to the diocesan priesthood than to monastic communities, where there is less outside surveillance. A member of the East Coast Franciscans estimates that as many as 300 of the 400 brothers are gay.[147]

Some priests convince themselves that sexual encounters with males do not violate their pledge of celibacy, according to a study completed in 1999 by the Australian Bishops Conference.[148] They rationalize their conduct by defining celibacy as avoiding being defiled by having intercourse with a woman. A seminary instructor says: "The canon law that is taught in the seminary makes it clear who the enemy is: it's women. Meet a girl and you disengage. Meet a man, and it's different."[149] An American survey of gay priests concluded:

> Most priests over thirty-five . . . became more comfortable in relationships with men because they were taught not to develop relationships with women. . . . The church almost forced these men into an arrested development with no affective relationships, so a lot got fixated on a fantasy level with patterns of eroticism. That's why so many visit pornographic magazine stores and movie houses.[150]

With the virtual collapse of junior seminaries in the past generation, the opportunity for confessors to discern the sexual fitness of adolescent boys for a celibate life has been lost. As the name "seminary" indicates, they were a seedbed where the cultivators of Catholic virtue not only nurtured growth but also attempted to weed out any who were perceived to be incompatible with the priestly vocation. With the age of seminarians continually becoming older, heterosexual or homosexual patterns of sexual activity have already to a large extent been formed before arrival. Theological seminaries are desperate to increase their enrollments, so little attention is given to excluding candidates based on their sexual past. Seminaries now tend to welcome "the man who has already dealt with these 'coming out' issues outside the seminary, perhaps even in the promiscuous gay subculture, and who has 'come to his senses' (Luke 15:17), and who decides to embrace celibacy and priesthood as a more genuine, a more fulfilling way of life."[151]

In America, AIDS has been spread mainly by gay sex. Journalist Judy Thomas researched the death rate of Catholic clergy from AIDS from the beginning of the epidemic in the mid-1980s through the 1990s. Interviews and death certificates in fourteen states, the only ones permitting public examination of those certificates, disclosed more than 150 AIDS-related deaths of priests, more than doubling the rate of all adult males in those states.[152] Extrapolating from that data, more than 500 priests have died of AIDS throughout the United States. The ratio of Americans who test HIV positive to those who die of AIDS is about three to one, so probably another 1,500 Catholic priests suffer with the infection.[153] Since the church does not condone male lovers living openly in long-term partnership, many gay priests engage in high-risk clandestine activity at parks and public toilets. Priest Richard Wagner interviewed fifty gay priests from across the United States, ranging in age from twenty-seven to fifty-eight.

He found that only two were having no sexual activity and the others averaged 227 partners each. One priest infected at least eight other priests. Sixty percent had engaged in group sex and one-third acknowledged that their partners were "distinctly younger."[154] An Arizona priest kept a file on nearly 2,000 sex acts he had engaged in with males.[155] Some priests with AIDS have spread their disease to the sexually less experienced.

The new Catholic catechism continues the medieval outlook of treating masturbation, along with homosexuality, as a grave moral disorder.[156] The 2003 edition of the *New Catholic Encyclopedia* rejects statements in the initial edition that masturbation is recognized in the Bible as "a serious sin," but it acknowledges that that has been the judgment of the church. Accordingly, the Vatican has denied permission for the obtaining of semen specimens by masturbation for detecting and curing venereal diseases. Catholicism also treats uterine artificial insemination and in vitro fertilization as immoral, in part because they involve masturbation.

Sipe indicates that "a classic pamphlet commonly distributed at the spiritual retreats of teenage boys in the 1950s was entitled *The Greatest Sin*," which pertains to masturbation and not to mass murder.[157] "All Catholic boys were supposed to be chaste—that is, not to have ejaculations except unwillingly and while asleep."[158] Richard Ginder observed in 1975 that "the conscientious Catholic who takes his training seriously is convinced that he is committing a mortal sin every time he 'plays with himself.'"[159]

While indulging in the most frequent of all sexual activities, many celibates over the centuries have been terrified by the recognition that this way of "sinning" cannot be kept secret from the all-seeing eye of God. When John Cornwell entered seminary at the age of puberty he found that community's anxiety over masturbation caused "psychological torture." When he acknowledged this sin, his confessor asked, "How can God's grace be visited upon his house when you have done such a terrible thing?"[160] One priest recalled being taught "that a single act of masturbation was sufficient for him to lose his soul and destroy all the good he had ever done." Another, overwhelmed by guilt after masturbating, risked his life searching late at night for another priest to whom he could confess and obtain forgiveness. Ginder has described the mindset of fellow priests: "To the rest of the country 'pollution' is an ecological term, but every time the professional Catholic sees the word he automatically thinks of orgasm."[161] According to Catholic casuistry, ejaculation is evil if the penis is hand-stimulated, but not if genital movement is made against a pillow. That dodge is derived from a possible etymology of "masturbate," which may be a compound from the Latin words *manus* (hand) and *stuprare* (to defile).

Contrary to the Catholic view of masturbation, David Gordon maintains that social protection can come from the hands-on stress reducer. If potential rapists were not affected by cultural taboos that constrict masturbating, fewer sexual crimes would be committed.[162] Even though Catholics persist in attempting to repress masturbation, it serves as a healthy cathartic for both individuals and society by releasing pent-up emotions in a manner that causes no personal or social damage.[163] For reducing sexual pressure and regaining composure, masturbating may have no more moral significance than sneezing or blowing mucus from one's nose.

The obsolete Vatican standards on birth control, masturbation, homosexuality, and celibacy have become increasingly ineffective in controlling conduct. Educated Catholics are tending more and more to make up their minds on these matters by examining empirical studies pertaining to sexuality and family life. In spite of the church's anti-choice position on abortions, in America there are more abortions among Catholics than among Protestants.[164] Catholic Italy is a European leader in the use of contraception.[165] The majority of priests dissent from papal teachings on masturbation and believe that it is seldom or never wrong.[166] Kinsey reported that four out of five devout single Catholic males, ages twenty-one to twenty-five, engage in masturbation to obtain sexual relief.[167] Sexologist William Masters found that 198 out of the 200 priests he had surveyed reported having masturbated during the past year.[168]

The structure of the Catholic Church in America has been shaken by stunning revelations of priests being involved in what is usually designated as pedophilia. Its literal meaning, child-love, is a euphemism that covers a range of pathological behavior. Pedophilia clinically refers to the sexual abuse of prepubescent children by adults, but until recent years, the term was applied to the molestation of all minors. As now strictly defined, pedophiliac predators are almost exclusively men, and research shows that young girls are more likely to be their victims. The most common setting for its expression is incest, which is often not exposed. However, in reference to the priesthood, it usually involves two males, because boys are more accessible.[169]

The majority of priests who are popularly accused of pedophilia should be placed in a different category, because they are attracted to adolescent youth rather than to prepubescent children.[170] The English term "ephebophilia," coined in 1988, refers to a sexual desire for teenagers, which corresponds more precisely than "pedophilia" to the practice of the ancient Greeks, who originated the words from which the present nomenclature has been formed. One of their main dual sports was what they called *paiderastia*, or boy-eroticism, which has been transliterated as "pederasty." Accepting it as normal, Greek literature and art documents adult males playing sexually with youth, *epheboi*.[171] The slogan of those pederasts was, "Women for breeding but boys for pleasure." Priestly ephebophiliacs are generally homosexuals, and few teenage girls are among their victims; some of their activity is rape and some is consensual. But homosexuals are no more likely to abuse minors than are heterosexuals. Ephebophilia and pedophilia are viewed as both immoral and criminal in our culture.

In the 1980s, Catholic clergy were publicly accused of abusing boys on the average of one case per week, and the pace has rapidly accelerated since then, although the year of the molestation is often decades earlier. Thomas Doyle, a Dominican canon lawyer, estimated in 1987 that as many as 3,000 U.S. priests could be pedophiles (then including ephebophiles), about 5 percent of the total number of priests. Unable to convince the prelates to stop hiding the perversion, he resigned from his post at the Vatican embassy.[172] Editor Tom Fox of the National Catholic Reporter, who has followed these cases for years, tells of "the almost invariable pattern of church response: first a denial by the local bishop, then the reshuffling of the accused priest to another assignment and the discrediting of the accuser by church officials, and finally, the lawsuit."[173] Sipe, to whom Fox appeals as one who "has probably studied the phenomenon of sexual abuse by clergy longer than any other Catholic professional," shows that a few bad apples are spoiling the lot in public perception. In 2003, Sipe estimated that 2 percent of American Catholic priests are fixated on prepubescent children and 4 percent on postpubescent minors.[174] Since consensual sex by the ephebophiles is not reported, the total number in that category is impossible to estimate. In 1993, University of Chicago sociologist Greeley extrapolated from research findings that several thousand American priests have sexually abused minors, involving more than 100,000 victims. He also reported that Cardinal Joseph Bernardin of Chicago estimated that he spent 30 percent of his time dealing with such abuse.[175]

Some cases of child predation are so gross that they can cause trauma for a long time. For example, a Nevada priest confessed in court that he had required five boys in his parish to spread their arms in a cruciform before he raped them.[176] Priest-professor Cozzens observes that the devastating effect of clerical abuse extends far beyond the large numbers that Greeley reports:

Thousands upon thousands of young victims have suffered the almost unimaginable effects of sexual abuse at the hands of Catholic clergy. I've sat with some of them and listened to their halting attempts to put into words the pain, confusion, disillusion, and sense of shame that followed the episodes of abuse.... The harm inflicted on their family members and friends is likely to raise the number directly touched by the scandal to a million. When the dismay and hurt of the accused parishioners are factored in, the number affected could be in the millions.[177]

Commenting on the "catastrophe" of "sexual crimes against the most innocent lambs in the flock," columnist Lance Morrow queries, "If trust dissolves into doubt and disgust, if God's representatives on earth turn out to be, many of them, child molesters and protectors of child molesters, then who will ever see such men at their priestly work ... without suspicion and unbidden loathing?"[178] Even a decade ago, "a significant percentage of Catholics connect[ed] clerical celibacy and child sexual abuse," and 42 percent of American priests thought sexual abuse in the church was a "very serious" problem.[179]

An extensive investigation conducted by the *New York Times* in 2002 has provided the most reliable hard data on the amount of priestly sexual abuse in the United States. But the public will never know about many more perpetrators and victims because neither party wishes to testify about the traumatic circumstances, and prelates would prefer to keep these matters hidden. Journalist David Gibson writes, "The sexual abuse of children is one of the most underreported crimes; the U.S. Department of Justice estimates that only 30 percent of abuse is reported."[180]

The *Times* survey discovered abuse in all but 16 of the 177 Latin Rite American dioceses. (In 1992, attorney Jeffrey Anderson, a specialist in clergy sex abuse, had reported cases in every one of the dioceses.[181]) The more than 4,000 victims who were willing to communicate with the *Times* investigative reporters have charged 1,200 priests with sexual molestation. Some 16 percent of the priests had five or more victims. Sixteen dioceses divulged lists showing that more than 5 percent of their priests ordained between 1950 and 2002 had been accused of abusive conduct, including Boston with 5.3 percent, and Baltimore with 6.2 percent. Five of the ninety-four priests accused in Boston were removed in 2002. Although the archdiocese of Boston has received the most scrutiny, "more than a dozen other dioceses had a higher rate of accused priests." Four-fifths of them have been accused of molesting boys, whereas nonpriests who have been accused of sexual abuse have girls as victims by about the same percentage. "While the majority of the priests were accused of molesting teenagers only, 43 percent were accused of pedophilia."[182]

The work of the *Times* reporters illustrates the difficulty of penetrating covert activity. A Mr. O'Connor told them of being raped by priests when he was ten. He dared not volunteer information about what had happened to anyone, but he had to tell his mother after she inquired about blood on his underwear. When his parents threatened to bring charges, Cardinal Spellman reassigned to other parishes the three involved priests. O'Connor knew of ten other boys who had been similarly attacked and whose mothers were aware of it but did not protest to church authorities. As psychiatrist William Reid reports, "careful studies have indicated . . . that child molesters commit an average of sixty offenses for every incident that comes to public attention."[183] Since victims usually come from devout Catholic families, outcries are often not forthcoming out of recognition that the protesting of debased assaults might besmirch the public image of the church they love. Some victims perceive that sexually active priests and bishops are reluctant to disclose molestation by fellow clergy for fear of exposing themselves.

Philip Jenkins has written much about these matters, including a book on pedophilia among priests.[184] Rejecting the findings of Sipe as well as others with similar data on clerical sexual molestation of children, he estimates that 2 percent of Catholic priests might be involved in misconduct, and claims that hardly any are "sexually interested in pre-pubescent children." Moreover, without supporting data, he opines that "virtually all" of these cases involve sex between older teenagers and priests, who "are likely to be involved with just one or two individuals."[185] Jenkins vilifies Catholic liberals, whom he charges with exaggerating sexual abuse in the church to support their contempt for patriarchal tradition. "The legend of the pedophile priest is a powerful weapon for feminist groups," he charges.[186] Greeley justifiably excoriates Jenkins for his unfounded judgment that the American media created a sexual abuse crisis in the church where none existed.[187] Recovery of the church will not come through distraught apologists attacking the media or the victims of clerical crimes but rather through thorough probing of the deep-seated causes and engendering openness to difficult cures.

Friar Richard Rohr specifies the way in which celibacy appeals to some unhealthy types of men:

> The demand for celibacy as a prerequisite for ministry is a setup for so many false takers: . . . insecure or ambitious men who need stature; passionate men who need containment for their passions; men who are pleasing

their pious mothers or earning their Catholic father's approval; men who think "the sacred" will prevent their feared homosexuality, their wild heterosexual hormones, or their pedophilia; men with arrested human development who seek to overcompensate by identification with a strong group; men who do not know how to relate to other people and to women in particular.[188]

Sexual attraction for children begins for most pedophiles while they are adolescents. When confronted by repressive sexual environments, males more than females tend to redirect their impulses in abnormal ways. Youth who go into training for the priesthood after their teens may have earlier been sexually disordered, so it may not be the repressed sexuality of celibacy that transforms them into sexual predators. If they come from strict Catholic families, they may assume that attending seminary and taking the oath of ordination will inoculate them spiritually against their evil stirrings. Glen Gabbard, director of the Menninger Clinic where dozens of clerical pedophiles have been treated, says, "The most striking thing is the number of them who went into the profession as a way of dealing with . . . impulses to molest children."[189] As Jesuit psychiatrist James Gill puts it, "Some young people deep down fear their sexual inclinations and think the ambience and lifestyle of the priesthood will protect them from acting out their sexual urges."[190] They fancy that becoming part of a sanctified community will relieve their conflict of conscience and will prevent them from acting out their yearnings, or provide sanctuary if they do.

McBrien, an authority on American Catholicism, has commented on cases of sexual abuse:

> No matter how many priests are exposed, defrocked and even sent to prison, the problem is not going to go away. . . . Because the problem isn't only in the pool; it's in the . . . seminary pipeline. And at the root of the seminary problem is celibacy. . . . Obligatory celibacy has the effect of excluding a lot of healthy men who are called to the priesthood. It has the effect of attracting a lot of unhealthy men into the system. The celibate priesthood is a magnet for people who are psychologically and especially sexually disturbed.[191]

Bishop Joseph Galante of Dallas reflects on his own training, "You basically came out of seminary emotionally an adolescent." Having been stunted there has helped him to understand why some priests become involved in child molestation.[192]

Leslie Lothstein, the director of psychology at a Hartford clinic that has treated many abusive priests, notes that immature priests are often assigned to work with boys, and they experiment with those whom they find sexually attractive. "Their rationalization is that they've preserved their chastity because they've not had sex with adults, and nobody gets pregnant," Lothstein says.[193] New priests with deep sexual problems come to realize that verbal acceptance of celibacy is not enough to protect them against their overwhelming aberrant desires. On the contrary, they find that the church provides a community where suspicions of sexual escapades by its single employees have been low, at least until the past decade. They find altar and choir boys who are more likely to be submissive to the suggestions of one who has the aura of holiness. Boosted by the respect their collar commands, priests may feel little shame from their immoral and criminal behavior. Cozzens attributes the "little genuine remorse" that he found in many of these sociopaths to defective conscience formation, which in part may have resulted from their having been abused as youth.[194] Psychologist William Perri has found that "unconscious feelings of victimization and sexual inadequacy, both of which can be associated with enforced celibacy, may lead to a search for power and abusive control in relationships."[195]

An infamous 1977 Texas court case illustrates the way sexual abuse has often been condoned by the staff of a local parish. Priest Randolph Kos was convicted of seducing eleven boys, ages ten to eighteen, but one committed suicide before the trial began. Mark Jordan, who attended the trial that the diocese paid more than $10 million to settle, reports:

> Kos would lure boys with candy, video games, cigarettes, and—later—alcohol or marijuana. . . . Many of them spent nights in the rectory. Next morning, they would be introduced to the parish's other priests at the breakfast table. . . . Kos pretended to adopt one sixteen-year-old in order to move him into the rectory for several years as a steady sex partner. The arrangement was written up in the diocesan paper as a shining example of priestly philanthropy.[196]

Cozzens provides some explanation for such clerical misconduct:

> Immature adults . . . find healthy friendships with their own age group difficult. Relationships with minors . . . are less threatening. . . . The clergy abuse scandal may be read as yet another indicator that mandatory celibacy isn't working. Indeed, the suspicion grows that it may foster or reinforce, at least in some, the very psychosexual immaturity that lends to compulsive and diverse manifestations of destructive behavior.[197]

Psychiatrist Jay Feirman, who has treated many pedophiliac priests, is convinced that the incidences of the disorder would be reduced if there were no celibacy requirement. He works at a the Servants of the Paraclete clinic, established by a Catholic order for priests with unusual sexual proclivities who have engaged in abusive behavior.[198] Similarly, an active Franciscan attributes "rampant psychosexual problems," such as cases of child sexual abuse, to the celibacy law that threatens to destroy the priesthood.[199] Likewise, a Newfoundland priest convicted of sexually assaulting boys has charged, "Celibacy has turned otherwise normal men into monsters."[200]

Murphy found that as many as 50 percent of women in Catholic orders, about twice the number of women generally, are survivors of child sexual abuse:

> These people are in double jeopardy in the relational arena: (1) they have been robbed of their ability to trust because of the role violation perpetrated by their abusers and (2) they have been taught distorted lessons about their sexuality and its role in their lives. To complicate matters, many adult survivors enter ministry or vow celibacy with no conscious memories of their abuse. It is not until they work through their childhood trauma that they can even begin to deal with intimacy and sexuality issues in an honest way as adults.[201]

Catholic researcher Ann Wolf reported in 1996 that as many as 40 percent of American nuns had experienced sexual abuse, frequently by priests but also by other nuns. To protect the church, nuns have usually reported nothing after being victimized, so as of 2003 only one criminal charge by a nun against a priest is on record.[202] This suggests that stories of priestly scandals are only beginning to surface. Recognizing that the decline of nuns in the United States has been more precipitous than that of priests— to less than half the 1965 number, with ages now averaging in the seventies[203]—one wonders how many have left silently so that Catholicism would not receive a bad press by public disclosure of their abuse.

Abusive Prelates

Victims of Catholic sexual abuse have often been doubly violated, first by a priest and then indirectly by the bishop who hid the offense. Abuse of power by diocesan priests reflects the similar abuse they have received from their prelates, reaching up to the pope. The current scandal has unmasked the systemic failure of the church's feudal hierarchy. Its duplicity, secrecy, and denial have enraged both Catholics and non-Catholics during the past decade.

The onus of sexual abuse, which often should be designated rape, has not fallen heavily on those who protect abusers. George Weigel, although a Vatican apologist, expresses this indignation: "The deepest angers of Catholics . . . have been reserved for bishops . . . who evidently did little to heal the personal and familial wounds caused by recklessly irresponsible priests."[204] Johanna McGeary tells about a cardinal virtue in the culture of prelates: "An obedient priest moves up in power by keeping his head down. . . . When cardinals are created, they take a vow before the Pope to 'keep in confidence anything that, if revealed, would cause a scandal.'"[205] Publicizing internal operations appears to perturb hierarchs more than the despicable issues themselves.

Jason Berry, a devout Catholic, after his lengthy investigation of child molestation by American priests and cover-ups by their superiors, wrote in 1992:

> The crisis in the Catholic Church lies not with the small fraction of priests who molest youngsters but in a power structure that harbors pedophiles. . . . For years, the bishops recycled offenders without telling parishioners. Rarely are the clerics defrocked . . . yet the church has no effective way to monitor offenders once they are put back in clerical life. The image of an all-seeing hierarchy ready to pounce on errant clerics is farfetched.[206]

Regarding the protection abusive priests have been given by their bishops and fellow priests, Greeley surmises, "Priests can do anything they damn well please to lay people and feel pretty confident that they can get away with it."[207] In 1993, when Massachusetts priest James Porter was on trial for sexual sadism against 200 minors, another priest who had watched one of his many rapes offered this defense, "Father is only human."[208] In 1983, the Vatican did modify its statutes so that the violation of celibacy law pertains to more than getting married. A cleric can now be punished or dismissed if he violates celibacy "by force, or with threats, or in public" with a minor under the age of sixteen. Raping a child might result in a priest's dismissal, but marrying a woman definitely would.[209] Presumably, if the violation is consensual and in private, punishment can be averted. Anthony Padovano comments on the abiding distorted values of Catholic prelates: "If you marry a woman, they are unrelenting in getting rid of you; they have a more benign attitude to pedophiles."[210] This outlook helps to explain why in 2004 the Vatican asked for a revision of the American bishops' "zero-tolerance" proposed policy on abusive clerics.

Laxity by the hierarchy may be due in some cases to bishops being involved themselves. Anthony O'Connell was sent in 1998 to replace Keith Symons as bishop of Palm Beach, who resigned after admitting that he had abused five boys. Four years later, O'Connell admitted that he provided "therapy" in 1975 for a teenage seminarian whom his clerical instructors had sexually abused. The treatment consisted of coaxing the boy to lie naked with him in bed. O'Connell resigned after being confronted with sex-related lawsuits.[211] Bishop Rembert Weakland of Milwaukee, prompted by the many heinous tales of clerical abuse of vulnerable children that have surfaced, expressed openness toward considering changing the hoary law of celibacy.[212] Yet Weakland subsequently resigned after acknowledging that he used $450,000 of charitable donations to silence a man who accused him of sexual assault. But the payment did not constrain the recipient, so the bishop had to resign after the accusation was made public.

Decades ago, Kennedy gathered data to inform the hierarchy about the arrested adolescence of many priests. When prelates disregarded such research, "the clerical scandal of pedophilia exploded as towering bins of grain do, not from outer attack but from within, out of the dangerous mist of dust that rises from the packed-down and airless conditions in the dark."[213] The church has often resisted professional therapy for psychopaths by placing aberrant behavior in the category of sin to be confessed, not realizing that it is also a sickness requiring quarantine and treatment. Victims are often given even less attention; dialogue with them is usually avoided. A counseling text used in several Catholic seminaries dismisses the sexual seduction of children in this way, "Nothing happens to the child if the parents keep their heads and do not behave as if some catastrophe has taken place."[214]

Edward Egan, while a bishop in Connecticut, permitted many priests accused of sexual crimes to continue their duties.[215] Also, by designating priests as "independent contractors," he maintained that the institutional church had no legal responsibility for their actions. A Jesuit authority at the Vatican in 2002 expressed a similar position: "From a canonical point of view, the bishop or religious superior is neither morally nor legally responsible for a criminal act committed by one of his clerics."[216] Egan's subsequent elevation in 2000 to archbishop of New York has stimulated Kennedy to ask, "Can we conclude other than that he has the Pope's approval for stonewalling on sexual abuse charges against the clergy, for practicing the equivalent of priest abandonment to protect institutional assets?"[217]

With his superior's approval, Terrance Sweeney surveyed American bishops regarding their viewpoint on celibacy. He found that the number who favored making celibacy optional had increased in 1990 to 32 percent.[218] Cardinal Joseph Ratzinger, head of the Vatican's Congregation for the Doctrine of the Faith—a position previously called the Grand Inquisitor—was disturbed by the finding and ordered Sweeney to destroy the data. Sweeney was under the obedience rule of Ignatius Loyola, the Jesuit founder, "To always be in conformity with the Church herself, we ought always to be ready to believe that what appears to us white is black, if she so defines it."[219] Although long an outstanding Jesuit, Sweeney had the integrity to resign from his order rather than comply with the Vatican's demand. Thus John Paul II, through his right-hand man for enforcing antiquated sexual policies, attempts to hide the truth that his own church's scholars discover if it deviates from his position.

Boston has become the Chernobyl of Catholicism, for practices in both cities were allowed to fester dangerously until an explosion occurred that continues to have a devastating and unprecedented fallout. Those epicenters have alerted people living elsewhere to inspect the region where they live to see if areas closed off to the public need to be cleaned up. In 2003, the attorney general of Massachusetts reported that 237 Catholic priests have been charged with sexual molestation in the Boston archdiocese since 1940 and that 789 minors have been their victims.[220]

The scandal in the flagship Boston archdiocese resulted in an open clash between higher and lower priests. The expression of a desperate need for new leadership was displayed when fifty-eight priests of the archdiocese petitioned for the resignation of Cardinal Bernard Law. Gibson describes him in this way: "He was the pope's man in America, a kingmaker whose word could make or break ecclesiastical careers. And from the bastion of Irish-Catholic America, Law spoke with the imposing voice of stern Catholic morality, reproving the faithful and excoriating the nation for its wayward behavior."[221] Americans were stunned to learn that for decades he had coddled sexual criminals. He retained an incorrigible serial sexual predator who had been accused of molesting more than 130 children, and there were dozens of other priests under his jurisdiction who allegedly have sexually abused children. Another such priest seduced girls studying to become nuns by telling them he was the second coming of Jesus.[222] Law used a sacrament for carrying out a cover-up after a victim informed him that one of his priests had sexually molested him as a child. The cardinal laid his hands on the man and said, "I bind you by the power of the confessional never to speak about this to anyone else."[223] James Carroll, formerly a Catholic university chaplain, comments, "The resignation-in-disgrace of Cardinal Law would be meaningful only in the context of an equivalent resignation by Pope John Paul II, of whose antireform policies—

closed, secretive, dishonest, totalitarian—Cardinal Law is a mere functionary."[224]

Yet the Boston revelations of long undeterred criminality are only the tip of the iceberg. Law was the nineteenth bishop worldwide and the tenth in the United States to leave office in recent years over such scandals. The news of celibacy-related defrockings of men of the cloth continue to make frequent headlines. Within a few days in 2002, not only were there subpoenas involving a Cincinnati archbishop and a Detroit bishop, but the pope also announced the resignation of Polish archbishop Paetz because of sexual abuse accusations. Those are in addition to the resignations in the 1990s of bishops and archbishops—not to mention ordinary priests—who were involved in sexual scandals.[225] In 2002, John Paul II summoned to Rome the eight American cardinals for what was widely said to be little more than a consultation on controlling the damage of the scandal publicity.

Priest Michael Baker informed Los Angeles Cardinal Roger Mahony in 1986 that he had sexually abused boys. But for the next fourteen years, Mahony continually reassigned him to six different parishes, where his spree continued. No warning was given to parishioners of the serial criminal in their midst, and of course no police were notified. The archdiocese paid more than a million dollars' hush money to the victims.[226] The Cincinnati archdioese was heavily fined in 2003 for failure to inform authorities about sexual abuse cases. Archbishop Daniel Pilarczyk pleaded no-contest to the charge of having "an institutional knowledge that certain felony sex crimes involving minors occurred."[227]

In 2003, Bishop Thomas O'Brien of the Phoenix diocese was granted immunity from prosecution for failure to report criminal misconduct. He avoided a prison penalty for obstructing justice by publicly admitting that he knowingly shielded sexually abusive priests and by agreeing to avoid handling personnel placements in the future. O'Brien disclosed that at least fifty church leaders have been accused of sexual contact with minors during his tenure as bishop. Because of this involvement, he submitted his resignation to the Vatican as spiritual leader of Arizona Catholics, but the church initially refused to permit him to step down.[228] Recognizing that seven American bishops have resigned in disgrace since 2002 over this abuse issue, it appears that Rome is attempting to halt a domino effect. However, after subsequently being charged with leaving the scene of a traffic accident for which he was not responsible, the Vatican decided that O'Brien had committed an offense significant enough to justify dismissing him as bishop.

The editor of the leading American Catholic magazine claims that the clerical scandal "has produced the greatest crisis in the history of the U.S.

Catholic Church."[229] The media has focused upon priestly sexual abuse in America, but the problem is global in scope and can be illustrated from the situation in Ireland. In 2003, more than a thousand lawsuits pertaining to this scandal were filed in that small country. Wags call the Curragh prison "the Vatican" because of the many priests who are inmates. In some Irish dioceses, convicted clerics have not been defrocked. Bishop Philip Boyce of Raphoe has been reluctant to expel a priest who was convicted and imprisoned for raping and molesting a dozen boys, some only ten years old.[230] The church has paid over a hundred million dollars "to Irish children who were sexually abused by priests, nuns and other church officials in decades past."[231] Looking beyond the American scene, McBrien thinks the scandal is "the most serious crisis the church has faced since the Reformation."[232]

Incredible inroads into church funds are now being made for settlements of abuse cases, for therapy costs to abusers, and for attorneys' fees. Attorneys have commonly been receiving much more than the victims.[233] Some fear that together, the legal and secret payoffs may leave the church financially as well as morally bankrupt. In 1985, a Louisiana jury awarded one million dollars in a child sex-abuse case because the predator priest was reassigned by his bishop to another parish where he abused more children. Afterward, it became almost impossible for dioceses to obtain liability insurance to cover future cases.[234] That should have been a wake-up call for prelates to become more aggressive to protect the children and defrock the perpetrators. Settlements increase each year, and now have exceeded more than a billion dollars in America alone with the implication of hundreds of priests in scandals during 2002. One notorious suit resulted in a $10 million settlement against John Geoghan, who was accused of molestation by nearly 150 boys over three decades, including raping some in the confessional.

The total costs of the plethora of recent lawsuits pertaining to clerical sexual abuse are difficult to estimate because each diocese operates as a separate corporation and reports directly to Rome. Moreover, bishops have often insisted on confidentiality agreements with victims to hide the terms of settlements. In the small Louisville archdiocese, several hundred plantiffs agreed to a $25.7 million out-of-court settlement of child-abuse suits against some twenty-seven priests. The payment is not covered by church insurance, so assets intended for charitable work have been depleted.[235] Later in 2003, the Boston archdiocese settled similar claims by paying $85 million plus therapy costs to 552 persons whose lives were devastated. Also, a California diocese has sued the Boston archdiocese for the damages it faced because of what a depraved priest did there after arriving with a letter certifying him to be in good standing.[236]

Lawsuits that may result in the highest settlements ever have been filed by native Americans against Jesuits who ran a dozen boarding schools on Sioux reservations across South Dakota for most of the past century. Many former students have charged that "predatory priests and nuns typically targeted children as young as six for sexual abuse."[237]

Change may be prompted by lay people who are voting with both their feet and their purses. Priestly predators and their protectors have caused 62 percent of members of the Boston archdiocese to lose confidence in their church, and one-third of that group said in 2003 that they have considered joining a non-Catholic church during the last year. Reforms may be effected if a pattern of decline in congregational contributions emerges, because the Vatican as well as Catholicism in the United States is dependent on the more than seven billion dollars that American Catholics give annually. In the Boston archdiocese, revenue from the annual fundraising appeal dropped 47 percent in 2002.[238] Catholics are now giving about 1 percent of their income to the church, about half of what they gave previously.[239] Increasing church finances was one of the reasons for the hierarchy's initiating mandatory celibacy, but now it may function as a reason for ending the requirement.

The pent-up anger over sexual violence in the church is also evidenced by the several lay advocacy groups that have sprung up in response to unconscionable assaults on innocence. The tradition of a passive laity who just pray, pay, and obey is over. A decade ago, a group called Survivor Connections collected more than five hundred cases of pedophilia among clergy of various faiths, but most of them pertained to Catholic priests.[240] An American support group made up of those who have been sexually traumatized is labeled VOCAL, for Victims of Clergy Abuse Linkup. Another such group is SNAP, Survivors Network of those Abused by Priests, which is composed of local units throughout the nation. Its membership was 4,600 in 2003, double that of the previous year. SNAP helps victims of "black collar" crimes cope with the emotional aftermath of exploitation, which is so serious that at least six committed suicide in 2002 and 2003. In addition, parishioners of a suburban Boston church who are eager for reform met together in 2002 to form the Voice of the Faithful (VOTF). Within a year, this grass roots movement evolved into more than 150 chapters nationwide with more than 30,000 members. A number of bishops in various states have refused to permit VOTF to meet on property under their jurisdiction, even though it is composed mostly of moderates seeking to restore trust between the laity and the hierarchy. VOTF recognizes that the long pattern of priestly sexual abuse will not greatly diminish until basic ecclesiastical changes are made.[241] VOTF has a reform agenda similar to the older Call to Action (CTA), which advocates discarding "the medieval discipline of mandatory priestly celibacy."[242]

Catholic hierarchs display institutional denial much like drug addicts who refuse to face up to their problem. In 1992, the National Federation of Priests' Councils voted sexual misconduct to be its top item of concern, but the princes of the church, who are unaccustomed to being challenged, took little notice. Judging from these prelates, one might presume that the seven last words of Jesus were: "Christians should never change the status quo." Columnist Maureen Dowd expresses her sense of betrayal by the church in which she was reared: "While teaching us not to lie or cheat, the church simply covered up its own sins, recycling abusive priests and putting parish after parish of children at risk, paying off victims and demanding their silence, refusing to admit that sexually assaulting children was a destructive crime and not merely a moment of moral weakness."[243] The Vatican is losing all semblance of integrity by continuing to scuttle discussion of the celibacy requirement No longer can the Church attempt to prevent the public from becoming aware of the requirement's violations.

Eugene Bianchi recognizes that the church's role of dispensing forgiveness is hampering its ability to weed out sexual deviants who find the priesthood a good place to hide.[244] Church officials, who seem to be unaware of the high recidivism rate of pedophiles, tend to accept assurances from them that their criminal behavior will never happen again. Priestly celibacy has provided a safe haven for child sexual abusers because of holiness and self-control expectations. The professed celibate has until recently been especially trusted by parishioners because of the presumption that he is an "athlete of sexual mastery." His dealings with youth have been thought of as "a meeting of the innocent with the innocent." Consequently he customarily has been given easy access to children by protective caretakers. Parents have previously given little thought to chaperoning children who are alone with a priest. Rather, the prevailing assumption has been that contact with someone who refrains from all sex will improve their moral fiber. But ordination bestows a power that can be used to dominate and intimidate children. Also, "the reverence due to heroic abstention has made civil officials chary of investigating, reporting, or prosecuting celibates' offenses."[245]

Ethicist Brian Linnane argues that sexual abuse has to do not only with immoral priests but with submission to the unbending patriarchal power structure of Catholicism. He observes that church authorities like "to claim that the problem of clerical sexual malpractice has to do with weak or deviant individuals and not with the discipline of celibacy as it is presently structured or the organizational character of the church." All of this is related to the theme of this study because, as sociologist Schoenherr concludes, "preserving compulsory celibacy in the Catholic Church is a smokescreen for preserving patriarchy."[246]

In 2002, John Paul II reacted to sexual scandals by scapegoating wayward priests rather than blaming also the sexual totalitarianism of the Vatican. But the problem cannot be solved "by better screening of candidates for orders or careful seminary training on respecting boundaries." When the hierarchy is confronted with cases of sexual abuse, it overlooks contributory systemic institutional culpability. According to Linnane, celibacy that is not experienced as freely embraced "can be symptomatic of a malaise that serves as a breeding ground for abusive relationships. While sexual renunciation itself does not explain clerical sexual malpractice, the experience of being a victim of sexually confining and controlling power might."[247] The celibate, in a powerless relation to his superiors, in turn exercises dominance over powerless males and females.

Linnane agrees with feminist Valerie Bryson who maintains that for celibates "sexual domination is so universal, so ubiquitous and so complete that it appears 'natural.'"[248] Linnane states, "The controlled sexuality of priests conforms with the power interests of the church hierarchy. . . . Sex and thus women are perceived as dangerous to this power structure." "Sexual abuse of adult women by members of the clergy is simply a blatant example of the destructive logic of patriarchy." "This same logic explains the homosexual abuse of men by members of the clergy."[249]

At the end of her historical study of celibacy, Abbott reflects on the unheeding Vatican in the face of the significant number of clandestinely uncelibate priests, as well as the many priests who have left the priesthood. "With the Vatican's intelligence system operating even more efficiently than the CIA's," she is sure that church officials cannot be unaware of the rampant sham. "Astonishingly, and pityingly, we are forced to conclude the Vatican chooses to trumpet the inviolability of clerical celibacy against a backdrop of a priesthood writhing, figuratively and literally, against that very ideal."[250]

In the "old-boy" network of prelates, an alibi occasionally given is that the sexual misconduct of Catholic priests is unlikely to be higher than that in other segments of the population. The Vatican fabricates that less than 1 percent of priests have abused minors. Cardinal Hickey, archbishop of the Washington archdiocese, similarly claims—without supplying any substantiating data—that sexual dysfunction is no more prevalent among Catholic clergy than among their non-celibate counterparts. Consequently, he argues that sexual misconduct in the priesthood would not be reduced by making celibacy optional.[251] Likewise, the late New York Cardinal John O'Connor asserted, "No one has ever been able to correlate celibacy with sexual abuse," and conservative Catholics continue to mouth that mantra. Tom Lynch, dean of a Toronto seminary, stonewalls, "Marriage does not change sexual abuse . . . and celibacy is not a factor."[252] Jenkins claims that evidence is lacking to suggest that Catholic clergy have a greater frequency of abuse than clergy of other denominations, so ending the celibacy requirement would have no bearing on solving the issue.[253]

Regardless of the hierarchy's stance, a wide sampling of Catholics in North America discloses that "a significant percentage of Catholics connect clerical celibacy and child sexual abuse."[254] A plurality of Catholics in the Boston archdiocese think celibacy is the primary cause of clergy sexual abuse.[255] Closer to the truth would be the slogan "Celibacy has nothing to do with perfection" rather than "Celibacy has nothing to do with perversion." Catholics are highly frustrated because their bishops prohibit discussion of celibacy as a cause of the current crisis.

Bishops usually dread to offer an opinion that deviates from that of the Vatican, but some have expressed their desire for more change in canon law. Irish bishop Willie Walsh, along with Bishop Pat Power of Australia, were the first senior Catholic churchmen to say that the Vatican's marriage ban on clergy may be a key factor in child sex horrors. Walsh advocates a probe of hundreds of priests who have preyed on children to test his theory. In 1998, bishops from the Pacific Ocean area, in recognition of abusive conduct toward both minors and adults by priests, were in Rome "clamoring" for the ordination of married men. In a pastoral letter that same year, Bishop Raymond Lucker of Minnesota urged that the celibacy law be dropped.[256] Monsignor Peter Conley of the Boston archdiocese raised and suggested an affirmative answer to this critical question, "If celibacy were optional, would there be fewer scandals of this nature in the priesthood?"

There are studies that suggest a linkage between sexual abuse and celibacy. Research by Mark Clayton and Seth Stern of the relationship between the denomination of clergy and imprisonment shows that although Catholics make up only 22 percent of the population of the United States, thirty-eight of the seventy-five clergy serving time for sexually abusing children between 1985 and 2002 have been Catholic priests.[257] To cite another example, Australia has approximately the same number of Catholic and Anglican clergy but more than three times as many Catholic priests have been convicted of sexual crimes—mostly against children— during the past decade.[258] Approximately 40 percent of Australian criminals claim to have been sexually abused as a child by a Catholic clergyman.[259] In prisons generally, pedophiles are treated harshly by fellow inmates who once might have been their victims. Monsignor Eugene Gomulka, supervisor of 250 chaplains in the U.S. Marine Corps from a

large variety of religious groups, has disclosed information on imprisonment or dismissal from the corps due to misconduct, which is not limited
to sexual abuse: "While priests comprised about 20 percent of the chaplains, they accounted for about 50 percent of the serious offenses." Over
three-fourths of the chaplains are Protestants, but they had less than half of
those problems. After carefully studying the matter, Gomulka concluded
that the significantly disproportionate ratio was due to the loneliness of
professed celibates.[260]

Psychotherapist and former monk Sipe, who has provided the longest
research into priestly sexuality and patterns of abuse, challenges the hierarchy's long-standing denial of a relationship between child predation and
obligatory celibacy:

> The scandal of priestly sexual abuse of minors . . . is primarily a symptom
> of an essentially flawed celibate/sexual system . . . based on a false under-
> standing of the nature of human sexuality. . . . To address the problem of
> sexual trauma in the church in any narrower context runs the risk of self-
> deception and certain failure similar to applying a bandage to a cancerous
> lesion. . . . If we can approach the original Christian perception of sexuality,
> there is hope of renewal and reform. . . . Celibacy is . . . a factor in the
> power system of the church and is intimately connected with its abuses.[261]

Sipe's focus on the basic cause of clerical sexual abuse brings to mind
Thoreau's observation, "There are a thousand hacking at the branches of
evil to one who is striking at the root."[262] Sipe implicates celibacy as an
accessory to crime: "When you glorify celibacy, rather than enlightenment
through fatherhood, children don't count for very much. That's why the
bishops and priests have no sense of the victims of pedophiles today—they
are not fathers."[263] Popular sentiment on this matter is expressed by a car-
toon that focuses on altar boys who are followed by an archbishop in a
cathedral procession. The prelate carries a placard expressing the shibbo-
leth, "Celibacy has nothing to do with pedophilia." One boy whispers to
the other, "If he were a father, I bet he wouldn't let anything happen to
kids." This aptly conveys that a real father, when dealing with a colleague
who has been convicted of child sexual abuse, would more likely be outraged by the crime and determined to be protective of the child.

A theological encyclopedia produced by Benedictines provides a concise
summary of the current questioning of celibacy in Catholicism:

> Clerical celibacy is called into question for various reasons: it is not intrin-
> sic to priesthood; it is not essentially more perfect than married love; its

historical origins are suspect, coming from a neo-Platonic view of sexuality and Old Testament ideas of ritual purity; there is evidence that its observance has always been problematic, at least for a significant minority, leading to the adage *si non caste, tamen caute* ("if unchaste, be discreet"); celibacy, being a charism, cannot be imposed; it can, and again for a significant number does, lead to a stunted affective life, and immaturity in relationships. The most significant argument against a law of celibacy, however, is the assertion that because of it the Christian people are in places being seriously deprived of the Eucharist.[264]

Tardily, the U.S. Conference of Catholic Bishops responded in 2002 to heavy criticism of their role in the clerical child abuse scandal by establishing an independent national review board composed of prominent lay Catholics. The board has attempted to compile statistics from 1950 to 2002 on the number, gender, and ages of victims as well as the number of abusers and how they were disciplined. About one-third of the 194 dioceses refused to disclose information on those matters. In 2003, frustrated board chair Frank Keating, a former prosecutor and Oklahoma governor, rashly compared obstructionist Cardinal Mahony, whose archdioese is the largest in America, to the Mafia, which resulted in Keating's resignation under pressure. Perturbed by the siege mentality of some prelates, he issued this parting shot: "To resist grand jury subpoenas, to suppress the names of offending clerics, to deny, to obfuscate, to explain away; that is the model of a criminal organization, not my church."[265] Gibson points out that the bishops who resisted Keating had Rome on their side, because to give laity any prerogative over bishops was a reversal of church tradition.[266]

In 2004, the board reported 10,667 allegations, mostly substantiated, of sexual abuse against minors, 81 percent of whom were boys. Under 4 percent of the 4,392 accused priests—4 percent of the total number of priests surveyed—were removed from the active ministry.[267] The reliability of this data is dependent on the willingness of bishops to make full disclosures, but their pattern has been to prioritize protecting their priests rather than diocesan children. The board did not make a thorough investigation because no attempt was made to verify what the bishops reported. Mandatory celibacy was not considered as one cause of the sexual misconduct.

Jesus directed his harshest criticism toward child abuse: "If any of you puts a stumbling block before one of these little ones who has faith in me, it would be better for you to be drowned in the deep sea with a large millstone fastened around your neck. . . . Be careful not to treat with contempt a single one of these little ones" (Matt 18:6, 10). Jesus also addressed hypocritical cover-ups: "Whatever you have said in the dark will be heard in daylight and what you have whispered behind closed doors will be shouted from housetops" (Luke 12:3).

Notes

1. Andrew Greeley, *The Catholic Myth* (New York: Scribner, 1990), 217.

2. Philippe Levillain, ed., *The Papacy* (New York: Routledge, 2002), 863.

3. John Paul II, *To All Pastors* (1992), 29.

4. Uta Ranke-Heinemann, *Eunuchs for the Kingdom of Heaven* (New York: Doubleday, 1990), 32–33, 37–38.

5. John Paul II, *The Theology of Marriage and Celibacy* (Boston: Daughters of St. Paul, 1986), 83–84.

6. John Paul II, *Letter to Priests* (9 April 1979), 8.

7. John Paul II, *The Theology of the Body* (Boston: Pauline Books, 1997), 157.

8. Jerome, *Letters* 22:5; *Against Jovinian* 1:49.

9. *Catechism of the Catholic Church* (Washington, DC: U.S. Catholic Conference, 2000), 882.

10. John Paul II, *On Priestly Ordination* (30 May 1993).

11. *Time,* November 5, 1990, 83.

12. *New Yorker,* April 1, 2002, 36.

13. *New Blackfriars* (March 1985): 277.

14. *Time,* November 5, 1990, 83.

15. *Time,* June 17, 2002, 63.

16. Richard Schoenherr and Lawrence Young, *Full Pews and Empty Altars* (Madison: University of Wisconsin Press, 1993), 30.

17. *Sociology of Religion* (Spring 1998): 15.

18. *U.S. Catholic* (December 2001), 26; *St. Louis Post-Dispatch,* January 7, 2003, B6.

19. *San Antonio Express-News,* May 20, 2001, G1.

20. CARA statistics.

21. Gordon Thomas, *Desire and Denial: Celibacy and the Church* (Boston: Little, Brown, 1986), 11.

22. Dean Hoge, *The First Five Years of the Priesthood* (Collegeville, MN: Liturgical Press, 2002), 60–64.

23. Elizabeth Abbott, *A History of Celibacy* (Cambridge: Da Capo, 2001), 384.

24. Thomas, *Desire and Denial,* 4.

25. Jonathan Kwitny, *Man of the Century* (New York: Holt, 1997), 614.

26. *National Catholic Reporter,* May 13, 1994, 9.

27. Paul Dinter, *The Other Side of the Altar* (New York: Farrar, 2003), 234.

28. Peter Steinfels, *A People Adrift* (New York: Simon & Schuster, 2003), 329.

29. Dean Hoge, *The Future of Catholic Leadership* (Kansas City: Sheed, 1987), 126.

30. Greeley, *The Catholic Myth,* 219.

31. Paul VI, *Priestly Celibacy,* 49.

32. Quoted in John Cornwell, *Breaking Faith* (New York: Viking, 2001), 152.

33. *U.S. Catholic* (December 2001), 27.

34. *Washington Post,* November 4, 1989, A21.

35. *New York Times,* August 20, 2003, 10; August 29, 2003, 14.

36. Associated Press, September 5, 2003.

37. *America,* December 1, 2003, 10.

38. *Fact Book on Theological Education* (Pittsburgh: Association of Theological Schools, 2003), 4–5.

39. David Rice, *Shattered Vows* (New York: Morrow, 1990), 24.

40. *Sociology of Religion* (Spring 1998): 30, 32.

41. Cornwell, *Breaking Faith,* 13–14.

42. *Daughters of Sarah* (Winter 1996): 16.

43. William Bassett and Peter Huizing, eds., *Celibacy in the Church* (New York: Herder, 1972), 154.

44. Ibid., 120.

45. John Carmody, "Celibacy and the Religious Experience of Roman Catholicism," *Religion in Life* (Spring 1971), 17, 23.

46. Elisa Sobo and Sandra Bell, eds., *Celibacy, Culture, and Society* (Madison: University of Wisconsin Press, 2001), 259.

47. Ibid., 250.

48. *New York Times,* May 6, 1993, A27.

49. Eugene Kennedy, *The Unhealed Wound* (New York: St. Martin's), 133.

50. Eugene Kennedy and Victor Heckler, *The Catholic Priest in the United States* (Washington, DC: U.S. Catholic Conference, 1972), 12.

51. Rice, *Shattered Vows,* 76.

52. Dinter, *Other Side of the Altar,* 89.

53. *National Catholic Reporter,* May 12, 1995, 21.

54. Dinter, *Other Side of the Altar,* 102.

55. *New Yorker,* June 17, 2002, 60.

56. Rice, *Shattered Vows,* 78.

57. *National Catholic Reporter,* March 19, 1993, 9.

58. Richard Schoenherr, *Goodbye Father* (New York: Oxford, 2002), xiv.

59. *Chicago Sun-Times,* June 13, 1992, 3.

60. *U.S. Catholic* (February 1999), 27.

61. Rice, *Shattered Vows,* 147.

62. Sheila Murphy, *A Delicate Dance* (New York: Crossroad, 1992), 135.

63. *America,* June 18, 1994, 22–23.

64. Schoenherr, *Goodbye Father,* 112, 176.

65. *Liechtenstein News Digest,* November 18, 2003.

66. David Gibson, *The Coming Catholic Church* (San Francisco: Harper, 2003), 256.

67. Rice, *Shattered Vows,* 80–81, 124.

68. *Raleigh Spectator,* July 10, 2002.

69. Edward Schillebeeckx, *The Church with a Human Face* (New York: Crossroad, 1985), 240.

70. *Christian Science Monitor,* September 4, 2003, 11.

71. John Cornwell, *Hitler's Pope* (New York: Viking, 1999), 94, 112, 176; Paul Murphy, *La Popessa* (New York: Warner, 1983).

72. Donald Goergen, *The Sexual Celibate* (New York: Seabury, 1975), 225–26.

73. Ibid., 159, 183, 203.

74. Peter McDonough and Eugene Bianche, *Passionate Uncertainty* (Berkeley: University of California Press, 2002), 96.

75. Goergen, *Sexual Celibate,* 189.

76. Raymond Hedin, *Married to the Church* (Bloomington: Indiana University Press, 1995), 202.

77. Cornwell, *Breaking Faith,* 155.

78. Dinter, *Other Side of the Altar,* 72.

79. Richard Sipe, *A Secret World* (New York: Brunner, 1990), 100.

80. Sheila Murphy, *A Delicate Dance,* 107, 133, 136.

81. *Washington Post,* November 4, 1989, A21.

82. *America,* November 4, 2000, 12.

83. Sipe, *Secret World,* 109, 124.

84. Ibid., 88–96.

85. Knight Ridder News Service, October 1, 1993.

86. Rice, *Shattered Vows,* 126.

87. Thomas, *Desire and Denial,* 7.

88. Rice, *Shattered Vows,* 120–21.

89. *Manila Standard,* March 11, 2003.

90. *Philippine Daily Inquirer,* June 26, 2003.

91. Andrew Greeley, *The Making of the Pope 1978* (Kansas City: Andrews, 1979), 99.

92. Rice, *Shattered Vows,* 123.

93. *America,* April 16, 1994, 12–13.

94. Sipe, *Sex, Priests, and Power,* 115.

95. *Katholische Nachrichien Agentur,* January 30, 1985.

96. Terrance Sweeney, *A Church Divided* (Buffalo: Prometheus, 1992), 28.

97. Abbott, *History of Celibacy,* 179.

98. John Mbiti, *African Religions and Philosophy* (Garden City, NY: Doubleday, n.d.), 174.

99. Bassett and Huizing, *Celibacy*, 155.

100. George Frein, ed., *Celibacy: The Necessary Option* (New York: Herder, 1968), 54.

101. Philip Jenkins, *The Next Christendom* (New York: Oxford, 2002), 33.

102. Emmett McLoughlin, *People's Padre* (Boston: Beacon, 1954), 92.

103. Gibson, *The Coming Catholic Church*, 256.

104. Jason Berry, *Lead Us Not into Temptation* (New York: Doubleday, 1992), 368.

105. *Newsweek*, May 6, 2002, 29.

106. *National Catholic Reporter*, March 16, 2001, 3–4.

107. *National Catholic Reporter*, August 10, 2001, 13.

108. *The Times of Zambia*, November 29, 2002.

109. *National Catholic Reporter*, September 7, 2001, 6.

110. Rice, *Shattered Vows*, 126–27.

111. Bassett and Huizing, *Celibacy*, 37.

112. Donald Cozzens, *The Changing Face of the Priesthood* (Collegeville, MN: Liturgical Press, 2000), 100.

113. Sipe, *Sex, Priests, and Power*, 136.

114. *Los Angeles Times*, April 10, 2002, B1.

115. Berry, *Lead Us Not into Temptation*, 183–84, 188.

116. James Wolf, ed., *Gay Priests* (San Francisco: Harper, 1989), 60.

117. *Commonweal*, June 14, 2002, 12.

118. *Newsweek*, May 6, 2002, 26.

119. Gibson, *The Coming Catholic Church*, 178.

120. Cornwell, *Breaking Faith*, 166–67.

121. Alfred Kinsey, *Sexual Behavior of the Human Male* (Philadelphia: Saunders, 1948), 651.

122. Edward Laumann et al., *The Social Organization of Sexuality* (Chicago: University of Chicago Press, 1994), 293–94.

123. *Newsweek*, May 6, 2002, 29.

124. Steinfels, *People Adrift*, 271.

125. *Catechism*, 2358.

126. *New York Times*, March 3, 2002, A1.

127. *America*, September 30, 2002, 8–9.

128. *Boston Globe*, August 1, 2003, A1.

129. Sipe, *Secret World*, 123.

130. *London Evening Standard*, April 30, 2002, 13.

131. Desmond Morris, *The Naked Ape* (New York: McGraw-Hill, 1967), 94.

132. Rice, *Shattered Vows*, 79.

133. Steinfels, *People Adrift*, 324.

134. *Commonweal*, June 19, 1987, 382–83.

135. Ellis Hanson, *Decadence and Catholicism* (Cambridge: Harvard, 1997), 297.

136. *Boston Globe*, April 23, 2002, E1.

137. Paul VI, *Declaration on Sexual Ethics* (1975), 3, 8.

138. *New York Times*, April 27, 2002, A14.

139. "Homosexuality," *New Catholic Encyclopedia* (New York: McGraw-Hill, 1967).

140. *Time*, June 17, 2002, 64.

141. Dinter, *Other Side of the Altar*, 72–73; Sipe, *Sex, Priests, and Power*, 173–75.

142. Sipe, *Sex, Priests, and Power*, 10.

143. Roger Peyrefitte, *Propos secrets* (Paris: Michel, 1977), 240–42; Mark Jordan, *The Silence of Sodom* (Chicago: University of Chicago Press, 2000), 92–93.

144. John Cooney, *The American Pope* (New York: Times Books, 1984), 109, 332 n. 25.

145. Sipe, *Secret World*, 128.

146. *Commonweal*, June 14, 2002, 12.

147. *Time*, May 20, 2002, 62.

148. *Sydney Morning Herald*, August 24, 2002, 37.

149. *National Catholic Reporter*, May 13, 1994, 9.

150. Berry, *Lead Us Not into Temptation*, 186.

151. Quoted in Jordan, *Silence of Sodom*, 156.

152. *Kansas City Star*, January 29 and November 5, 2000.

153. *Society* (March/April 2003): 13.

154. Richard Wagner, *Gay Catholic Priests* (San Francisco: Sexuality Institute, 1980), 12–14.

155. Gibson, *The Coming Catholic Church*, 164.

156. *Catechism*, 2352.

157. Sipe, *Secret World*, 143, 152.

158. Jordan, *Silence of Sodom*, 147.

159. Richard Ginder, *Binding with Briars* (Englewood Cliffs, NJ: Prentice-Hall, 1975), 172.

160. Cornwell, *Breaking Faith*, 70.

161. Ginder, *Binding with Briars*, 92.

162. David Gordon, *Self-Love* (Baltimore: Penguin, 1972), 39.

163. William Phipps, "Masturbation: Vice or Virtue," *Journal of Religion and Health* (September 1977): 191–93.

164. John Cornwell, *Breaking Faith*, 137.

165. *National Geographic*, September 2003, n.p., opening map.

166. *America,* July 16, 1994, 8.

167. Kinsey, *Sexual Behavior,* 471.

168. Sipe, *Secret World,* 139.

169. Thomas Fox, *Sexuality and Catholicism* (New York: Braziller, 1995), 189.

170. *Newsweek,* August 16, 1993, 44.

171. Francis Mondimore, *A Natural History of Homosexuality* (Baltimore: Johns Hopkins University Press, 1996), 6–9.

172. *Washington Post,* September 17, 1989, C1.

173. Fox, *Sexuality and Catholicism,* 187.

174. Richard Sipe, *Celibacy in Crisis* (New York: Brunner, 2003), 203.

175. *America,* March 20, 1993, 7.

176. Gibson, *The Coming Catholic Church,* 164.

177. Donald Cozzens, *Sacred Silence* (Collegeville, MN: Liturgical Press, 2002), 97.

178. *Time,* March 25, 2002, 54.

179. *America,* June 18, 1994, 23; July 16, 1994, 7.

180. Gibson, *The Coming Catholic Church,* 167.

181. *National Catholic Reporter,* November 3, 1992.

182. *New York Times,* January 12, 2003, 20.

183. Quoted in Cornwell, *Breaking Faith,* 165.

184. Philip Jenkins, *Pedophiles and Priests* (New York: Oxford, 1996).

185. *Society* (March/April 2003): 9; Philip Jenkins, *The New Anti-Catholicism* (New York: Oxford, 2003), 139–41.

186. Jenkins, *Anti-Catholicism,* 88, 152–54.

187. *Society* (March/April 2003): 40.

188. *Sojourners* (July 2002): 29.

189. Frank Bruni and Elinor Burkett, *A Gospel of Shame* (New York: Harper, 2002), 51.

190. *Newsweek,* August 16, 1993, 44.

191. Bruni and Burkett, *Gospel of Shame,* 228–89.

192. *Times-Picayune,* March 15, 2003, 16.

193. *USA Today,* July 16, 2002, D6.

194. Cozzens, *Sacred Silence,* 105.

195. William Perri, *A Radical Challenge for Priesthood Today* (Mystic, CN: Twenty-Third Publications, 1996), 66.

196. Jordan, *Silence of Sodom,* 95.

197. Cozzen, *Sacred Silence,* 102–3.

198. *The Economist,* July 18, 1992, A28.

199. *St. Anthony Messenger,* August 1986.

200. *Toronto Star,* July 30, 1990, C1.

201. Sheila Murphy, *Delicate Dance,* 110.

202. *Toronto Star,* February 1, 2003, K1.

203. Cozzens, *Sacred Silence,* 69.

204. George Weigel, *The Courage to Be Catholic* (New York: Perseus, 2002), 29.

205. *Time,* April 1, 2002, 31.

206. *Washington Post,* November 15, 1992, C5.

207. Ibid.

208. Sipe, *Sex, Priests, and Power,* 11.

209. *Code of Canon Law,* 1394–95.

210. *Washington Post,* August 8, 1993, C3.

211. *Palm Beach Post,* March 9, 2002, A1.

212. Bruni and Burkett, *Gospel of Shame,* xvi.

213. Kennedy, *Unhealed Wound,* 136.

214. *Washington Post,* August 8, 1993, C3.

215. *Hartford Courant,* March 17, 2002.

216. Gibson, *The Coming Catholic Church,* 40.

217. Kennedy, *Unhealed Wound,* 138–39.

218. Sweeney, *Church Divided,* 33, 58.

219. Ignatius Loyola, *Spiritual Exercises* (1540), 2:13.

220. *Time,* August 4, 2003, 20.

221. Gibson, *The Coming Catholic Church,* 4.

222. Associated Press, September 10, 2003.

223. James Carroll, *Toward a New Catholic Church* (Boston: Houghton Mifflin, 2002), 6.

224. *New Yorker,* April 1, 2002, 35.

225. *National Catholic Reporter,* June 16, 1995, 28.

226. *Los Angeles Times,* May 16, 2002.

227. Associated Press, November 20, 2003.

228. *New York Times,* June 3, 2003, A18.

229. *Commonweal,* December 20, 2002, 10.

230. *News of the World,* November 3, 2002.

231. Associated Press, January 31, 2002.

232. *Boston Herald,* December 5, 2002, 8.

233. *America,* July 7, 2003, 11.

234. *America,* February 18, 2002, 3.

235. *Washington Post,* June 11, 2003, A10.

236. *New York Times,* April 9, 2003, 18.

237. *Washington Post,* June 2, 2003, A1.

238. Associated Press, May 11, 2003.

239. Steinfels, *People Adrift,* 30.

240. *Newsweek,* August 16, 1993, 44.

241. *America,* November 25, 2002, 30.

242. Gibson, *The Coming Catholic Church*, 121.

243. *New York Times*, March 20, 2002, A29.

244. *National Catholic Reporter*, April 27, 1993, 23.

245. Garry Wills, *Papal Sin* (New York: Doubleday, 2000), 183–84.

246. Schoenherr, *Goodbye Father*, 10.

247. Gary Macy, ed., *Theology and the New Histories* (Maryknoll NY: Orbis, 1999), 231, 233, 236.

248. Valerie Bryson, *Feminist Political Theory* (London: Macmillan, 1992), 185.

249. Macy, *Theology*, 234–35, 243.

250. Abbott, *History of Celibacy*, 381.

251. *Washington Post*, August 15, 1993, C7.

252. *Edmonston Journal*, February 2, 2003, D6.

253. *Survey* (March/April 2003): 9.

254. *America*, June 18, 1994, 22–25.

255. Associated Press, May 11, 2003.

256. *U.S. Catholic* (February 1999), 30.

257. *Christian Science Monitor*, March 21, 2002, 1, 4.

258. (Sydney) *The Age*, April 17, 2003, 4.

259. Thomas Plante, ed., *Bless Me Father for I Have Sinned* (Westport, CN: Praeger, 1999), 127.

260. *America*, August 27, 2001, 17.

261. Sipe, *Sex, Priests, and Power*, 4, 5, 7, 46.

262. Henry Thoreau, *Walden*, part 1.

263. *Washington Post*, August 8, 1993, C3.

264. "Celibacy of the Clergy," *Ecclesia* (Collegeville, MN: Liturgical Press, 1996).

265. *New York Times*, June 17, 2003, A16.

266. Gibson, *The Coming Catholic Church*, 41.

267. *New York Times*, February 28, 2004, A1; The National Review Board, *A Report on the Crisis in the Catholic Church in the United States*, February 27, 2004.

Chapter 9

CONCLUSION

❧

The Heritage in Summary

This historical study has exposed much in the church that is incongruous with the biblical doctrine of the goodness of creation as set forth in Genesis, and as endorsed by Jesus. Assumptions about the intrinsic depravity of sex have been attributed throughout most of church history to a presumed curse conveyed by Adam's semen. The shame associated with organs that have both sexual and eliminative functions is derived not from the "fall of our first parents" when they disobeyed what the Creator ordained, but rather from personal phobias arising from childhood training by our immediate parents and their surrogates who have treated sex as dirty. By contrast, the Song of Songs, a book in the Hebrew Bible whose title is an idiom meaning "the finest song," tells of naked spouses entwined and achieving a guiltless satisfaction.[1] Apropos is a New Testament proverb, "To the pure all things are pure" (Titus 1:15, NRSV). Those who view sex as defiled and marriage as second best to virginal life have not been inspired by either testament of the Christian Bible.

Lifelong celibacy was completely foreign to the ancient Judeo-Christian outlook, both in theory and in practice. A Jewish editor expresses a characteristic repulsion toward the sexual attitudes of ascetic Christians: "The ancient Hebrews and the later Jewish scholars have not been troubled by

237

the fantastic imbalance of attitudes that, springing in part from the vicious and repugnant idea of original sin, has so harassed Christian marriage in the past, and works havoc still. . . . Also, the theory that enthrones celibacy has always been to Judaism alien and abhorrent."[2] Nor can priestly celibacy be traced to a strong celibate tradition during the formative years of the church. My survey has shown the error of Vatican II's assertion that "the Church has always held in especially high regard perfect and perpetual continence."[3] The church started when Jesus accepted the testimony of Simon ben Jonah, a.k.a. Peter, but the sexual key entrusted to him was lost as "the keys of the kingdom" were transferred to bishops in "apostolic succession" (Matt 16:16–19). Unfortunately, the marital status of that alleged premier bishop of Rome did not become petrified in tradition. The Apostle Paul was de-married while on his missionary journeys, but he pointed out that he was atypical among the apostles and asserted that all Christians have the right to marry (1 Cor 9:5). Philip Jenkins engages in pseudo-history when he declares that "priestly celibacy is a product of the very early Church" and that it is "simply wrong" to maintain that priests were generally married during the first millennium of the church.[4] As has been shown, marriage was common for Christian leaders during the first ten centuries. Without warrant, Jenkins dismisses those who read history differently on this matter as "anti-Catholic."

The church was nurtured under the wing of Hebrew culture, but before the fledgling had matured, the Jewish state was destroyed, separating the early church from its native habitat. The popular veneration for virginity in pagan cults of the Mediterranean area partially eclipsed the biblical emphasis on both the integration of the spirit-body and the sanctity of the physical. Abstention from marital sex was an ascetic virus transmitted into Gentile Christianity from currents of its surrounding culture, especially from Neopythagoreanism, Neoplatonism, Stoicism, and Manichaeism. Subsequently, by subtle eisegesis, some biblical texts were interpreted to support alien ideas often inimical to the main outlook of its ancient Jewish and Christian authors. The two verses most often quoted out of context as endorsements for clerical celibacy were Matt 19:12 and 1 Cor 7:8.

After several centuries of Christianity had passed, lifelong continence was praised by bishops, and centuries more passed before it was generally enforced. Priests, who began in the second century to take charge of individual congregations, were not expected to abstain from marital sex any more than were the laity. In the third century, temporary sexual continence of married priests before administering the Eucharist began to be advocated. In the fourth century, a local synod in Spain enacted a rule demanding that priests stop having sex with their wives, which a succession of popes attempted to make applicable to all churches. In the twelfth century, the Catholic Church exercised supremacy over secular and sacred matters in western Europe by declaring all clerical marriages invalid. Subsequently, many or most priests interpreted the restriction to mean that sexual relief would need to come from outside of marriage by means of one or more of the following: concubines, whores, boys, or masturbation.

Priestly celibacy in church history displays the emergence of sexual attitudes markedly different from those of original Christianity. After dealing with this subject, William Cole drew this severe but sound conclusion, "The church has been guilty of preserving and preaching a point of view not generic to Christian faith, an attitude which originated in Hellenistic dualism and which is not only un-biblical but also anti-biblical."[5]

In the second millennium of Christianity, policies concerning clerical marriages have been the best-known differences between Roman Catholicism and all of the other Christian denominations. The schisms between Greek and Latin Catholics in the eleventh century and between Protestantism and Roman Catholicism in the sixteenth century were occasioned in significant part by conflict over celibacy. The conflict reflects broader ethical disagreements over birth control, virginity, sexual pleasure, family responsibility, charismatic gifts, women's status, community living, personal dignity, and human rights.

In her *History of Celibacy*, which is vast in scope, Elizabeth Abbott comments:

> Most pagans and Jews considered it peculiar and unnatural, detrimental to society, and fatal to the species. . . . But as the struggling cult of Christianity swelled in number, its leaders began to argue that a permanently celibate priesthood should be established. It was never a popular notion, especially among married priests and, one must presume, their wives. To this day, clerical celibacy is the most divisive, difficult, and draining issue in the Roman Catholic Church, the only Christian denomination to demand it.[6]

Opposition to mandatory celibacy has been smoldering for the past generation in the liberal sector of the Catholic clergy. Following the relative openness of John XXIII on the topic, this matter is now a frequent topic of internal discussion among the lower priests. Ukrainian priest Petro Bilaniuk echoes the words of that pope when he writes about the celibacy law: "It originates not from above, but from below. It comes from a positive will of a human ecclesial authority which requires more of priests than the positive will of God expressed in divine revelation."[7] Contrasting current Catholic training with the historical reality, Paul Dinter recalls, "Leading authorities always assured us [seminarians] that God would not allow us to be tempted beyond our capacity, but it was clearly not God who was demanding celibacy of us—no matter what the bishops claimed."[8] James Kavanaugh speaks for many of his fellow priests when he calls celibacy "a senseless law" and claims that it "hides the very Christian love it once was meant to serve."[9] The latent antagonisms of priests have been reflected in polls showing that the majority favor having the freedom to marry. Were the issue to be decided by secret ballot, they would no doubt vote to reject the medieval celibacy requirement.

Ex-Jesuit Peter De Rosa, who was trained in Rome and knows Vatican history well, excoriates the fiasco even more severely than Abbott:

> The Catholic church has nearly always been in crisis over clerical celibacy. . . . The fact is that priestly celibacy has hardly ever worked. In the view of some historians, it has probably done more harm to morals than any other institution in the West, including prostitution. For everyone is on his guard against women of the streets, whereas ministers of the Gospel, even when unfaithful, are given respect and personal confidences.[10]

Strange as it may seem, a priest's church position is severed by entering into holy matrimony but not by participating in trysts that are customarily deemed immoral. A priest can obtain absolution for sexual irregularities from an ordinary confessor, but pardon for marriage can be obtained only from the Supreme Pontiff and on the condition that he abandon his wife. Clerical marriage is recognized as a more serious evil than promiscuity in canon law because marriage is by its very nature is an open acknowledgement of cohabitation. The church officially tends to wink at affairs that are kept discreetly silent inasmuch as they do not damage its virginal public image. In dealing with reported clerical sexual misconduct, the operating procedure of Catholic hierarchs has usually been to scold the abuser, condemn the victim, and—if possible—sweep all iniquities out of public sight.

When accounts of priests' sexual misconduct with children and with adults are made public, the Catholic hierarchy has launched desperate efforts to control the damage. The harm done to the personalities of the individuals involved in this exploitative and surreptitious behavior has been secondary to keeping the establishment's sepulcher whitewashed. All of this is done in the name of the one who alerted his followers about encountering lovely tombs with corruption inside (Matt 23:27). Hypocrisy, which was for Jesus one of the most deadly of vices, has become commonplace in the celibate system that tends to esteem outward respectability more than inward character. Significantly, Pope Gregory the Great, who strongly advocated celibacy, did not include hypocrisy in his famous list of the "seven deadly sins." The few priests who pray on their knees on Sunday and prey on women or children during the week are like the lambskin-garbed wolves whom Jesus denounced (Matt 7:15). Over the past millennium, irreparable harm to the cause of religion has been done by such priests and by their overseers who have tolerated diabolical dissemblance with regard to celibacy.

Even apart from condoning sexual malfeasance by shifting erring priests from parish to parish, the hierarchy has failed the church by not permitting full debate on areas where sexuality impinges on canon law. These areas include not only celibacy but the status of women, homosexuality, masturbation, artificial contraception, abortion, and divorce. Currently prohibited are artificial insemination, in vitro fertilization, and surrogate motherhood, methods that can enable married women to conceive who would be otherwise unable to procreate.[11] This ban runs counter to what Catholics have held to be the first purpose of marriage.

Meanwhile, the church has retreated into its institutional tower along the Tiber and refuses to face the reasons why thousands are departing from the priesthood. But church closets previously sealed from public scrutiny are now being pried open. As secrecy is removed and frankness expressed, blatant immorality and criminal behavior in the exploitation of children and women is being exposed. Required celibacy is seen to fester and foster the very injustice that the gospel opposes.

Especially poignant is the sexual abuse of children by priests, which clearly is not only a recent phenomenon. Recognizing that laws are enacted historically in response to violations of community standards, it is significant that "Do not seduce boys" is included in the first church manual.[12] One of the earliest councils decreed that men who had sexually abused boys could not be accepted by the church even when dying.[13] Subsequently, the medieval church ruled, "Any cleric or monk who seduces young men or boys, or who is apprehended in kissing or in any shameful situation, shall be publicly flogged and shall lose his clerical tonsure."[14] Disclosures by the Protestant Reformers of sixteenth-century practices illustrate that the requirement of priestly celibacy has exacerbated sexual immorality in every century in which it has been present.

Research data confirms a saying of Horace, a pre-Christian Roman writer. His words aptly describe the result of the Vatican's attempts over the centuries to lock out sex: "If you drive out nature with a pitchfork, she will still find a way back."[15] Her reentry into one's personal abode is more likely to be through the sewer below than through a window above. To remain honest and credible, the church will have to reject what has been developed on a misunderstanding of Holy Scripture and human nature. Of course, removing celibacy will not eliminate sexual abuse any more than removing handguns will eliminate homicides. Pedophilia will continue to have its largest expression in incest involving a father and daughter. Moreover, since a significant number of married ministers are unfaithful, and even abusive sexually, having a publicly acknowledged permanent partner is no guarantee of proper sexual conduct. However, studies show open-minded persons that crime and immorality can be significantly lessened if fundamental changes are made in policies toward guns and celibacy.

On Imitating Jesus

The dominant church in many nations has been a poor conduit for Jesus' views on marriage. Some of his major interpreters in the postbiblical period have assumed that he conscientiously objected to marriage for himself and encouraged his disciples to take a similar stance. Beginning with ascetic church leaders who lived more than a century after Jesus, claims were made that he was indubitably a celibate. Appeal to the founder of Christianity continues to be the main support that prevents the church's ruling on priestly celibacy from collapsing. Paul VI cited as an alleged fact the example of Jesus as the compelling reason for the law of celibacy: "Christ remained throughout his whole life in the state of celibacy, which signified his total dedication to the service of God and men. . . . [The celibate priest is likewise] more free from the bonds of flesh and blood."[16] That pope called celibacy a "sign of the values of faith, of hope, of love, an incomparable condition for full pastoral service."[17] Catholic sister Margaret Maxey observes, "Advocates of mandatory celibacy . . . presume that an unquestionable and divinely advocated celibacy of Jesus provides everyone concerned with . . . a convincing social legitimation . . . and a sufficient personal motivation [for religious celibacy]."[18]

However, nowhere in the New Testament are any followers of Jesus asked to follow his personal example in deciding whether to become married or to remain married. The only mandatory requirement that he gave his disciples was to be of humble service to one another. Maundy Thursday was so named in the medieval church because the Latin Bible refers to Jesus' command (*mandatum*) at the Last Supper to wash one another's feet (John 13:14). Christians should follow the example as well as the order of the church's founder and focus on lowly assistance to the needy—going beyond a ceremonial foot-washing sign to the reality.

Recognition of Jesus' true humanity and concomitant libido can benefit both clerics and non-clerics, married or single. An honest look and revitalized understanding of how Jesus' manhood might have been expressed should encourage a healthier outlook on our own sexuality, and on sex education for others. If historical probability favors a married Jesus, as I think would be concluded from a judicious examination of his life and times, this subverts the celibate Christian's claim that he or she is following Jesus' pattern more closely.[19]

If Jesus blessed marriage by personal practice as well as by lofty tribute, then more could result from this discovery than the removal of the legalized celibacy excrescence that has long disfigured the body of Christ. Christians could more clearly perceive, as he did, that the Yahwist's theology of marriage is ongoing truth for the general population. "It is not good for the human being [*adam*] to be alone" is not only the rationale for stable sexual partnership in the ancient Israelite culture; anthropological investigations disclose that it is universally valued as a means for obtaining individual and social fulfillment.[20] Throughout history, marriage has developed whole persons, integrating body and soul.

Since celibacy etymologically means "alone," what God said in the symbolic paradise could read, "It is not good that the human should be celibate; I will provide a partner" (Gen 2:18). Study after study of Catholic priests reveal that "loneliness" is one of the most frequent terms to arise in describing their privations, and it is a factor in the alcoholism problem that a significant number of them confront. According to a 1995 study, more than 10 percent of American priests are alcoholics,[21] which is several times the rate for American males generally. How ironic it is for loneliness to be prominent among those representing the gregarious person who compared life with his disciples to a wedding party, and who deprecated withdrawal from sensuous enjoyments (Mark 2:19).

After reviewing what the Gospels say about Jesus' sexuality, Rosemary Ruether judiciously concludes:

> Jesus' life gives no exclusive sanctification to a particular sexual life style, whether celibate or married, hetero- or homosexual, as the normative model for Christians. On the other hand, there are aspects that are open to all of these options. None of these options is enshrined. None is ruled out as irretrievably contrary to the Gospel. Most of all, the Synoptic world is not a world obsessed with sexuality, either as the darkest sin or as the path of fulfillment.[22]

Clinical psychologist Eugene Kennedy evaluates the celibacy model: "That model, nowhere to be found in the attitudes of Jesus, explicitly says that the spirit is good and the flesh is not; that the soul is imprisoned in a betraying body."[23] That theory, on which celibacy is based, was held by monks who lived after the second century, especially Jerome, Augustine, Gregory VII, and Aquinas. As we have seen, they molded subsequent Catholic thought and practice when they projected back onto Jesus the celibacy notions they had unwittingly imported from pagan philosophy and cults. By way of monasticizing the church, they gave higher status to monks, who were "regular" clergy, in contrast to the "secular" priests in parishes.

The considerable attention given to Jesus' alleged celibacy in this study has not been because his marital status is of central importance in considering his life and mission. Rather, a thorough probe has been presented to ascertain the way he might have expressed his sexuality in order to discover if his example is indeed that of celibacy. The apostles did hold that Christ's life is the paradigm for Christians (Phil 2:5; 1 Pet 2:21), but undiscriminating attempts to duplicate that pattern without attention to the difference between his culture and one's own culture can do violence to the integrity of his message and lifework. Jesus lived in a specific time and place, and his actions were relative to that historical environment. To follow him does not involve adopting his particular marital arrangement, sharing his economic class, working in a building trade, living in a rural area, or worshiping in a synagogue on the seventh day of the week. The pattern he provided is not a cookie-cutter type intended for reproducing the externals of his life. One of the challenges of the Christian life is to discern which elements of Jesus' life are dated and dispensable, and which are integral and necessary for followers to use as examples.

Jesus testified that he came "to set at liberty those who are oppressed," and Paul reaffirms that "where the Spirit of the Lord is, there is freedom" (Luke 4:18; 2 Cor 3:17; Gal 3:6, 13). "The only thing that counts is faith working through love," the apostle said; "for you were called to freedom, brothers and sisters." Consequently, those who accept Jesus as their superlative model seek to make life's sexual choices responsibly. True love is neither sexual anarchy nor sexual abnegation; such polarization is the negation of authentic love. Freed love is the full expression of spirit through flesh, which gives partners long-range obligations as well as delightful liberties. Unless the imitation of Jesus is interpreted broadly, it can involve surrender of individuality and make a travesty of Christian freedom.

Qualities that can be embodied by either the unmarried or the married are what count most in genuine Christian living. Christians should attempt to exemplify in their diverse cultures the most Christlike expression of loving attitudes, enabling relationships, and courageous deeds. Jesus' qualities for emulation are compassion, worship, justice, and joy—not the way he expressed, or restrained from expressing, his testosterone.

Some are called to the priesthood and not to celibacy, and vice versa; others are called to neither or to both. In the context of discussing the option of marriage, Paul advised, "Let each of you lead the life that the Lord has assigned, to which God called you" (1 Cor 7:17, NRSV). The vocation for each individual is to express love in a way that harmonizes with his or her situation. To advise a minister that celibacy is best for "the sake of the kingdom of God" in one situation or that marriage is best for another situation is one thing, but to require either for all who choose church careers is against the spirit of Jesus' teaching. The New Testament counsel that a church leader should be married may fit a particular historical situation, and indeed, many contemporary situations, but if taken as legislation to be applied to all, it can rob the church of many valuable ministers.

William Hoyt aptly questions the strong marriage sanctions in some professions:

Does one have to be sexually active to be sexually authentic? Rather, is it not the fully sexed person who can decide what his sexual role will be without feeling the need to prove to himself or anyone else that he is virile? . . . One may ask whether the unofficial but widely enforced rule that Protestant ministers must marry has always had wholesome results. A man can be called to be a minister without being called to be a husband and father. Indeed, is not marriage a requirement not only in the ministry but in many other segments of our society for those who wish to be promoted in the organization, or included in the social life, or become eligible for income shelters? . . . We need liberation for those who wish to live a celibate life; we must grant them the recognition that they too may be dealing authentically with their sexual nature.[24]

A problem arises in this regard in Semitic religions, where marriage has traditionally been viewed as necessary for self-completion. Because of the need for many offspring in the underpopulated ancient world, where high infant mortality was the norm, the children of Abraham understandably regarded marriage as obligatory for all humans. Procreation was prerequisite to continuity of their society. That value undergirds a promise of God to Abraham, "I will bless you abundantly and make your offspring as numerous as the stars in the sky and as the sand on the seashore" (Gen 22:17). The perspective of classical Judaism is expressed in the judgments that "any man who has no wife is no proper man,"[25] and that "the Divine Presence rests only upon a married man, because an unmarried man is but half of a man."[26] Robert Gordis, a contemporary rabbi, less stringently states, "Judaism regards marriage and not celibacy as the ideal human state, because it alone offers the opportunity for giving expression to all aspects of human nature."[27]

Islam, another Semitic religion, has traditionally made marriage obligatory.[28] The Qur'an teaches that Muslims should marry at least once, and Muhammad was frequently espoused.[29] He said, "When a man marries he has fulfilled half of the religion; so let him revere God regarding the remaining half."[30]

Christians have occasionally joined historical Judaism and Islam in assuming that the humanity of an unmarried adult is necessarily diminished. As the Russian church developed in Eastern Orthodoxy, the marriage of diocesan priests was demanded. A canon of eleventh-century Georgios, metropolitan of Kiev, reads, "If anyone is unmarried he is not worthy to be a priest; once he has taken a wife let him be ordained a priest, for it is good to marry, and that there be children." Ukrainian priest Roman Cholij tells how the priestly profession was transmitted from father to son for centuries: "All priests who lived in village parishes were required to be married; their sons furnishing future candidates for the clerical state. . . . In seventeenth century Russia, Tsar Peter the Great reinforced the practice by establishing special schools for the sons of priests."[31]

Some Protestants have been almost as rigid in expecting clergy to marry as Catholics have been in demanding the opposite. According to the contemporary popular Lutheran pastor Johann Hampe, "It is inconceivable that the clergy should abstain from marriage."[32] The eminent theologian Karl Barth has criticized fellow Protestants who, in reaction to Catholic priestly celibacy, have declared marriage to be an obligation for every able-bodied person.[33] Taunting his fellow Protestant ministers, Charles Smith observes, "A clergyman who remains unmarried for more than a year after graduation from seminary is suspected of being abnormal, immoral, or chicken."[34]

There are many unmarried adults who are well adjusted, responsible, reverent, and skillful in interpersonal relations, as well as married folk who lack such pastoral qualities. Celibacy can be chosen for reasons other than gender hang-ups or intimacy timidity. Personal responsibility for a significant task may prompt an individual to opt not to marry or propagate. Occasionally one hears of a person who has forgone matrimony out of a sense of duty to care for a handicapped family member. Bishop Francis Asbury, who rode thousands of miles on horseback to establish Methodism in early America, realized that marriage was inappropriate for circuit riders who had no home base of operation. He lamented that hundreds of his itinerating preachers had quit out of preference for a settled family life.[35]

Consider Beethoven, a lifelong bachelor who was warmly disposed toward matrimony. To maintain that he was less of a man than Bach, who was married and had many children, is both unfounded and uncharitable. Erasmus and Pope John XXIII are likewise superb examples of the divinely inspired human spirit, even though, as Catholic priests, they presumably were not sexually active. Celibacy was a good thing for Asbury but he can be faulted for advocating the single life as the only acceptable way for Methodist evangelists to live.

Married Christians can be oppressive unless they acknowledge the legitimate lifestyle of those who have, without compulsion, accepted celibacy. Many who select that "road less traveled by" often inspire others by the loving way they live. Writer Kathleen Norris has described some joyous female and male celibates who befriended her during her years of affiliation with the Benedictine order.[36] My wife and I have similarly established an abiding friendship with Sister Teresa Reddington, whom I have affectionately called the bishop of Belington, a town in the West Virginia highlands without a resident priest. I doubt if the famous Mother Teresa surpassed her in cheerful and effective Christian service.

During this third millennium, lifelong sexual abstinence—whether for religious or nonreligious reasons—will probably have a status similar to vegetarianism or abstinence from alcohol. Those who participate in such atypical modes of living are generally deserving of respect. A person should have no more anxieties over abstaining from coitus than over renouncing meat or alcohol. Individuals who reject marriage because of patriarchal constrictions in their communities, or because they do not want to contribute to global overpopulation, can be compared to teetotalers who realize that they cannot otherwise control the consumption of spirits, or to vegetarians who believe that their bodies will be more healthy if they do not consume animal fat. Some with limited financial means or various other conscientious concerns may decide that marriage, alcohol, or meat is unnecessary for them.

But unwholesomeness results from those in minority lifestyles who feel morally and religiously superior to others. In weighing the single versus the non-single status, Paul's counsel of tolerance is helpful: "Meat eaters and vegetarians should not pass judgment on one another, for God has accepted them. . . . Meat eaters have the Lord in mind, since they thank God for their food; while those who abstain have the Lord in mind no less, since they too give thanks. . . . All that I know of the Lord Jesus convinces me that nothing is intrinsically unholy" (Rom 14:3, 6, 14).

⊚⍦⍩

The Vatican has not only made Jesus' alleged lifelong virginity the standard for its priests but has asserted that women cannot be ordained because they do not look like the male Savior. Issued during Paul VI's reign was an explanation as to why "the Church, in fidelity to the example of the Lord, does not admit women to priestly ordination": "When Christ's role in the Eucharist is to be expressed sacramentally, there would not be this 'natural resemblance' [Aquinas's words] which must exist between Christ and his minister if the role of Christ were not taken by a man: in such a case it would be difficult to see in the minister the image of Christ. For Christ himself was and remains a man."[37]

While calling for the "full participation" of women in the life of the church, the Vatican insists that this does not mean that they should be ordained.[38] John Paul II explains, "Precisely because Christ's divine love is the love of a bridegroom, it is the model and pattern of all human love, men's love in particular."[39] Since a "bridegroom" is male and the church is referred to as female, only males can represent Christ in the "bride's" sacrament of the Eucharist. In an apostolic letter, the pope defiantly declared, "The Church has no authority whatsoever to confer priestly ordination on women," because God in his wisdom planned otherwise.[40] So male superiority has been determined by a divine decision pertaining to Jesus' gender. Alas, in the church, biology continues to be destiny, now as in the medieval era. According to the official Catholic catechism, no women can be ordained because Jesus chose only males (Latin, *viri*) as apostles: "The Church recognizes herself to be bound by the choice made by the Lord himself. For this reason the ordination of women is not possible."[41]

Yet John Paul II has acknowledged that Mary Magdalene was given the title "Apostle to the Apostles" in the early history of the church because, according to John's gospel, she was the first to be "sent forth" (*apostello*) to proclaim to male apostles what the risen Jesus had disclosed to her.[42] According to Luke's criteria for selecting an apostle, namely companionship with Jesus throughout his public ministry and witnessing his resurrection (Acts 1:21–22), Magdalene better fits those two qualifications than does the Apostle Paul. Also, a letter of fifth-century Pope Gelasius recognizes that Christian women had been officiating at sacred altars, and inscriptions dating to that century refer to women ordained as priests.[43] It is mind-boggling to think of the policies regarding women that might have transpired if Magdalene had retained prominence and if Petrine primacy had not evolved. Would there have been women bishops with no gender subordination? Would there have been military crusades sponsored by the Church?

In spite of papal pronouncements, Jesus' gender is not relevant to imitating Jesus. As we have seen, he had both male and female followers, but called none of them to the ordained priesthood. Gender was deemphasized in the nascent church, for baptism symbolized a Christian oneness in which "there is no longer male and female" (Gal 3:27–28). Christ is proclaimed as the enfleshment of the perfect image of God that both females and males reflect (Gen 1:27; Col 1:15). Jesus is referred to as male (*aner*) only several times in the Greek New Testament, but he is frequently called *anthropos* (human being). Paul referred to him only as *anthropos*, showing that he did not view him primarily as a male but as the generic man who defines for both genders what it means to be genuinely human. Also, the creeds of the early ecumenical councils at Nicea and at Chalcedon use *anthropos* several times to describe Jesus' manhood. His maleness had little significance, especially since he did not advocate patriarchy or other kinds of oppression. As Catholic theologian Leonard Swidler discerns: "Jesus vigorously promoted the dignity and equality of women in the midst of a very male-dominated society: Jesus was a feminist, and a very radical one. Can his followers attempt to be anything less—*De Imitatione Christi*?"[44] The perennial issue is not which gender Jesus physically resembles but whether Christians, male or female, resemble their exemplar in how they live their lives. Happily, the majority of American Catholic men and women now favor ordaining women, whether celibate or married.[45]

Christians should pattern their lives after only those qualities of Jesus that are essential to full humanity. Attempts to imitate him should be relevant to the situation of all Christians regardless of whether they are single, married, separated, divorced, male or female, young or old. Because of nature or circumstance, no one can participate in all those modes of living. Jesus did not experience the gratifications and difficulties of old age or of being female, but that fact does not make him less relevant as a matrix for individuals in those groups, who make up the vast majority of humankind. Likewise, marriage and parenthood are not essential for full humanity, so a married or unmarried person of either sex has the potential for representing Jesus, the paradigm of true humanity.

Now that the reproductive function of marriage is no longer generally recognized as primary, it can be seen more clearly that the life of bachelors, or those earlier stigmatized as "spinsters," need not be judged as less than fully human. A Christian might decide that he or she can aim at expressing the "mind of Christ" by choosing to remain unmarried, and concentrate on maximizing the quality rather than the quantity of life. The sharp increase in the number of single adults in the past generation in the United States demonstrates that the single-status option is now more appealing than in the past. However, modern medical technology has effectively isolated the procreative from other functions of marriage. Methods of birth control have given individuals the freedom to decide the question of becoming wedded independent of the question of adding new life to a crowded planet. Commendable chastity should include not only abstinent singles but also couples who have exclusive love for one another, regardless of sexual orientation. Hopefully, the church of the future will accept lay and clerical persons of those types.

Devoted gay and lesbian couples focus on companionship rather than on reproduction, and they may find in the gospel of Jesus an acceptance of their lifestyle. Some adopt children, and occasionally lesbians obtain them by artificial insemination. Being involved in a stable and exclusive relationship has religious as well as health benefits. When love and fidelity are mutually covenanted, whether the pair bonding is between those of the same or of the opposite sex, the church has questionable authority for shunning those who cannot obtain a marriage license or who are not publicly wed. An affectionate and committed couple who "cling together in one flesh" may be more "joined by God" than two who have obtained a clerical blessing or a state license. If those who have participated in formal nuptial rites are in a situation of permanent alienation, it is they who are "living in sin." Ironically, many Christians regard cohabitation to be wicked if not sanctioned by a public official, even though neither priests nor state officers performed weddings in the biblical culture. Christianity had been underway for centuries before religious officiants or government agents were either expected or required for performing marriages.

Moving toward Recovery

A six-year investigation by Richard Schoenherr and Lawrence Young accurately documented that "the Roman Catholic Church faces a staggering loss of diocesan priests in the United States as it moves into the 21st century." The continual increase in responsibility for already overloaded parish priests is causing a serious malaise. Compounding the problem is the barring from the priesthood even celibates who happen to be female. Leadership by a fulsome number of priests who are intellectually able and emotionally healthy is needed as never before. "To preserve the more essential elements of Roman Catholicism," Schoenherr and Young conclude, "the nonessentials, first compulsory celibacy and later male exclusivity, will need to be eliminated as defining characteristics of priesthood."[46] The critical shortage of priests and candidates for the priesthood, which is not just an American problem, should be causing the Vatican to view the future anxiously. Recognizing the adequate supply of clergy in most denominations without obligatory celibacy, a good case can be made that the shortage of priests would soon end if celibacy were optional.

Disturbed by that sociological assessment, Cardinal Roger Mahony of Los Angeles responded, "The Catholic Church in our country has been done a great disservice by the Schoenherr report." Mahony's preference to remain ignorant of scientifically gathered and analyzed information about the church's plight is revealed by the dichotomy he imposes, "We live by God's grace, and our future is shaped by God's design for his church—not by sociologists."[47] (One might ask if God has not sometimes worked through scientists.) Mahony predicted that there would be more than twice as many priests ordained in his archdiocese by 1995 than Schoenherr had projected; actually, the decline in priests there was greater than Schoenherr forecasted for 1995.[48] Catholic journalist Thomas Fox cites Mahony's reaction as symptomatic of "institutional denial, an unwillingness by the hierarchy to accept and face bad news."[49] Mahony's outlook stands in bold relief to that of Vatican II, which stated: "The forms of the apostolate should be properly adapted to current needs. . . . Religious and social surveys, made through offices of pastoral sociology, contribute greatly to the effective and fruitful attainment of that goal, and they are cordially recommended."[50]

Another example of the recalcitrance of American Catholic leadership to consider ordination policy modification has come from John O'Connor. That former New York cardinal predicted, "Anyone awaiting a change in the future is going to wait well beyond an infinity of lifetimes."[51] O'Connor reflected the view of John Paul II, who reaffirmed in 2003 that the celibacy rule is nonnegotiable.[52] His stance deserves to be dismissed with a bit of levity conveyed by an imagined colloquy he had with God: "Will the law of celibacy be discontinued?" "Not in your lifetime." "Will celibate women ever be admitted to the priesthood?" "Not in your lifetime." "Will your future Vicars preserve the law?" "Not in my lifetime."

John Paul has planned carefully to assure that his declarations will continue without modification after his death. During his long tenure, he has appointed nearly all of the cardinals who will elect the next pope. He has not selected those who would provide diversity of outlook on sexual matters in the College of Cardinals, but rather those who agree with papal policies that have caused much controversy with the lower priests and laity. One exception has been Keith O'Brian of Scotland who, after being appointed cardinal in 2003, indicated that he favors admitting married priests.[53] Recognizing the conservatism of the next "red hat" conclave, Gary Wills comments that finding a new pope who will be open to change on celibacy places "heavy duty on the Holy Spirit, but she'll do it."[54] Tim Matovina, who directs the Cushwa Center for the Study of American Catholicism at Notre Dame University, has observed, "In history, the longer a pope has been in office, the more likely there will be a pendulum change in one direction on the other."[55]

Strange as it may seem, recent popes have shown by word and deed their willingness to accept as genuine the combination of marriage and sacramental ministry by converted Protestant clergy. In his 1967 encyclical, Paul VI expressed a willingness to admit "married sacred ministers of other Churches . . . to full priestly functions."[56] Following up on that announcement in 1969, he accepted the first married Anglican clergymen for re-ordination as Catholic priests. The converts are permitted to live in Catholic rectories with wives and children. These priests can continue conjugal relations but they lose their positions if they remarry as widowers.

Continuing that policy, John Paul II has quietly admitted to the priesthood male ministers, mostly married, from several Protestant denominations in Europe and America. Several hundred of these clergy have been attracted to a church that absolutely rejects abortion and women priests. Graham Leonard became a Catholic priest because he was disgruntled by the failure of the resistance he had led to women's ordination in the Church of England. The pope was so pleased by the apostasy of that former Anglican bishop, and by his bringing in other sexual conservatives for re-ordination, that he met with him and his wife at an audience in 1995.[57]

Examples can be given of varied results that have come from accepting former Protestant clergy as Catholic priests. One such priest tells of officiating at his son's wedding.[58] In another case, William Shields, a former Episcopalian, became the first active divorced Catholic priest in America.[59] Catholicism officially declares that divorce for any member is "a grave offense against the natural law,"[60] but no penalty has been established for a priest who is so involved. Or again, Archbishop Francis Hurley of Anchorage, anguished over the extreme shortage of priests in Alaska, re-ordained a former Methodist minister who had been converted through the influence of his Catholic wife and children.[61]

This new idiosyncratic policy of accepting a special group of married priests into the Catholic priesthood pokes a hole into the celibacy dike because it illustrates that marriage is no longer thought of by the Vatican as an inviolable obstacle for Catholic ordination in Western nations. These married priest exceptions have de facto destroyed any inherent basis for the

Vatican's absolute celibate law. If this is a test run on the general acceptance of ordained fathers who may also be daddies, it has already proved to be highly successful. A survey of American Catholics shows that four out of five think that allowing Protestant ministers to become Catholic priests is a good policy,[62] and a 2002 survey reveals that 72 percent of American priests also approve.[63]

The acceptance of married priests into the Latin Catholic Church is invidiously more generous toward converts than toward lifelong Catholics. Marriage is not permissible for a Catholic layman who is called to the priesthood, and if he marries after taking Holy Orders, his service as an active priest is abruptly ended. He is held in dishonor, but if he reverts to his former unmarried state by separating from his wife or by burying her, he can return to active duty in the church. Thousands of married Catholic priests would like to continue in their vocations and help relieve their church's acute shortage of clergy, but the Vatican treats them as pariahs and has no intention of inviting them to resume diocesan work. Having devoted many years of their lives to learning about and continuing Catholic traditions, they are understandably peeved that they have been forced out of the church because they have opted to marry, while other married clergy from denominations traditionally treated as heretical are, after some evaluation and instruction, welcomed as priests in full communion with the church. A Protestant minister who has forsaken his denomination and has become re-ordained is treated more kindly than a married Catholic who is convinced that he continues to be divinely called to serve as a priest. If I were to become disenchanted with my status as a Presbyterian minister and converted to Catholicism, I, along with my spouse, might be more acceptable to the Vatican than a married career Catholic priest with excellent education in Catholic theology and with high parish ratings. Perhaps due to Catholic officialdom's awareness of this double standard, converted priests sign a pledge not to give "undue publicity" to their new status.[64]

Another anomaly has surfaced: several dozen married priests who have been lifelong Catholics are serving churches in a capacity that appears to be valid despite objections from hierarchs. According to canon law, the church's prohibition of sacramental celebrations by a dismissed priest "is suspended whenever a member of the faithful requests a sacrament" in facing death.[65] Because of the critical priest shortage in Germany, and the belief that the Eucharist is the sine qua non of Catholicism, some parishes that otherwise would have no access to a priest have requested married priests to say Mass in order to strengthen those who are spiritually dying. For Catholics, the Eucharist is the Alpha and Omega of life, celebrating the first communion and the last rites. Canon law expert Klaus Ludicke agrees that those parishioners express a legitimate right because they are confronted with an emergency sacramental deprivation.[66] Similar appeals to that canon law might be repeated by priestless Catholic groups elsewhere who need relief, recognizing that half of the world's parishes are now without resident priests.

The Vatican has also initiated a change in celibacy regulations pertaining to deacons that gives hope of more substantial changes before long. That apostolic-originated office, which had required celibacy for the past millennium, has been opened to married men. Becoming a deacon is no longer merely a step toward becoming ordained as a priest. Vatican II decided that diaconate ordination can be conferred "upon men of more mature age, even upon those living in the married state."[67] Paul VI provided additional guidance, "Care should be taken that only those are promoted to the diaconate who have lived as married men for a number of years and have shown themselves to be capable of running their own house, and whose wives and children lead a true Christian life and have good reputations." The pope expected that the wives should not only give consent but also be supportive of their husbands' vocation.[68] These requirements resemble what the New Testament established for that office, with the major exception that female as well as male deacons were recognized in early Christianity (Rom 16:1; 1 Tim 3:8–13).[69]

Archbishop Thomas Roberts, a participant in Vatican II, cites this diaconate restoration as evidence that "the ice of Trent is cracking."[70] These deacons, nearly all of whom are married, portend the gradual redeployment of a practice that is more ancient than the unbiblical one that has long been unquestioned by the Vatican. Many thousand have been ordained during the past generation and it appears that none have been accused of sexual abuse. They perform many of the duties previously reserved for priests, excepting consecrating the Eucharist, administering the reconciliation sacrament, and anointing the sick. They perform baptisms, bless weddings, officiate at funerals, lead in worship, preach the Word, distribute the Eucharist, and care for parish facilities.[71]

Another giant step toward removing the clerical celibacy requirement could come if marriage were to be permitted at least for all diocesan priests. Clerics in monastic orders of the Latin Church, along with those of the Eastern Church, would continue with their threefold vows of poverty, obedience, and celibacy. There is some residual rationale for an expectation of celibacy in religious communities, although homosexual activity is increasingly apparent there.

の✦の

The hierarchical priestly system is gradually being transformed by the empowerment of the laity, appropriately symbolized by Mass celebrants turning toward the congregants. Also, the replacement in the liturgy of the vernacular for the Latin is indicative of the move away from spiritual colonialism. Emerging is a fresh awareness that the Spirit of God is not owned by the hierarchy but resides among all of God's people. In accord with the New Testament, Vatican II stated: "The laity . . . are assigned to the apostolate by the Lord himself. They are consecrated into a royal priesthood and a holy people in order that they may offer spiritual sacrifices through everything they do. . . . The apostolate of married persons and of families is of unique importance for the Church and civil society (1 Pet 2:9–10)."[72] As resignation, retirement, death, and inadequate recruitment for replacement priests take their heavy toll, much of the work of the priesthood in America is being transferred to lay people. This movement has demonstrated that religion is no more dependent on clergy than patriotism is on politicians. In visiting Catholic churches, I am impressed by the vitality of congregations that are mainly operated by the laity. Widespread appreciation is found for the many thousand American Catholic lay ministers, who now greatly outnumber active diocesan priests.[73] Many of these nonordained employees are married and most of them are female. Parishes could not function without them because they handle church business, instruct the young, comfort the sick, and distribute the Eucharist. Journalist Peter Steinfels, who has his fingers on the pulse of the American Church, writes: "Laypeople are taking charge of the church's vast network of institutions and activities. They are coming to constitute the bulk of theologians, church historians, perhaps even canon lawyers. They staff Catholic schools and pass on the faith in catechetics and adult education programs, prepare people for the sacraments, hold key posts in parishes and increasingly dioceses, too."[74]

Catholic laypersons are no longer content to accept that the magisterium should make all the rules, especially pertaining to their sexual lives. Rejection by rank-and-file Catholics of the church's proscription of artificial birth control displays their awareness that the Bible's first command for humans to "multiply" must be interpreted in a historical context. Failure to multiply was associated with homicide in the ancient world, and with the decline of the Roman Empire; now population multiplication must be viewed as a means of mass destruction. Contributing to the historic large birth rate of Catholics was the belief that semen is human life and therefore any "spilling" of it outside a vaginal receptacle was condemned. The continuing obsession by Catholic officialdom with increasing the quantity of life by neglecting birth control, or by declaring embryos and deformed fetuses to be persons with full human rights, is counterproductive to reducing the enormous overcrowding and accompanying misery in many areas of the world. Yet popes continue to stress the first injunction in the Torah, "Be fruitful and multiply, and fill the earth" (Gen 1:28). In visiting some of the most overpopulated areas of the world, John Paul II has insisted that married couples "will not have recourse to contraception, which is essentially opposed to love and parenthood."[75] But the biblical command does not sanction overfilling, so the appropriate multiplication factor is now one. Jerome and John Chrysostom announced that procreation is no longer a moral imperative because the earth is fully inhabited.[76] That message may have been wrong for the era of those patristics, when the earth's population was about 5 percent of what it is today, but surely its time has now arrived.

Congregants' widespread repudiation of the Vatican's birth control regulations is symptomatic of their disdain for the church's denigration of women as priests' wives or as priests. Anthony Padovano, a past president of CORPUS, perceptively ties obligatory celibacy with the denigration of women: "When you tell every priest in the world that they can't marry, what you're saying is that a relationship with a woman is not holy enough for the priesthood, women are inferior and marriage is a second-rate institution."[77]

A future pope would be truly revolutionary if he simply ruled that a Y chromosome should not be a prerequisite to ordination. A poll of German Catholics shows that 78 percent favor ordaining women,[78] and a survey of American Catholics indicates a 65 percent acceptance rate, almost as high as the percentage of those who favor permitting priests to marry.[79] A 2003 survey of Boston archdiocese members indicates that 80 percent would support ordaining women.[80] Catholics in most of the 19,000 American parishes are well prepared to accept women priests, due in part to the positive impact of the roles that nuns have traditionally had in religious education.

A case can be made for women priests even if, in an intermediate transition, they are required to be celibate. Judging by the comparatively few nuns who have been accused of sexual abuse, it appears that women in Catholic orders deviate less from their celibacy goal than male clerics. They would resist the men's club on the Tiber who operate with the de facto canon law that clandestine sexual relationships are permitted so long as they do not besmirch the virginal image of the church. At a protest meeting, a layperson said: "The only way to purge the Church is to allow priests to marry and to open the seminary doors to women. . . . The abolition of confession [is needed] so that fallen priests wouldn't have an easy means of homing in on their victims."[81]

The unhappiness of Catholic laypersons over the church's positions on sexual ethics continues to reduce financial contributions. The ban on artificial contraception may have decreased church offerings in America by one-third,[82] and the loss from the priestly sexual abuse issue is yet to be figured. Currently, religious donations of Catholics are about half of what Protestants give, even though the average per capita income of Catholics is not lower.[83] Economic—not sexual—concerns have always been the main reason for mandatory celibacy. As we have seen, celibacy was mandated by the papacy to make sure that children of priests could not inherit church holdings; it still "allows the Church tight control over its priests, who have no dividing loyalties to wives and offspring and thus require minimal salaries."[84] Housing, feeding, and moving an unmarried priest is much less expensive, but prelates do not publicly admit their secular rationale. Fergus Kerr, the renowned Dominican scholar at Oxford, believes that priestly celibacy will soon become an option even though that change will heighten the fiscal anxiety that has fueled the practice: "Historically, it was about property; now it's about salary. It's easy to support a celibate priest, but supporting a married priest with children would be a big drain on resources."[85] In 2003, according to a Duke Divinity School survey, the median compensation for American Protestant pastors, including family allowance, is 60 percent more than for priests.[86] But if the church changed its arcane regulations, and established practices that aim at liberty and justice for all, increased offerings from appreciative parishioners could well cover the higher salaries needed for housing and for educating offspring. An increase in Catholic giving would not be unduly burdensome.

French writer Victor Hugo remarked at the conclusion of one of his works, "An invasion of armies can be resisted, but not an idea whose time has come."[87] Recognizing the current composition of the College of Cardinals, it may be overly sanguine to think that the electors of the next pope will respond to the pressing need for a progressive leader. But within this century, the law of priestly celibacy, Catholicism's festering thorn in the flesh, will probably be eliminated and Christians will look back on the medieval ruling in the same way we now look on laws denying freedom to slaves. A generation ago, suspended priest Donald Hayne viewed the jettisoning of obligatory priestly celibacy as an issue of when, not if:

The Roman Catholic Church will eventually allow its priests to marry. . . . It took us four centuries to catch up with the Protestant reformers in the matter of a vernacular liturgy, . . . and three centuries to catch up with William Penn and Roger Williams in the matter of religious liberty. The time-lag is lessening now. . . . The growing consensus on contraception is an example of that.[88]

Hans Kung, one of the most respected Catholic thinkers and writers alive, has been an outspoken critic of Vatican declarations on priestly celibacy and indeed, on other matters. Primarily because of his opposition to papal infallibility, he was stripped of his Tübingen position as a Catholic theologian a year into John Paul II's pontificate. Kung thinks that practical church politics, more than theological principle, will soon cause the Vatican to open discussion on celibacy. "Because of the current scandals and the pastoral emergency arising from the dearth of priests," he is confident that the celibacy requirement will be rejected before long.[89]

Padovano visited with me and expressed the ardent hope that the next pope will accept married priests, not merely out of pragmatic necessity to fill empty altars, but out of faithfulness to the optional status of celibacy during the first millennium of church history. He recognizes that when candidates present themselves for ordination, their central commitment is to becoming a priest, not a celibate. But the official church treats the ordinance of celibacy as de facto of more importance than the sacrament of Holy Orders, so a priest cannot continue to carry out his priesthood promise if he decides to accept for himself the sacrament of Holy Matrimony. Padovano thinks that the acknowledgment of a married Jesus could provide a sound basis for reversing the error of the priestly celibacy law, which is manmade in every sense of that word. At the 1995 conference of CORPUS, he charged:

> I believe that mandatory celibacy may have done as much or more evil than any other Church policy, especially when one considers all its consequences in terms of the exclusion of women and the negative reading it gives the laity on sexuality. . . . Is it not more likely that a married Jesus would more easily equate the Reign of God with weddings, with the joy of the bridegroom, with the embrace of a lost son, with an expansive role for women?[90]

The removal of the marriage barrier to the Catholic priesthood is almost inevitable during this century. At a time when the institution of matrimony is losing some of its traditional hallowedness, Catholics cannot afford to continue to appear to be saying that marriage is debasing for priests. The crown jewel splendor that Paul VI saw in celibacy can be found at least as brilliantly in holy wedlock. Deprived of the imitation of Jesus as that pontiff's ultimate justification for banning clerical marriage in the largest branch of the Christian church, the prohibition can in good conscience go the way of all flesh. Forced celibacy is dying and not even the artificial inspiration from a succession of popes can resuscitate it. If the Catholic hierarchy were to reassess its assumptions regarding Jesus' marital status and his view of the body in an unbiased way, they could find a way to escape the impasse that has developed over the celibacy law. A pope has to make the simple choice between continuing to require celibacy, while dangerously diminishing the quantity and quality of priests, or embracing early church traditions that had no celibacy requirement.

In accord with its recognition that the church must be "continually reforming,"[91] Vatican II set a healthy precedent for admitting egregious errors in church pronouncements. Medieval Pope Boniface VIII gave theological justification for the crusades against Muslim "infidels" by declaring, "It is absolutely necessary to salvation for every human creature to be subject to the Roman Pontiff."[92] Repudiating such arrogance, Vatican II stated: "The plan of salvation includes those who acknowledge the Creator. First place among these are the Moslems, who, professing to hold the faith of Abraham, along with us adore the one and merciful God."[93] But the Vatican has yet to consider reversing its similarly non-apostolic position on celibacy, which has been held even longer than its condemnation of non-Catholic religions.

Centuries after educated earthlings accepted the heliocentric theory, John Paul II appointed a commission to inquire if the church erred in condemning Galileo for demonstrating that the earth revolves around the sun. After the issue was studied for a dozen years, the pope exonerated that astronomer. In 2003, Richard Sipe gave this sanguine forecast: "In ten years there'll be a reformation. . . . In terms of human sexuality, the Church is at a pre-Copernican stage of understanding."[94] He hopes that Catholicism will similarly catch up with general human understanding on sexuality and admit its errors over many centuries. The longest running travesty in human history has been attempts to separate priesthood from marriage; the two should complement one another in expressing incarnational love. But if the Vatican remains intransigent, the church in its third millennium could repeat its tragic second millennium splits over this issue, and Catholics in some areas of the globe might declare independence from Rome.

The Reformation inaugurated by Catholic priest Martin Luther five centuries ago was motivated in part by the fiasco over celibacy that had been mandated some five centuries earlier. Needed now is a new reformation with changes at least as sweeping to meet the present crisis. *Krisis* is a concept attributed to Jesus in the Greek New Testament (John 3:19), meaning an occasion for great opportunity. As in medicine, a "crisis" is a situation in which the patient may rally and regain health if responses soon occur. An ominous situation will arise if the next pope has similar sexual values as his predecessor, and as great a longevity.

According to church demographers, African and Latin American Catholics comprise about half of the one billion Roman Catholics worldwide. By 2025, about 60 percent of all Catholics will live in the Southern Hemisphere, while the number of Catholics in Europe, the birthplace and traditional heartland of Catholicism, is projected to decrease from its current membership.[95] Brazil, which is by far the largest Catholic country in the world and the one where priestly celibacy is especially a sham, may be the nation from which a pope comes this century. Or, a pope may be selected from Africa, where in the past century the church has moved from no bishops to ten cardinals. With the shift in Christendom's center of gravity, non-European cardinals will increase, and popes may be elected from continents where prelates are more sensitive to the critical need for married priests.

Church history from the postbiblical era until this century can be divided into two major epochs, the first extending from the patristics until Vatican II. During those eighteen centuries, power was largely controlled by a Eurocentric and patriarchal Catholic hierarchy. Perpetual virginity, celibacy, and subordination of women was praised and exploited by the dominating male bishops. Bishop Michael Kenny of Alaska rightly views the prohibition of women priests as "an expression of a patriarchal era that tended to view females as inferior to males."[96] The epoch of the world church, which began a generation ago and may extend 'til kingdom come, will probably be characterized by more equal partnership in both ecclesiastical and marital matters.

Assuming there will be another Vatican council in this century, as there have been for the past two, hopefully the agenda will feature replacing mandatory celibacy and male-dominated autocracy with the best of the practices of early Christianity. Then, when Vatican IV meets in the twenty-second century, one can imagine that most bishops will be married and some of them will be women. Within the foreseeable future, another married bishop may ascend to the papal throne and, as has occurred with numerous married popes of the past, eventually be canonized as a saint.

Removing the celibacy debacle cannot be accomplished without adopting some of the radical egalitarianism of the New Testament community, with its priesthood of all believers and its confession of sin to one another. The role of women in the earliest church was much greater than in the Judaism of that era.[97] Hope would brighten for Catholicism were there a democracy in which all members, from the cardinals to the 98 percent of lay members now disfranchised, were significantly represented in governing the church. The church's hoary theocracy, which has exercised awesome power in past centuries, needs a massive overhaul to gain full respect from both religious and nonreligious people in this century. British Catholic Lord Acton, perturbed by the unlimited ecclesiastical power that might ensue from the dogma of papal infallibility over "faith and morals" that was declared during his day by Pius IX, wrote, "Power tends to corrupt and absolute power corrupts absolutely."[98] Even though no subsequent pope has infallibly pronounced celibacy to be a moral requirement for priesthood, many Catholics have been conditioned through ecclesiastical authoritarianism to associate holy persons with sexlessness.

Decentralization of power will involve the sharing of leadership roles with men and women who have been trampled on at the bottom of the church's social pyramid. Pope Gregory the Great conceived of his role as "servant of God's servants,"[99] a humble self-designation that should guide the practice of all popes. The women who followed Jesus understood better than the men that ministry meant service (*diakonia*; Mark 15:41; Luke 8:3), not rule. From their diaconal role of waiting on others they grasped and lived by these words of Jesus: "You know that among pagans the recognized rulers lord it over their subjects, and strong men tyrannize them. It should not be like that for you; whoever wants to become great must be your servant. . . . For the Son of Man did not come to be served but to serve" (Mark 10:42–43, 45).

Jason Berry concludes his diagnosis of the sickness in institutional Catholicism with this realistic judgment: "Optional celibacy will not be a panacea, but opening the diocesan clergy to married men and women will be a major step in . . . revitalizing parish life. . . . This transition will be fraught with conflicts. Celibates who have honored their vow may well wonder why they have done so."[100] The practical necessity of an acute shortage of priests, or the sharp decline in church offerings by those voting with their purses against mandatory celibacy, or the perception that the priests are becoming predominantly homosexual may be the basic motivations for the change. A more principled reason is needed; namely, that the perpetual pledge of celibacy was a historical and theological misunderstanding of what the early Christian community expected. Mandated celibacy has always produced more theological and moral problems than it has solved.

A prerequisite for major ecumenical advance is papal willingness to rescind the ban on clerical marriage and a jettisoning by all Christians of views on sex that are contrary to the generally wholesome biblical outlook. The prominent Catholic theologian Edward Schillebeeckx asks, "How can the church, in view of Paul's statement 'concerning the unmarried I have no command from the Lord,' make celibacy obligatory for the clergy?"[101] Cutting away the celibacy tumor on the body of Christ could do much to restore oneness, holiness, catholicity, and apostolicity among the Eastern Orthodox, Roman Catholics, and Protestants—all of whom profess to belong to "the one, holy, catholic, and apostolic church."

All religions with Semitic roots will also come closer in understanding when they emphasize themes of their common history. An important element in the scriptural sources of Judaism, Christianity, and Islam is that marital sexuality is an untainted gift of God.[102] Celibacy is a block to fraternal relations among the major monotheistic religions. Rabbi Herbert Weiner states, "There are few aspects of Christianity more difficult for Jews to understand than the principle of celibacy." He affirms that for Jews "spiritual and physical love not only do not conflict with each other, but to diminish one is to diminish the other."[103] In the face of current pervading secularism and mounting violence in the name of religion, shalom-loving Jews, Christians, and Muslims need more than ever to stand together with a common message.

A parable of Jesus can provide inspiration for the basic revisions needed in church canons crafted for a bygone age. When criticized for not having his comrades participate in the established twice-a-week fasting for pious Jews (Luke 18:12), Jesus responded, "No one puts new wine into old wineskins, for the wine will burst the skins, and the wine is lost along with the skins. Fresh skins for new wine!" (Mark 2:22). Jesus perceived that some traditional cultic forms were like dry and hard old leather, unable to stretch when used to encompass the potent gospel. Jesus warned that the fermentation resulting from his "new wine" would cause outworn "skins" to explode. Attention should be given to constructing elastic structures that will retain his precious eucharistic gift.

Notes

1. William Phipps, *Recovering Biblical Sensuousness* (Philadelphia: Westminster, 1975), 139–62.

2. Leo Jung, ed., *The Jewish Library* (New York: Soncino, 1934), 362.

3. *Decree on the Ministry and Life of Priests*, 16.

4. Philip Jenkins, *The New Anti-Catholicism* (New York: Oxford, 2003), 183.

5. William Cole, *Sex in Christianity and Psychoanalysis* (New York: Oxford, 1955), 285.

6. Elizabeth Abbott, *A History of Celibacy* (Cambridge: Da Capo, 2001), 107.

7. George Frein, ed., *Celibacy* (New York: Herder, 1968), 66–67.

8. Paul Dinter, *The Other Side of the Altar* (New York: Farrar, 2003), 101.

9. James Kavanaugh, *A Modern Priest Looks at His Outdated Church* (New York: Trident, 1967), 10–11.

10. Peter De Rosa, *Vicars of Christ* (New York: Crown, 1988), 395.

11. *Catechism of the Catholic Church* (Washington, DC: U.S. Catholic Conference, 2000), 2376–77.

12. *Didache* 22.

13. Council of Elvira, Canon 71.

14. Burchard of Worms, *Decretum* 17:35.

15. Horace, *Letters* 10:24.

16. Paul VI, *Priestly Celibacy*, 21.

17. Paul VI, address, February 1, 1970.

18. Martin Marty, ed., *New Theology, no. 9* (New York: Macmillan, 1972), 219–20.

19. I first discussed this probability in my groundbreaking *Was Jesus Married?* (New York: Harper, 1970), and subsequently, there has been substantial scholarly agreement with this position.

20. Ruth Anshen, ed., *Moral Principles of Action* (New York: Harper, 1952), 652.

21. David Gibson, *The Coming Catholic Church* (San Francisco: Harper, 2003), 263.

22. *Christianity and Crisis* (May 29, 1978): 135.

23. *Calgary Herald,* March 23, 2002.

24. *Christian Century* (July 14, 1971): 862.

25. *Genesis Rabbah* 17:2.

26. *Zohar Hadash* 4:50b.

27. Robert Gordis, "Rejudaizing Christianity," *Center Magazine* (September 1968): 15.

28. Alfred Guillaume, "The Influence of Judaism on Islam," in *The Legacy of Israel* (ed. Edwyn Bevan; Oxford: University Press, 1927), 165.

29. Qur'an 4:3; William Phipps, *Muhammad and Jesus* (New York: Continuum, 1996), 138–43.

30. *Mishkat* 13:1.

31. Roman Cholij, *Clerical Celibacy in East and West* (Leominister, UK: Wright, 1988), 135, 137.

32. Stanley Jaki, *Theology of Priestly Celibacy* (Front Royal, VA: Christendom, 1997), 149.

33. Karl Barth, *Church Dogmatics* (Edinburgh: Clark, 1961), 3:4:141.

34. Charles Smith, *How to Become a Bishop without Being Religious* (Garden City, NY: Doubleday, 1967), 21.

35. Elmer Clark et al., eds., *The Journals and Letters of Francis Asbury* (Nashville: Abingdon, 1958), 2:474.

36. *Christian Century* (March 20, 1996): 331.

37. Paul VI, *On the Admission of Women to the Ministerial Priesthood* (1976), 27.

38. *San Diego Union-Tribune*, June 29, 2003, A30.

39. John Paul II, *On the Dignity and Vocation of Women* (1988), 25–26.

40. *Ordinatio Sacerdotalis* (22 May 1994).

41. *Catechism*, 1577.

42. John Paul II, *The Theology of the Body* (Boston: Pauline Books, 1997), 466, 491; John 20:17–18.

43. Bruce Metzger and Michael Coogan, eds., *The Oxford Companion to the Bible* (New York: Oxford, 1993), 818.

44. *Catholic World*, January 1971, 183.

45. Gibson, *The Coming Catholic Church*, 71.

46. Richard Schoenherr and Lawrence Young, *Full Pews and Empty Altars* (Madison: University of Wisconsin Press, 1993), xvii, 354.

47. *National Catholic Reporter*, November 5, 1993.

48. *Sociology of Religion* (Spring 1998): 20.

49. Thomas Fox, *Sexuality and Catholicism* (New York: Braziller, 1995), 173.

50. *Decree on the Bishops' Pastoral Office*, 17.

51. *National Catholic Reporter*, June 17, 1994.

52. *San Diego Union-Tribune*, June 29, 2003, A30.

53. *Edinburgh Evening News*, September 9, 2003, 16.

54. Book TV, March 30, 2003.

55. *Miami Herald*, October 11, 2003.

56. *Priestly Celibacy*, 42.

57. *National Catholic Reporter*, March 10, 1995, 24.

58. *London Times*, April 19, 2002.

59. *National Catholic Reporter*, June 2, 1995, 3.

60. *Code of Canon Law*, 2384.

61. *America*, February 28, 1998, 3.

62. *U.S. Catholic*, February 1999, 29.

63. Dean Hoge and Jacqueline Wenger, *Evolving Visions of the Priesthood* (Collegeville, MN: Liturgical Press, 2003).

64. Gibson, *The Coming Catholic Church*, 255.

65. *Code of Canon Law*, 1335.

66. *National Catholic Reporter*, February 21, 1997, 3.

67. *Dogmatic Constitution on the Church*, 29.

68. *Basic Norms for the Formation of Permanent Deacons* (Washington, DC: Catholic Conference, 1998), 44.

69. *Didascalia Apostolorum* 2:26; Pliny, Letters 10:97.

70. James Colaianni, ed., *Married Priests and Married Nuns* (New York: McGraw-Hill, 1968), 107, 119.

71. Bryan Froehle and Mary Gautier, eds., *Catholicism USA* (New York: Orbis, 2000), 142–44.

72. *Decree of the Apostolate of the Laity*, 3, 11.

73. *America*, May 13, 2000, 5.

74. Peter Steinfels, *A People Adrift* (New York: Simon & Schuster, 2003), 349.

75. John Paul II, *Fruitful and Responsible Love* (New York: Seabury, 1979), 26.

76. Jerome, *Against Helvidius* 23; John Chrysostom, *On Virginity* 19.

77. Knight Ridder News Service, October 1, 1993.

78. *Forsa Institut* (April 2000).

79. *Newsweek*, May 6, 2002, 25.

80. Associated Press, May 11, 2003.

81. Philip Jenkins, *Pedophiles and Priests* (New York: Oxford, 1996), 109.

82. *National Catholic Reporter*, February 12, 1993, 13.

83. Gibson, *The Coming Catholic Church*, 137.

84. Frank Bruni and Elinor Burkett, *A Gospel of Shame* (New York: Harper, 2002), 231.

85. *Scotland Sunday Herald*, April 21, 2002, 11.

86. Associated Press, February 16, 2003.

87. Victor Hugo, *Histoire d'un Crime* (1852).

88. Colaianni, *Married Priests and Married Nuns*, 217.

89. United Press International, April 23, 2002.

90. *CORPUS Reports* (July 1995): 16.

91. *Decree on Ecumenism*, 6.

92. Boniface VIII, *Unam Sanctam* (1302).

93. *Dogmatic Constitution on the Church*, 16.

94. *National Catholic Reporter*, January 10, 2003, 9.

95. David Barrett et al., eds., *World Christian Encyclopedia* (New York: Oxford, 2001), 12.

96. *America*, August 22, 1992, 77.

97. Wayne Meeks, *The First Urban Christians* (New Haven: Yale University Press, 1983), 81.

98. Lord Acton to Bishop Creighton, April 5, 1887.

99. Gregory I, *Pastoral Rule* 1.

100. Jason Berry, *Lead Us Not into Temptation* (New York: Doubleday, 1992), 368.

101. 1 Cor 7:25; Edward Schillebeeckx, *Celibacy* (New York: Sheed & Ward, 1968), 62–63.

102. Genesis 2:24; Mark 10:9; Qur'an 24:32.

103. Herbert Weiner, *The Wild Goats of Ein Gedi* (New York: Doubleday, 1961), 89–90.

SELECTED BIBLIOGRAPHY

Abbott, Elizabeth. *A History of Celibacy.* Cambridge: Da Capo, 2001.

Abbott, Walter, ed. *The Documents of Vatican II.* New York: Guild, 1966.

Barstow, Anne. *Married Priests and the Reforming Papacy.* New York: Mellen, 1982.

Bassett, William, and Peter Huizing, eds. *Celibacy in the Church.* New York: Herder, 1972.

Berry, Jason. *Lead Us Not into Temptation.* New York: Doubleday, 1992.

Brundage, James. *Law, Sex, and Christian Society in Medieval Europe.* Chicago: University of Chicago Press, 1987.

Bruni, Frank, and Elinor Burkett. *A Gospel of Shame.* New York: Harper, 2002.

Carroll, James. *Toward a New Catholic Church.* Boston: Houghton Mifflin, 2002.

Catechism of the Catholic Church. Washington: U.S. Catholic Conference, 2000.

Colaianni, James, ed. *Married Priests and Married Nuns.* New York: McGraw-Hill, 1968.

Cornwall, John. *Breaking Faith.* New York: Viking, 2001.

Cozzens, Donald. *The Changing Face of the Priesthood.* Collegeville, MN: Liturgical Press, 2000.

———. *Sacred Silence.* Collegeville: Liturgical Press, 2002.

De Rosa, Peter. *Vicars of Christ.* New York: Crown, 1988.

Dinter, Paul. *The Other Side of the Altar.* New York: Farrar, Straus & Giroux, 2003.

Dodds, Eric. *Pagan and Christian in an Age of Anxiety.* New York: Norton, 1970.

Fox, Thomas. *Sexuality and Catholicism.* New York: Braziller, 1995.

Frein, George, ed. *Celibacy: The Necessary Option.* New York: Herder, 1968.

Gibson, David. *The Coming Catholic Church.* San Francisco: Harper, 2003.

Ginder, Richard. *Binding with Briars.* Englewood Cliffs, NJ: Prentice-Hall, 1975.

Hoge, Dean, and Jacqueline Wenger. *Evolving Visions of the Priesthood.* Collegeville, MN: Liturgical Press, 2003.

Jordan, Mark. *The Silence of Sodom: Homosexuality in Modern Catholicism.* Chicago: University of Chicago Press, 2000.

Kelly, John. *The Oxford Dictionary of Popes.* New York: Oxford, 1986.

Kennedy, Eugene. *The Unhealed Wound.* New York: St. Martin's, 2001.

Lea, Henry. *History of Sacerdotal Celibacy.* London: Watts, 1932.

McBrien, Richard. *Catholicism*. San Francisco: Harper, 1994.

Migne, Jacque, ed. *Patrologia Graeca*. Paris, 1844–1866.

———. *Patrologia Latina*. Paris, 1867–1879.

Murphy, Sheila. *A Delicate Dance*. New York: Crossroad, 1992.

Phipps, William. *Influential Theologians on Wo/Man*. Washington, DC: University Press of America, 1980.

Ranke-Heinemann, Uta. *Eunuchs for the Kingdom of Heaven*. New York: Doubleday, 1990.

Rice, David. *Shattered Vows*. New York: Morrow, 1990.

Schillebeeckx, Edward. *The Church with a Human Face*. New York: Crossroad, 1985.

Sipe, Richard. *Celibacy in Crisis*. New York: Brunner, 2003.

———. *Sex, Priests, and Power*. New York: Brunner, 1995.

Schoenherr, Richard. *Goodbye Father*. New York: Oxford, 2002.

Schoenherr, Richard, and Lawrence Young. *Full Pews and Empty Altars*. Madison: University of Wisconsin Press, 1993.

Sweeney, Terrance. *A Church Divided*. Buffalo: Prometheus, 1992.

Thomas, Gordon. *Desire and Denial: Celibacy and the Church*. Boston: Little, Brown, 1986.

Wills, Garry. *Papal Sin*. New York: Doubleday, 2000.

INDEX

Limited to cross-references of names and terms used more than once in different passages.